DEAD WRONG

Violence, Vengeance, and the Victims of Capital Punishment

RICHARD A. STACK

Foreword by Rob Warden

Westport, Connecticut
London

Library of Congress Cataloging-in-Publication Data

Stack, Richard A.
    Dead wrong : violence, vengeance, and the victims of capital punishment /
    Richard A. Stack ; foreword by Rob Warden.
        p.   cm.
    Includes bibliographical references and index.
    ISBN 0–275–99221–7 (alk. paper)
    1. Capital punishment—United States—Moral and ethical aspects.
    2. Judicial error—United States.   3. Judicial corruption—United States.
    I. Title.
    HV8699.U5S48   2006
    364.660973–dc22   2006020997

British Library Cataloguing in Publication Data is available.

Library of Congress Catalog Card Number: 2006020997
ISBN: 0–275–99221–7

First published in 2006

Praeger Publishers, 88 Post Road West, Westport, CT 06881
An imprint of Greenwood Publishing Group, Inc.
www.praeger.com

Printed in the United States of America

The paper used in this book complies with the
Permanent Paper Standard issued by the National
Information Standards Organization (Z39.48–1984).

10 9 8 7 6 5 4 3 2 1

Dedicated to the
memory of my Father, Norman Arthur Stack
and in honor of my Mother, Ida Hankin Stack.

By their words and deeds,
I learned right from dead wrong.

Contents

Foreword

When the United States Supreme Court, in the 1972 case of *Furman* v. *Georgia*, temporarily laid capital punishment to rest—finding that it had been imposed in an arbitrary, capricious, wanton, freakish, and racially discriminatory manner—Justice Thurgood Marshall said in a concurring opinion that, if Americans were fully informed of the purposes and liabilities of the death penalty, they would reject it.

As unacceptable as Marshall found the death penalty then, it is more so today. Indeed, in view of our experience in the intervening years, it is tempting to dismiss proponents of capital punishment as culpably uninformed, or disingenuous, or close-minded, or delusional, or some combination thereof. On the other hand—more disquietingly—Marshall may have been wrong. Perhaps a well-informed public would continue to embrace capital punishment. But more likely he was right—and what we have here, in the immortal words of Cool Hand Luke, "is a failure to communicate."

If you happen to be among the sizable but dwindling portion of the population who would tell Gallup today you consider the death penalty an appropriate punishment for murder, the very act of opening this book suggests that you are interested in more information and are open to reassessing your position. If so, as you read on, you will test the Marshall thesis and, in all likelihood, arrive at the view that the death penalty is simply awful social policy.

In a sweeping historical context, Rick Stack explores the purposes and liabilities of the death penalty. With few exceptions, the issues central to a reasoned verdict on the death penalty are not new. Voltaire advanced the principal ones in the 1750s—that capital punishment was unnecessarily cruel (although not unusual), that inherent in it was the danger of executing the innocent, and that it had no demonstrable deterrent effect on crime. Although it took more than two centuries for Voltaire's wisdom to gain traction in the policy arena, since World War II capital punishment has been abolished in all of Europe and the Western Hemisphere—with the exception of the United States.

As the accounts of recent death row exonerations in this book show, Voltaire's concern about executing the innocent persists as a modern reality. Stack's narratives expose the criminal justice system's persistent and stunningly ubiquitous problems—coerced confessions (in some cases extracted by physical torture), erroneous eyewitness identifications, uncorroborated testimony of so-called jailhouse snitches and other witnesses with incentives to lie, misleading and sometimes fraudulent forensic evidence, the withholding of exculpatory evidence and other police and prosecutorial misconduct, juries from which minorities have been systematically excluded by prosecutors, and drunken or otherwise incompetent defense lawyers.

Alone or in concert, these problems have been documented repeatedly in capital cases under state laws enacted after *Furman* and since the resumption of executions with that of Gary Gilmore by a Utah firing squad in 1977. In just under three decades, more than 120 men and women under sentence of death have been exonerated, while just over 1,000 have been executed. Thus, of the 1,100-plus capital cases that have reached finality, the error rate was more than one in ten. As a result, the most salient issue in the death penalty debate shifted from fundamental fairness, which only a small minority of Americans ever bought, to accuracy, which has more popular appeal.

U.S. District Court Judge Jed S. Rakoff, of the Southern District of New York, found the accuracy issue sufficiently appealing that he stunned the legal establishment in 2000 by holding the federal death penalty unconstitutional on the basis of the prevalence of mistakes. Wrote Rakoff: "The best available evidence indicates that, on the one hand, innocent people are sentenced to death with materially greater frequency than was previously supposed and that, on the other hand, convincing proof of their innocence often does not emerge until long after their convictions. It is therefore fully foreseeable that in enforcing the death penalty a meaningful number of innocent people will be executed who otherwise would be able to prove their innocence."

These realities, Rakoff continued, violate procedural due process, by depriving the innocent of important opportunities to make their cases, and substantive due process, by creating an undue risk of executing an innocent person. Not surprisingly, given how deeply invested those who administer the criminal justice system have been in the death penalty since *Furman*, the decision was soon overturned on appeal. Rakoff's frontal assault, nonetheless, was remarkable and certainly right about the ubiquity of inaccuracy in capital cases.

The demonstrated inaccuracy, however, is but a harbinger of another fundamental problem with the death penalty—a point that Governor George Ryan made when he commuted 167 Illinois death sentences in 2003. Noting that, in the previous quarter century, Illinois had seen thirteen exonerations and only twelve executions, Ryan asked rhetorically, "If the system was making so many errors in determining whether someone was guilty in the first place, how fairly and accurately was it determining which guilty defendants deserved to live and which deserved to die?" And he answered, "Our capital system is haunted by the demon of error—error in determining guilt, and error in determining who among the guilty deserves to die."

One issue that affects the guilty and innocent alike is capital punishment's inherent cruelty, which ironically seems to register with less salience today than it did in Voltaire's time because the mode of execution is more humane. While lethal injection probably entails physical pain, it is hardly in the league of drawing and quartering, burning at the stake, electrocution, or hanging. Nonetheless, it is no stretch to brand the anguish of anticipating one's own death as torture and, by any name, the pain is not restricted to those facing execution. It extends—before, during, and afterward—to their innocent spouses, parents, children, siblings, other relatives, and friends.

Another issue that affects all defendants is discrimination. Americans are imbued from childhood with the notion—rather the myth—that their criminal justice system is based on a fair and objective assessment of fact and application of the relevant law without regard to social differentials. Miscarriages of justice are portrayed as only rare and regrettable deviations from normality. In truth, however, the outcome of the typical criminal case may well be less dependent on fact or law than on sociology—the race and social status of the defendant and the victim, the cultural distance between them, their gender, and various attributes of the lawyers, the judge, and jurors. As a result, in terms of race alone, the group most likely to be sentenced to death is blacks convicted of killing whites, followed by whites convicted of killing whites, then by blacks convicted of killing blacks, and—a distant fourth—whites convicted of killing blacks.

While innocence has surpassed cruelty and discrimination as issues in the death penalty debate, the latter underlie the view to which Rick Stack subscribes—that capital punishment would be unconscionable even if the system could be made perfectly reliable in its threshold determination of guilt or innocence.

The problems might be tolerable, of course, if significant steps were taken to minimize them and if they somehow were outweighed by social benefits—if, for instance, the death penalty were shown to save lives either by permanently incapacitating dangerous criminals or by deterring murder. But there is precious little effort at either the state or federal level to fix the glaring problems associated with capital punishment. And there basically are no social benefits. Given that escape from modern maximum-security prisons is all but impossible, incapacitation is effectively accomplished by imprisonment, and the death penalty seems never to have been much of a deterrent. Until 1830, England executed pickpockets, yet pocket picking flourished even at executions of pickpockets. In the final analysis, it makes no sense to assume, as deterrence theory does, that the least rational members of society—those prone to commit murder—are likely to engage in some sort of risk–benefit analysis before acting on their violent impulses.

If federal and state policymakers actually believe in the tenets of the Chicago School, they would do well to weigh the benefits of the death penalty, if they can come up with any, against the costs—social and financial. The latter are difficult to estimate, but capital cases are more expensive at every stage of the judicial process—and the costs are staggering. The *Sacramento Bee* found that—while California averages only one execution a year—the costs of capital trials alone are roughly $78 million more than the costs would have been if the death penalty were off the table. In Florida, the *Palm Beach Post* found that the incremental costs of the death penalty system came to $24 million per execution. Studies in North Carolina and Texas put the incremental costs in those states at more than $2 million per execution—a bargain by California and Florida standards.

Regarding costs, Richard C. Dieter, Executive Director of the Death Penalty Information Center in Washington, D.C., has pointed out: "Surely, there comes a point where such exorbitant expenditures to achieve one execution raise not only fiscal questions, but moral ones as well. How many lives could be saved if the same money was spent on health care, nutrition, education, or crime prevention? Even if the death penalty itself is morally permissible, it does not follow that the state should bankrupt other vital programs to wreak such retribution."

As perverse as it may seem that so many self-styled fiscal conservatives choose to ignore the financial drain of death, it is morally and ethically indefensible that they have ignored persuasive evidence that three innocent men have been executed in recent years—Larry Griffin, in Missouri, based on dubious eyewitness testimony flatly contradicted by newly discovered witnesses; Cameron Todd Willingham, in Texas, based on erroneous evidence that an accidental fatal fire was arson; and Ruben Cantu, also in Texas, based on the testimony of a surviving victim who now accuses police of pressuring him to lie.

Oblivious to the ramifications of those cases, Congress blithely advanced a bill known as the Streamlined Procedures Act. The bill would radically limit the scope of federal review of state capital cases. As the *Washington Post* editorialized, "Calling what this bill does 'streamlining' is a little like calling a scalping a haircut. A better name would have been the Eliminating Essential Legal Protections Act."

Unfortunately, the Streamlined Procedures Act typifies political pandering to uninformed prejudices regarding the death penalty. Were it otherwise, the debate would have ended long ago and capital punishment would now be smoldering in a grave alongside such other failed social policies as separate-but-equal public accommodations, alcohol prohibition, and eugenics.

At some point, of course, the status quo is likely to change, as it has in Europe. Hopeful signs abound, notwithstanding the so-called streamlining initiative in Congress.

In Virginia, Frank D. Hargrove, Sr., a conservative Republican state legislator who once advocated bringing back public hangings as a means of deterring crime, changed his view on the basis of the danger of mistakes and became the principal sponsor of legislation to abolish the death penalty. Similarly, in Kentucky, State Representative Tom Burch, a former supporter of the death penalty, sponsored abolition legislation, saying of his former stance, "I was just wrong. I've seen the death penalty applied unjustly around the country. I've seen it used for political gain by unscrupulous prosecutors. I've seen it used in a discriminatory fashion against minorities."

In Florida, Gerald Kogan, former chief justice of the state Supreme Court and former chief prosecutor of capital crimes in Dade County, came to oppose the death penalty, concluding that innocent persons had been executed. Also in Florida, Mark Schlein, an assistant attorney general, switched from supporter to ardent opponent of the death penalty after discovering that, in his earlier career as a police detective, he had been instrumental in sending an innocent man to prison for murder.

In Illinois, Governor Ryan experienced a gradual epiphany after he began studying the death penalty in 1999 as a result of the exoneration and release of Anthony Porter, a death row prisoner from Chicago. Porter had come within two days of execution the previous year before the Illinois Supreme Court delayed his execution—not because the justices entertained doubt about his guilt but rather because he had tested so poorly on an IQ test he might not be capable of comprehending what was about to happen or why. The reprieve afforded time for a reinvestigation of the case as a Northwestern University student journalism project, which uncovered evidence of Porter's innocence, leading to his exoneration.

Ryan was a Republican who, at the time of Porter's release, was the Illinois chairman of George W. Bush's presidential campaign. As a legislator twenty-two years earlier, after *Furman*, Ryan had voted to reinstate the Illinois death penalty. Heinous crime also had struck close to him. In 1987, Steven Small, his neighbor and friend in their hometown of Kankakee, was abducted for ransom and hidden in a shallow hole, where he suffocated. Thirty-year-old

Danny Edwards, also of Kankakee, was convicted and sentenced to die for the crime.

While Ryan found the Porter case deeply troubling, it did not result in his instant conversion to the abolition camp. The month after Porter walked free, in fact, Ryan signed the death warrant for a man convicted of abducting, torturing, and killing prostitutes. That execution would be the only one of Ryan's tenure as governor, although surely there would have been others had Ryan not begun absorbing the realities of the death penalty.

What Ryan learned, essentially, was that Porter's wrongful conviction was no anomaly. Although others had been released from Illinois' death row—Porter was the tenth—Ryan previously had not appreciated either the strength of their innocence claims or the nature of the systemic flaws that led to the miscarriages of their cases. But he soon realized that all ten almost certainly were innocent. He also learned that so-called cooperating witnesses—jailhouse snitches, alleged accomplices, and other witnesses with incentives to lie—had testified against seven of the men. False confessions had been introduced against six, and erroneous eyewitness identifications against four. Police and prosecutorial misconduct, although not as easy to quantify as the other factors, also was prevalent in the cases.

By early 2000—after the exonerations of three more death row prisoners—Ryan had not the slightest doubt that the Illinois capital punishment system was dysfunctional, and that there almost certainly were other innocent prisoners on death row who simply had not been as fortunate as the thirteen who had won freedom. Consequently, Ryan followed the dictates of his conscience, declaring a moratorium on executions and appointing a blue-ribbon commission to study the problems and recommend reforms to improve the accuracy and fairness of the system.

The commission comprised fourteen members, none of whom, like George Ryan, had ever been accused of having bleeding hearts. Eleven of the fourteen were sitting or former prosecutors. After studying the system for more than two years, however, a majority of the members voted to recommend abolishing the death penalty. The recommendation was not made part of the official report because it exceeded the commission's mandate, but the vote was a testament—like Ryan's epiphany—to the accuracy of Justice Marshall's thesis. Supporters of the death penalty, once aware of its realities, will change their minds.

Apprising a wider audience of the realities is, of course, the purpose of this book—and in the dissemination of its message lies the hope of abolishing the death penalty while the twenty-first century is still young.

Rob Warden
Executive Director,
Center on Wrongful Convictions,
Northwestern University School of Law

Preface

Ideas for this book evolved over a seven-year span. In the life of an academic, the notion of seven-year timeframes elicits a Pavlovian response: sabbatical. The root of this cherished ideal is, of course, Sabbath. The Bible proclaims that on the seventh day, God rested after creating heaven and earth. Similarly, the ancient agricultural tradition was to leave fields fallow every seventh year so they may rejuvenate. Academia permits professors the privilege, with an approved plan, to withdraw from normal duties for a year in order to recharge one's batteries. The time away is to be spent pursuing relevant research interests.

One's first sabbatical is granted following a favorable tenure decision. The lifetime job security of tenure is another anomaly in university labor practices. Tenure is intended to afford professors protection to cultivate new ways of thinking. Without worry that one's job is at stake, an instructor is encouraged to expand ways of looking at the world.

Before achieving tenure, however, one's work is painstakingly scrutinized. As I came to "the academy" after years of social service work, I was not schooled in the ways of tenure. This made me particularly attentive to my colleagues' tips. I scoffed when one half jokingly suggested I preserve every Kleenex I touched on campus. Her point, though, was that there would be some committee somewhere along the line that would want to examine everything I had done. My research, writing, teaching, service to the university, and professional development were closely analyzed.

During the final-year review, my life was reduced to a three-ring binder, six inches thick, crammed with everything I'd written, outlined, presented during the previous six years. Nearly every piece of paper (other than Kleenex) I'd used during my scholarly career was carefully positioned in that binder, organized by sections and subsections, cross-referenced, and divided by tabs. Each section was prefaced by a flowery summary of my accomplishments. Each summary was steeped in self-praise.

The intent of my file for action was to convince the reader that I was worthy of tenure. The process of persuading reviewers of my merit was a most self-indulgent exercise. To be so intensely self-centered for so long felt awkward, uncomfortable.

When I received the call notifying me I'd been awarded tenure, I met the news with relief, exhilaration, and a twinge of bitterness. A sabbatical comes with tenure, I suppose, to allow time to remove any residual resentment. I was pleased that I could let a cleansing process begin, that I could reverse the preoccupation with self.

Two months before receiving official word of my status, my wife and I celebrated Valentine's Day by taking in a movie. Our son, three years old at the time, was in day care, and our daughter was still six months from being born. I must say, we didn't pick the most romantic matinee. *Dead Man Walking* was a thoughtful depiction of the complexities of capital punishment. The film explored the painful, raw emotions surrounding an execution from both the victims' and perpetrators' perspectives.

I was so moved by the experience that upon exiting the theatre, I walked across the sprawl mart to a bookstore and purchased a copy of Sister Helen Prejean's work. As I pored over the text with its exhaustive footnotes, I realized the death penalty could be fertile ground for the research I'd been doing in litigation public relations. I wasn't sure how to make my work apply, but I was determined to try.

Prior to teaching, I had been involved in antihunger/antipoverty work. I was the founding Executive Director of the Capital Area Community Food Bank, the largest hunger-fighting nonprofit organization in metropolitan Washington, D.C. I had served on the Board of Directors of Second Harvest, the national network of Food Banks. I was the first Board Chair of the D.C. Central Kitchen, an innovative job training program that rechanneled surplus prepared food.

Now it was time to rechannel my energies and return to my law school roots and days in the Jackson County (MO) Public Defender's Office. It was time to draw on my research interests and leverage the blessing of sabbatical. The internal preoccupation that resulted in tenure could now be turned outward.

I followed one of Sister Helen's footnotes to the desk of Steve Hawkins, Executive Director of the National Coalition to Abolish the Death Penalty (NCADP). Steve is a wise and gentle person, a man with a young face that covers an old soul. Although issues of life and death engulf his office, a collected calm permeates the organization.

I am grateful that Steve didn't dismiss me outright, some johnny-come-lately do-gooder. Instead, we had a lengthy talk about death penalty philosophies. We commiserated about the challenges of fund raising and managing a nonprofit. We exchanged reasons for our opposition to capital punishment.

One of the core arguments cited in support of the death penalty is its ability to deter crime. True, the person executed won't be committing more offenses. But as for lessons learned by others, it is difficult to draw conclusions that favor the ultimate punishment's deterrent capabilities. Scientific studies consistently fail to find convincing evidence that executions prevent other acts of violence more effectively than alternative sentences. One state-to-state comparison suggests the opposite. The murder rate is lower in Michigan than in neighboring Illinois. The two states have comparable demographics, urban-to-rural ratios, and racial compositions. A major difference exists, however. Unlike Illinois, Michigan is a jurisdiction without the death penalty. Does state-sanctioned killing jangle the nerves of citizens sufficiently to stir violent reaction? Is the government unwittingly modeling murder as a means to resolve problems?

Steve noted the discriminatory way in which the death sentence is imposed. Capital punishment is so riddled with class and race bias that it is unleashed almost exclusively on the poor and people of color. Some examples from NCADP's brochure:

A study of death sentences in Philadelphia found African-American defendants nearly four times more likely to receive the death penalty than people of other ethnic origins who committed similar offenses.

More than 80% of those executed since 1976 were convicted of murdering white victims, although people of color comprise more than half of all U.S. homicide victims. Is the message, white life is more valuable than black?

A defendant who has the means to hire his own lawyer is much less likely to be sentenced to death. Ninety-five percent of people sentenced to die in the U.S. could not afford counsel. Fifty-five percent of those sentenced to die are people of color.

Before such executions were categorically banned, the mentally retarded and juveniles on Death Row were more likely to be black, Latino, Asian or Native American.

The United Nations Commission on Human Rights passed a resolution seeking suspension of executions with an eye toward abolishing the death penalty. Each year since 1976, three more countries have added their names to the list of nations that have eliminated the death penalty. A majority of nations have ended capital punishment in law or practice.

Despite international human rights standards some countries still execute their citizens. Among the family of nations, the United States is a leader in executions. The United States, China, Iran, and Saudi Arabia account for more than 80 percent of the executions recorded by Amnesty International. Since the year 2000, only four countries—the United States, the Democratic Republic of Congo, Pakistan, and Iran—are known to have executed juvenile offenders. The United States is the world leader in this category. It has executed more than 1,000 people since 1976, and has more than 3,500 inmates on death row.

I explained to Steve that my experience in the Public Defender's Office taught me that mistakes are made every day in the criminal justice system. I questioned how we (as in "We the people . . . ," the same people that comprise "the State") can take human life on the basis of such a flawed system.

Steve responded with his own bottom line. "If we eliminated the death penalty, we'd remove a layer of violence from society." This struck me as counterintuitive. These weren't Boy Scouts we were talking about. Those on death row were a layer of violence unto themselves. Maybe. But Steve's point was that the way we, as a society, choose to treat these people speaks to other dimensions of violence—physical, emotional, and spiritual—in our world.

Steve also addressed the moral implications of capital punishment. He emphasized how it devalues human life, how it denies the possibility of redemption, rehabilitation, and compensation from the convicted individual to the victim's survivors.

I shared more of my background with him and asked how I might help. Steve seized upon my experience as a professor of communication. He wanted to improve his organization's written materials—newsletters, fact sheets, brochures. Also, NCADP was beginning to consider an Internet presence.

I took my involvement further. I called on some of my best graduate students and cobbled together a Communication Team. In addition to helping produce written collaterals, the team helped organize NCADP's annual conference and helped conceptualize a public education campaign aimed at halting juvenile executions.

Steve appreciated my support as his media advisor. We'd brainstorm campaign strategy and message development. I'd help him craft talking points before media appearances.

After our initial chat, Steve had me peruse the organization's reading room. I scoured shelves, looking at books, videos, pamphlets, and reports. I studied the makeup of the coalition. I concluded that two of the coalition's constituencies had extremely powerful stories that mostly weren't being told.

The two groups consisted of those who had been sentenced to die but lived to tell about it and those who had lost a loved one to murder yet found it in their hearts to reconcile with the killer. In the unthinkable suffering these people endured, I believed, might lie the answers to why the death penalty must be abolished.

The universe of the exonerated encompassed my original opposition to the death penalty. As long as we have such a punishment administered by humans prone to err, we risk executing the wrong person. Whether one argues from the political left or right, no one wants to see an innocent person executed. It doesn't take a bleeding-heart liberal to sympathize with the injustice of wrongful conviction. Death row exonerations shake everyone's confidence in the system.

The other set of individuals, organized into the support group Murder Victims' Families for Reconciliation, represents Steve's attitude toward diminishing violence in society. That these individuals can seek an understanding with the person who brought such pain to their lives, to me, exemplifies the highest of human ideals.

The perspectives of these extraordinary groups were missing from the literature in NCADP's reading room. I suggested to Steve that the compelling accounts of the exonerated or the moving stories of members of the Murder Victims' Families for Reconciliation could stir people's emotions and sway public opinion. Polls consistently indicate that about three-quarters of respondents favor capital punishment. However, studies also show that when people are pumped with more information—how racially biased the administration of the death penalty is, for instance—support for executions levels off at 50 percent. The critical support for this sanction is soft.

This is encouraging news for those wishing to put an end to the irreversible punishment. The public could be evenly split on this issue, making the political future of executions a toss-up. But to produce this stalemate requires dissemination of information. And information is much more palatable when it takes the form of personal stories.

I started gathering compelling stories. I read books and articles, attended conferences, and spoke with people whose lives had been profoundly impacted by violent crime, either as alleged perpetrator or victim. My intention was to compile a set of memorable depictions of one of the most basic evils of capital punishment: wrongful convictions.

I want to raise awareness of Americans who either do not give executions much thought or, when they do, naively think of the death penalty as a law enforcement tool that safeguards society. I am aiming at that cross section of survey respondents who are sitting on the fence. I want to chip away at capital punishment's soft support and convert the "undecideds" to the "opposed" column.

My original idea was to cull together thumbnail sketches of the first 100 people exonerated from death row. Such a collection of accounts had never been published. This would be eye-opening reading for people who assume those on death row are guilty. I wanted to convey what it was like to have one's life ruined, nearly extinguished, by the state's legal, but fallible, criminal justice apparatus. I wanted readers to conclude that if so many people came so close to dying for crimes they didn't commit, reliance on capital punishment is not in society's interest.

As I engaged in my research I encountered two detours. I applied for a Senior Research Fellowship with the Soros Open Society Institute. During my interview with the foundation's panel, the phrase "new and different" kept surfacing. What was my book going to bring to the national death penalty debate that was "new and different?"

I explained that the anthology I was proposing had never been written. I tried to redirect the interview from "new and different" to "more and better." I pointed out that members of this review committee were so steeped in the issue that "new and different" was a natural desire for them. However, as they were already firmly in the anti-death penalty camp, they were not the audience for whom I was writing. "More and better" information was critical to change the minds of those in the vast middle of this dialogue.

My proposal was good enough to gain me finalist consideration as a Research Fellow. My interview performance, however, didn't push me over the top. All the while, the phrase "new and different" kept ringing in my ears.

A few months following my Soros interaction, I had a discussion with a literary agent. I explained my concept of crafting the profiles of those exonerated from death row. To this, she responded, "You're going to write a book that has a hundred characters and no plot?" I knew she was playing devil's advocate. But I couldn't deny the truth in her assertion. I respected her knowledge of publishing. She explained that readers can only follow so many protagonists in one book. She underscored the need for weaving characters together and creating a plot device that carries the reader's interest from one story to the next.

I reconceived my plan. My intent remained the same. I wanted to create a book that raised the visibility of the death penalty's evils. I wanted to concentrate on a basic issue that is both a bridge between political right and left, and a wedge that can penetrate the consciousness of those in between. For maximum effect, I wanted to humanize the issue by telling the stories of those victimized by the system. I wanted to aim my message at those in the middle, whose consequent change of heart could influence public policy.

I felt vindicated when another author, independent of my plan, wrote a compilation of stories about the first hundred death row exonerees. I also felt relieved I hadn't gone far down that path, for the other writer clearly had me beat.

Incorporating the literary agent's advice and suggestions from the Soros Foundation, I came up with a different approach. I would revisit the accounts of the exonerated. I would determine what the various causes were that led to all the wrongful convictions. I would synthesize the recurring reasons and choose particularly compelling cases to exemplify the system's flaws.

My analysis revealed that the factors contributing most to the miscarriage of justice in capital cases could be placed in four main categories. The leading cause of wrongful convictions, capital case or otherwise, is mistaken eyewitness identification. Systemic corruption, due to police or prosecutors overstepping their bounds, often results in an innocent person being convicted. Another major consideration accounting for wrongful convictions is ineffective defense counsel. And, often, a fourth factor undergirding the previous three is racism.

After placing the cases into their various categories, I appointed a committee of former graduate research assistants and asked them to read the synopses of the exonerees' stories. I asked them to recommend the stories they believed best characterized the particular reason for wrongful conviction. Thoughtful discussions ensued. I took the recommendations and added a few other screens. I was looking for individuals who (a) were still alive, (b) could clearly articulate their unusual tale, and (c) hadn't had much written about them recently. (Do I detect "new and different"?)

Each category of recurring reason could be represented by any number of cases. But applying the predetermined screens to the committee's consensus resulted in a set of very powerful stories.

News was breaking constantly as I researched the book. On the anti-death penalty front, no news was bigger than Governor George Ryan's decision to commute the sentences of all 167 Illinois' death row inmates to life without parole. I decided to unearth the Governor's transformation from capital punishment proponent to abolitionist advocate. The story of one man's change of heart and its enormous consequences provides the backdrop for the chapters to follow.

On the world stage, the most important story unfolding was the U.S. confrontation in Iraq. As the drumbeat to war grew louder and the consequent quagmire got deeper, I questioned the relevance of a book on the death penalty. After all, thousands of people were getting injured or killed in battle. The turmoil of the Mid-East was sending shockwaves reverberating through Europe. But I pressed on and found relevance in Steve Hawkins' observation that capital punishment adds another "layer of violence" to society. It diminishes us all. Like a war machine difficult to derail, the violence wrought by the death penalty could cease only if enough American minds will it so.

Then, in April 2004, revelations emerged from the Abu Ghraib prison forging an ugly connection between U.S. criminal justice and our country's military efforts to ready Iraq for life after Saddam Hussein. The world watched in horror as images of abuse surfaced: hooded prisoners sexually humiliated in a public display; physical torture captured on home video as a sick souvenir for G.I.s; prisoners paraded naked by female soldiers, led around on all fours like dogs on leashes. The international community had long loathed U.S. capital punishment. The mistreatment of prisoners only compounded the world's negative view of American "justice." It appeared to the global community that by exporting our brand of justice, the cycle of violence perpetuated by the U.S. system had come full circle.

The sort of abuse heaped on Iraqi prisoners is endured by American inmates everyday, according to those in the know. Corrections officials, human rights advocates, and incarcerated individuals attest to routine mistreatment. It is accompanied by no fanfare or formal apology, so the public has little awareness it is happening.

In some states, such as Pennsylvania, inmates are routinely stripped in front of fellow prisoners before being relocated to a new facility. Male inmates in the Maricopa County jail in Phoenix, Arizona, are made to wear women's pink underwear as a form of humiliation.

At Wallens Ridge maximum security prison in Virginia, new inmates have reported being forced to don black hoods, Abu Ghraib–style. This practice is meant to prevent prisoners from spitting on the guards. The inmates said they were often beaten and cursed by prison personnel.

Corrections experts claim some of the worst violations have taken place in Texas, whose prisons were under federal consent decree for much of the latter half of the 1990s. This was due to overcrowding and violence perpetrated by guards against inmates. Judge William Justice of Federal District Court imposed the decree after finding that prison staff permitted gangs to buy and sell inmates as sex slaves.

The experts note that the man who directed the reopening of the Abu Ghraib facility and trained its guards, had earlier resigned under pressure as director of the Utah Department of Corrections in 1997 following the death of an inmate who expired while being shackled to a restraining chair for 16 hours. The prisoner, who suffered from schizophrenia, was kept naked the entire time.

Lane McCotter, the Utah official, later became an executive of a private prison concern. One of the company's facilities was under investigation by the Justice Department when McCotter was sent to Iraq. He was part of a team of prison officials, judges, prosecutors and police chiefs chosen by Attorney General John Ashcroft. The team's mission was to rebuild the Iraqi criminal justice system.

McCotter is director of business development for Management & Training Corporation. The Utah-based firm is the third largest private prison company in the United States. The operation encompasses thirteen prisons. In 2003, the Justice Department and the New Mexico Department of Corrections criticized the company's Santa Fe facility. Management & Training Corporation was cited for unsafe conditions and lack of medical care for inmates.

Such conditions should not be surprising in a private prison facility, where profit is the driving force. "Corrections" or "rehabilitation" become subordinate to the mission of maximizing revenue. A burgeoning prison industrial complex, particularly in rural America, is predicated on cheap labor, high occupancy, and low overhead. Minimal investment is made to train staff. Corners are cut when it comes to services and support for inmates. Scrimping on food and medical supplies is another way to hold down expenditures. Offering few, if any, literacy or job skills courses also contains costs. Making sure cells are filled is the best way to maintain cash flow.

During the past twenty-five years, more than forty state prison systems have come under court order for brutality, overcrowding, poor food, or lack of medical care, according to Marc Mauer, Executive Director of the Sentencing Project, a research and advocacy group that seeks alternatives to incarceration.

Judge Justice, in 1999, commented on the situation in Texas. "Many inmates testified to the existence of violence, rape and extortion in prison and about their suffering from such abysmal conditions."

An inmate at the Allred Unit in Wichita Falls, Texas, claimed he'd been raped repeatedly by other prisoners, even after he appealed to guards for help. Penitentiary staff allowed him to be treated like a slave. He was bought and sold by various prison gangs. Inmate Roderick Johnson has filed suit against the Texas Department of Criminal Justice.

Corrections experts are careful to say they do not know to what extent the humiliation and brutality at Abu Ghraib were meant to break the inmates for interrogation or were merely random acts.

Former secretary of corrections in Colorado and Washington state, Chase Riveland, has said that in some jurisdictions there is a prison culture that tolerates violence. Riveland, currently a Seattle-based prison consultant, believes this prison culture has been around a long time.

This culture has been exacerbated by the quadrupling of inmates to 2.1 million during the previous quarter century. The result is overcrowding. According to Riveland, conditions have been compounded by the need to hire large numbers of inexperienced guards.

Some states have difficulty recruiting guards. Often pay is very low. Because retention is a problem, unqualified people can get quick promotions. Something similar may have transpired in Iraq, where Americans initiated a prison system with undertrained military police from Army reserve units.

When Attorney General Ashcroft announced the appointment of the team intended to restore Iraq's criminal justice system, including Mr. McCotter, he declared that Iraqis now could taste liberty in their own land. The United States, in Ashcroft's opinion, would help make that freedom permanent by helping establish an equitable criminal justice system based on standards of human rights.

McCotter had a long history in prison administration. He had been a military police officer in Vietnam and had risen to the rank of colonel in the Army. His last post was warden of the Army prison at Fort Leavenworth,

Kansas. After retiring from the military, McCotter was head of corrections in New Mexico and Texas prior to accepting the Utah position.

In Utah, in addition to the death of the mentally ill inmate, McCotter was criticized for employing a prison psychiatrist whose medical license had been suspended and who was accused of Medicaid fraud and writing prescriptions for drug addicts.

In an interview with Corrections.com, an online trade journal, McCotter was quoted in January 2004 saying that of all the Iraqi prisons, Abu Ghraib "is the only place we agreed as a team was truly closest to an American prison. They had cell housing and segregation."

But nearly 90 percent of the prison had been destroyed, so McCotter set about rebuilding it and restoring its functionality. He engaged 100 Iraqis who had worked in the facility under Hussein. McCotter paid for everything with large wads of cash.

Another problem McCotter encountered was that Iraqi personnel, despite American training, soon reverted to their old methods, shaking down families and inmates, letting prisoners buy their way out.

So the American team fired the guards and hired former Iraqi military staff who hadn't developed bad habits and did as they were trained. McCotter also worked closely with U.S. military police.

It is no coincidence the abuse abroad bears close resemblance to that at home. Some of the principal players in the Iraqi scandal come from the U.S. criminal justice system. From terror tactics employed to solicit confessions, to targeting the poor and people of color in the United States, to deceptions of the police and prosecutors, and to the conditions of death row and the ultimate moment of execution, the death penalty is the most visible and controversial symbol of those abuses.

In mid-May 2004, with no end in sight to the skirmishes in Iraq, Supreme Court Justice John Paul Stevens chose to comment on the faults of the death penalty. "I think this country would be much better off if we did not have capital punishment," he told hundreds of lawyers and judges attending the 7th Circuit Bar Association dinner in Chicago.

Referring to the death penalty as "an unfortunate part of our judicial system," Stevens said he would feel better if more states would "consider whether they think the benefits outweigh the very serious potential injustice, because in these cases emotions are very high on both sides and ... there is special potential for error."

The Court ruled the death penalty unconstitutional in 1972. But after Georgia established the model, amending its legislation to satisfy the Court's concerns that state standards were too "arbitrary and capricious," the Court reinstated the sanction in 1976. Stevens, the Court's oldest member, joined in 1975.

Although he does not take issue with the constitutionality of the punishment, Stevens' comments are the most pronounced statement against the death penalty made by a Supreme Court justice in years. He has raised objections to executions previously, through written opinions. Choosing to speak so publicly about capital punishment, amidst the swirl of world events, keeps a spotlight shining on the issue.

FLOW OF THE BOOK

Following this Preface, the introductory chapter provides a historical perspective on executions. It focuses on the American evolution of the practice and how present-day attitudes have been forged.

The second chapter describes one man's transformation from advocate to opponent of capital punishment. That one man was the governor of Illinois. What were the pressures influencing George Ryan's thinking when he decided to commute the death sentences of 167 inmates? Chapter 2 examines Ryan's struggles, which resulted in his concluding that the death penalty was too flawed to be workable.

Chapters 3, 4, and 5 explain recurring reasons behind the basic flaws of capital punishment. Wrongful conviction should unite political left and right. No one wants an innocent person punished. Such miscarriages of justice undercut confidence in the system. Such misdirected violence diminishes us all. Maintaining death penalty statutes leaves open the possibility of executing the innocent.

Chapter 3 explores the most common reason for wrongful convictions of any sort, not just capital prosecutions. Mistaken eyewitness identification, often unwittingly, is the basis of the state's case. Such was Jennifer Thompson's situation when she testified against her alleged rapist, Ronald Cotton. This chapter deviates from death row, as Cotton was serving a life sentence. But for Thompson's story to be told, it could be no other way. A first-degree murder, which lands its perpetrator on death row, leaves no victim to recount events. Jennifer's experience shows that even when nose to nose, a victim/witness determined to get the facts straight can be dead wrong. The Cotton/Thompson story includes a postrelease reconciliation, 11 years after their courtroom confrontation, that transcends forgiveness.

Freddie Pitts is featured in Chapter 4. Freddie's story depicts systemic corruption laced with racism. The police in the Florida panhandle went out of their way to nail Pitts and his codefendant for the murder of two white gas station attendants. Even when the real killer confessed, prosecutors weren't willing to arrange a deal that would have exonerated Pitts and Wilbert Lee. The state attorneys were content that they had two black men behind bars. As if to stamp the case with an ironic, historic footnote, the very day Pitts and Lee were being sentenced in Florida, thousands of miles north, at the base of the statue of Abraham Lincoln, Martin Luther King Jr. was proclaiming he had a dream. The notion of judging others by the content of their character, not the color of their skin, fell on deaf ears in the Deep South.

Chapter 5 tells the story of Greg Wilhoit, a man who would not have shuttled for eight years between the courts and death row had he had a competent lawyer. One catastrophic event simultaneously initiated Wilhoit's dual status in two extraordinarily sad constituencies. Although living apart from his wife, Kathy's killing qualified Greg as a grieving victim's family member. But because they were separated, Greg also became the crime's prime suspect. Greg's case was first in the hands of lazy lawyers who did little in the year and a half leading to trial. With just weeks before his scheduled court date, Greg replaced his legal team with an aging trial lawyer whose best days were behind him. Turns out his new counsel was addicted to a mix of alcohol and painkillers. The medicine had been prescribed to offset the effects of a brain trauma. A once highly skilled advocate now occasionally wet himself in court and threw up in judges' chambers. The old hired hand failed to counter key evidence presented by the state. The lawyer's negligence wound up costing Greg a death sentence.

The final two chapters, preceding the afterword, comprise a collective call to action. What becomes of the exonerated once innocence is established and they are set free? What are the problems they face upon reentering society? After prison has assaulted their spirit and broken them down, body and soul, after the erosion of whatever job skills and personal relationships they may have had prior to incarceration, is there life after death row? Can the psyche ever heal? Can one ever escape the stigma of incarceration?

Pursuing answers, I came across an astounding fact from the Bureau of Justice Statistics. About 600,000 individuals annually—approximately 1,600 a day!—are released from prisons and returned to their communities. While circumstances surrounding release are different for the exonerated than for those who complete serving their time, the struggles of reintegrating into society carry similarities.

The connection between reentry and the death penalty only matters for the fortunate few who have been exonerated. The intersection of wrongful conviction and capital punishment opens a window to an enormous societal problem. Kirk Bloodsworth's postpenitentiary experience illuminates difficulties inmates face trying to piece together their lives on the outside. As prisoner reintegration has far-reaching ramifications for the individual, his/her family, employer, and neighborhood, it is incumbent upon society to develop policies that enhance the chances of success. The cost of failure is too great. The policies discussed in Chapter 6 expand well beyond the death penalty.

Chapter 7 returns to an issue more germane to the exonerated: compensation. What does it say about our judicial system that it is easier to get the government to reimburse you if a state-owned truck ran over your petunias than if your municipality mistakenly locked you up for years? Here, too, a call to action is delivered so that more humane policies may be implemented.

That which seeks to correct injustice moves us toward a more peaceful civilization.

For the final word, I turned to the other abolition coalition constituent with an overwhelming stake in the issue. If there are angels walking this earth, they may well be members of Murder Victims' Families for Human Rights. How they are able to find the love and strength to seek an understanding with the individual who caused them so much pain is beyond me.

I wanted the book's epilogue to slam a powerful exclamation point behind my message. The previous seven chapters explain the ins and outs of wrongful convictions. What causes them? How they erode confidence in the system? How, being a result of human error, they are unavoidable? And, if that's so, the criminal justice system should not be taking human life.

Then comes the epilogue, written by a representative of Murder Victims' Families for Human Rights to say, "We are a group of people who have lost loved ones to violence. No one in society has been more affected by senseless killing than we have. We want the killing to stop. We think the death penalty is a bad idea. We want the killing to stop."

In November 2002, I was planning a message development workshop for NCADP's annual conference. I asked Kate Lowenstein to be a panelist and represent the murder victims' families' perspective. Kate was completing a joint law and masters of social work degree at Catholic University. Kate is a thoughtful, soft-spoken person whose father, Congressman Allard Lowenstein, was murdered when Kate was a little girl.

By the time I asked Kate to consider contributing to my book, she was employed full-time by the victims' families' organization. She shared her interest in my project. She lamented that although she often picked up books about the death penalty she rarely finished them because her point of view was rarely represented. She was eager to interject the MVFHR position.

Months later, I called Kate to activate her involvement. As happens with a small staff in an overworked office, Kate was overwhelmed with assignments. For one, she was preparing an amicus brief for a Supreme Court case, letting the justices know not all victims are in favor of capital punishment.

Kate delegated my epilogue to Susannah Sheffer, the group's Writer in Residence. Although not related to a murder victim, Susannah is very perceptive. She is a student of many aspects of the criminal justice system and has recently written *In a Dark Time: A Prisoner's Struggle for Healing and Change*.

Thoughts about naming this book: The main title, "Dead Wrong," works as a succinct summation of my feelings toward capital punishment. "Dead" is an emotionally charged word suggesting the finality and irreversibility of the sanction. "Wrong" not only expresses my opinion but also ties into the miscarriage of justice perpetrated by erroneous convictions.

I struggled to develop a subtitle. I had amazing accounts of individuals to make my points. There was hope in that these individuals beat the odds and regained freedom. There was redemptive value in what exonerated inmates have been able to make of themselves and in the relationships they have restored.

My "aha" moment came in the alliteration of "Violence, Vengeance and the Victims of Capital Punishment." The idea connects to Steve Hawkins' notion of peeling away a layer of violence from society by eliminating the death penalty. This theme runs throughout the book.

There is one more reason, most important to me, why I oppose the death penalty. I referred to my children earlier. Gabriel, now thirteen years old, and Reva, ten, are central to my worldview. I feel strongly that I do not want my government telling my kids violence is an acceptable solution to problems.

As I conducted research for my book during the autumn of 2002, the Washington, D.C., area was gripped by the fear of snipers on the loose. The anxiety at school bus stops was palpable. Playgrounds and ball fields were shut down for weeks in October. Students were denied outdoor recess. Any extracurricular activities on school grounds were out of question.

It was a most challenging time to be a parent. Keeping kids safe was paramount. For the sake of the children, adults tried to maintain a sense of normalcy. Parenting became a communal, village-like endeavor and neighbors rose to the occasion.

The close bonding and protective love that shielded the kids during the crisis gave way to the urge for revenge as soon as the perpetrators were apprehended. I have great sympathy for those who lost a loved one as a result of the snipers' rampage. I am sorry that senseless violence caused them such pain. The community's energy is well spent comforting the mourners. The kids could learn a lot about taking care of each other from the behavior modeled by their parents. That affected jurisdictions had to rush to see which one would have the right to kill the killers first is not the behavior I want my kids learning.

Acknowledgments

Without the kindness, encouragement, and wisdom of the following, this book would not have been written: Steve Hawkins, Dick Dieter, Kate Black, Marc Mauer, Larry Kirkman, Rosaline Juan, Kristen McGuire, Rebecca Harrison, Stacey Mayuga, Jennifer Thompson, Ronald Cotton, Freddie Pitts, Greg Wilhoit, Ida Mae Wilhoit, Nancy Vollertsen, Kirk Bloodsworth, Kate Lowenstein, Susannah Sheffer, Shujaa Graham, Hilary Claggett, Rebecca Ballard, Elana Setton, Rob Warden, Sister Helen Prejean.

1

The Death Penalty in Context

The 1960s are remembered for many things—the Free Speech Movement, spirited protests against the Viet Nam war, heated civil rights demonstrations, feminism's emergence, the flexing of consumerism's economic muscle, to name a few. It is not surprising that in this climate a major death penalty milestone—though unheralded—was achieved. Public opinion polls in 1966 revealed that only 47 percent of Americans endorsed capital punishment.[1] This marked the first time in the nation's history that a majority of the citizenry sided with abolitionism.

Eleven months later polls indicated that 13 percent of respondents had changed their minds—maybe in response to growing concern about crime and urban unrest. The proportion opposed to the death penalty fluctuated at around 45 percent between 1969 and 1972. In fact, no convict was put to death between 1967 and 1977. The key case was the Supreme Court's 1972 decision in *Furman* v. *Georgia*, which struck down the nation's death penalty laws on the basis of the arbitrary and discriminatory nature in which capital punishment was administered.[2] The ruling came on a five-to-four vote. Each justice in the majority wrote a separate opinion. *Furman* represented a fragile victory. Death penalty opponents recognized that their goal had not been totally achieved. The justices left open the prospect that jurisdictions might yet draft statutes that were constitutionally permissible, kicking off a new round of struggles.

In *Furman's* aftermath the public adopted an increasingly hard line. In November 1972, two-thirds of Californians backed a referendum amending the state constitution to revive executions.[3] The following March, national surveys indicated 63 percent favored return of death sentences. The figure climbed to two-thirds a year later.[4] Abolition had arrived in the midst of rising support for executions.

Post-*Furman* backlash was swift in terms of legislation as well. The wheels of restoration began spinning within weeks of the decision. Florida Governor Reubin Askew signed a death penalty bill in December 1972. This made the Sunshine State the first to reinstitute capital punishment. Within six months, twelve more states had revived the sanction. By spring of 1975, thirty-one jurisdictions had followed suit. In their haste to put the nation's executioners back to work, state legislators faced a dilemma. It was not clear what sort of death penalty the Supreme Court would allow.

Two forms of capital laws emerged. Some state lawmakers concluded that all arbitrariness could be eliminated from capital sentencing if death were made mandatory for specific offenses. Mandatory death sentences began to disappear from U.S. jurisprudence in the early nineteenth century and vanished by the time courts started looking into the constitutionality of capital punishment.[5] Nonetheless, sixteen states reacted to *Furman* by passing mandatory death penalty legislation: Delaware, Idaho, Indiana, Kentucky, Louisiana, Mississippi, Nevada, New Hampshire, New Mexico, New York, North Carolina, Oklahoma, Rhode Island, South Carolina, Tennessee, and Wyoming.[6] The most common crimes for which death was required were the murder of a police officer, multiple murder, a killing by a person already serving a life term, and murder-for-hire.

The other tack for devising an acceptable death penalty involved strategy the Court previously refused to require: the formalization of sentencing guidelines based on specific aggravating circumstances. Five jurisdictions—Georgia, Illinois, Montana, Texas, and Utah—permitted death sentences only when such circumstances were found. They included many of the factors drafted into mandatory schemes: the killing of a law officer, the commission of murder during another felony, multiple murder, and murder by an inmate. Arkansas, Colorado, Florida, and Nebraska went further, delineating mitigating circumstances that sentencers were required to balance against aggravating factors such as mental impairment, youth, and extreme emotional disturbance. California, Connecticut, Ohio, and Pennsylvania enacted laws requiring a death sentence where aggravating circumstances were present but no mitigating circumstances found.[7]

The situation post-1972 was uncertain. The executioner made a comeback while several different sorts of sentencing schemes awaited Court scrutiny. Abolitionists were aware that another landmark decision was in the pipeline.

During the four years in between the Court's striking down executions and its ruling in *Gregg* v. *Georgia*, allowing the introduction of more rationalized capital sentencing plans, abolitionists continued to place faith in the judiciary.[8] Some were confident that litigators could manage the reinstitution challenge. Others were concerned their recent success might be reversed, but believed they had bought time. The longer it took the Court to determine the constitutionality of mandatory sentencing and guided discretion laws, the better prepared lawyers would be to make their case and the harder it would be for justices to reintroduce a punishment for which many shared a distaste. Immediately following *Furman*, anti–death penalty forces marshaled empirical ammunition for upcoming legal skirmishes, took steps toward reconstructing a political wing for the movement, and continued to litigate.

Leading up to *Furman*, lawyers for the Legal Defense and Educational Fund (LDF) of the National Association for the Advancement of Colored People drove the abolitionist movement. The fight against the death penalty was in the litigators' lap. Everyone else, including American Civil Liberties Union (ACLU) officials, deferred to them. Such legal campaigns require careful coordination. Cases must be handled in proper sequence to erode adverse precedents. Although the anti–capital punishment campaign exhibited little of the deliberation that characterized previous LDF litigation on housing and school desegregation, it was nonetheless helpful for the non-lawyer abolitionists to stay out of the way of LDF attorneys. Actions that might adversely affect the climate in which federal judges determined legal issues were best avoided. By 1972, even the ACLU was mostly on the sidelines.

In spite of the consensus that capital punishment's future would be decided by the "nine old men" behind the bench in Washington, many recognized that resistance to restoration would need to be backed by lobbying and public education. These factors had been missing from the movement, and the LDF had neither the expertise nor the resources to provide them. The ACLU was the only organization capable of directing the nonlitigational elements of the struggle.

Some ACLU affiliates were trying to prevent the executioner's return. ACLU of Northern California provided funds and staff for the state's "No on Proposition 17" initiative. In 1975 and 1976, several state affiliates were active in the struggle. They launched a statewide letter-writing campaign and telephone chain in Kansas, sponsored public hearings on a restoration bill in New Jersey, and supported a series of community meetings on the death penalty in Vermont. Capital punishment was given low priority by most state ACLU offices. Many members felt this was an effort that could slide until the issue was before the Supreme Court. The size of the anti–death penalty movement between 1972 and 1976 remained small, and the intensity of work low.

Attorneys who led the fight against capital punishment in the 1960s could not relax after their victory in 1972. For *Furman* to take effect, the highest court in each jurisdiction had to implement it. So the Legal Defense Fund's first job was seeking implementation of *Furman* in every capital punishment state and commutation of every death sentence. The LDF filed challenges to new death penalty statutes as swiftly as states enacted them. The justices had painted themselves into a corner: *Furman* declared arbitrary application of death sentences unconstitutional. Yet a year earlier, in *McGautha* v. *California*, the court's ruling pushed the most likely remedy, sentencing guidelines, off the table.[9] Abolitionists hoped the Court would go further and ban death sentences altogether. That didn't seem likely in the short run. Maintaining LDF litigation was meant to extend the five-year-old moratorium. If that could happen, the possibility of a tidal wave of executions would make it difficult to reopen death chambers.

The first case the Supreme Court agreed to hear was *Fowler* v. *North Carolina*.[10] The matter involved one of the twenty-nine death row inmates represented by LDF. Under the revised statute, Jesse Fowler had received a mandatory death sentence for killing an acquaintance during a dice game. The case promised to be a showdown on the most common type of post-*Furman* death-sentencing law. Oral argument took place in April 1975. An ominous development from LDF's perspective was the filing of an amicus curiae brief by Solicitor General Robert Bork supporting North Carolina's death penalty. Bork attacked the characterization of capital punishment as cruel and unusual. He cited research by economist Isaac Ehrlich to maintain that frequent expressions of doubt about the deterrent effect of executions were unfounded. Bork's involvement in the *Fowler* case placed the weight of the solicitor general's office behind LDF's opponents. Bork's position amounted to the assertion of a federal interest in capital punishment.[11]

Owing to the illness and retirement of Justice William O. Douglass, *Fowler* did not resolve anything. Absent Douglass, the Court was split four-to-four on the death penalty. Rather than rehearing arguments before a fully reconstituted Court, the justices agreed to rule on a package of five cases in October, after Douglass's successor had been seated. Two of those cases, *Woodson* v. *North Carolina*[12] and *Roberts* v. *Louisiana*[13] pertained to mandatory death penalty laws. *Gregg* v. *Georgia*, *Proffitt* v. *Florida*,[14] and *Jurek* v. *Texas*,[15] involved challenges to guided discretion statutes. The cases were unusual in two respects. Each of the defendants had been convicted of "felony murder," killing in the course of committing another crime. Such offenses constituted less than a third of all homicides. While most homicide victims were black, the victim in each of these cases was white. These five cases were chosen because they were straightforward, presenting no tangential issues.[16] Differences among them concerned details of sentencing schemes that had delivered men to death row.

In *Woodson* and *Roberts*, LDF lawyers claimed that "mandatory" death penalties, as applied in North Carolina and Louisiana, failed to resolve problems the justices found objectionable in 1972—the arbitrariness and capriciousness in determining who lives and who dies. It transferred discretion from juries to others in the process: prosecutors who determined the initial charge, judges who accepted or rejected plea bargains, higher courts that either heard or refused to hear appeals, and governors who could grant or deny clemency in the convict's final days. The attorneys restated their conviction that capital punishment entailed excessive, cruel punishment regardless of the legal formalities that preceded it.

Arguments made in other cases were similar. Briefs filed by lawyers for Gregg, Proffitt, and Jurek asserted that bifurcated trials and aggravation/mitigation schemes installed in Georgia, Florida, and Texas did not produce evenhanded justice. Like mandatory sentencing, "guided discretion" laws had minimal influence on one of several decision points, and aggravating factors were defined too vaguely to make sentencing rational. Procedural fine-tuning did not alter the fact that state-sanctioned killing violated evolving standards of decency. Executions could not be reconciled with the Eighth Amendment.

Opposed to abolitionists were lawyers representing states whose statutes were being challenged. They contended that where discretion existed, it was justifiable, not arbitrary; that capital punishment cannot be seen as "unusual" or unconstitutionally cruel; and that racial discrimination does not play a significant role in choosing who's to be executed. Solicitor General Bork submitted another amicus brief, asserting that death was not qualitatively different from other constitutional punishments. He reintroduced Ehrlich's deterrence findings to discredit the argument that death penalty served no purpose.[17]

In March, arguments were heard in the *Gregg* package of cases. They did not go well for abolitionists. Some justices seemed hostile. The lawyer leading the charge against the death penalty, Anthony Amsterdam, came off as self-righteous and disrespectful. Justice Stewart, who had sided with the majority in *Furman*, sparred with Amsterdam over whether discretion in death cases was any less acceptable than in other criminal matters. Other justices were equally aggressive. The questions they posed to state attorneys were less sharp than those aimed at Amsterdam and his colleagues. Bork made his appearance during the second day of arguments, when the *Woodson* and *Gregg* cases were heard. He was speaking to a sympathetic audience. If the inclinations of the Court were not already apparent, they became so when Justice Powell encouraged Bork to elaborate on his views of deterrence, and then gave him five additional minutes to do so.[18]

Abolitionists waited months before the decision was delivered. They braced for the worst. The ACLU braintrust planned a "Governors' Commission Against Execution," consisting of present and past governors willing to urge fellow state executives to exercise clemency powers. They scheduled an emergency meeting for the week the Supreme Court was to announce its ruling, to devise strategies in case the *Gregg* decision permitted some or all of the capital-sentencing laws to stand.

GREGG AND *WOODSON*

John Paul Stevens replaced Douglass on the Supreme Court before the 1976 death penalty cases were argued. Abolitionists assumed the fate of capital punishment would be in his hands. Because Stevens had never offered a ruling on the issue, no one could predict which way he'd go. But when the Supreme Court announced its decision in *Gregg* v. *Georgia* and its companion cases on July 2, 1976, Steven's vote was not as crucial as had been expected. By a seven-to-two vote, the premise was laid to rest that capital punishment is inherently cruel and unusual under the Constitution. The justices allowed the death-sentencing schemes of Georgia, Florida, and Texas to stand, concluding that three factors were sufficient to safeguard against arbitrary sentencing: (1) guided discretion—sentencing guidelines detailing elements of crimes that make state-imposed death an appropriate punishment; (2) special consideration of mitigating circumstances; and (3) the requirement of automatic review by state appeals courts.

Justices Stevens, Stewart, and Powell cast swing votes. They agreed the Framers of the Constitution had accepted death as legitimate punishment. They dispensed with the "evolving standards" claim by noting that elected representatives in at least thirty-five states had already reinstated the sanction in the wake of *Furman*. Could they all be acting contrary to the wishes of their constituents? And how could the U.S. Supreme Court justify substituting its moral judgment for that of the people? Thurgood Marshall and William Brennan dissented, seeing nothing in the revised laws to change their 1972 assessments.

The same day the Court upheld guided discretion schemes, it struck down North Carolina's and Louisiana's mandatory death penalties. In the rulings on *Woodson* and *Roberts*, the majority reasoned that rigid sentencing structures that failed to account for particular circumstances of a crime and the criminals responsible were inconsistent with *Furman*. To require execution for all persons convicted of certain crimes eliminates unbridled discretion, but at too high a cost. The Court wanted the life or death decision to be bounded and rationalized, but was not willing to sacrifice individualized sentencing completely.[19] The margin in *Roberts* and *Woodson* was five to four. Justices Burger, Rehnquist, White, and Blackmun, dissenting, would have permitted the mandatory sentencing schemes to stand.

In granting its blessings to sentencing standards, the Court was forced to find a way around its *McGautha* ruling, decided five years earlier.[20] In May 1976, Justices Stewart, Powell, and Stevens struggled for a theory with which to declare guided discretion schemes constitutional without explicitly overturning the 1971 decision. To do so would be admitting the Court reasoned poorly in *McGautha*.[21] The task of reconciling *Gregg* and *McGautha* was assigned to Justice Stewart. His solution was to emphasize that the Court was not now making sentencing standards and bifurcated trials an absolute requirement in states that desired to retain capital punishment; it was merely declaring this approach to be constitutionally permissible. White and Stevens thought this approach contrived, but with time running out before the end of the 1976 session, they concluded that it was the best they could do. Justice Steven's hands shook as he read the *Gregg* decision to the packed chamber on July 2.[22]

It is reasonable to wonder why the Court did not abolish the death penalty and be done with the legal mess. Impending executions and the inconsistencies in the Court's decisions caused enough agony for several justices to make a final resolution appealing. Outright abolition could have been the next logical step after *McGautha* and *Furman*, as Lewis Powell predicted when the cases were adjudicated in 1976. But it is not a safe assumption that Supreme Court justices behave like philosopher-kings, gravitating toward conclusions dictated by precedent and logic. They are not immune to pressure from the public and the president.[23] So why did the Court opt against abolition? Why, in 1976, did it change direction on the death penalty? The answer is not simply that the Court moved to the right politically as the conservative Nixon/Burger Court took over for the liberal Warren Court, since the shift was from five to four against capital punishment to seven to two for it. A more likely explanation for the Court's change of position lies in public opinion. White and Stewart, who voted with the majority in *Furman*, but switched sides four years later, referred to the post-*Furman* legislative and public reaction in their opinions. Both cited California's constitutional referendum, a Massachusetts referendum in support of the death penalty, and trends of opinion polls. The *Gregg* decision initially was rendered in the court of public opinion.[24] A Supreme Court rubber stamp of this lower court would be considered abdication of judicial responsibility. Justices are to interpret the Constitution regardless of how acceptable the decision may be. The Legal Defense Fund's strategy to apply an "evolving standards" argument invited the Court to consider public backlash. If the people wanted to reinstate the death penalty, standards must not have evolved as much as abolitionists contended.

Gregg opened the door to America's death chambers. The long-dreaded bloodbath was now a possibility. As it happened, executions occurred infrequently for several years. From 1976 to 1983, the Court continued to grant certiorari to a large number of appeals by condemned prisoners. The justices refined the legal machinery that would result in the demise of a small proportion of inmates. Abolitionists struggled to reassert themselves at the forefront of legislative action and public education.

One hundred ninety-nine days after the Supreme Court declared its ruling in *Gregg v. Georgia*, Gary Mark Gilmore was strapped to a chair in front of a Utah firing squad. As bullets pierced his heart, America's historic moratorium on executions ended.

Abolitionist reaction to the *Gregg* decision was grim. From their perspective, the critical point was that the Court rejected constitutional arguments against the death penalty, arguments that had stopped executions in America for nearly a decade. Death penalty opponents had good reason to worry. Almost 500 post-*Furman* death-sentenced convicts now were locked up in thirty-five states. Expectations were that these jurisdictions would be swift to execute their death row denizens now that they had permission. But the long-awaited "bloodbath" was not imminent. The Supreme Court would spend the next several years fine-tuning the death penalty process. It would not be until the mid-1980s that the nation would experience executions in significant numbers.

REFINING THE DEATH PENALTY PROCESS

Between 1976 and 1982, the Supreme Court contained capital punishment within the bounds of law that began with *Furman*.[25] It reviewed a series of appeals to individual post-*Furman* death sentences. In bringing cases before the Court, defense bar sought to overturn as many sentences as possible and to prove to the courts that it was intellectually and administratively impossible to make executions constitutional.[26] Many of the Court's decisions during this period adhered to the principle that "death is different" from other punishments. This required enhanced due process protections. The effect of the rulings was to constrain the way death sentences were imposed.

One set of decisions concerned the range and specificity of aggravating and mitigating factors admissible in the penalty stage of a capital trial. The Court struck down a Louisiana law, in 1977, that made a sentence of death mandatory for the murder of a police officer because it did not allow for consideration of mitigating circumstances.[27] In 1978, the Court prohibited statutory restrictions on the types of mitigating elements that defense counsel could present to juries.[28] While aggravating circumstances had to be spelled out in law, the same was not true of evidence that might produce more merciful results. Defense attorneys assumed an advantage over prosecutors—the freedom to introduce aspects of a defendant's record or character, or anything about the crime, that might prevent a death sentence.

Other Court decisions during the post-*Gregg* period further expanded due process rights for capital defendants. Protection was established against death sentences for crimes in which no life was taken, forcible rape for instance.[29] Courts were restricted from basing death sentences on vaguely defined aggravating factors[30] and from excluding prospective jurors who simply acknowledged that they may be "affected" by the fact that execution was a possible outcome.[31] The justices prohibited the imposition of a death sentence on retrial when the initial proceeding had resulted in a life sentence,[32] as well as the introduction, during the penalty phase, of damaging psychiatric testimony drawn from pretrial examinations in which the accused had not been warned their statements could be used against them.[33] The cumulative thrust of the Court's reasoning through 1982 was that capital punishment was constitutionally permissible only under higher due process standards. States were allowed to put their worst offenders to death, but not before negotiating a procedural obstacle course unique to capital cases.[34]

The advantage given capital defendants did not cease with their conviction and sentencing. They were granted access to an elaborate appellate process, one that saved many lives and delayed the demise of others. The process varies from jurisdiction to jurisdiction, but typical outlines during the years prior to 1983 were as follows: Death sentences automatically were appealed to the highest state court, regardless of the desires of condemned inmates. First-round appeals were limited to the trial record and any procedural errors it might contain. If the state's highest court confirmed the conviction, the prisoner could appeal to the U.S. Supreme Court. However, the Supreme Court agreed to review only 2 or 3 percent of such requests—generally those that contained legal questions of widespread significance.

If the petition for review was rejected, a second round of appeals, called state postconviction proceedings, was available. The claim would be filed first in lower court, often the tribunal in which the trial took place, then in the higher state courts, and, finally, in the U.S. Supreme Court again. In this cycle, appeals were not restricted to trial transcripts. An inmate might contend that his lawyer had represented him in an incompetent way, or that newly unearthed evidence indicating innocence merits further review.

If, following two rounds of appeals, the prisoner was still under sentence of death, he or she could seek federal habeas corpus review. Only alleged violations of constitutionally guaranteed rights could be considered. Federal habeas proceedings were initiated in U.S. district courts, and if denied there, proceeded through the U.S. Circuit Court of Appeals and, finally, to the Supreme Court. When all these opportunities were exhausted, there remained the possibility of "successor" habeas petitions predicated on new issues. Only direct appeals in state courts were guaranteed to prisoners under sentence of death. They could request further appeals, but there were no promises such petitions would be granted. Convicts were not guaranteed right to counsel beyond initial appeal. This varied by state. Many death row residents had to draft their own appeals. The appellate process was often different from what the public believed. Only those convicted of a capital offense had access to such elaborate appellate procedures. The result was significant delay in carrying out executions. For those convicts who ultimately had their death sentences implemented, "justice" was usually not administered for years.

THE RETURN OF EXECUTIONS TO AMERICA: "KILL GARY GILMORE FOR CHRISTMAS"

After *Gregg*, it was not certain which jurisdiction would be first to put a convicted offender to death. Texas, Georgia, and Florida were front-runners, but the "winner" turned out to be Utah. Gary Gilmore was convicted on October 7, 1976, of two killings earlier that year, and was scheduled to face a Utah firing squad on November 15. Through its state affiliate, the American Civil Liberties Union initiated proceedings to block the execution. The ACLU won a stay a week before the death sentence was to be implemented. Gilmore, however, preferred "to die like a man" rather than spend his days in prison. He persuaded Utah's Supreme Court to lift the stay.

As New Year's approached, Gilmore was still alive. Those wishing to prevent his demise managed to obtain two more stays. These were granted—over the condemned man's objection—by the governor and by the U.S. Supreme Court. Abolitionists were in the awkward position of acting against the expressed desires of a death row denizen, aggravating his psychological distress by doing so. So upset was Gilmore he attempted suicide on November 16. His refusal to appeal forced the ACLU to explain repeatedly their quarrel was not with the inmate but with the state. The ACLU's bone of contention was not about the "right to die" but about the state's right to kill. The warped nature of the controversy was captured by *Saturday Night Live* satire, when the cast, attired in Charles Dickens–style garb, gathered to sing a most macabre carol, "Kill Gary Gilmore for Christmas."

The last of Gilmore's scheduled execution dates was January 17, 1977. However, the day before, ACLU attorneys pleaded with a federal district judge to issue another restraining order on grounds that the Utah Supreme Court had not upheld the constitutionality of the state's death penalty statute. The judge complied at 1:05 A.M., January 17, sparking a chaotic battle during Gilmore's final hours. State attorneys set off to Denver in a Utah National Guard aircraft, hoping to get the Tenth Circuit Court of Appeals to overturn the stay. A Utah ACLU lawyer was with them to argue that the circuit judges lacked authority to render such ruling. Meanwhile, prison officials maintained preparations for an early morning execution. So did Gilmore, who, learning of the judge's order in the middle of a surprisingly cheerful visit with family, became so enraged he needed sedation.

At 7:37 A.M., a specially convened panel of the Tenth Circuit determined the execution could proceed. The ACLU, ready at the U.S. Supreme Court, pressed for one final desperation stay. At 7:45 A.M., Justice Byron White denied the application. As the condemned man was being led to the prison warehouse that would serve as his execution chamber, Justice Thurgood Marshall also rejected the ACLU's petition.

Without further delay, Utah authorities proceeded to carry out Gilmore's death sentence. He was strapped onto a chair that faced a black-sheet curtain. Behind the curtain stood five anonymous riflemen. The warden asked the prisoner if he had any last words. Gilmore paused, then said, "Let's do it!" A hood was placed over Gilmore's head. At 8:07 A.M., he was shot in the chest. One rifle fired a blank. Four other bullets pierced Gilmore's heart. Two minutes later, he was pronounced dead.[35]

As if the nation needed to catch its collective breath after Utah's melodrama, no one was executed in 1977 or 1978. The cause of delay was the deliberate functioning of the country's legal machinery. Executions remained rare in the United States through 1983.

Only two of the six men put to death between 1976 and 1982, John Spenkelink and Charlie Brooks, put up a legal struggle. The rest (Gilmore, Jesse Bishop, Steven Judy, and Frank Coppola) were "consensual" executions, meaning they refused appeals. Justices Marshall and Bennan referred to them as "state-administered suicides."[36] The eagerness of these inmates to die and to confront through the media those who wanted to keep them alive served death penalty proponents well. So did the fact that five of the six prisoners were white. This went a long way to ease the return of a practice accused of being racist.[37]

EXECUTIONS IN THE FAMILY OF NATIONS

Capital punishment remains controversial. "The death penalty is an anachronism that survives because we hide it from our awareness and deny its violence."[38] When we place the punishment in context, we can acknowledge its true nature. Only then will the sanction be abolished.

If Western Europe's experience is any model, capital punishment, two generations removed from abolition, would no longer be a political consideration. It would devolve into a barbaric relic, akin to branding and slavery. This would be quite a contrast from today, where the United States finds itself aligned with—take your pick—nineteenth-century Western democracies or such twenty-first-century repressive regimes as Iraq, Iran, and China, countries that flaunt commitment to executions and suppression of human rights.

Executions, for much of history, were public rituals of pain inflicted with a terror-like strike upon hapless offenders. Often, the condemned endured torture. Executions were scheduled shortly after convictions. Much of the community was directly or indirectly involved with implementation of punishment. Some crimes punishable by death were trivial. Executing petty thieves, for instance—some of whom were children—strikes a modern observer as bloodthirsty and primitive. In the United States, minority children—African American and Native American kids—have been sentenced to die for crimes committed when they were as young as ten. In the United States, and around the globe, members of poor and otherwise marginal groups have been targeted for execution at disproportionately greater rates.

Things have changed today in the United States, although not as much as one might hope. Executions are preceded by years of incarceration; inmates are no longer subjected to the indignity and pain of torture. Now the condemned are held captive until they have exhausted their legal remedies. Then they are killed with great dispatch and, one hopes, little pain. Modern executions are hidden from public view. They are somber, restrained, calculated procedures reserved almost exclusively for adult men who have committed aggravated murder. The offenders have been sentenced pursuant to legal guidelines intended to minimize racial and other forms of discrimination and to maximize accuracy in judicial deliberations. The system has been designed to foster the appearance of justice and humanity. The reality of the modern death penalty is just the opposite. Too often, death sentences are meted out to defendants who, subsequent to incarceration, have been found factually innocent. True to the past, there is an overrepresentation of the poor, particularly minorities, for whom the injustice of racism shapes the administration of capital justice.

Until two recent Supreme Court rulings, moral innocents—the young and the retarded—also were the targets of death sentences. In March of 2005, in *Roper* v. *Simmons*, the Court declared that the Eighth and Fourteenth amendments forbade the execution of offenders who were under the age of 18 at the time of the crime. Writing for a five-to-four majority, Justice Kennedy reaffirmed the necessity of referring to "the evolving standards of decency that mark the progress of a maturing society to determine which punishments are so disproportionate as to be cruel and unusual."[39]

In *Roper*, the Court paralleled the constitutionality of executing juveniles and the constitutionality of executing the mentally retarded. Before 2002, the Court refused to categorically exempt mentally retarded individuals from capital punishment.[40] In *Atkins* v. *Virginia*, the Court held that standards of decency had evolved in the thirteen years since its prior consideration and that national consensus had formed against such executions, demonstrating that executing the mentally retarded is cruel and unusual.[41]

Nearly fifty death row inmates had been sentenced to die as juveniles. Since 1976, nine persons were executed for crimes committed when they were juveniles. These were kids, heartbreakingly immature, assigned to die before they approached any meaningful notion of adulthood. Until *Atkins*, a similar injustice had been in effect for retarded adults, people whose reduced intelligence made them children in adult bodies. Some had the mental capacity of six-year-olds. This was akin to executing a first-grader. Almost thirty retarded offenders were executed since 1976. These offenders had little comprehension of the meaning of their crimes or punishments. Some went to the death chamber expecting to wake up in the morning, ready to resume life. Such naivety brings to mind the notion of lambs led to slaughter.

More offenders, though not minors yet still young in body or mind, may be sentenced to death in the future. Youth and reduced intelligence were once powerfully mitigating factors in the court of public opinion and, consequently, in the minds of elected representatives. Attitudes change. Youth may even work against the offender, on the premise that a young outlaw has a long criminal career ahead that could be halted by execution. Accordingly, twelve jurisdictions had no minimum eligibility age for the death penalty. Prosecutors sought death for children as young as thirteen. These offenders faced death for incidents that occurred when they were little more than children. Many cases involved defendants who were victimized by domestic abuse.

Errors in capital sentencing are common, despite safeguards. Between 1900 and 1985, approximately 350 people were wrongfully sentenced to death. Since 1977, there have been more than 120 people mistakenly banished to death row, the watershed for modern legal protections. According to researchers Michael Radelet, Hugo Bedau, and C.M. Putnam, twenty-three legally innocent people were executed in the twentieth century.[42] Legal innocence is no bar to execution if evidence of innocence is found too late; that is, after so-called discovery statutes have expired. "Even a compelling claim of innocence, such as a videotape of someone else committing the crime . . . does not guarantee a review in state or federal court."[43] The politically appealing concept of streamlining the capital appeals process—by shortening discovery and restricting appeals—points toward innocent people winding up on death row.

The most salient injustice of capital punishment is racism. This is particularly true of post–Civil War America, following emancipation. During slavery, blacks were punished by means of the "domestic discipline" that dominated plantations. Rarely were slaves subject to criminal courts or mob violence, as they were protected, if miserably treated, chattel. In their slaves, masters had made a substantial investment.

Once former slaves became freedmen, they were vulnerable to a racist criminal justice system and to the "popular justice" of lynch law administered by mobs and vigilante gangs like the Ku Klux Klan. It is a toss-up as to which punishment was worse—the criminal justice system or the lynch mob. For the period from 1870 to 1930, African Americans were the nearly exclusive targets of Southern lynching. This also was the case for technically legal executions. Racism was so pervasive during these decades that legal executions, occurring at approximately the same frequency as unauthorized hangings and without much more due process, were little more than "legal lynchings."

Blacks were swept off the streets and into captivity, sometimes for little more than loitering. Their future consisted of doing hard labor as contract prisoners and, later, plantation prison inmates. Often, these people worked the same fields their ancestors had as slaves. According to historian David Oshinsky, penal processes were "worse than slavery" because inmates, unlike slaves, were cheap and hence expendable labor units. They could be worked to death, then replaced by new convicts acquired at little cost.

Lynchings, legal or otherwise, are a thing of the past, as a regular practice. These egregious injustices symbolize an enduring legacy of racism in the use of executions. Overt and often pronounced discrimination in the deployment of the death penalty in the South dragged on into the 1960s and early 1970s. A less harsh but persistent racial bias survived in the North as well during this period. A public opinion survey reported in the *Journal of Research in Crime and Delinquency* revealed "support for capital punishment is associated with prejudice against blacks."[44] For many whites, violence is seen as a black problem. They see the death penalty as a black punishment. Unfortunately, there's something to this: Blacks have been overrepresented among condemned inmates throughout U.S. history. The major reason for this is bias—in society and the justice system—rather than a natural proclivity for crime.

Since the 1976 reemergence of the death penalty, approximately 350 people have been put to death. Roughly 40 percent of those executed were African American, although African Americans comprise just 12 percent of the population. The overrepresentation of blacks among the executed was much higher in the past, especially in the South. It might be detected that blacks commit a disproportionate number of violent street crimes—roughly 40 percent—in a way placing themselves at greater risk of execution. Before reaching conclusions, a key question is, why do black Americans have a high rate of violent street crime? A significant part of that answer surfaces as enduring social injustice.

Evidence suggests that high rates of violent crime among blacks can be traced to the persistent and destructive interaction between race, poverty, and injustice in U.S. history. This damaging mix began with slavery, gave way to decades of indiscriminate mob lynching, judicial execution, and incarceration in prisons patterned after plantations, and continued through to ghettos and penitentiaries that virtually hold captive society's poor black population. Variously characterized as "truly disadvantaged" and consisting of a hard-core "underclass," many African Americans, past and present, see "little reason to respect the law or look down upon those who were punished and sent to jail"[45] and a lot of reason to view authorities with contempt. Few minority groups have ever faced such conditions of continuing deprivation and injustice, often under the guise of the law. Few groups have been forced to live for so long under what Robert Johnson calls "criminogenic conditions." Our past cloaks the death penalty in a mantle of racism.

Racial bias in the administration of capital punishment takes different forms. One relates to the victim's race: nearly 85 percent of those executed in the United States were convicted for killing a white person. This is so even though 50 percent of murder victims are black. When an African American man kills a white person, his chances of receiving a death sentence are four to eleven times greater than the killer of a black person.[46]

The crimes in which blacks kill whites might be considered legally more serious. Many are armed robberies gone astray, qualifying for felony murder penalties. This crime pattern reinforces the effect of race and poverty in America. To borrow philosophy from outlaw Willie Sutton, who robbed banks because "that's where the money was," blacks disproportionately rob whites because they are the ones with money. The severe penalties these crimes carry reveal vestiges of a racial caste system in the United States, a system formally dismantled only a few decades ago but which still surfaces in segregated patterns in housing, schooling, and other aspects of American life. Crossing the color line in commission of violent crime is seen as legally more serious than violence among blacks, in part because social arrangements dictate that crossing the color line is itself threatening to the larger social order. It has been considered sinister throughout our country's history.

By comparison, whites have rarely been executed for capital offenses against blacks. Of the roughly 1,600 American executions carried out since 1608, only thirty whites (spread over twenty-six cases) have been executed for crimes against blacks. This comes to about two-tenths of the 1 percent of known U.S. executions. Only two white offenders have been executed for killing black victims in the past twenty-five years. The conclusion one draws is that the lives protected by our death penalty have been white; the lives sacrificed are those of persons of color, specifically young African American males. It isn't surprising that among those wrongfully convicted, most are black.

Shifting focus from race to class, it may be said that the death penalty is largely the province of the poor. "Only those without capital get capital punishment," posits an old gallows adage. No one of means resides on death row. There are several reasons. The rich can employ good legal counsel who help privileged clients avoid death sentences by artful plea bargaining or skillful courtroom tactics. The poor, meanwhile, too often get shoddy legal defense. If one is poor, his attorney is apt to be young and inexperienced or old and incompetent. Class and race bias often converge. According to the National Law Journal, "Indigent defendants on trial for their lives are being represented by ill-trained, unprepared court-appointed lawyers. One death case in Georgia was tried (and lost) by a third-year law student, and in four other trials that led to Death Row, defense counsel referred to clients in open court as 'niggers.'"[47]

More profound biases are operating. White-collar crimes, most perpetrated by wealthy white offenders, sometimes result in death and destruction on a far larger scale than the typical murder case. For instance, negligently maintained work environments, such as factories and mines, pose life-threatening hazards. Sometimes such conditions are the cause of mass injuries and deaths. These offenses often are treated as tragedies, as civil indiscretions with a commercial bent, or as minor criminal matters but never as capital criminal cases, even though cold-blooded calculation—the willingness to risk lives for money—can be established in many situations.[48] If the death penalty were ever warranted, would it not apply to a person of privilege acting with due deliberation and displaying disregard for the welfare of others?

The claims of Jesse Jackson, senior and junior, ring true. The outspoken civil rights leader and his Congressman son cowrote *Legal Lynching: Racism, Injustice, and the Death Penalty*.[49] The point of their text is that, even today, capital punishment is so riddled with injustice that it can be considered legal lynching. The authors speak metaphorically—concentrating on extreme cases rather than widespread social practices—but theirs is a powerful thesis. At one time, legal executions in the South were routinely comparable to lynching. Those days may be past but substantial injustices remain, resulting from the arbitrariness of death penalty law and from residual biases linked to race and class. These miscarriages of justice strain our faith in the legal system. We should be troubled, as the Reverend and Representative Jackson are, that a punishment so readily embraced by lynch mobs lives on. Remnants of injustices that marked the death penalty as a primitive type of violence should be relegated to the trash heap of history.

Even if the death penalty were administered evenhandedly, it would still be unjust because the modern execution process is profoundly inhumane. Executions today amount to a slow death by psychological torture. No criminal should be tortured as punishment. Torture is tantamount to a violation of our most basic human right—the right to remain a person with a distinct personality. Yet today's condemned prisoners are dehumanized. They are reduced to the status of objects—bodies not persons—then put to death following an impersonal bureaucratic script. The executioners are dehumanized also, although only partially and symbolically, in the context of implementing punishment. This dehumanization permits authorities to operate as impersonal agents of violence while remaining unaffected in their personal lives.

The bottom line in the relationship between executioner and prisoner is that capital punishment strips both of their humanity and, therefore, is an actual, not merely a metaphorical, instance of torture. Since torture can never be just, that leaves the death penalty as unjust punishment.

SOME HISTORICAL PERSPECTIVE

Sensibilities about violence—especially about the killing that is the heart of the death penalty—have evolved. These sensibilities impart a different form and significance to capital punishment at different points in history. There was, first, the raw, passionate, unfettered rage that underscored stonings in antiquity (3000 B.C.E. to 500 C.E.) In those days, the violence was face-to-face and the entire community was involved as spectators or executioners.

Later, the rage of communal stoning, softened but not tamed, came to be expressed in the primitive marketplace hangings of the early medieval village (500 to 1000 C.E.). These hangings were rough-and-tumble events, featuring the aggrieved party as executioner. During the late Middle Ages (1000 to 1500), executions still were held in the marketplace or on the village square, but by then had become more formal, dignified, ceremonial affairs. Procedures were elaborate. Rage was blunted by formalities. For the dire offenders of this day—a group that included heretics—executions were finely detailed exhibitions of state authority orchestrated by high officials. Rage was removed from these pageants, but other strong emotions were left intact. There was excitement and awe, especially before the majesty and might of the Inquisition.

Executions characterized by a restrained ceremony were the norm during the early modern period (1500 to 1800). Crowds of spectators might have lapsed into unseemly behavior, but such conduct was an aberration from the formal execution script. These proceedings featured ritual and etiquette, as in the late Middle Ages, but with little of the pomp or circumstance. Milder emotions, such as those of devotion, were given outlet in ceremony. Neither awe nor excitement were deemed appropriate. Officials and spectators were expected to express a quiet reverence, tinged by sadness.

In the modern period (1800 forward), ceremony gave way to bureaucratic procedure carried out behind prison walls, out of the community's sight. Feelings are absent, or suppressed, in bureaucratically administered executions. With rigid procedure comes a functional routine dominated by hierarchy and assignment. Officials perform mechanically before a small, silent gathering of authorized witnesses who behave with measured restraint. Executions have come to be considered "dirty work." There is no communal component. The process is antiseptically conducted. Few have to get their hands soiled.

The trend in executions is to remove ourselves from the violence. First, physically—we no longer throw stones. Then, existentially—we are no longer involved in the process in any meaningful way. This trend reflects our growing awareness of the humanity of others, which makes it more difficult for us to kill criminals—particularly in public, with bloody hands— even when we are convinced they are guilty. Executions have become more formal affairs detached from community life. What was once a public, communal event has developed into the private preserve of prison officials, who approach the task of execution with the impersonality of the modern bureaucrat. The result is that capital punishment has become a commodity dispensed without redeeming social or communal purpose.

Executions today are isolated undertakings carried out impersonally—in cold blood—to the detriment of all. This is not violent justice, as was the case with death penalty past. This is violence pure and simple. This violence must be recognized for what it is and should be rejected. Society will discover it can live with its worst offenders—although some must spend the rest of their lives behind bars.

Executions once were public, passionate events. The earliest executions were acts of spontaneous, explosive violence. Stonings had a savage tone to them even as they united the community against the offender. Later executions featured hanging and took a formal, restrained character, although the crowds could be festive. In fact, the word *gala* derives from *gallows*, an association that evokes the scene at many hangings. The death penalty was both a confirmation and a celebration of community values and community life. One might cry for the condemned, but in general they were considered demonic figures, destined for Hell, beyond the care of the community against which they had offended. The violence inflicted on them met with little or no repugnance.

Accounts of executions from olden days reflect a familiarity with violence: a sense that people were not put off by the way in which criminals met their fate. The threshold of accepted violence is lower in later times, indicative of more refined sensibilities. Repugnant reaction was elicited when heads rolled in England or bodies were broken on the rack in Germany. At each phase of history up to the early modern period, citizens showed a considerable capacity for witnessing crude acts of violence without being repulsed. One sees sadness at some of the condemneds' plight, suggesting a compassion typically missing in earlier executions. The civility of proceedings implies that neither executioner nor crowd were terribly troubled by the events. There was no apparent repugnance at the bloody fate about to befall those facing decapitation. There are no reports of public revulsion at the sight of stonings during the biblical era. Nor is there evidence of revulsion at the sight of the gross bodily torture that accompanied medieval executions.

Paintings of European execution scenes during the early modern period portray the ritual and its aftermath as normal and unremarkable. Decent citizens are pictured going about their everyday business, oblivious to the gallows and the corpses hanging from them.

London during this era was colloquially known as the City of Gallows. Gibbeted bodies, hung up in chains and left to rot at major crossroads, were visual reminders of hometown justice. This was considered standard fare by the English. "No matter by what approach the stranger entered London, he had the fact of the severity of English criminal law painfully impressed upon him by a sight of the gallows."[50]

Actual executions were another matter. "Then the crowd came specially to watch the spectacle and did not want to miss a minute."[51] A public killing was exciting and worthy of interest, a communal and political affair of some moment; residual bodies were empty of larger meaning. Executions took place. Public attention rose and fell, not in response to the tragedy of life lost but in reaction to the drama of life taken. The bodies of the dead may have lingered, but life in the community went on.

EXECUTIONS AMERICAN-STYLE

The history of execution procedures in America roughly parallels that of executions in Continental Europe and England. Executions in the colonial period and on through the mid–nineteenth century were comparable to the early modern executions across the ocean. Later executions in the United States followed a script that, with its focus on technical method and bureaucratic procedure, is uniquely American.

Colonial executions, similar to those in Europe, were public. They were conducted on scaffolds, centrally situated and elevated to accommodate the audience. Procedures were restrained and dignified, merging civil and religious authority. Ministers and magistrates jointly designed public executions, intending to flex religious and civil muscle. As civil ceremony, executions demonstrated state power. They reinforced order and encouraged conformity. As religious ritual, clergy used hanging day to remind those assembled of their mortality and to highlight that only God redeems the sinful. Ministers instructed spectators that the truly penitent could earn salvation. Execution day functioned as lesson and celebration. At the gallows, the crowd received a warning about crime's consequences. Hanging day was an opportunity for clerical and civic leaders to provide proof that society worked properly and that God saved souls.

Colonial executions were well-attended, attracting high officials and common citizens. The behavior of the crowd generally was restrained, although an aura of celebration—of confirmation of one's righteousness—was present. The execution process was seen to have a beauty all its own.

Executions during this period were a communal undertaking. These and subsequent American executions shared a communality with capital punishment as practiced in Europe; the community typically saw themselves as insiders and the condemned as outsiders. Such outsiders were thought to be minorities or foreigners or, literally, those not from the immediate community. Execution lore, especially with a European slant, makes much of the wealthy or noble who meet their demise on the scaffold. But those are a small minority of the condemned. Generally, those publicly executed were common folk of no distinction. In the colonial context, the condemned "were people for whom spectators might feel the least sympathy, and, authorities hoped, the assembled would unite against the condemned to defend social stability."[52] This characterization of the condemned—as outsiders, marginal to the community—applies to virtually all public executions in America and Europe.

Those condemned to public executions often served as scapegoats. Their sentences were a variant of human sacrifice. Throughout history, vengeance, sacrifice, and criminal justice have been intertwined in the same process, needed alike to safeguard the state against the wrath of the gods. As all scapegoats, the condemned typically are "in" but not "of" the community. Unlike strangers, marginal members of a group are suitable substitutes for the entire group and so can be appropriate vessels for the group's impurities. Scapegoats can serve as stand-ins for the group's fears, since the dominant group typically fears and loathes its marginal members, on whom it projects its worst fears.

The scapegoat, sufficiently invested with group guilt and symbolizing all the group fears, can be banished on the scaffold in a ritual of righteous power, the object of which is to appease God, to unite the "insiders" in their shared status as special in God's eyes and in their own, and to render the greater group safe from the type of earthly dangers represented by the criminal they have offered up for punishment. No wonder public executions attracted large crowds and generated a spirit of festivity, celebration, and smug self-congratulation. Those assembled would be drawn together and imbued with a special sense of community. This was no ordinary gathering. The spectacle of the execution offered the exclusive sight of the dominant group asserting raw power, reveling in that power, and celebrating their clarified identity. The gala made the group whole by killing off a deviant pretender to the esteemed ranks of society.

An ordinary death by hanging was not the harshest sanction at the disposal of the seventeenth- and eighteenth-century state. Just as there were stages shy of death, there were stages beyond it. "'Tis well known there are some kinds of Death more sharp and terrifying than others," an English writer observed. "An Execution that is attended with more lasting Torment, may strike a far greater Awe."[53] These more severe penalties were meted out to apply terror where it was thought appropriate.

Hanging sometimes caused a quick and seemingly painless death. When government authorities wanted to ensure that death would be slow and painful, and all the more frightening, they turned to an alternative—burning alive. Burning had a tradition in English jurisprudence. In the late medieval period it was a common form of execution for witchcraft and heresy.[54] By the time of colonization of North America, burning was no longer used as punishment for religious offenses. Those convicted of witchcraft at Salem were hanged, as were other colonists executed for witchcraft. Burning was reserved for two categories of offenders whose crimes were considered unusually disruptive of the social order—slaves convicted of murdering their owners or plotting revolt and women convicted of killing their husbands.[55]

Public execution procedures didn't vary much in America or Europe. In America, many aspects of the killing ritual barely changed throughout the seventeenth and eighteenth centuries. The officials presiding over executions saw in the assembled crowds the assertion of a social order united against the threat posed by the offender. Sermons were a vital facet of executions. The themes, intended to apply to offender and spectator alike, were notably enduring. Clergy used the language of *salvation* and *penitence*. Sermons, with their reusable arguments, held enormous sway on hanging day.

Sensibilities began changing around the turn of the nineteenth century. A middle class was emerging that valued restraint and private punishments. For this sector of society, the suffering and dying of the condemned were increasingly perceived as painful since others were increasingly considered fellow human beings. The broadening scope of people believed to be human was a consequence of a growing mutual dependence among social groups. This mutually dependent middle class was characterized by the merchant, trading, and service strata of an increasingly civilized society. This privileged group identified to some extent with the convict on the scaffold. In the offender they could glimpse their own humanity. These increasingly civilized people did not enjoy the sight of physical suffering, even that of the guilty. This is because the guilty, no matter how serious the offense, were still considered fellow human beings. The public display of suffering provided by executions, variously entertaining and edifying in past eras when applied to marginal and demonized groups, had become a source of distress, a cruel spectacle that was to be avoided.

Changing sensibilities shifted the perception of capital punishment in the abstract, and the nature of the turnouts at executions. Those of more re-fined sensibilities strictly avoided executions. Those who remained attracted to the deadly affairs were of a more coarse ilk. Ironically, many in that crowd were outsiders to the community who would travel to executions for the entertainment. Their conduct often resembled that of unruly English mobs. Their behavior was a far cry from the hushed and penitent—even if smugly self-righteous—community members who had been praised for their restraint by Puritan ministers over the centuries. The condemned, also, could prove unruly—refusing to confess, claiming innocence—and would have to be coerced into their assigned roles of the execution's morality play. The depiction of hanging day as a spectacle of social and religious order was no longer so predictable. The event no longer shared the same meaning for all citizens, God-fearing and criminal alike. The claim could no longer be made that on hanging day the whole community came together for a powerful lesson in piety and morality.

Executions came to resemble county fairs, attracting crowds of onlookers to small villages. Matters were worse in urban areas. While a small-town execution might draw a crowd of mostly outsiders totaling 1,500, city ex-ecutions could pump up crowds of 40,000. Regardless of where a public execution was held, it became a commercial event, complete with admission tickets, preferred seating, and refreshment stands. For the enlightened, these were disgusting spectacles because the crowds attracted to them came for the crass carnival atmosphere. The elite viewed these crowds as a threat to social order and state power, both of which were called into question by the rowdy behavior of spectators. The executioner always won out and the rowdies always dispersed and went home. The greater threat may have been to the image of civility central to the elite vision of society. If public executions can be stretched to be considered human sacrifice, such sacrifices would have been offered to satisfy the vanity of people who reveled in the primitive violence that gave lie to the idea of death penalty as civilized sanction.

Public executions were banned state by state in New England and the Mid-Atlantic. They were outlawed in these regions by 1845. The practice was replaced by private hangings discreetly held behind prison walls. Prison hangings became the new execution-day ritual. These were modest secular operations performed in front of a small group of elite citizens who were obligated by class etiquette to behave with decorum. Private executions were not intended to be spectacles. Nor were they ceremonies, with sacrificial overtones. Proponents of private executions claimed that condemned inmates would repent sincerely if removed from the stare of onlookers. There was concern that public hangings produced confessions concocted for the masses instead of genuine professions of guilt. The handbills distributed at executions, featuring a standard repentance formula, suggest this was so.

Repentance, real or contrived, was not central to private executions. The key was to maintain a quiet, uncontroversial execution, in contrast to the unpredictable undertakings of the public gallows. Drugs were used to anesthetize the condemned before they were privately hanged, so that emotional control was preserved. A tame execution with the appearance of the condemned's cooperation would result. The prisoner to be hanged would stand alone. There was no scaffold platform from which to vent feelings, protest innocence, or secure forgiveness from the community. The condemned was denied any emotional support that might be derived from the energy of the gathering. The ill-fated inmate was held secure in the uncontested grasp of officials, who asserted control of the event. Isolated from human passions, executions could proceed in calculated, antiseptic fashion. In hushed tones, from behind opaque walls, the deadly deed would be done. The paradoxical result, in a foreshadowing of contemporary executions, was that "a polite nation's brutality [was] camouflaged" as an act of humaneness.[56]

The elimination of public executions only served to hide their cruelty. This procedural modification intensified the experience. The transition from public passionate executions to cold, clinical, private ones is the start of the bureaucratic regimen of modern executions. Today, psychological dehumanization triggered by social isolation serves as the anesthetic that facilitates efficient, impersonal killing. These executions are devoid of emotion from the governing authorities' perspective. With the advent of lethal injections, many jurisdictions tranquilize the condemned. This medication works to numb the human spirit and expedite a process that so camouflages executions as to render them unrecognizable as premeditated acts of violence carried out in the guise of an ostensibly civilized society.

SOUTHERN-STYLE PUBLIC EXECUTIONS—LEGAL AND OTHERWISE

The retreat from public executions in the United States was delayed in the South. There the condemned were nearly always blacks, considered by Southern whites to be less than fully human. In the eyes of Southern white society, blacks were a marginal, demonized group almost completely excluded from the safeguards afforded members of the human community. It is revealing that one rationale for American slavery was the misconception that blacks possessed racial traits making them, like primitive beasts of burden, uniquely qualified for bondage. Following the termination of slavery, whites anticipated the demise of African Americans on the premise that blacks, being naturally dependent on whites, couldn't survive on their own.

According to historian David Oshinsky, "Many believed that blacks would perish in freedom, like fish on the land. The Negro's 'incompetence,' after all, had been essential to the understanding of slavery itself."[57]

A corollary belief held by many Southern whites was that black people were natural criminals. As quoted by Oshinsky, in the smugly self-righteous words of a nineteenth-century Southern planter, "You can't find a white streak in 'em. . . . All the men are thieves, and all the women are prostitutes. It's their natur' to be that way, and they'll never be no other way." Slavery, it was thought, had contained criminality. With freedom, the thinking went, came constant, violent crime, requiring severe punishment.

The sanction of choice was public execution, either by legal means or illegal. None of the day's social elites considered blacks fellow human beings worthy of compassion. No one thought to protect ex-slaves from humiliation and suffering on the public scaffold. The annihilation of blacks—there was talk of black extermination after Emancipation—framed punishment debates. For one political party, the Radicals, "the 'Negro Problem' was how to control blacks as they passed through bestiality and into extinction."[58]

A 1905 Texas editorial stated, "Almost every day some negro brute assaults a white woman in this state, and often one to a half-dozen murders are committed to hide the crime. . . . If rape and murder by brutish negroes are to become common, the negro must expect extermination."[59] Confronted with a violent "criminal race," Southerners resorted to legal and illegal executions, and routine brutal punishment.

Lynching was a Southern phenomenon that sprouted with the passing of slavery, when blacks became subject to severe sanctions. There were hangings in the South prior to the freeing of the slaves, but they were infrequent.

The targets of this justice, pre-Emancipation, were mostly poor whites considered marginal to the community. This contradicts the image of slavery in America, which features the indiscriminate lynching of slaves. Slaves were rarely executed. Slaves had great value as commodities of labor. To kill a slave was to squander a considerable financial investment.

The social control imposed by executions was superfluous to the slaves. They already were imprisoned on plantations and subject to corporal punishment. Those seeking to abolish slavery referred to the South as a prison for blacks. William Lloyd Garrison writes of "the Southern prison-house of bondage" in his preface to Frederick Douglass's narrative about his slave experiences.[60]

The emancipation of slaves ended the mass incarceration of African Americans. It set in motion forces that hammered the Southern way of life. The class structure of Southern society and the caste system upon which it was built were in danger of being toppled. Approximately four million slaves were set free. A tidal wave of humans, previously considered chattel, was now unleashed to become potential competitors. Southern whites—fearful, beleaguered, and increasingly vengeful in the face of social and economic competition from free blacks—looked for alternatives to slavery that would enable them to control the black population. The dominant undertone was the preservation of white supremacy, undisputed during slavery.

White supremacy meant racial purity. Brutal violence was one approach to maintaining supremacy. The idea was to break the spirit of newly liberated African Americans the same way one might tame a beast. Reduce the poor being through debilitating fear. Turn the object of your scorn into someone who would submit willingly to the demands of the dominant caste, quietly living out a segregated, inferior life. This strategy is exemplified by the actions of vigilante groups like the Ku Klux Klan and other terrorist gangs that would frighten, torture, and lynch black citizens.

The word *lynching* probably derives from Captain William Lynch, a back-country settler of Scotch-Irish descent who lived in Virginia before moving to South Carolina. In the 1760s, he and his neighbors started administering swift justice to "lawless men" by flogging or killing them. Evidence and due process weren't a consideration.[61] Lynchings are no longer defended, but they once earned praise as noble acts of "popular justice" throughout the South after the Civil War and far into the twentieth century.

"Lynch law is a good sign," according to Tom Watson, the Georgia populist. "It shows that a sense of justice lives among the people."[62] The popularity of illegal executions followed the migration of Southerners west to Texas. Lynchings delighted the public and local officials in the South. Several governors, deferring to the public will, reflected its demands for vengeance. Former Mississippi governor James K. Bardaman's thoughts were indicative: "If it is necessary every Negro in the state will be lynched; it will be done to maintain white supremacy."[63]

Lynching rituals were reminiscent of the mob violence of biblical stonings. Southern sanctions sometimes took on the flamboyant aura of medieval executions. An 1856 Maryland statute "provided that a Negro convicted of murder should have his right arm cut off, head severed, body divided into four parts and ... the head and quarters ... set up in the most public place near where the crime was committed."[64]

The victim of mobs often would be seized by outraged citizens who would assault him savagely. The beaten victim might be mutilated while still alive. Many lynchings turned the victim into a human sacrifice. These immolations were known as "Negro barbeques." This excruciating procedure had long been abandoned in legal executions. Such barbarism recalled medieval witch hunts. Immolation had been reserved for the worst offenders, criminals who had to be instantly wiped from the face of the earth. The dominant group believed execution was not enough for these violators. They needed to be reduced to ash. Effort was made to prolong the killing, the better to inflict agony while entertaining the assembled. Southerners, perceiving themselves surrounded by a brutal subhuman enemy, reacted accordingly with primitive violence, undeterred by any empathy for the targets of their fear and anger.

Lynchings characterized by ferocious violence were the norm. Lynchings followed a script. That script often called for exercises in frenzied mob violence. The resulting scene was ruled by blood lust.

Elements of human sacrifice were present in many lynchings. The victims were marginalized and transformed into demonized stereotypes. They were imbued with blame for all that had gone wrong in Southern society after the Civil War. The blame game carried through to the Great Depression. In cases of human sacrifice, the target group is subjected to two transfigurations, so that "the victims are transfigured into aggressors," allowing the dominant group to convert its brutality into a scared rite, reaffirming the purity of those committing the retaliation.[65]

Thought to harbor intense resentment against white Southerners who had enslaved them, newly liberated blacks were objects of hysterical fear. That fear resulted in lynchings for vague violations of racial etiquette (i.e., "acting like a white man") and for violent offenses. Paranoia sometimes led to lynchings of obviously innocent people—friends or relatives who were consciously selected by mobs as surrogates when the alleged offenders could not be located. As members of a scapegoat class, any black could—once a mob gained momentum—serve as a candidate for hanging.

Some offenses and lynchings were worse than others. The murder of one's employer had special meaning. This crime could be linked to deep-seated fear stemming from slavery. The situation evoked visions of docile slaves revolting to kill masters, reversing white supremacy. Such fearful concerns intensified as slavery was called into question with the impending Civil War. These fears ran rampant following Emancipation, when concerns of "Negro retribution" for the abuses of slavery were common.

Rape, an especially heinous offense, resulted in some of the most horrible lynchings. Rape threatened white supremacy at its supposed genetic core by "polluting" the white gene pool. "It is small exaggeration to describe white preoccupation with miscegenation and racial amalgamation as a regional paranoia" during this period. The paranoid nightmare was rape.[66] Racial discrimination in the use of capital punishment has been most pronounced in the matter of rape. Marquart, Ekland-Olson, and Sorensen write that "When males from an African-American background raped an Anglo female, the case was approximately 35 times more likely to result in capital punishment than a prison sentence," while few white men were executed for rape in the South. "In only one case did the rape of a black female result in a death sentence and actual execution."[67] This disparity leads to the conclusion that rape laws were intended to protect white women far more than black and to punish black perpetrators to a greater degree than white.

Lynchings attracted crowds composed of a broad cross-representation of society—the poor and rich, the old and young, women and men. This was possible because lynchings often were publicized in advance. This tactic further frightened blacks with the threat of imminent violence. It encouraged attendance by whites from surrounding vicinities. Railroads added special trains to accommodate larger lynching crowds.[68] A hanging in Mississippi in 1902 offered strategically situated reserved seating for women who might want a closer view.[69] As blacks were perceived as subhuman, empathy was no deterrent to the elite finding places at lynchings. No concerns about humaneness interfered with attendance. Such sentiment was reserved for humans. With a demonized scapegoat, a member of the assembled could think of the lynching as a humane exercise in service to the community. The lynching victim was being sacrificed for the greater good.

Photographs of hanging scenes captured the festive, gloating mood of public executions. Members of the dominant group smile broadly while toting their picnics. Others raise their arms triumphantly and point with pride at the ravaged corpse, as if to say, "long live the whites; the evil black is dead." Pictures catching the mob in action portray another impression. Mob members appear infused with rage, straining to get at the victim, kicking and spitting to tear at their prey. Rocks were thrown, bats and clubs wielded. Sometimes members of the gang hurt each other. Even children got into the fray. It's hard to miss the resemblance to out-of-control biblical stonings.

Lynching participants would recall the experience and retell it to others. A desire for relics, akin to craving souvenirs—body parts, parcels of clothing, a chunk of burnt wood or rope; all attesting to the sacrificial nature of the event—was a universal aspect of lynchings, underscoring their memorable quality and bringing to mind the days of the Middle Ages. Picture postcards of the proceedings, hawked by enterprising photographers, became prized keepsakes. Descriptions of hangings were reported in newspapers. Such accounts included stories of citizens prominently engaged in the violence. Like contemporary legal executions, lynchings typically were a matter of civic and racial pride.

Statistics regarding lynchings of African Americans in the South, incomplete though they may be, tell a frightening tale of violence. Hangings were common during Reconstruction (1865 to 1877). This was a time of remarkable violence against blacks, a paranoid reaction to the concerns of many whites that "the region was threatened by the prospect of 'Negro domination.'"[70] As reliable numbers are not available, the extent of carnage is not easily determined. During the "lynching era" (1882 to 1930), statistics are better. Local records reveal that "on average, a black man, woman, or child was murdered nearly once a week, every week ... by a hate-driven white mob."[71] Capital punishment during this period, almost interchangeable with the peculiar Southern oxymoron, "legal lynching," claimed approximately as many black lives and helped reinforce the reign of terror sought by Southern whites. The death toll during this period attributable to all executions—mob violence and capital punishment—tallied an amazing 4,291 black lives. Over the forty-nine years of the notorious lynching era, "an African-American was exterminated—legally or illegally—somewhere in the South nearly every four days. Adding lynchings from the Reconstruction period, the deadly era extends for more than sixty years and covers a full three generations of free African-Americans."[72]

Racism is at the core of slavery and the cavalcade of killing that followed Emancipation. The tidal wave of imprisonment of freemen following the Civil War also was the result of racism. The Southern prison system, originally based on contract labor, then on plantation prisons, was created to replace slaves with prisoners whose punishment, marked by an alarmingly high death rate, was in many regards "worse than slavery."[73] Racism also explains why the majority of those sentenced to die in the South during this period were black, why their alleged victims were white, and why many of these black men were publicly hanged well into the twentieth century— a primitive, degrading procedure for a legal system to perpetuate at such a late date. Public hanging as a legal sanction was introduced as a "conspicuous symbol of indignity" intended to deter and shame; hanging often produced "a slow and agonizing death," the embarrassing manifestations of which—kicking, twitching, choking, loss of bowel and bladder control— were readily visible to sizeable gatherings.[74] All execution techniques spawn macabre death scenes, but the spectacle of a dangling corpse is among the most degrading of all.

One might imagine that in such an environment it must seem fitting that a group of law-abiding whites would assemble to witness and celebrate the degradation of a black criminal. The victim might well be resigned to his fate; after all he lived in a world in which lynching gangs could wreak havoc on his race at will, and in which law boiled down to white rule. A lawful public hanging might well be, for prisoner and audience alike, a routine and decent endeavor, a kind of tame lynching with antecedents from days long— and not so long—ago. Such events most notably recalled the early modern period, with its staged executions scripted to conceal human emotion that might mar the proceedings.

The record bears out these speculations. The ritual of twentieth-century public executions in the South was streamlined relative to early modern executions. The process offered echoes from that distant period. There was a sort of ceremony, characterized by a bucolic simplicity. Conducted in pastures, these hangings were unobtrusive, routine events. The condemned, generally, betrayed no profound sentiments. The gatherings ranged from raucous to subdued in their reactions. Occasionally, onlookers expressed sadness or resignation that a young black life was about to be prematurely snuffed at the scaffold.

An execution described by Alan Mencken depicts the dichotomy between inner turmoil and outward appearance characterized by public hangings. In Snow Hill, Maryland, in 1902, a black man named Asbury Dixon was put to death. On the eve of his execution, Dixon, family, and fellow inmates freely congregated in the jail, singing hymns. Dixon sang "with a fervor and solemnity unsurpassed by any of them." He was resigned to die. Dixon's young son, Tema, "much interested in the singing of hymns and the farewells of the prisoners to his father," grew tired and fell asleep in his father's cell. The jailor, seeing no harm, allowed the boy to sleep the night "in his father's arms." The parting of father and son the following morning was heart wrenching for Dixon and his boy, as well as for the jailer. This was the private reality. Dehumanizing stereotypes could be discarded. The public reality, of white justice demanding black death, awaited Dixon on the scaffold. Whatever the jailer's feelings, he conducted his business absent sentiment. Dixon, too, assumed his role in the morality play, betraying no emotion. He ate a hearty last meal and puffed a cigar. Before the assembled, Dixon acknowledged the error of his ways, spoke of receiving the Lord's forgiveness, and bade a gentle farewell to the onlookers. Resignation to a force beyond the condemned's control permeated the proceedings. The execution was not a time for sadness, but one of "the quiet little hangings [that] made a pleasant break in the monotony of farm life."[75]

Public executions would be conducted in Southern states deep into the twentieth century. Such executions held sway in Mississippi and Louisiana well into the 1950s. Executions were held in local jails in these jurisdictions as recently as 1957. After this point, the execution procedure was centralized and moved into state penitentiaries. Mississippi is home to the first portable electric chair. This device was used in the state from 1940 through 1955. Of the seventy-three prisoners put to death in this chair, 77 percent were black. The executions usually were conducted in local jails. Occasionally they were for public consumption. Newspaper reports during this period sometimes carried photographs of these electrocutions. The condemned was depicted as a specimen, nothing more. The person strapped into the chair was merely a test subject to help examine the workings of the curious killing machine. The condemned was an entity whose demise could be dissected dispassionately.

Although executions employing the portable electric chair were conducted within local jails, they had a semipublic patina. When the executioner arrived with the chair in the back of his truck, it would generate buzz in the community. Photos exist of executioner, Jim Thompson, posing with the chair in front of a school. Surrounding the chair are kids from an all-white Mississippi school, holding books and gazing admiringly.[76] Actual executions drew considerable attention. People would surround the jail straining to detect signs of electrocution. A crowd would form late at night on the courthouse square. Seated on chairs, gathered with their children, people would wait for the current to be turned on and the street lights to dim.[77]

Nowhere do the Southern-fried roots of injustice run deeper than Texas. Justice Lone Star–style has resulted in 336 executions since 1976. This exceeds the next five states combined. The Texas proclivity to execute may be explained by its unusual judicial system. Texas is the only state with two separate, equal courts of last resort. The Texas Supreme Court adjudicates civil matters. The Court of Criminal Appeals handles criminal cases. Each has nine judges sitting for staggered six-year terms.

According to some experts, this bifurcated system results in a criminal appeals court devoid of general practitioners and the sort of legal talent that occupies corporate boardrooms. Seven of its nine members are former tough-on-crime prosecutors who embody the court's antidefense leanings. "No one runs for the Court of Criminal Appeals on a platform of vindicating constitutional rights," said Jordan Steiker, law professor at the University of Texas.[78]

To the contrary, this court has permitted instructions encouraging jurors to lie during capital deliberations. From the Supreme Court's reinstatement of the death penalty in 1976 to 1989, Texas juries were asked two questions at the sentencing stage of a capital trial: Was the killing deliberate? Does the defendant pose a danger to others? If the jurors unanimously replied yes to both, the judge was required to impose a sentence of death. In 1989, the Supreme Court determined the Texas procedure to be flawed as it did not allow the jury to consider mitigating evidence that might cause it to spare the accused's life. But the state legislature did not amend the procedure for two years. In the meantime, Texas judges adopted ad hoc instructions that kept the two questions while also telling jurors they could falsely answer "no" to one or both questions if they believed the mitigating evidence to be sufficiently strong. In its 2001 *John Paul Penry* decision, the Supreme Court ruled that instructing a juror to lie was unconstitutional. Justice Sandra

Day O'Connor wrote, "It would have been both logically and ethically impossible for a juror to follow both sets of instructions."[79] The Texas Court of Criminal Appeals continued to uphold death sentences imposed under the unconstitutional procedure, saying that some juries considering some mitigating evidence actually could have followed the seemingly inconsistent instructions. Such defiance explains why Texas leads the nation, by a wide margin, in killing convicts.

EXECUTION INSIDE PRISON WALLS: PRIVATE, BUREAUCRATIC, PROCEDURAL

The informality of so many executions played out as though it were only natural that these alien creatures be put to death. Executions of this kind now are a thing of the past. Executions came to take on new meaning and a new, impersonal form in response to the increasing perception of the humanity of the inmate. This reciprocal process—acknowledgement of the humanity of the condemned and a corresponding need to distance oneself from that humanity in order to kill the convict—occurred first in the North and much later in the South. The attitude toward blacks in the South was nothing short of primitive and, of course, blacks were the primary target of executions.

Executions came to be seen as acts of violence that reflected poorly on the community, hardened the public, and demeaned the condemned. Executions became less frequent and less public. They were moved inside jails, where they would stay until state prison systems were sufficiently constructed to take over the deed. Eventually, all executions took place within prisons. Originally, these procedures were conducted in the center of the prison yard, which accommodated large crowds. Later, executions were performed in remote corners of the yard, restricting the viewing audience. Finally, executions were moved inside prison buildings, to the basements of death rows. Such isolation centers were housed within the bowels of the prison compound.

Attempts were made to make executions as tame as humanly possible. Effort was extended so that those on the scene might conclude the endeavor was decent and humane. This concern with humanity meant that officials wanted executions to be quick, painless, minimally disfiguring, and private. One avoided anything that would alert the condemned to his impending execution, such as a peek at the killing apparatus. Unnecessarily heightening the prisoner's apprehension would result in those final torturous moments becoming even more unbearable. In the process of trying to shield inmates from such suffering—and no doubt to diminish the discomfort of prison personnel as well—executions became strained, hidden, and hurried affairs. From the executioner's perspective, one laid low, laboring quickly and quietly.

The present-day process could hardly be more different from executions of the past. Modern executions are conducted in secluded zones within penitentiaries. A restricted number of spectators attend, most doing so for professional purposes. Witnesses maintain a discreet silence, although many are understandably shaken. Neither death nor killing is any longer a routine part of daily life. Killings by officials are rare occurrences, siphoned of emotional potency by secrecy (few people see them) and semantics (few refer to executions as killings).

Efficiency and speed weaken the emotional clout of the proceedings. Contemporary executions are over within minutes. In early London, by contrast, it took nearly two hours to get from prison to gallows. In extreme situations today, executions can take mere minutes from the moment the inmate departs his cell. Observers barely realize that a killing has taken place. Nor, according to an efficient hangman, does the prisoner. Once in a while, an inmate would flee from a lynch mob and, preferring the more humane snuffing by the state, seek the safety of the official executioner.

Modern executions are highly bureaucratic operations with finely drawn roles and responsibilities, spelled out in state protocols. Conduct is closely proscribed by prison authorities and occurs in the context of enforced routines. Most prison work is bureaucratized nowadays. But the execution of inmates presents an extreme example. Killing and dying are fundamental activities. Prisons sanitize the procedure to make it as reassuring and comforting as possible. The process is ritualistic owing to its mechanical precision. But bureaucratic executions are a far cry from true rituals. Similar to bureaucratic functions, rituals permit people to disengage from their customary roles. But with true rituals, disengagement takes place in the service of a greater undertaking—some sort of celebration or cleansing—that carries a deeper communal significance. The bureaucratic execution is an end in itself, recognizing only its own internal rationale.

Citizens who are not officially affiliated with an execution play a diminished role in the proceedings. Crowds may gather during executions, although today's turnouts are a fraction of crowds past. Executions have become so routine that some barely register with the media. People may mill about outside prison gates, sometimes cheering or jeering the scheduled execution, but they have no actual awareness of what's transpiring. Prison personnel are barely cognizant of these groups. Such crowds lack a meaningful involvement in the process. Even the execution of notorious serial killer Ted Bundy, considered by many the personification of evil, attracted a gathering of two thousand, small by past standards.

The loved ones of the condemned and of the victim are on the periphery of contemporary executions. The family and friends of the condemned have restricted opportunities to visit in the death house. Although some jurisdictions allow relatives and friends of the offender or victim, or both, to attend executions, their numbers are limited. So, too, their conduct is circumscribed, in keeping with the bureaucratic principle of impersonality. Sister Helen Prejean paraphrases the admonitions given witnesses at Louisiana's Angola Prison. The warden "emphasizes to all witnesses—victims' families included—that during an execution there must be 'no emotional outbursts, no obscenities uttered, no undignified behavior of any kind.' They have designed a process that 'protects everyone's rights,' including those of the executed. 'They have family, too. A circus atmosphere is not in anyone's interest.'"[80]

Surely no one wants witnesses from the victim's family to celebrate the execution in the death chamber. But the warden's premise seems to be that any strong emotions are inherently out of place. This sentiment holds despite the execution's being an event that pulls together those deeply affected by violence and is itself a powerfully affecting violent act.

Even the condemned are curiously removed from modern executions. They are present more in body than spirit. The condemned spend years on death row awaiting their fate. This breaks from the past when the inmate's wait was merely days or weeks. A corollary of our contemporary preoccupation with humanely administered capital punishment is our desire to allow prisoners to pursue every avenue of appeal before execution. This expands the inmate's stay on death row. During their barren and lonely incarceration, the condemned die a slow psychic death. Darby Tillis was the first of thirteen men exonerated in Illinois. This was the group that inspired Governor George Ryan to empty his state's death row. Speaking at a rally in Takoma Park, Maryland, two weeks prior to the execution of Steven Oken, Tillis shared his outlook of life on death row. "You struggle for your sanity, your humanity, in an environment intent on destroying you." Numb submission becomes the norm in the death house.

HUMANE ILLUSIONS OF MODERN EXECUTIONS

The United States has tweaked the execution process, seeking the "perfect" technique. Perfect means the most tame and reliable way of killing made possible by prevailing technology. Our preferred methods have evolved. Starting with the simple, straightforward violence of hangings and firing squad shootings—we moved to the relatively complicated but tamer killings made feasible by twentieth-century technology: the gas chamber, the electric chair, and lethal injection. Our tradition lives on in modern execution methods, as each is still in use since the advent of the contemporary death penalty in 1976. In descending order of frequency, execution by lethal injection tops the list, occurring nearly twice as often as electrocution. A very distant third is the gas chamber, followed by just a few hangings and two firing squad executions. When one looks back over the twentieth century, the predominant method of killing has been the electric chair, which has taken more than four thousand lives. The mode of the future appears to be lethal injection. Authorized in more than thirty jurisdictions, lethal injection is the most frequently employed method. Execution by lethal injection or electrocution share an important facet: each lends itself to impersonal bureaucratic procedures and the appearance of quick, bloodless, and even painless deaths.

Modifications in the state's killing apparatus are revealing. Society has distanced itself from the reality of capital punishment. Our system now terminates life efficiently and impersonally—as so many functionaries in the business of justice. The modern execution procedure is unlike any of those before. Although contemporary executions are obviously violent in that they involve the forcible taking of life, the technical process is typically quick, clean, and precise. Apparently, this is the way of progress. Society has traveled a long way from the spectacles of time past.

It is easy to question this progress. One normally thinks of modern execution techniques as humane because they appear painless. But appearances can be deceiving. Doubt has been cast on the presumed painlessness of electrocution. Scientific evidence has been collected that raises the unsettling possibility that despite expert disclaimers, "death by electrocution may inflict 'unnecessary pain,' physical violence and 'mutilation'" in direct violation of the Eighth Amendment.[81]

Justice William Brennan delivered an eloquent dissent from the denial of certiorari in *Glass* v. *Louisiana*.[82] He advanced a compelling argument against the violence of electrocution. Brennan maintained such violence made this punishment "cruel and unusual." Brennan made his case that gas chamber executions also were an Eighth Amendment violation. He cited evidence that criminals executed by asphyxiation suffered great pain over several minutes. The gas chamber was intended as the electric chair's successor. There was no mutilation, no overwhelming surge of electrical power. Gas was thought to end life quietly and quickly. Few jurisdictions adopted the technique, however. For one, it was expensive. A gas chamber is a fairly elaborate device, requiring considerable maintenance. Also, it is risky. Deadly gas can escape the chamber, endangering witnesses. Further, the gas chamber fell into disfavor because of its association with the genocidal campaigns of the Nazis. The first American gas chambers only slightly preceded Nazi use. Another reason this method was abandoned was that prisoners in the gas chamber appeared to suffocate in a slow, painful way. In a 1994 case, *Fierro* v. *Gomez*, the U.S. District Court for the Northern District of California reviewed evidence on the effects of the gas chamber and concurred with Brennan's contention that its use violates the Eighth Amendment. The court "concluded that the time it takes for the lethal gas to kill an inmate combined with the degree of pain inflicted on the inmate warrants the use of another method of execution."[83]

Today, most executions use lethal injection. This is the tamest and seemingly most pain-free method yet concocted. Here, too, controversy exists. There are anesthesiologists who question whether injections are as painless as they appear. Experts claim injections, like hangings, may produce a paralysis that masks a slow, painful demise by suffocation. In *Chaney* v. *Heckler*, the court referred to "known evidence concerning lethal injection which indicates that such drugs pose a substantial threat of torturous pain to persons being executed."[84] The court observed that when using the cocktail of barbiturates and paralytics prescribed by law, "even small error in dosage or administration can leave a prisoner conscious but paralyzed while dying, a sentient witness to his or her own slow, lingering asphyxiation." Such errors could result in botched executions. Other glitches surface, as well. It can be difficult to find veins in which to insert the needle on offenders with histories of abusing drugs, a description that covers many contemporary inmates. Malfunctions of medical equipment, also, may plague the technique.

Lethal injection provides a paradoxical execution scene. A supine prisoner, apparently at rest, seems to drift into sleep intertwined imperceptibly with death. This is the ideal modern death—one that transpires peacefully. Reality may be entirely opposite. The wait on the gurney, resembling rest but actually a forced restraint, can be thought of as a sort of torture. Once the drugs are introduced, what unfolds may be death by slow suffocation. All of this plays out as society congratulates itself for its humaneness. More macabre, the immobilized offender realizes the deception of lethal injection and, unable to struggle, recognizes his inability to communicate distress. His dignity may suffer a final insult through sheer helplessness as others smile benignly, as if all is well when murderers are killed with kindness.

Pain is highly subjective. It is not possible to know the experience of those who are executed. No one comes back to tell what it was like. Even botched executions, where the condemned languishes before death, do not provide much insight. Since no one knows with certainty, it is possible that contemporary executions are pain-free or at least comparatively painless, as professed by numerous proponents. A lethal injection process could be envisioned in which the anesthetic used is powerful enough that no consciousness of pain is plausible—akin to a medicinal overdose. Even this benefit of the doubt leaves open to question the psychology of modern executions. The significant point is that, although by historical standards modern methods may be restrained, today's executions, even if pain-free, are purely destructive undertakings. On this ground alone, capital punishment should be dismissed outright.[85]

DEHUMANIZATION

Modern executions neither appease God nor affirm community. Rather, contemporary execution procedures reflect a mechanized, mindless, moral void. A former San Quentin chaplain, Byron Eschelman participated in many executions. He offers this astute critique:

Society is expert at cold-blooded, unemotional, businesslike, professional killing. The death penalty is routine, ritualistic, even-tempered, assembly-line annihilation. The state becomes a legal "Murder, Inc.," serving respectable citizens who pay taxes to get the job done. There is even a "countdown for death" detailing the condemned's final hours, as if his execution were a technical drill.[86]

No community, including that of the penitentiary, can derive emotional nurturing or deeper significance from the pseudoritual scripted in modern execution protocols. Such details are as lifeless as the corpses the procedures produce. Nor can the prisoners find purpose in these undertakings. Earlier execution procedures had the advantage of affording the offender the chance to establish a public character and die demonstrating dignity. Even with lynchings, the fortitude of the condemned was met with reluctant approval. One's conduct on the scaffold offered the opportunity for redemption—of one's character, at least in a limited, public sense, and of one's private soul. And with redemption comes hope.

This no longer seems the case. Brave or cowardly, penitent or not, the offender's death is immaterial since almost no one witnesses it and few attach a spiritual meaning to the way an inmate approaches his death. The intent of the modern bureaucratic execution procedure is to suppress any real-life human responses by the condemned or the executioner. Human reactions—of character or faith—would get in the way of efficiently administering the sanction. Such reactions would draw unwanted attention to the true violence of the affair.

The impersonality of the modern death penalty makes it brutal in a distinctive way. This notion is a bit curious. Humane executioners are explicitly sought. Whereas in times past, the condemned was physically assaulted by the community or by an executioner brutal enough to do the killing before the public's eyes, today execution personnel are chosen because they can be civil and accommodating to the needs of prisoners during their final hours. The interpersonal skills of such officers perpetuate a decent social control and facilitate the seamless execution drill that characterizes contemporary capital punishment. Perhaps the inmates sense the duplicity in this, no matter how well meaning it may be. Although most of the condemned appreciate the attention they receive from the deathwatch officers, both the inmates and the prison personnel remain emotionally distant. The consequences are a civil, impersonal, undertaking that provides company but not comfort to the condemned.

Modern executions are disturbingly dispassionate. Executions today entail the pain of a lonely, anonymous death. Such a demise is predicated upon the inmate's personal insignificance. Death is a profoundly personal experience.

Today's condemned prisoner suffers the dishonor and disgrace of an impersonal death inflicted by faceless bureaucrats. This inmate is reduced to an
object and disposed of according to schedule.

Executioner and condemned alike are dehumanized. Both are morally
numb, as they reciprocate movement in their macabre dance. Each partic-
ipates in a peculiarly subtle form of torture that prepares them for their
respective parts in the script. This is not justice so much as it is, in the
words of Albert Camus, "administrative murder."[87] These arrangements
make executions more manageable. Given modern sensibilities, there may
be no other way to execute an individual. But it must be acknowledged that
these dehumanizing procedures mask a reality that society must confront—
that the death penalty is completely out of step with current standards of
decency and does not belong in the justice system.

CAPITAL PUNISHMENT AND CIVILIZATION

Changes in the administration and meaning of the death penalty are intertwined with the civilization of punishment. Civilization advances in fits
and starts, sometimes moving in reverse before righting itself. Civilization
progresses over time. In each succeeding era, people's empathy for the humanity of others increases. This growing sensitivity includes even deviant
others. Supreme Court decisions restricting the use of capital punishment
against the mentally retarded and juveniles attest to this. A revulsion has
emerged against public infliction of pain once integral to punishment. This
has led to rejection of punishments involving infliction of bodily pain. Psychological pain also has become less tolerable as punishment. Where once
society intended to create terror among those sentenced to confinement, now
incarceration most powerfully evokes shame. Often, the community will accept simple submissiveness or contrition as evidence that the inmate is being
adequately punished. Modern, highly civilized sensibilities reject violence as
punishment, especially public violence.

It is reasonable that when a civilization is at its zenith, its members'
awareness of their shared humanity and their emotional bond are strong.
One consequence is that criminal sanctions are less severe. This holds relative to the norms of the period. People reject as cruel the punishments they
have inherited from their ancestors. Violence intrinsically becomes objectionable. It is diminished by the available methods of execution. Classical
Greece offers an example. Solon oversaw a time of burgeoning civilization.
Although he inherited Draco's arbitrary and brutal judicial system, in which
virtually all crimes were capital offenses, he rejected the "draconian" code
and replaced it with one of the more progressive criminal codes known to
any historical period. The death penalty was rarely imposed. Incarceration
was rarer still. In late republican and Augustan Rome—Rome at the height
of its civilization—voluntary self-banishment was institutionalized as a legal

sanction. Magistrates were ordered to grant the condemned individual time to escape before implementing the capital sentence.

When an execution took place in classical Greece, the preferred mode was ingestion of hemlock. This comparatively painless poison would be self-administered. The potion would be consumed in private, in a supportive environment. The prime example of such an execution was that of Socrates, who chose the hour of his demise, conversed freely with his students until the end, and died in their comforting presence. By the standards of the time—for that matter even by today's norms—execution by hemlock was exceptionally humane. Executions were private affairs. Only the prosecutor had the right to observe up-close the imposition of the sentence. This restriction spared the condemned the insults of the community's antagonism. Like Socrates, those destined to die would have the supportive companionship of others for their final moments.[88]

The violence of executions is muted by ritual. Such procedures operate as a psychic barrier, separating community from the condemned. The executions of ancient Greece serve as an extreme example. That the execution ritual was private and self-administered eliminated the need for an executioner and hid the underlying violence. As holds today, capital punishment becomes an isolated, bureaucratic, mechanical event. In the context of tightly choreographed bodily punishment, the community is removed from the undertaking. Even the ritual's participants have no meaningful contact. It is a paradox of the modern death penalty that, having attained a finer appreciation of the humanity of the condemned, society must suppress its awareness of that humanity. Society must suppress the humanity if it is to conduct executions. The moral entity that is the condemned is first killed by dehumanization. Then the criminal justice system kills and disposes the body. This has developed into an efficient procedure. But it cannot be a just one.

With the civilization of punishment comes the recognition of the finality of death and the irrevocability of the sanction. The finality of death deepens the awesome and awful reality of capital punishment. It deepens society's need to distance itself from the process. However painless and impersonal the penalty of death may become, there is no escaping the perception of execution as annihilation. This is a distinctly modern point of view. In prior times, people shared the comforting belief that the death penalty left the truly final matters in God's hands. People did the Lord's bidding, sticking closely to recognized rituals. God, and often the condemned, understood and approved. Today society can take cold comfort in the death penalty. The extreme nature of such punishment gives society further reason to distance itself from executions, even to the extent of employing bureaucratic procedures that physically and morally numb people to the reality of the sanction.

The evolution of the death penalty can be characterized like this. Killing criminal offenders, particularly in public, came to be seen as a revolting spectacle as citizens began to appreciate the humanity of the condemned. People empathized with the humiliation and degradation brought on by the punishment. In response, executions became tamer, with savage communal stonings becoming a thing of our past, giving way to increasingly restrained, impersonal execution rituals. Killings in early modern Europe, though flagrantly violent, were civilized compared with earlier executions. Hangings in twentieth-century America were so civil as to hide the violence of the death penalty. Executions were concealed from the public by relocating them behind prison walls until finally, today, executions are conducted in remote penitentiary cell blocks, beyond the awareness of all but a few official witnesses. The violence of executions came to be hidden from the participants themselves. This was accomplished by bureaucratizing the undertakings, thereby dehumanizing the participants and muting their moral sensibilities. Executioners know they kill people. They are so absorbed in the procedural concerns that characterize modern execution drills that the violence of executions is hidden from their consciousness.

In times past, society was less aware of its shared humanity. The enormity of executions escaped the average citizen. Violence against others was unremarkable. The community could execute criminals spontaneously, without remorse. Even planned executions could be cordial or festive, because participants did not acknowledge the finality of the event. As society came to sense a shared mortality, and recognize the violence of capital punishment, executions became morally and psychologically problematic. Public execution rituals became less accepted and were replaced by private procedures. Today, executions advance this evolution to its logical conclusion. Society has substituted meaningful ritual with mechanical ritualism. The result is bureaucratic execution that negates community humanity under the guise of justice.

2

Dead to Rights

As the door to the Governor's mansion was about to hit him on his way out, Illinois' conservative Chief Executive, George Ryan, took the boldest anti–death penalty action since the Supreme Court put the sanction on ice in 1972. "Because the Illinois death-penalty system is arbitrary and capricious—and therefore immoral—I no longer shall tinker with the machinery of death," he announced, borrowing language from the late Supreme Court Justice Harry Blackman. "The legislature couldn't reform it. Lawmakers won't repeal it. But I will not stand for it. I must act."[1]

And act he did. On January 11, 2003, with forty-eight hours remaining in his term, Governor George Homer Ryan became the most unlikely champion of the anti–capital punishment cause. He stunned the world by clearing out his state's death row. Ryan reduced the sentences of three inmates to forty years and commuted 164 others' to life without parole.

"The only other thing that would match what he's done is in 1972, when the U.S. Supreme Court overturned the death penalty, and 600 death sentences were reduced to life with that decision," said Richard Dieter, Director of the Death Penalty Information Center.[2]

The governor also granted pardons to four death row prisoners who had been tortured by Chicago law enforcement authorities. To placate the police and end the abuse, the four men made false confessions that landed them in prison. Collectively, the four served nearly seventy years, waiting to die for crimes they didn't commit. Their pardons bring to seventeen the number of death row inmates Illinois has exonerated since 1976, when the Supreme Court allowed states to reconfigure their capital punishment systems.

Ryan's decisions were met with searing criticism, lavish praise, monumental media attention. His mug, with the perpetual scowl that earned him *The Chicago Sun-Times'* title Governor Grumpy, made the rounds of the talk show circuit. In Italy, Romans—notorious for despising the death penalty—lit up the Coliseum in the Governor's honor. His gesture merited a Nobel Peace Prize nomination. True to the controversial nature of the issue, even this most noble of acclimations stirred skepticism. A Chicago-born writer for the *St. Louis Post Dispatch* accused Ryan of seeking the Nobel Prize for the prize money he would need to pay legal fees to defend himself from possible state indictments.[3]

Scandal dogged Ryan from his days as Illinois Secretary of State. Ryan was the sort of chummy politico a citizen could count on if a favor needed to be done. First as Chairman of the Kankakee County Board in the late 1960s, then as Speaker of the Illinois House of Representatives, and then as lieutenant governor, Ryan mastered his state's patronage system. Real trouble began brewing in the '90s when, as secretary of state, Ryan and his cronies appeared to manipulate a process prone to abuse.

"The scandal," as it came to be known in the Land of Lincoln, began with a horrible car crash in 1994 that killed six children in a minivan. Federal prosecutors discovered that the truck driver responsible for the accident was one of dozens of unqualified truckers who had gotten licenses through bribing officials in Ryan's office. Much of the bribe money, the feds alleged, was diverted into Ryan's campaign warchest.

The corruption was not without coverup. At least four key officials from Ryan's office knew—within a week of the fatal crash—that unqualified truck driver Ricardo Guzman shelled out bribes to obtain his license. Ryan's close friend and former inspector general, Dean Bauer, knew it. Bauer wound up serving time for obstruction of justice.

The accident that smashed and burned the six siblings could have occurred with a qualified driver. But a qualified driver was not behind that wheel. It was Guzman. He didn't heed repeated warnings from fellow truckers to pull his dangerous rig from the road.

In the final weeks of his gubernatorial campaign, Ryan repeatedly proclaimed that Guzman got his license legally. Thus, it could be asserted that Ryan won high office on the basis of a falsehood.

As Ryan prepared to move into the governor's mansion in January 1999, the federal investigation of his office's misdeeds splashed across the front pages. As the dragnet spread, the investigation was not simply about swapping truckers' licenses for kickbacks. Bribes, money laundering, and extortion seemed to be part of the regular agenda of Ryan's secretary of state office as determined by prosecutors. Ryan's campaign machine was accused of racketeering. Dozens of indictments and guilty pleas followed.

While publicly apologizing for the scandal, the new governor denied personal knowledge of misdeeds committed by his subordinates. To the contrary, according to prosecutors. They believed Ryan was aware of document shredding taking place in his office. They believed he allowed aides to blur the boundary between official state assignments and political maneuvers.

On the first day of Ryan's retirement, his former chief of staff and top confidant, Scott Fawell, went on trial facing charges of mail fraud, racketeering, conspiracy to obstruct justice, theft of government funds, perjury, and filing false income tax returns. Seasoned observers of the Chicago political machine sensed that Ryan's day in court could be soon to follow.

Ronald Safer, a former federal prosecutor, was quoted in *The Chicago Tribune* as referring to Ryan as "the second defendant" in the Fawell case. The former governor's "just not in the courtroom" yet.[4]

During his last strange weekend in power, Ryan's controversial commutations triggered an avalanche of emotion. Paul Edwards, astute analyst of the local political scene, remarked, "Ryan seems to have the reverse Midas Touch. Whatever he touches turns to . . . let's just say it isn't golden."[5]

The timing of the governor's announcement didn't allow for reflection of the repercussions. Had he acted sooner, there would have been more time for public consideration. But he seemed calm in the eye of the hurricane he created.

No one can know what was in Ryan's heart. He could have been motivated by goodness or guilt. Maybe he was moved by an urge to atone. His apparent humanitarianism could be little more than a ploy—redemption through public relations. Perhaps it was a stunt to appeal to a potential jury pool. It may have been the last noble gesture of a tormented politician. From deep within, the battle may have raged between tortured nobility and cynical self-preservation.

Amidst all the media blitz, one question was not asked. Perhaps it would've spoiled the spirit of the moment. But it is worth pondering. As Ryan was under investigation, even though charges had yet to be filed, there was a pervasive sentiment, based on the court actions swirling around his colleagues that the governor may yet be indicted. Such charges were not to be filed for another eleven months.

On December 17, 2003, a federal grand jury did indict the former governor on charges of racketeering, mail and tax fraud, and lying to law enforcement officials. U.S. Attorney Patrick J. Fitzgerald alleged that Ryan improperly accepted free vacations; passed confidential information to friends, who used it for personal gain; and brokered deals for a personal cut of public contracts. The value of the gifts, services, and loans allegedly totaled $167,000—coincidently, $1,000 for each commutation. Ryan also wound up being charged with directing more than $300,000 worth of gifts, services, and loans to a friend, hiding transactions and subsequently lying about them to investigators. The allegations prompted

Fitzgerald to declare that "the state of Illinois was for sale," thanks to Ryan's "cronyism."[6]

The question on so many minds was: Mr. Ryan, are you offering mercy now mindful that you may be in need of some soon? It is not a pretty question to pose. But that was the ugly thought that lurked in newsrooms, courthouses, and smoke-filled, backroom bars across the state.

Ryan's political rise and fall has been a peculiar journey for a pharmacist from Kankakee, Illinois, a rustbelt town in decay. Other than as a port of call for Arlo Guthrie's relic railroad line, "The City of New Orleans," Kankakee may be known most for its mental institution. A quirky piece of political trivia also centers on Kankakee. From this town of 28,000, three of Illinois' governors hail. This is small consolation for a berg where plant closings and the brain drain of its young have become commonplace.

Many of Ryan's oldest chums were astounded that he wound up governor. They still consider him more the neighbor, the town pharmacist. And given Kankakee's familiarity with murder and its ramifications, many citizens were floored by his capital punishment flip-flop.

Kankakee's experience with homicide came in 1987. Stephen Small, the Ryans' next-door neighbor, was kidnapped and held for ransom. He was buried in a box and suffocated. As a kid, Small took on many jobs for his neighbors, including mowing the Ryans' lawn and shoveling snow from their walk. He babysat the Ryans' six kids. The Ryans held him in fond esteem, especially future first lady Lura Lynn.

The Small family was a Kankakee fixture. Great-grandpa Len was governor of Illinois in the 1920s. The Smalls were local media magnates, owning the town's newspaper and operating radio stations elsewhere. Stephen himself was well-to-do, tooling around town in flashy cars while remodeling a Frank Lloyd Wright home.

Small's conspicuous lifestyle made him an easy target for enterprising trouble-maker Danny Edwards. Edwards later admitted building the box that became Small's coffin. He contended it was never his intention to kill Small. He maintained that he incorporated air holes and tubing to keep his victim alive. Nonetheless, Small was found asphyxiated when the police located him. Edwards was convicted, along with his girlfriend, in 1988. For the murder of Stephen Small, father of three young children, Edwards was given the sentence of death.

Ryan believed justice had been served. He was raised in the Republican stronghold of Kankakee, played high school football, ventured to college, administered to the wounded in a MASH unit during the Korean conflict and launched his local political career without a lingering thought toward capital punishment. Being tough on crime, which meant being supportive of the death penalty, was second nature to a staunch Midwestern conservative. Ryan saw no reason to be opposed to the ultimate sanction. That was the sort of mushy-headed thinking of liberals.

For a *Washington Post* Sunday Magazine piece, Ryan shared his perspective with Lee Hockstader. He recalled James Cagney saying in the movies—"*Don't take me to the chair.*" It was entertaining, but not something to which he gave a lot of thought. Ryan added, "I just thought the death penalty was good … something that was needed. That if there was a bad guy, they caught him, and if it was a really bad guy, they executed him."[7]

In 1972, months after the Supreme Court ruled the death penalty unconstitutional in its landmark *Furman* decision, Ryan won election to his first term in the Illinois House of Representatives. Many jurisdictions responded to *Furman* by enacting new death penalty legislation. Four years later, the Court declared that with appropriate modifications, states could impose death sentences.

Such was the climate in 1977, when Illinois confronted the momentous decision of whether to reinstate capital punishment. Ryan was among the majority in the General Assembly voting in favor of reinstating the death penalty. He did so believing that whatever ailments plagued the capital punishment system were being fixed. He was confident that most of his colleagues who voted with him shared this position.

When Ryan became a gubernatorial candidate in 1998, eleven Illinois inmates had already been executed and dozens more awaited similar fates. Among the condemned was Danny Edwards, the murderer of Stephen Small. Neither Ryan nor his Democratic opponent bothered to debate the death penalty. There was no point, as both favored it. As he stumped for office, he couldn't have imagined that capital punishment would become the issue that would frame his governorship.

Then came Ryan's revelation. He had become the executioner.

George Ryan's metamorphosis began the day he was inaugurated governor in January 1999. He would soon become familiar with the case of Anthony Porter. An African American male with an unusually low IQ, Porter was a sixteen-year resident of Illinois' death row. He had been convicted of the shooting deaths of a Chicago couple in a park in 1982.

Porter maintained his innocence, although those pleas fell on deaf ears. His lawyers had just about played out his appeals. Fifty hours separated Porter from his appointment with the executioner when, in September 1998, a state court stayed his sentence. Concerns over Porter's mental competence interrupted the execution process.

News of the reprieve registered immediately with Professor David Protess, a member of Northwestern University's journalism faculty. Protess often assigned his graduate students semester-long investigations of murder cases in which he determined the sentencing didn't sit quite right. Porter's conviction raised questions for the professor. Protess's charges began their own investigation, searching for clues as the inmate's day of reckoning drew near.

In a few weeks, the students unearthed critical evidence. After eyeballing the crime scene, the young investigators concluded there was no way the state's star witness could have observed what he swore under oath to have seen. Subsequently, accompanied by a private detective, the students sniffed out another suspect, who confessed to the killings. An emotional throng bellowed its approval as Porter cleared the prison gates on February 5, 1999. The next day's papers ran a front-page photo of the jubilant professor leaping into the freed man's arms. Shortly thereafter, the state's lead witness, William Taylor, recanted. According to Taylor, one police officer kept badgering him before the trial with the taunt, "Who are you more afraid of? Porter or us?"[8]

This episode took the governor aback. Ryan had been in office just weeks when Porter bounded from prison. By the state constitution, Ryan was authorized to review the sentences of inmates condemned to die. Now he had seen how close the Illinois machinery had come to executing the wrong man. He had long believed the system worked. Now he wasn't certain. Ryan determined an additional precaution was necessary. He pondered the Illinois safety net, not sure what that safeguard should be.

Thinking back to his administration's early days, Ryan recalled the death penalty was not on his radar screen. He never intended to be an activist on this issue.

As if to reassure Ryan that being pro–capital punishment was the proper opinion, spokesman Dave Urbanek let slip the ironic statement that Anthony Porter's exoneration was evidence "the system worked."[9]

While still in anguished uncertainty, Ryan let an execution proceed a few weeks following Porter's reprieve. The governor denied Andrew Kokoraleis' eleventh-hour appeal. For the brutal murder of a young secretary, Kokoraleis was executed on St. Patrick's Day, 1999. As he struggled to authorize Kokoraleis' execution, the first public indications of the governor's private doubts became visible. Ryan agonized over his decision, briefly considering staying the sentence, then settling on a convoluted explanation allowing the execution to stand.

Ryan's rationale: "I must admit that it is very difficult to hold in your hands the life of any person, even a person who, in the eyes of the many, has acted so horrendously as to have forfeited all right to any consideration of mercy."[10] He added, "Some crimes are so horrendous and so heinous that society has a right to demand the ultimate penalty."[11]

The system's shock waves kept reverberating for Ryan. In a matter of months, two more death row inmates would be exonerated. The state Supreme Court overturned one conviction. New DNA evidence triggered the other exoneration.

As the governor's position on capital punishment began to change, critics viewed his evolution as a handy diversion from his political and legal dilemmas.

"The governor campaigned in favor of the death penalty," said John Gorman, a spokesman for Cook County State's Attorney Richard Devine, a staunch opponent of blanket clemency. "He was the last governor to execute a person in Illinois. Apparently, he didn't have any philosophical or religious problems with that, and he did that a week or so after Anthony Porter was let free." With a skeptical emphasis, Gorman added, "One questions whence came this great metamorphosis."[12]

The Chicago Tribune kept the issue hot by publishing an enlightening series, "The Failure of the Death Penalty in Illinois," in November 1999, detailing the serious flaws of the state's death penalty. *Tribune* reporters Steve Mills and Ken Armstrong exposed several of the system's shortcomings. Their findings included the following: thirty-three condemned inmates had been represented by lawyers who had been subsequently disbarred or had their license to practice law suspended; of more than 160 death row inmates, thirty-five were Blacks convicted by all-white juries. Ryan would later remark that these African American defendants were not tried by a jury of their peers. Further reflection of bias was the increased likelihood of a death sentence if the case involved a white victim and black defendant; symptomatic of prosecutorial abuse, forty-six of the condemned had been found guilty on the basis of snitch testimony elicited from fellow inmates in exchange for consideration of a lesser sentence. Roughly half of the nearly 300 capital convictions in the state had been reversed for a new trial or resentencing.[13]

A Columbia University study released in 2000 showed that Illinois' woes were consistent with the country's. Of all death sentences imposed since 1976, 68 percent have been reversed for serious errors such as those cited by the *Tribune*.[14]

Following the newspaper exposé, Ryan asked his staff, "How does that happen? In America, how does it happen? I'm not a lawyer, so somebody explain it to me."[15]

The governor took the bold step on January 31, 2000, of imposing a moratorium on executions. By this time, thirteen Illinois death row inmates had been exonerated. State-sanctioned killing would cease, Ryan determined, until he could be certain that everyone sentenced to death was truly guilty.

Ryan's action intensified the national debate about the death penalty and prompted groups like Murder Victims Families for Reconciliation (MVFR) and others opposed to capital punishment to concentrate their energies on Illinois. That thirteen innocent Illinois citizens had been found guilty and sentenced to die compelled the governor to recognize that his state's death penalty system had major problems.

Ryan's moratorium was met with skepticism. His announcement followed the federal indictment of Dean Bauer, Ryan's former inspector, for obstructing politically embarrassing investigations.

The countervailing theory was expressed by Jane Bohman, executive director of the Illinois Coalition Against the Death Penalty. "I don't think anything else influenced [Ryan's moratorium decision], other than his own understanding of what was at stake. Picking the death penalty as a diversionary tactic isn't like giving out candy on the street corner to make yourself popular. I think he was confronted by the fact he's the last person to sign off."[16]

Before announcing the moratorium, Ryan had created a legislative task force to study Illinois' capital punishment system. In Autumn 1999, nine MVFR members testified at one of the task force hearings. Victims who testified in favor of the death penalty had been organized by the Cook County Victim Assistant. They were shown deference and treated with respect. The members of MVFR, on the other hand, were provided no support from the Victim Assistant. They were given less time to speak. They were made to feel marginalized throughout the hearing process.

Because of that, those in the abolitionist camp knew they had to keep pushing their message. Opponents of capital punishment know that the way to influence public opinion is to demonstrate, through personal example, the system's flaws, to illuminate the moral perspective, and to express the perspective of victims' loved ones who oppose executions.

"It's not that our numbers were that significant," MVFR Board Chair Jennifer Bishop notes. Quoted in her organization's newsletter, *The Voice*, she notes, "We made sure we were present enough and vocal enough that we could talk about the victims' perspective." Bishop added that those who supported her point of view did not want to "let the pro-death-penalty side own that perspective."[17]

From the moment the moratorium was declared, a scramble ensued to influence the governor's thinking. Ryan appointed a blue-ribbon commission to study the state's system and correct its kinks. The commission was a diverse lot: two active prosecutors, two current public defenders, a former Chief Judge of the Federal District Court, and a former U.S. senator. The commission included three women and four members of racial minorities, and prominent members of both major political parties. Twelve of the fourteen were attorneys. Of those, nine had experience representing defendants and eleven were seasoned prosecutors, including William Martin, the successful District Attorney in the state's 1967 high-profile case against mass murderer Richard Speck. One commissioner, Roberto Ramirez, a Mexican American immigrant and self-made businessman, bore personal experience with violent crime. His father had been murdered—his grandfather subsequently shooting and killing the murderer. When the members of this commission were introduced at a March 2000 press conference, they were asked who among them opposed the death penalty. Four hands were raised.

Ryan charged the commission with one task. The deliberative body was to determine what reforms would render imposition of capital punishment fair, just, and accurate. The governor's instincts reflected the general uneasiness of the citizenry toward crime and its consequences. For while a specific transgression, say the Washington-area sniper shootings, elicits the public's retributive wrath, there seems to be a growing skepticism about implementing the death penalty. A significant percentage of people question the system's evenhandedness and, in light of the cases in which DNA evidence has demonstrated that the wrong person was convicted, its facility to distinguish the guilty from the innocent.

In January 2001, MVFR Chair Bishop testified before the Governor's Commission. Her experience on this occasion differed greatly from the cold shoulder received by MVFR members when they spoke to the legislative task force a year earlier. Although only ten minutes had been reserved for her testimony, Jennifer wound up answering commissioners' questions for an hour and a half. Members of the panel were attuned to her challenging the folk wisdom that somehow executions deliver peace of mind, and closure, to the families of the victims.

"I told them about victims' family members who thought they would feel better after the killer was executed but didn't," explains Jennifer.[18] This line of thought was eye-opening for Commission members.

The impact of MVFR's perspective was immediate. One commissioner wept during Jennifer's comments. Two other Commission members reported that her comments were what convinced them to change their positions regarding the death penalty.

Uncertainty over the ultimate sanction is rooted in American history. When the nation was founded, all the states, pursuant to Common law, imposed capital punishment. But as democracy flourished, with its humanistic leanings, doubts arose over the state's authority to take the lives of citizens on whose consent government was grounded. Thomas Jefferson was among the first to advocate limiting executions. Michigan, in 1846, became the first state to eliminate the death penalty, outlawing the punishment in all circumstances except treason.

The public's sentiment continued to waiver. After World War II and the decline of several totalitarian regimes, countries in Western Europe ceased executing criminals. Their model may be of questionable applicability to the United States, as our murder rate is about four times Europe's. Stare at American TV for any stretch of time and you'll grasp the country's obsession with violence. The debate over the death penalty splits our moral fiber and is driven by the competing notions of retribution and reconciliation.

Capital punishment is supposed to be reserved for the most heinous offences. It is exactly those instances, however, because of the strong emotions they stir, that most mightily challenge the impartiality of those engaged in the pursuit of justice. This, ironically, can put the innocent more at risk. Most defendants facing capital charges avoid death sentences through plea bargaining. This process generally does not appeal to someone who is actually innocent. Why negotiate a lesser sentence when you've done nothing wrong? Innocent individuals are apt to insist on a trial by jury. When such a trial transpires, the jury will not include anyone who might resist on principle the imposition of a death sentence. Such an individual is barred from jury service in capital matters by *Witherspoon* v. *Illinois*,[19] a Supreme Court ruling that some legal scholars believe makes juries prosecution-friendly.

It also is a fact of communal life that when a horrible crime occurs, a frightened public clamors for results. Someone must be apprehended and put behind bars before the jangled nerves of the community can be calmed. The heat is on the police and prosecutors to capture a culprit and restore safety as quickly as possible. This pressure can lead to the use of questionable practices. Coerced confessions, unduly influenced eyewitnesses, and the abuse of snitch testimony are the consequences of police and prosecutorial overreaching.

If these flaws surface frequently, why bother with a death penalty? Deterrence is a resounding reason often cited in support of capital punishment. That many murders are committed in the heat of passion suggests perpetrators are not considering consequences when engaged in violent acts. And while studies do not focus on the vast majority who are nonoffenders to determine what they were thinking when they decided not to kill someone, empirical evidence demonstrates that states with the death penalty fare no better in deterring homicides than states without one. In fact, the numbers hold the opposite. Illinois, which has been a death penalty jurisdiction, has a murder rate greater than its neighbor Michigan, which lacks capital punishment. The comparison is especially appropriate as these two upper Midwestern states have comparable demographics regarding racial composition, income levels, and population spread between urban and rural areas. Furthermore, in the last decade the murder rate in states that do not execute has stayed steadily less than in jurisdictions that do. Polls of police chiefs and criminologists indicate that significant majorities of both groups doubt capital punishment substantially reduces homicides.[20]

Another argument advanced in favor of the death penalty is that it saves the state money. The reasoning goes that an execution spares tax payers the expense of lifetime incarceration. However, the severity and irreversible nature of an execution are such that the government goes to great lengths to get the punishment right. When the enormous costs of capital litigation are factored in, any savings an execution may generate are negated. The average span between conviction and execution in the United States in 2000, was eleven and a half years. All the while, attorneys are churning out briefs and courts are cranking out rulings. The appellate process is packed with expensive endeavors.

Security is another legitimate concern. An execution puts an end to any fear of recidivism. But so does a sentence of life without parole. A notion central to survivors' sense of justice is restitution. By no means ought the criminal wind up better off than his victim. This explains the uproar caused by the profit and notoriety garnered by jailhouse authors. Another way to understand the concept of restitution is to revisit the biblical mandate "an eye for an eye."

"That's probably the most misconstrued of all the passages in the Bible," explains Rabbi Yitzhak Husbands-Hankin. "It wasn't meant to be a criminal punishment, but rather a civil sanction. In other words, if I did something to impair your vision it was incumbent upon me to make it right. Perhaps that means providing you with a seeing eye dog or a permanent reader. It doesn't mean that if I'm responsible for your losing vision then poking out my eyes would make us even."[21]

Perhaps the most compelling case for capital punishment comes from those most immediately affected by an execution—the loved ones of the murder victims. It would seem that death brought on by a random force, cancer or a hurricane for example, is easier for survivors to accept than the loss of a family member through the deliberate act of another human being. What is it exactly that survivors hope to gain from the execution of a murderer? Proper vengeance, retribution, restitution? Or, to borrow from pop psychology, closure?

The term *closure* gets kicked around a lot by victims' families. It refers to the end of the legal process that allows survivors to come to terms with their grief. Families may find the execution of their lost loved one's murderer becomes a significant emotional crossroads.

Eyeballing an execution may have its own unintended traumatic consequences. Such were the findings of three Stanford University School of Medicine researchers. David Spiegel, Andrew Freinkel, and Cheryl Koopman studied the effects on journalists who watched the 1992 execution of Robert Alton Harris, the first California convict to suffer a death sentence after the Supreme Court's reinstatement of the punishment. They found the impact surprisingly damaging, even on witnesses who had no emotional connection with the crime. Their conclusion: witnessing trauma is not far removed from experiencing it.

Fifteen of the eighteen reporters assigned to Harris's execution participated in the study. These seasoned journalists suffered severe short-term aftereffects. One was tearful for weeks; several felt listless and had trouble concentrating; and a number reported nightmares. Several sought counseling. One ambitious scribe declined to cover the Los Angeles rioting that ensued shortly after the execution.

These individuals were displaying reactions associated with acute stress. They had difficulty handling emotions stirred by the execution. More than half said they felt removed from their own emotions. A third said they felt "confused and disoriented." Sixty percent reported being "estranged or detached from other people." More than half claimed to "avoid thoughts or feelings about the execution." One-third felt "despair or hopelessness," while 20 percent experienced "uncontrollable and excessive grief."

Drawing a parallel between these reporters and other citizens who have a more personal stake in the outcome of an execution, the researchers concluded that witnessing the killing of a killer is apt to inflict additional trauma. The experience may lead to more pain rather than to so-called closure.[22]

That Attorney General John Ashcroft acceded to the wishes of many of the Oklahoma City bombing survivors and allowed closed-circuit viewing of Timothy McVeigh's execution is testament to the power of the victims'-rights movement. The muscle flexed is tending to put victims in the driver's seat of the capital justice system. This trend can exacerbate glaring inconsistencies where two defendants, having committed similar offenses, receive dissimilar punishments. Perhaps one victim's family, pursuing their version of justice, presses for a death sentence, while another family, desiring a speedier resolution and hoping to dodge the spotlight, prefers a penalty of life without parole. But, as noted by Scott Turow, lawyer, novelist, and member of Governor Ryan's blue ribbon panel, it makes as little sense to let victims decide the capital process as it would to determine what will be built on the World Trade Center site solely based on the wishes of the survivors of those killed on September 11th. In a democratic society, no minority, even those with seemingly the most at stake in an issue, should be entitled to speak for everyone.

Ryan's commission didn't dwell on philosophical niceties. Those who were supportive of the death penalty reiterated a major theme: at times a crime is so horrendous that killing the perpetrator is the most just response. A strong argument of capital punishment proponents is that it debases the deep indignity of murder by punishing it the same way as lesser offences. Under California's "three strikes" system, for instance, one may receive a life sentence for a third felony of shoplifting. How disorienting is it to a community's moral compass when the unlawful taking of human life is treated similarly? The point is not so much retribution or even vengeance, as it is a sense of moral balance. Lacking conclusive data, it may well be speculated that a primary reason most Americans continue to support the death penalty is this concept of moral order—the ultimate evil demands the ultimate sanction.

This drive for moral proportion sets a powerful demand on the judicial system for precision. Executing the innocent or the undeserving undermines the need for moral proportion and shakes confidence in the courts.

The burden of precision also is affected by discrepancies between cases. Such disparities often are magnified by social factors, like race, which carry nuances not always clearly understood. Ryan's commission approved an investigation that revealed that in Illinois, defendants are two and a half times more likely to receive death sentences if they're white. One explanation is that in a racially divided society white people tend to associate with, and consequently to kill, other whites. Targeting a white victim, however, makes a perpetrator three and a half times more prone to be punished via death than if he'd murdered a black person.[23] Is the message: white life is worth more than black? In Illinois, at least, whites and blacks who killed whites were sentenced to die at approximately the same rate, an equality that hasn't always been the case elsewhere.

Geography also is influential. One is five times as likely to draw the death penalty for first-degree murder in a rural area, as in Chicago's Cook County. Gender matters, too. Murdering a woman results in a death sentence three and a half times more often than killing a man.[24] When one examines the system's numerous x factors—who is trying the case, who is serving as judge and jury, what are the victim's characteristics, where did the crime occur—the ambiguities that cloud morality become apparent.

Capital punishment proponents in Ryan's state often refer to Henry Brisbon as their ace-in-the-hole argument. Eliminate the death penalty, they say, and what do you do with the Henry Brisbons?

More than thirty years ago, on a June night in 1973, Brisbon and three friends diverted several cars from Interstate 57, south of Chicago. Brisbon forced a woman from one of the vehicles to remove her clothes. He then took a shotgun and blasted her at close range. He ordered another couple to lie down together in a field. While they held each other in a trembling embrace he shot them both in the back. His part in these murders was discovered years later when, while serving time for rape and armed robbery, he confessed to a fellow inmate. Since the I-57 shootings occurred after the Supreme Court deemed the death penalty unconstitutional, Brisbon was not subject to capital punishment. Instead, he was given a prison sentence of 1,000 to 3,000 years, the longest punishment in the state's history.

Barely a year after sentencing, Brisbon struck again. In October 1978, he overcame a prison guard by holding a homemade knife to his throat. Then Brisbon, with several other prisoners, went to the cell of another inmate and stabbed him to death. By early 1982, when Brisbon stood charges for this crime, Illinois had reinstated capital punishment. As he was being sentenced to die, evidence came to light of another homicide allegedly committed by Brisbon before he went to prison. He was responsible for another gruesome shotgun killing. While incarcerated, he had collected more than two hundred disciplinary actions and had been a leader in the violent 1979 prison revolt at Stateville. A sentence of death had not motivated improvement in Brisbon's demeanor. In the years since being condemned, Brisbon had been accused of several serious assaults, including injuring an inmate by heaving a thirty-pound weight on his skull.

Brisbon now resides at the Tamms Correctional Center, a "super-max" complex that holds 250 of Illinois' most incorrigible convicts. Gleaned from a state prison population of 45,000, those taken to Tamms are considered either gang leaders or men with intractable conduct problems.

Tamms' terms of imprisonment are harsh. Inmates get no physical contact with other human beings. Each man is confined twenty-three hours a day inside a seven-by-twelve-foot cinder block cell. Each space has a single, small window. Cells are equipped with a stainless-steel fixture containing a toilet bowl and a sink. A concrete slab covered by a foam mattress completes the furnishings. The doors are reinforced so that small holes allow conversation but prohibit the havoc possible when inmates can slip their hands through the openings. Once a day, a remote-controlled system allows a prisoner to leave his cell and walk down a grim corridor to an outside area. This space is twelve by twenty-eight feet, surrounded by thirteen-foot-high concrete walls, with a roof covering half the area. An inmate may breathe fresh air, but only for an hour. A similar remote-controlled system allows twenty-minute showers, several times a week.

As Tamms does not operate at full capacity, it costs about two and a half times more to house an inmate there than the $20,000 annually spent to incarcerate a prisoner elsewhere in Illinois. Tamms, however, claims quite a successful track record in containing misconduct. Can such a facility, with its rigorous terms of confinement, keep the likes of Henry Brisbon from killing again?

Commission member Turow posed this question to the Tamms' warden, George Welborn. Welborn cautiously replied, "Yes," then added, "Henry is a special case. I would be foolish to say I can guarantee he won't kill again. I can imagine situations, God forbid ... But the chances are minimized here."[25]

Reasonably satisfied with the containment of such incorrigibles, Ryan's commission reconvened. The members realized the death penalty in Illinois would not be abolished in the foreseeable future. Consequently, the commission's considered opinions focused on reforms. The primary concern was diminishing the chances of executing the innocent. Of the state's thirteen death row exonerees, several had rendered questionable confessions, statements that had been coerced or fabricated. To safeguard against such dubious admissions, the commission recommended videotaping all interrogations in capital cases. The panel suggested modifying lineup procedures to address the disappointing degree of trustworthiness generated by eyewitness testimony. The commission proposed pretrial procedures to assess the reliability of jailhouse snitches. These inmates, who exchange testimony for lighter sentences, have emerged as a force in capital prosecutions.[26]

Attempting to decrease some of the system's randomness, the commission recommended reducing the number of eligibility criteria for capital punishment from twenty to five. It was urged that crimes warranting a death sentence be restricted to multiple murders, murder of a law enforcement official or firefighter, murder in a prison, murder intended to obstruct the judicial system, and murder accompanied by torture. Murders committed during another felony would be dropped from the list. The commission also proposed an oversight authority that would impose uniformity across the state's process of selecting death-penalty cases.

The commission addressed the distress of survivors. To prevent the process from devolving into an endless and bewildering loop of litigation, it was recommended that life sentences without parole be levied when qualified cases didn't result in the death penalty. Commission members delineated reforms meant to expedite postconviction reviews and clemency appeals.

Following two years of research and deliberation, it dawned on former U.S. Senator Paul Simon, commission cochair, that perhaps the group was missing the big picture. Simon, an avowed opponent of capital punishment, wondered if the commission was sidestepping the ultimate question. He forced members to cast a vote on whether Illinois should even have a death penalty. The vote was to be considered an expression of sentiment, rather than a binding resolution. Laying aside political realities, what would be the panelists' best advice to their fellow citizens? A narrow majority prevailed. Capital punishment should be abandoned.[27]

In April 2002, the Governor's Commission on Capital Punishment released its report. Although the panel focused on recommendations for reforming the system, the report duly noted that a slim majority of the Commission favored abolishing executions in Illinois. Those who held this position felt even more strongly about their views if the governor were to surmise that the legislature would not substantially enact the Commission's recommendations.

While the governor had created the context for the debate and his blue-ribbon commission had responded with eighty-five reforms to control systemic abuse and minimize error, it turned out the legislature lacked the will to implement change. Besides, polls indicated a majority of Illinois' citizens supported capital punishment.[28]

Back on the scandal scene, the federal probe of Ryan's former secretary of state post deepened. Those critical of the governor accused him of fanning the flames under the execution issue to create a smokescreen to hide personal problems. The scandal destroyed any hope of a political future Ryan may have harbored. By 2001, he had determined there would be no campaign for reelection. As a sitting governor with no pretense of another term, he liberated himself from the political consequences shackled to the death penalty. With decisions concerning death sentence commutations bearing down on him, Ryan was cleared to follow his conscience.

In October 2002, following the governor's instructions, the state's Prisoner Review Board held clemency hearings for nearly all death row convicts. Absent from the list was Danny Edwards, Stephen Small's murderer. He was in the minority of those who didn't seek to have their sentences commuted. Over two weeks, in four conference rooms packed with prosecutors and the mourning survivors of murder victims, board members were begged to let the executions go forward. The pleas also were directed at Ryan, who chose not to attend the proceedings. For many, the concept of balanced restitution resounded. They were convinced the guilty should not live and fare better than their victims.

There was an overwhelming outpouring of emotion. The sadness was palpable. At the close of proceedings, Ryan claimed he had "pretty much ruled out" sparing all those sentenced to die. After arriving at his final decision, in fact, Ryan admitted that he unintentionally misled the families and friends of those slain by death row murderers when he told them he was leaning away from blanket clemency. That was the position he expressed to more than one hundred victims' family members at a meeting in December. All over Illinois, newspaper editorials concurred, opposing a blanket commutation. They urged the governor to select wisely and use his power sparingly. Certainly some on death row deserved to die.

Even before the proceedings commenced, the anti–capital punishment movement was developing its strategic approach. These forces were led by Northwestern University law professor Lawrence Marshall, a brilliant visionary.

Under Marshall's auspices, the university's Center on Wrongful Convictions had organized a national conference of those interested in eliminating executions. The 1998 event attracted hundreds of attorneys, clergy, journalists, academics, and activists. The "guests of honor" were the thirty-nine men and women who had spent time on death row and lived to tell about it. Every panel during the three-day gathering included death row survivors among the experts.

The conference's most moving moment came during the plenary session. Accompanied by the rhythm of a solo African drum, one by one the exonerated marched from backstage to a podium front and center. They introduced themselves by name and each concluded with the eloquent, powerful couplet, "Had the state of _____ had its way, I'd be dead today." Each placed a radiant sunflower in a crystal vase before taking his/her place at the riser. There was an electricity charging the packed auditorium strong enough to jolt the pro–death penalty current.

On December 15, 2002, Marshall's Center on Wrongful Conviction created another event. This one was shorter and simpler, but with a fine focus and deliberate intent—to persuade the one man who could bring the state's death penalty to its knees, to do so. The second gathering of the exonerated was at the heart of a campaign Marshall crafted to influence the governor's convictions. Marshall enlisted lawyers, prominent jurists, and celebrities and encouraged them to woo Ryan. The 2002 affair was a three-hour celebration. Many of the individuals who attended the first conference reconvened to honor the exonerated and reinforce each other for the next big push. Those who had been released from death rows across the country signed a petition urging Ryan's commutation of the death sentences of Illinois' inmates.

The following day, before dawn, Marshall orchestrated the media event that began the final onslaught on Ryan's conscience. Thirty-seven former death row residents from various states engaged in a "Dead Men Relay Walk." They began outside the Illinois death chamber in Joliet. With each man advancing one mile, they delivered their document, relay-style, to the governor's Chicago office. In time for the evening news, the last man, Anthony Porter, placed the petition for blanket commutation squarely in Ryan's hands.

That evening, *The Exonerated*, an emotionally charged play was staged for the benefit of Governor Ryan. The theatrical work, written by the young team of Jessica Blank and Erik Jensen, is based on the testimony of six former condemned inmates, some of whom were present for the special gubernatorial performance. Ryan sat mesmerized from his front-row seat. After the show, the governor mingled with the star-studded cast. The performers included Richard Dreyfuss, Mike Farrell, and Danny Glover. So the charm of celebrity was added to Professor Marshall's strategic mix.

As he departed the theatre, Ryan referred to the play as "gut-wrenching." For the governor, it was a vivid demonstration of what was wrong with the system.

A week prior to the Center on Wrongful Conviction's activities, Murder Victims Families for Reconciliation held a special Victims' Voices event in Chicago. Civil Rights Activist Mamie Till Mobley, whose son Emmett Till was murdered in Mississippi in 1955, participated with fellow MVFR members.

Emmett was a fourteen-year-old black boy at the time he was dragged from bed and beaten to death by two white men for supposedly whistling at a white woman. His slaying and the subsequent acquittal of the two half brothers charged with the crime sparked national outrage. Emmett is widely remembered as a martyr of the Civil Rights movement.

Till, who was from Chicago, was naïve about the Jim Crow South at the time of his visit with relatives in Money, Mississippi. While shopping at a five-and-dime store, he whistled at a white store clerk and possibly touched her hand. One night in late August, he was abducted from his uncle's home, beaten, and shot. His body was dumped in the Tallahatchie River.

In Chicago, Till's mother insisted on an open-casket funeral. Thousands filed past and saw the boy's mutilated face. Photographs of the event in *Jet* and *Ebony* magazines elicited a powerful emotional response that helped ignite the modern civil rights movement.

About a month following the funeral, an all-white Mississippi jury acquitted Roy Bryant and half brother, J.W. Milam, after their lawyer admonished jurors their forefathers would roll over in their graves if the men were convicted. The jury deliberated about an hour before deciding to set the two defendants free.

Later, the brothers confessed to a magazine reporter that they had kidnapped Till, driven him to a shack, beaten him unconscious, shot him in the head, wrapped barbed wire about his neck, secured it to a heavy metal fan, and dropped his corpse into the river.

Referring to Mamie Till Mobley's dedication to Emmett and his cause, Till's cousin Earlene Green said, "Not a day went by when she didn't think about her son."[29]

On December 8, 2002, Mamie Till Mobley addressed the MVFR gathering. "I am pleased that I am able to stand here today and say with a pure and meaningful heart that I am against the death penalty," she said. "There is no purpose that it serves except to further the damage that has already been done."[30]

These words, uttered by Ms. Mobley, would help influence Governor Ryan's thinking. The Victims' Voices event would be Mamie Till Mobley's last public appearance.

During Ryan's historic speech announcing his commutation decision, he paid tribute to Ms. Mobley's life of courage. After discussing the racial disparity in death penalty sentencing, the governor said, "This week, Mamie Till died. Her son was lynched in Mississippi in the 1950s. She was a strong advocate for civil rights and reconciliation. Just three weeks ago she was the keynote speaker at the Murder Victims' Families for Reconciliation event in Chicago."

Added Ryan, "This group, many of whom I've met, opposes the death penalty even though their family members have been lost to senseless killing. Mamie's strength and grace not only ignited the civil rights movement—including inspiring Rosa Parks to refuse to go to the back of the bus—but inspired murder victims' families until her dying day."[31]

Ryan confessed he had felt the heat from both sides of the capital punishment argument. It was unlike anything he had previously experienced. "It's the toughest thing I've ever had to do in my life," is how Ryan characterized clemency decisions.[32]

One thing became apparent. After two emotionally draining weeks of hearings, Ryan had said the notion of blanket commutations was "off the table." Now, Ryan was reversing himself and putting across-the-board commutations back "on the table" after experiencing the play.

Ryan's case-by-case review was in full swing. The governor devoted himself to the thorough examination of every prisoner's appeal and the victims' survivors' counterarguments. For Ryan, the research had been reduced to eight thick white binders. One hundred sixty index tab dividers marked the case of each convict being held on death row. These binders were the governor's constant companion.

Everyone in Ryan's inner circle supported some number of commutations. All believed that some, although not necessarily the same, death row residents were deserving of clemency. The inevitable issue emerged as to just how many clemencies should be granted. Should blanket commutations be favored? Or were some cases just so heinous that the juries' verdicts should stand and the prisoners die?

During the speech in which he explained his decision, Ryan mentioned that "as long as a week to ten days" before his announcement, he didn't think he would be commuting all the sentences. "I didn't believe that I would I do it myself," mused the governor.[33]

Ryan was lobbied hard by activists on both sides. Rob Warden, executive director of the Center on Wrongful Convictions and an accomplished crime beat journalist, believed the work of advocates for blanket commutations was to overwhelm the governor's emotions. "We had to win his heart," were Warden's words. "That was our job."[34]

Defense lawyers and other capital punishment critics kept Ryan's focus on the errors made repeatedly in the death penalty system. Those pushing for blanket commutations emphasized the coerced confessions, the DNA exonerations, and the fact that authorities continually failed to learn from the mistakes.

Ryan was targeted by Desmond Tutu and the Vatican, pleading for blanket commutations. During a memorable corned beef sandwich at a favorite deli, Nelson Mandela telephoned to discuss the clemencies. The South African statesman and world-renowned human rights activist urged Ryan not to miss this opportunity to help America regain moral high ground. Decreeing a blanket commutation would deliver a mighty statement to the world, that freedom and fairness are cherished American values. Capital punishment, practiced by only a few dictatorships and authoritarian regimes, undercut America's image.

"For a guy like me to get a call from Nelson Mandela, that's pretty impressive," quipped the governor.[35]

Although Ryan gave Mandela reason to be hopeful, his political advisers weren't certain how the governor would end his long-awaited speech on the death penalty. His comments, containing the most monumental decision of his political life, were just days away.

Correspondence, pro and con, inundated the governor's office. A documentary film crew dogged Ryan's moves in anticipation of an archival piece.

Pressure came from prosecutors and victims' families who relived the gory details of crimes committed over a quarter century. It was a gruesome story of pain and suffering they told. Prosecutors, particularly Cook County State's Attorney Richard Divine, complained they had little access to the governor. Ryan countered, saying that he was willing to meet with anyone who wanted to discuss the matter.

Ryan took every opportunity to use close friends and aides as sounding boards, prospecting for the best advice. On one side were those who warned against embracing the extreme. Even colleagues who favored blanket commutations cautioned against the repercussions. Wouldn't this be turning his back on everything he once represented, they reasoned. He would be left isolated and friendless, according to this line of thought. The other point of view pressed him to be bold, encouraged him to make a mark on history that would be an inspiration for criminal justice reform.

One technique Ryan employed to more fully comprehend the cases was to have top aides bring him crucial breakdowns of the files. Deputy Governor Matt Bettenhausen and attorney Jean Templeton were key personnel in assisting with the analyses. Their summaries informed Ryan how the men and women on death row would have fared had the eighty-five reforms been implemented as proposed by his Commission. This information enabled the governor to know, for example, how many prisoners had been hampered by inadequate counsel and how many made claims of innocence.

This examination went on till January 3rd. It was just a week until Ryan would determine his only choice was to issue across-the-board commutations. He absorbed information, but said he wasn't ready to arrive at a conclusion. Ryan still needed to deliberate. The governor was engaged in deep soul-searching, trying to decipher what his conscience was telling him to do.

According to the governor's spokesman, Dennis Culloton, Ryan left the January 3 meeting thinking there was much more to discuss. Ryan believed the issue was fraught with subjectivity. The more Ryan and his staff reviewed the cases, the more he seemed to gravitate toward declaring blanket clemency.

Late on January 5th, another pivotal discussion took place. The debate centered on what to do about death row inmates who had been convicted of killing police officers. In Ryan's view, these murderers were "the worst of the worst." When the dialogue ended, the matter was still not resolved. Ryan cautioned his staff that there would be more discussion.

Another hotly contested topic was whether Ryan would grant a pardon and, if so, to whom. Ryan and his advisors wanted to be sure that the most powerful form of clemency was used judiciously. After all, many inmates had claimed they were innocent.

William Heirens, convicted of three murders in the 1940s and Illinois' longest-serving inmate, was given consideration. But then, the governor determined that pardoning Heirens would send the wrong signal. He didn't want the gesture interpreted as meaning that a sentence of life in prison meant something less than the convict's life.

Ryan and his aides seemed more certain about some of the cases involving Chicago police commander Jon Burge. According to members of the governor's staff, evidence in these cases was weak. This was especially so in four situations where there was little to corroborate a questionable confession. In the most controversial cases, inmates long maintained their confessions were uttered only after they'd been tortured.

Officials in the governor's office knew well that a weak case would be most vulnerable to the certainty required for execution. After all, this punishment is irreversible. For such a penalty, a strong case, one beyond a reasonable doubt, was necessary.

"The governor had no doubt that in those cases there was not the evidence you should have," according to Culloton. "He was convinced."[36]

Ryan also was concerned that prosecutors, particularly those in Cook County, seemed to learn little from all the episodes of wrongful convictions. A spokesperson for State's Attorney Devine let slip a remark that especially rubbed Ryan the wrong way. The comment that the governor was "buying into the mantra" of criminal defense lawyers who think the capital punishment system is broken, made the governor and his staff believe that prosecutors would never back real reform. It appeared prosecutors were not likely to admit, much less learn from, the errors of their ways.

One night in the final week, Ryan discussed with his aides cases such as Henry Brisbon's, the interstate killer who was slated for execution for a murder committed in prison while he was serving time for the highway murders. But as much as the governor pondered creating exceptions for certain horrendous cases, there always seemed to be a hitch. In this instance, Ryan's staff was aware that Capital Punishment Commissioner Scott Turow had previously written that Brisbon's conviction was dubious. That conversation, said Culloton, "brought [the governor] back to where he was with the picking and choosing, and he felt uncomfortable doing that."[37]

The governor continued to pore over cases, replete with the gut-wrenching details of awful crimes. Twice he conferred privately with the families of victims. Overcoming his own reservations, Ryan also met with the friends and relatives of the prisoners.

The latter category included Claude Lee from Kankakee. Ryan recalled Lee from their high school days together. Lee's deeply distraught son, Eric, was on death row for gunning down a local police officer, shooting him in the face. Now the father was pleading with his old high school acquaintance to spare his son's life.

It began to dawn on Ryan that playing God was beyond him. Making last-resort, Solomon-like selections of who's to live and who's to die at the end of an error-prone process was not within the ken of any governor. Ryan concluded that most of those sentenced to die would have avoided such a fate had they been tried under the rules proposed by his blue-ribbon panel. Many of the convicts had endured abusive childhoods. Shouldn't every killer be considered disturbed on some serious level? And with a system as fraught with mistakes as Illinois', how could the governor be 100 percent certain that the innocent weren't being mistaken for the guilty?

As the hours passed, Ryan's resolve grew firmer. He determined that, given the irreversible nature of capital punishment, if the system were to err it must do so in the direction of caution. If innocent people resided on death row, reasoned Ryan, commuting their sentences at least gave them a chance to work toward exoneration. Once executed, claims generally died with the convict.

By Thursday, the governor was leaning strongly toward complete commutation. He and his aides began composing a letter to victims' families informing them that he had decided to issue the blanket commutation—a choice he knew they would view as "betrayal." "They have a right to feel betrayed," Ryan would say in an interview following his speech. He blamed his own vacillation. "I probably misled them, certainly not intentionally.... I apologize to those people."[38]

That apology was not well received by many of the murder victims' friends and family members. They believed that Ryan had always meant to issue a pardon or commutation to every condemned inmate. Their view was that the governor's action was intended as a misdirection ploy to veer attention away from his corruption scandals. Many believed Ryan merely was playing politics.

There were those, like Police Sgt. Bill Stutzman, who figured long before that Ryan had made up his mind to issue a blanket commutation. Stutzman, whose colleague Kenneth Dawson was killed in 1985, believed it was obvious from the beginning what the governor was going to do. He felt that Ryan had disrespected the victims' families, police, prosecutors, and judges. Stutzman considered Ryan's action to be a tragedy, the governor's personal agenda.[39]

The governor drew criticism from Thomas Ramos, Jr., whose sister and her two children were murdered in 1988. Referring to Ryan, Ramos said, "This man is stepping on the graves of my sister and her children."[40]

Following the pardon of Leroy Orange for the 1984 murder of her son, Lorraine Pedro did not mince words. "I think he made jackasses out of us." Pedro, along with other relatives of the slain, had pleaded with Ryan not to grant complete clemency. They wondered what sort of message the governor was sending? Would thugs running around now feel they could get away with anything?[41]

Mid-afternoon Friday the tenth, several hundred letters, stuffed in special red-white-and-blue envelops, were sent from the governor's office to the friends and families of the slain. These letters would be delivered an hour before Ryan's Saturday speech. In his two-page correspondence, Ryan said he had wrestled with whether to issue an across-the-board commutation. He admitted he was contradicting himself when he previously said he had ruled out the possibility.

Ryan wrote how he reflected on the numerous times the system had failed to nail the appropriate culprit. He acknowledged that many of those receiving his letter would be displeased. But he added that he had come to peace within himself concerning his decision.

This isn't the spin that Crystal Fitch would put on the governor's choice. Fitch's sister and her boyfriend were murdered by Anthony Brown in 1994. Fitch is clear there was no doubt who killed her sister. A decade after the homicides, DNA evidence has come back linking blood found on Brown's clothing to the victims. Fitch believes the governor never meant to keep any of the condemned on death row. She must now try to make sense of the situation for her sister's son, who was born two months before his mother was murdered. The boy's concerned whether the convicted inmate will be released. Fitch believes Ryan lied. She's bothered that Anthony Brown is going to live off her tax money.

On Friday night Ryan phoned close friends to let them know his intentions. He also broke the news to his wife. Lura Lynn didn't take it well. She felt close to Stephen Small's family. She believed the execution of his murderer was necessary to serve justice. Ryan referred to Lura Lynn's reaction when he made his announcement. "My wife is even angry with me, just like many of the victims will be. They have a right to feel betrayed." Recall, Ryan had told them he would not issue an across-the-board commutation, then changed his mind. He explained, "My obligations are broader than their desires or wishes."

During his speech, Ryan referred to his family's affectionate relationship with Small and what became of their family friend. "I share this story with you so that you know I do not come to this as a neophyte without having experienced a small bit of the bitter pill the survivors of murder must swallow."[42] The governor also raised the case of Eric Lee, the Kankakee cop killer. Although he stated there was no doubt that Lee perpetrated the 1996 murder of police officer Anthony Samfay, Ryan said it was evident that Lee was mentally ill at the time of the crime. Ryan, knowing Lee's family, said he couldn't send another man's son to his death under what was a deeply flawed capital punishment system.

The governor noted after his speech that even though he had told victims' families he was moving away from blanket clemency, he cautioned against completely ruling it out. He recognized that may not have been clear. "I told families it was on the front burner, the back burner, that I wouldn't do it at all," he said. "I'm hoping that they have an understanding of the process that I have been through."[43]

Ryan made assurances he had kept his pledge to consider each case individually. "The facts I have seen in reviewing each of these cases raised questions not only about the innocence of people on death row, but about the fairness of the death penalty system. The Illinois capital punishment system is broken. It has taken innocent men to a hair's-breadth escape from their unjust execution."[44]

Many of the survivors weren't buying what Ryan was offering. "I think all the cases are being punished because of a few. If he had reviewed them individually, he would see that some of the cases were done on the up and up," said James Dudovick, whose daughter Dawn was murdered in 1988.[45] She was stabbed forty times by William Peeples. Peeples' guilt had been solidly substantiated by DNA evidence.

While the governor's mass mercy spared the lives of condemned prisoners who insisted they were innocent, it equally affected those who admitted guilt. Ryan's ruling meant that Illinois' most notorious murderers would not be executed. Among those who fell into this category were Fedell Cafey and his former girlfriend, Jacqueline Williams. The two were convicted for the 1995 killing of Debra Evans and her two children, and cutting a full-term fetus from Evan's womb. Sam Evans, Jr., Debra's brother, explained that the governor's announcement means his family will experience no peace. "He's seen to it that us and all of the families waiting will never have closure. We've been robbed of our justice." According to Evans, "[Ryan] cannot state there was any error in our specific case. It was just wrong. There's no other way of putting it."[46]

Some of the family members were more ambivalent. Gregory Jackson, whose eleven-year-old son was slain in 1987, said he could see the need for clemency in certain situations. He added, though, that blanket commutations were difficult to accept. "I don't want an innocent person to die. I don't want anyone to go through what I've gone through. . . . But I feel cheated. I feel cheated by the governor and I feel cheated by the detective and the system that caused this mess."[47]

A few of the surviving kin were conflicted. There were those whose cases were resolved by the blanket commutation who were not upset with the decision. Patty Davis spoke after the governor's speech. She noted four members of her family had been murdered by James Ashford. Still, she felt Ryan made the right decision. That seventeen men had been exonerated for something they didn't do underscored the flaws in the system and affirmed her family's support of the governor's position.

Others, too, were torn. Larry Harp's daughter was murdered in 1997 in Chicago. He said he accepted the commutation of his daughter's killer, William Riley. Harp does not believe in the concept of capital punishment. Yet he disliked the governor's decision-making process. The issue that haunts Harp is how the clemencies were conducted and the emotional distress that everyone had to relive to get to that point.

In Northwestern's Law School auditorium where both emotional gatherings of the exonerated occurred, Governor Ryan expressed his profound convictions. Reporters hung on every word. Referring to capital punishment as "arbitrary and capricious—and therefore immoral," he proceeded to commute the death sentences of 167 Illinois convicts. He termed the number of exonerations—a figure that expanded to seventeen when he pardoned four men from death row—"an absolute embarrassment" and "a catastrophic failure."[48]

Ryan reiterated that he reviewed every case with an eye toward distinguishing the innocent from the guilty. He was preoccupied with separating situations in which the system worked properly from those in which the system failed.

He couldn't make such clear-cut distinctions.

"Hell, I know some of those people are guilty. But you can't pick and choose. That's what drove us to mass commutations," explained Ryan. "How many more cases of wrongful convictions have to occur before we can all agree that this system is broken?"[49]

Prosecutors all over Illinois slammed Ryan's decision. They believed the governor should have left these cases for the courts to resolve. Critics continued to assert that it was the federal corruption probe that motivated Ryan's grandstanding actions.

"That had nothing to do with this at all," retorted Ryan.[50]

Responding to Cook County State's Attorney Richard Divine's blast that the governor's action was "outrageous and unconscionable," Ryan said, "If you really want to know what's *outrageous and unconscionable* ... it's 17 exonerated death row inmates. It is nothing short of catastrophic failure."[51]

Secure in the knowledge that the governor's power to pardon and commute is immune from challenge, Ryan responded to those who viewed his action as a mistake. Illinois' prosecutors, he said, "have the ultimate commutation power. They decide who will be subject to the death penalty, who will get a plea deal or even who may get a complete pass on prosecution. By what objective standards do they make these decisions? We do not know, they are not public."[52]

Ryan noted that death sentences were issued differently depending on where defendants lived in the state, how poor they were, what race they and the victims were, who their defense counsel was, and who was prosecuting the case. "Prosecutors across our state continue to deny that our death penalty system is broken—or they say if there is a problem it is a small one and we can fix it somehow, someday."[53] Ryan said it was hard for him to believe that the process could be mended when "not a single" reform proposed by his Commission had been enacted by the legislature.

"These reforms would not have created a perfect system, but they would have dramatically reduced the chance of error," according to the governor. "I don't know how many more systemic flaws we need to uncover before [the legislature] would be spurred to action."[54]

Attorneys representing death row inmates raced out of the rally at Northwestern, working their cell phones in a euphoric attempt to break the news to their clients. While all but three will receive life prison terms, Ryan commented that some speculate that is "a fate worse than death."

Ryan recognized that his announcement to commute the death sentences of all his state's inmates would "draw ridicule, scorn and anger from many." He felt compelled to explain that "even if the exercise of my power becomes my burden, I will bear it. ... I sought this office, and even in my final days of holding it, I can't shrink from the obligations to justice and fairness that it demands." The governor added, "I'm going to sleep well tonight knowing I made the right decision."[55]

On his final Saturday in office, Ryan commuted 164 death sentences to life without parole. The previous day he pardoned four death row inmates, resulting in the outright release of three. Ryan commuted the death sentences of three condemned men—Mario Flores, Montell Johnson, and William Franklin—to forty-year prison terms, thus completing the clean sweep of Illinois' death row.

Following his speech, during interviews with journalists, Ryan expressed the hope that his action would trigger deeper investigations of the death penalty systems in other jurisdictions. "If it's this bad in Illinois, it's probably just as bad across the country."[56] Ryan's action smashed the modern record of eight commutations issued by former Ohio Governor Richard Celeste. And although other states' chief executives have taken sweeping clemency actions before, experts believe Ryan's decree compares in scope only with the Supreme Court's overturning the death penalty in 1972. That ruling reduced hundreds of death sentences to life.

What impact Ryan's decision will have on national death penalty debate remains to be seen. Nancy Bothne, Midwest regional director for Amnesty International, called the blanket clemency "absolutely monumental." She added, "It is significant for every political leader in every one of those thirty-eight states that still has the death penalty. This will be a defining moment in the abolition of the death penalty in the United States."[57]

Ryan could hear the cheers of 500 law students, anti–death penalty activists and men liberated from death row as he addressed the gathering. "Like it or not, the decision I make about our criminal justice system is felt not only here, but the world over." Looking beyond his final days in office, Ryan determined, "I could not leave without getting something done."[58]

The governor certainly secured his status as a champion of the anti–death penalty movement. He drew praise from world leaders such as Nelson Mandela, Desmond Tutu, and Rev. Jesse Jackson. Ryan's extraordinary move prompted predictable outrage from prosecutors. Richard Devine, the Cook County State's Attorney, dubbed the decision "stunningly disrespectful to the hundreds of families who lost their loved ones to these death row murderers." With the governor's course of action, said Devine, Ryan had "once again ripped open emotional scabs of grieving families."[59]

The State's Attorney for Peoria County, Kevin Lyons, referring to Ryan's remarks commented, "It was so offensive for him to compare himself to Lincoln and say 'I am a friend to these men on death row.'" Lyons added, "My reply is, yes, your excellency, you certainly are. Now go home before you make any more friends who are murdering the good people of Illinois."[60]

Illinois' death row may be empty at the moment, but there are more than sixty capital cases scheduled for the state's docket. Prosecutors have already declared their intention to seek death sentences. Most of these cases will be adjudicated in the Chicago area. In dozens of other situations, defendants are eligible for the death penalty, but prosecutors have yet to indicate their intentions. In Cook County, there are approximately fifty capital cases in the pipeline. There are three capital cases pending in Kane County and one in Will County. In DuPage County, prosecutors are mulling over the death penalty in six matters.

At the Mexican Consulate, relatives of Mario Flores, Juan Caballero, and Gabriel Solache—the three Mexican nationals on Illinois' death row—gathered to express their gratitude. Carlos Sada, Mexico's general consul in Chicago, claimed Ryan's decision a triumph for Mexico, which has four nationals on U.S. death rows, making Mexico the country with the greatest number of foreign nationals among condemned inmates in this country.

Three of the four men Ryan pardoned the previous day received a hero's welcome at the Northwestern affair. "I think he saved a whole lot of people today," commented Madison Hobley. He was pardoned of setting a blaze that killed seven people. Hobley was one of those suspects who claimed former Chicago police Lt. Jon Burge tortured him to extract a false confession. "I just really saw justice yesterday after 16 years in the system."[61]

When asked if he considered that he had saved so many lives, Ryan responded to a reporter's question by saying, "I never thought about that. ... My goal was to improve a broken system in Illinois."[62]

Also present for the governor's announcement was Gary Gauger, whose conviction for murdering his parents was overturned and whom Ryan had pardoned previously. "This is not a time for celebration," cautioned Gauger. "This is a time for people to start looking at all the other cases in prison. Ten years ago, Jon Burge was fired for torture. But they haven't done anything yet. The courts are not handling it."[63]

Ryan concurred. He noted that capital punishment as administered in his state is extremely uneven. Paraphrasing Supreme Court Justice Potter Stewart, Ryan said that the imposition of the death penalty on defendants in this country is as freakish and arbitrary as who gets hit by lightning.

Plenty of retired politicians were on hand for Ryan's event. Other than the governor himself, no current officeholders attended. This conspicuous absence was not overlooked by Ryan. He noted, "It is easier and more comfortable for politicians to be tough on crime and support the death penalty. It wins votes." Then he commented, "But when it comes to admitting we have a problem, most run for cover. Prosecutors across the state continue to deny that our death penalty system is broken. ... Will we actually have to execute an innocent person before the tragedy that is our capital punishment system in Illinois is really understood?"[64]

For following through on what he believed, Ryan earned the admiration of many and incurred the wrath of others. Ryan will feel the heat of this controversy for some time. His detractors accused him of undermining the roles of judge and jury, of overreaching with his executive powers, of attempting to distract the focus away from his political scandal. He made the mandatory rounds of the television talk show circuits and made himself accessible to the media, all the while resisting the notion that this decision would be his legacy. "If the debate ends up in abolition someplace, that may be a legacy. That certainly wasn't my goal."[65]

Reflecting on Ryan's monumental action, Marlene Martin of the Campaign to End the Death Penalty said that she didn't really know what the governor was going to do until he did it. She acknowledged that he was under pressure from both sides, and he was vacillating. Martie noted that the governor first opposed blanket commutations especially when the state clemency board held hearings and prosecutors paraded murder victims relatives in front of the cameras. But, she added, the abolitionists kept the pressure on until the very last day with demonstrations and different events by different groups. Those tactics obviously made an impression.

Martin observed that listening to Ryan's speech made her think she was hearing a member of the Campaign to End the Death Penalty. He came across as though he was lifting whole passages out of the Campaign's newsletter calling for justice for the Death Row 10. The abolitionists had long wanted to make the plight of the Death Row 10—those who were torture victims of Chicago police—a household word. In Illinois, at least, that's been achieved.

Alice Kim, also a member of the Campaign to End the Death Penalty, commented that it was the work of activists, lawyers, reporters, students, death row family members and death row inmates themselves that exposed the Illinois death penalty. Activism, especially, led the charge for blanket commutations. The families of those on death row organized to meet with the governor to describe the devastation suffered by having a loved one sentenced to die.

Kim explained how the Campaign to End the Death Penalty and other groups conducted press conferences, town hall meetings, and rallies. She highlighted the media events masterminded by Northwestern's Center on Wrongful Convictions and Rev. Jesse Jackson's New Year's Eve visit with the Death Row 10 as particularly effective examples of activism that helped influence the commutation decision.

Martin offered a few political observations. She noted that Ryan is a conservative Republican. And although he could be heartless when making cuts in the state budget, on the issue of the death penalty he was far more radical than any politician in Illinois.

Even a pro–death penalty prosecutor like Cook County State's Attorney Richard Devine had to admit that the capital punishment system now has been "so bludgeoned that there's grave doubt about its viability." Devine has called for "a full debate about whether we should have a death penalty at all."[66]

3

Eyewitness Testimony: Seeing Isn't Always Believing

Picture yourself a smart (as in 4.0 Grade Point Average–sharp), attractive (Home Coming Queen–pretty) student, living alone, off-campus in a small college town in North Carolina. It's a hot, July night. You've long since finished your studies. It's three o'clock in the morning. You're deep asleep. A rustling sound disturbs your dreaming. From a sleepy stupor, you manage, "What's that? Who's there?"

Your answer comes in the form of a knife to your throat and a shadowy figure suddenly on top of you. Before you know it your arms are pinned to the side of your head. You realize your apartment's been broken into and your body is about to be violated. Your pulse races and a panic-stricken fear floods your veins.

Such was the hour-long horror of Jennifer Thompson, whose serene, twenty-two-year existence was about to be shattered. "I remember feeling frightened. I remember feeling sick. I also remember feeling an overwhelming sense of guilt," Thompson recalls.[1]

Unlike the typical victim of assault, Jennifer neither froze nor panicked. She was determined to extract her measure of revenge. Although she was repulsed by her attacker and didn't even want to look at him, she knew she had to overcome that instinct. Rather than look away, she had to force herself to sharpen her focus, absorb every characteristic she could about her assailant.

She studied every detail of the rapist's face. She looked at his hairline. She searched for scars, tattoos, anything that would help identify him. To make

DOONESBURY   **BY GARRY TRUDEAU**

the rapist pay, Jennifer resolved to become the most accurate eye-witness she could. When they caught the culprit, she wanted to be his worst nightmare. If she survived the attack, she was going to make certain the perpetrator would be put in prison to rot.

As her ordeal began, the intruder ordered Jennifer to stay silent. If she screamed, she'd be killed. And he had the knife to do it. Jennifer strained to see the assailant's face, hoping that it was someone she knew playing an awful trick on her. When she realized it wasn't, Jennifer thought perhaps this was merely a robber out for her money. She offered this to her assailant. But it wasn't money he was after.

Her heart pounding, Jennifer asked, "What do you want?" He proceeded to remove her underwear, slid down her body and began performing oral sex. Jennifer knew she was about to be raped. She didn't know if the attack would go further, if she was going to be hurt or killed. At this point she decided she would outsmart her attacker.

Throughout the night, Jennifer tried to turn on lights, if only for a moment. Each time her intruder demanded she shut the lights. At one point, he stooped to turn on the stereo. A dim blue light shone from the control panel and reflected on his face. Jennifer was able to catch a glimpse of her attacker's features. When she went into the bathroom, she turned on the light. Again, he told her to turn it off. But even such short glimmerings were enough to get Jennifer thinking, "Okay, his nose looks this way" or "His shirt is navy blue, not black." She used whatever flashes of light she could spark to patch together a composite picture of the assailant, a disjointed portrait she would try to memorize.

As he slithered up her body, he tried to kiss Jennifer's lips. This attempted intimacy enraged Jennifer, made her feel sick to her stomach. She turned away. He looked down at her and with a twisted affection called her "Baby." Jennifer sensed this was the moment to make her move. She returned his glance and encouraged his transition from being aggressive to being amorous.

"You know, if you would put your knife outside, I would feel much more at ease," Jennifer offered. He fell for it and got off her. Unfortunately, he didn't go outside to discard his weapon. He merely dropped his knife outside the apartment door and returned. Jennifer had to rethink her strategy. She needed to maintain momentum now that she'd worked up the courage to overcome her paralysis.

She said, "I'm really thirsty. I need to get something to drink." She headed to the kitchen. Her refrigerator was near the back door. As she walked in that direction, she saw that the back door was open and realized this was the intruder's point of entry. Nervously, she began running water and tossing ice cubes in the sink. She clanked open drawers and cabinets, raising as much racket as she could. All the while, Jennifer was building her courage to make her break. A deep breath. An adrenaline rush. And through the open back door she burst.

She ran to a neighbor's home that had a light on in the carport. Desperately, she banged on the door. When a man answered, Jennifer screamed, "I've been raped by a black man. He's after me. Please let me in." The neighbor became hysterical, losing his composure. Fortunately, his wife recognized Jennifer. She was a professor at the school Jennifer attended. Though she didn't know Jennifer by name, she told her husband, "I've seen her. She's a student at college. Let her in." Once safely inside, Jennifer was overcome by anxiety, terror and relief. Conscience thought, mercifully, failed her. Jennifer fainted.

Meanwhile, Ronald Cotton spent much of that July night across town, sprawled on the sofa of his mother's living room. Ronald slept soundly as his sisters came and went during the evening. He was the same age as Jennifer Thompson. He was a local fellow, who'd had his run-ins with the law. Cotton had served eighteen months in prison for attempted sexual assault.

When Jennifer regained consciousness, her neighbors took her to the hospital. After attending to her physical needs, the medical staff introduced Jennifer to Detective Mike Gauldin. Gauldin was a six-year veteran with an outstanding reputation. The investigation of Jennifer's sexual assault proceeded on several fronts. While Gauldin interviewed her, police were searching the neighborhood, trying to find Jennifer's assailant. Physicians were collecting samples of hair and vaginal smears, trying to gather evidence. Jennifer found the process intrusive and demeaning.

The police received a second call that night involving another woman who was heard screaming in a nearby neighborhood. This woman was the second victim of the perpetrator in Jennifer's case.

When the detective talked with Jennifer, while still in the hospital, she heard a woman crying a few stalls away. Jennifer asked Gauldin, "Did she get raped also?" Gauldin replied, "Yes, and we think it was the same person."

"That was a horrible feeling," Jennifer recalled. "He had hurt two women in one night. I can remember feeling so sorry for her because I knew how much pain I was feeling. I could only assume she was feeling the same."

Jennifer's nightmarish journey continued from the hospital to police headquarters where she was asked to provide a statement. According to Gauldin, "She was so determined during the course of the sexual assault to look at her assailant well, to study him well enough so that, if given the opportunity, she would be able to identify her assailant."[2]

At the police station, Jennifer was asked to study a directory containing pages and pages of facial features. "It can get very confusing," notes Jennifer. "All of a sudden, you've seen 20 noses and you're not really positive how the nostrils were."

Jennifer worked on a composite sketch to the best of her ability. She perused hundreds of different facial features. Days later, studying a series of police photos, she identified the attacker. She knew this was the man. She was certain.

Gauldin's confidence also was high in Jennifer's ability to identify her attacker. He knew that most victims become so traumatized, so overwhelmed by fear during the course of sexual assault, that Jennifer's ability to maintain her composure was highly unusual.

Jennifer was conflicted. She was trying to keep her presence of mind, to keep her memory straight. At the same time, though, she yearned to lose her mind.

Gauldin's strategy centered on Jennifer's memory of her attacker. He counted on her description leading to a suspect. He planned to publicize the composite sketch broadly, hoping someone would recognize the rapist.

Jennifer's determined recollection portrayed the perpetrator as a black male in his late teens or early twenties. The man had short hair and a pencil-thin mustache. He stood six feet tall. Jennifer figured he weighed about 175 pounds.

Following news reports broadcasting the rapist's description, a lead surfaced. An anonymous informer said that a man resembling the sketch worked at Somer's Seafood restaurant. The tip pointed police to Ronald Cotton. The restaurant was in the same neighborhood where the rapes occurred. As a result of the anonymous call, police assigned a detective to run a background check on Ronald Cotton.

Cotton had a police record. At age 16 he was convicted of attempted rape. His target was a fourteen-year-old white girl with whom he was acquainted. He was currently on parole for a second conviction for breaking and entering. The owner of Somer's Seafood said Cotton had a habit of touching white waitresses and teasing them about sex. The owner mentioned that Cotton possessed a blue shirt similar to the one Jennifer saw.

Cotton's name, along with five others, was brought to the authorities' attention. These six individuals became the starting point for developing a photo spread. A photo album filled with volumes of mug shots was handed to Jennifer. Careful not to bias her impressions, the police cautioned, "He may or may not be in here. Take your time. Think through it."

It didn't take Jennifer long to reach a conclusion. She pointed to the photo of Ronald Cotton. After Jennifer picked it out, police officers looked at her and said, "We thought this might be the one, . . . because he had a prior conviction . . . the same type of circumstances."

This matter seemed to fit the mold of the archetypal Southern crime. A black man accused of sexually assaulting two white women in a small Southern town is a familiar script. But upon closer examination, this case didn't match the archetype. The authorities had a description of a black individual. They handed a photograph to the victim in a fair photographic line-up and she selected Ronald Cotton. Then they tried to find evidence to support the identification.

Armed with Jennifer's eyewitness identification and a search warrant, Gauldin set out to track down Ronald Cotton. The police were moving in the right direction, but they picked the wrong Cotton.

"I had a knock on my door. My door flew open and they came in on me," said Calvin Cotton, the suspect's brother. "They reached and grabbed me, spun me around. They threw me in the bed and pulled my hands behind my back and asked was I Cotton."[3] Unaware of Ronald's predicament, Calvin said, "Yeah."

One of the officers said, "Cotton, you're under arrest." Another officer pulled Calvin's wallet out of his pocket. After perusing the contents, the policeman realized he had the wrong brother. At that, the police headed for the Cotton family home.

The police didn't find Ronald at his mother's house, but they did discover evidence. Under Ronald's bed, Gauldin found a pair of black shoes similar to those described by both victims. The police had recovered a piece of foam rubber at Jennifer Thompson's crime scene that appeared to have come from the inside of a shoe. The authorities found a flashlight similar to one described by the second victim.

The police began piecing together tidbits in support of their witness's story. No matter how circumstantial, the authorities pressed on, their enthusiasm increasing as the evidence mounted. Even though the foam rubber could have come from any one of a thousand athletic shoes in Alamance County, the possibility that it might have matched one of Ronald Cotton's shoes provided police reason to believe they may have been onto another link to the perpetrator. With dogged determination, they collected evidence upon which prosecutors constructed their case.

As the investigation intensified, Cotton voluntarily walked into the police station saying he wanted to clear the air. He identified the flashlight and shoes as his, but insisted he had not done anything wrong. He told police he had been out with friends on the night of the crime.

Several detectives were assigned to follow up on Cotton's alibi. The people he claimed to be with couldn't back up his story. Taking the unsubstantiated alibi offered by Cotton and combining that with Jennifer's positive identification, supported by evidence gathered from under the suspect's bed, the police believed they had the culprit.

Defense attorney, Phillip Moseley, was appointed to represent Cotton. He hurried to the jail and met with his client. They were rushed to the Burlington Police Department and brought to a viewing room. Seven young African American males were positioned in a line-up. Each held a number. One at a time, the victims were escorted in to view the line-up. Each of the men was asked to repeat a phrase, turn around, then step back. The voice presentation consisted of saying some of the lines the rapist uttered the night of the assault. This aspect of the line-up was significant as Jennifer believed the man had a distinctive voice.

After careful consideration, Jennifer narrowed the lineup to suspects number 4 and 5. She asked that these two men repeat the routine. Once both had, she selected number 5, who turned out to be Ronald Cotton.

"I picked the same man in a lineup. Again, I was sure," Jennifer declared confidently. "I picked the right guy, and he was going to go to jail. If there was the possibility of a death sentence, I wanted him to die. I wanted to flip the switch."[4]

When her viewing session was over Jennifer left the room. One of the detectives walked over and said, "That's the same guy. That's the one you picked in the photo." That reassurance was a relief to Jennifer. Knowing she had been consistent with her photo and line-up choices gave Jennifer a sense of esteem as a witness. She believed her credibility had been established.

When Jennifer left the line-up room, victim number 2 entered. She went through the same drill. She had the men say a slightly different phrase. They said the line, going through the same physical motions. When they finished, she said, "It's number 4." This was the same number 4 over whom Jennifer stumbled. As if to reinforce the confusion, this victim asked, "Did I get the right one?"

Ronald Cotton's case came to trial in January 1985. The prosecution decided to pursue charges only for Jennifer's rape, figuring the second victim's failure to identify Cotton could diminish the case. Despite extensive forensic investigations, the state had little physical evidence. There were neither fingerprints nor hairs. Blood typing of semen samples had proven inconclusive. The prosecutor believed that Jennifer Thompson alone would be far more persuasive than any physical evidence.

Research has shown that jurors are impressed by confident eyewitness testimony. How does such evidence compare to the weight jurors give other testimony? In a study that explored this question, mock jurors were offered testimony in a hypothetical bad check case. The defendant was charged with writing a check to buy a television set; the check had insufficient funds. The jurors were divided into four groups and were provided numerous details about the crime. Each group was presented one of four critical facts.

One set of jurors was told that an eyewitness—the clerk who sold the TV—had positively identified the defendant as the person who passed the check. A second group of jurors was informed that a polygraph operator had tested the defendant and found that he was lying when he said that he had not written the check. Another quarter of the jurors was told that a fingerprint specialist had examined the prints left on the counter by the person who had passed the check, and that they matched the defendant's prints. The fourth group was told that the handwriting on the check matched that of the defendant.

After all the testimony was in, the jurors reached a verdict. Convictions were highest in the scenario featuring the eyewitness (78 percent), and lowest in the circumstances focusing on the handwriting expert (34 percent). The testimony of the fingerprint and polygraph experts produced intermediate numbers for guilty verdicts (70 percent and 53 percent, respectively).[5]

One of the prosecutors working the Cotton case, James Roberson, in interviews subsequent to trial, spoke of the star witness's convincing style. "Jennifer had a very good rapport with the jury. When a question was asked, she would turn to the jury and explain what happened. It was almost as if she was taking the jurors back to when it happened."[6]

From the witness stand, Jennifer described how the intruder had rifled through her wallet while she lay sleeping. This allowed the rapist to know her name. "He had robbed me," Jennifer declared to the jury. "He had gone through private articles of mine. He completely violated me. In every way a person can be violated, I was violated."

One juror, interviewed for the PBS show, *Frontline*, shared his impressions. "As I listened to Jennifer's testimony," commented Dallas Fry, "I thought she was very, very brave. It had to be terrible for her to tell these

people all these intimate things. The part that infuriated me most was that
he scared her to death. The rape was bad enough and everything that he
made her do was bad enough, but the fear he instilled in her is what really
made me the maddest."

In another case that underscores the power of eyewitness testimony, jurors
in a trial in Hartford, Connecticut, chose to believe an eyewitness identification of a criminal defendant over the categorical testimony of an FBI laboratory director. The federal agent offered DNA findings that conclusively
proved the defendant could not have committed the rape. This example
illustrates that no lawyer opposing an eyewitness can afford complacency.[7]

Jurors may attribute more credence to eyewitness testimony than to other
testimony because an eyewitness typically gives a more complete report of
events. An eyewitness account is a detailed description that contributes matter for the reconstruction of events in jurors' minds. An eyewitness offers a
story. Research supports the idea of the story format as a powerful instru-
ment in juror decision making. Contrast this to testimony of other witnesses,
such as a handwriting specialist, who provide only an isolated sliver of evidence. It may just be easier for jurors to work with a seamless account,
tweaking it depending on subsequent evidence, rather than take snippets
and fashion them into a coherent whole.

Why does eyewitness testimony carry such clout? One explanation is that
throughout our lives exact memory is not demanded of us. People often do
not catch mistakes of memory that are made, leading individuals to believe
memory is more accurate than it is. Since people tend to trust their own
memories more than they should, they give the same credence to the memories of others. Information presented by a confident eyewitness is accepted
by jurors and incorporated into the mental construction of whatever event
the witness is recalling.

Jurors also place stock in an eyewitness account because they are unaware of the variables that influence its accuracy. The type and phrasing of
questions posed by authorities and attorneys can influence witness accuracy.
Several studies show what lay citizens believe about eyewitness testimony.[8]
One common misconception is that police officers make better witnesses
than do ordinary citizens. Roughly half of a large sample of Miami, Florida,
residents said yes to the question, "Do you think that the memory of law
enforcement agents is better than the memory of the average citizen?" Research with police officers shows that neither their training nor experience
increases their ability to be accurate witnesses.

Studies have uncovered other misconceptions about eyewitness testimony.
A couple that are pertinent to Jennifer Thompson include the following:

(a) *Witnesses recall the details of violent events better than those of nonviolent ones.*
Research demonstrates the opposite. The stress generated by violence tends to
blur perception and memory, especially for peripheral details.

(b) *The more confident a witness appears, the more accurate the testimony is apt to be.* Research suggests there may be little relationship between confidence and accuracy, particularly when viewing conditions are poor.

In the early 1980s, the Knowledge of Eyewitness Behavior Questionnaire (KEBQ)[9] was created to gauge whether people in general and jurors in particular understand the factors that influence eyewitness accuracy. When administered to an American sample, the result was that the public often was incorrect about the factors shaping eyewitness accounts. The results were similar with samples from other countries.

Another attempt to garner information regarding the public's views was made when the KEBQ was modified and given to 190 jurors who had been seated in criminal trials in the District of Columbia.[10] The jurors revealed several misconceptions about eyewitness testimony. The following illustrates the point:

Q: Some say it is more difficult for people of one race to identify people of a different race. Do you think this is:

(a) true

(b) false

(c) more true for whites viewing nonwhites than for nonwhites viewing whites?

Thirty three percent of the jurors selected (a); 45 percent chose (b); and 20 percent (c). The remainder responded "I don't know." The most commonly offered answer, (b), is wrong. The answer coinciding with the data is (a).

Misconceptions about how eyewitness memory operates are not limited to lay people. The KEBQ was given to a sample of British police authorities. They, too, carried a number of misconceptions. These officers held their erroneous opinions regardless of rank or length of service.

These misconceptions present a challenge for attorneys. It may prove counterproductive for a lawyer to elicit on cross-examination the fact that the event was violent if the jurors will use that detail to enhance their confidence in the eyewitness. A fact that, according to psychological findings, should undermine jurors' confidence in eyewitness accounts may wind up bolstering it.

Another contributor to the *Frontline* exposé was University of North Carolina law professor Rich Rosen. Rosen studied the Cotton case extensively. He observed, "If the victim is somebody the jurors can identify with and sympathize with, if the victim is really an innocent victim, then it's probably the most powerful testimony that could be presented." Rosen added, "This is somebody who's been hurt, who's been brutalized, who sits in front of the jury and ritualistically says, 'Yes, I can identify the person who did this to me. He is sitting at counsel table. That is the man who hurt me so

badly.' It is incredibly powerful evidence and jurors want to believe the victim. They identify with the victim. And especially when there is no motive
for the victim to lie, it is very hard evidence to overcome."[11]

Defense counsel tried to counter Jennifer's testimony by arguing she had
been mistaken, that Ronald Cotton was not involved. But Moseley knew
it would be a difficult sell. Lawyers know that eyewitness identification
is not the most reliable evidence. Unlike experienced legal professionals,
however, the general public, and hence jurors, believes the testimony of
eyewitnesses to be solid. Furthermore, the case had a racial component that
troubled Moseley. A white female victim accosted by an African American
male generally drew the jury's sympathy. That Cotton had a prior criminal
record added to the obstacles defense had to overcome.

Then there was the alibi. By the time of trial, Cotton said he'd gotten
his dates confused. He had given mistaken information to the police. His
original alibi was that he had been with friends on the night of the assaults.
He even named those friends. In trying to confirm Cotton's tale, detectives
couldn't match his dates and places with the recollections of his friends.
Then Ronald, conferring with his defense team, told his lawyers that his
alibi witness would be his girlfriend with whom he spent the night, before
going home. In the final version, he said he was at his mother's home. His
family claimed that he was asleep on the sofa. Three of Cotton's sisters
testified to walking past him several times over the span of Friday night to
Saturday morning. So the defense was in the untenable position of juggling
three alibis.

That Ronald's siblings repeated the same story didn't necessarily
strengthen his case. For some, it left the impression that these witnesses had
been rehearsed. Such a hollow presentation makes jurors think something's
being covered up.

The defense believed its best strategy was to focus on the second rape.
After all, although Jennifer identified Ronald Cotton as the assailant, the
second victim fingered an innocent bystander. There was such similarity
in how each crime was committed, the modus operandi was like leaving a
fingerprint. Defense counsel reasoned that since Ronald didn't commit the
second offense, he didn't perpetrate the first either.

Although police connected both assaults to the same man, Cotton stood
trial only for Jennifer's rape. The judge dealt the defense a damaging blow
by denying the motion seeking to enter into evidence facts pertaining to the
second attack. The jury was never allowed to learn about the night's other
crime.

The prosecutor concurred with the judge. Both believed the defense motion was merely a ploy, creating a collateral issue. This view held that what
defense counsel was really trying to do was develop a diversionary tactic that
would draw the jury's attention away from actual evidence, distract from
the powerful eyewitness identification that Jennifer was about to present.

Defense counsel knew the state's star witness believed she had made an accurate identification. Anticipating the powerful impact Jennifer's testimony was likely to have on the jury, the defense began developing a counterstrategy. Without appearing too aggressive, an attack needed to be mounted against the credibility of her memory. How reliable is anyone's ability to recall past events? In a delicate, yet forthright, manner, the jury needed to be shown that Jennifer's memory could be honestly impaired.

Attorney Moseley turned to Dr. Reed Hunt, a psychology professor at the University of North Carolina at Greensboro. Hunt explained that people tend to believe others when they say they remember something. If the person claims to recall an event with great confidence, such a statement is going to have enormous influence on a jury.

The professor added that Moseley wanted Hunt as an expert to offer testimony that would allow the jury to hear of possibilities that confusions in memory occur. Hunt was to discuss with the jury the importance of having multiple line-ups with Cotton as the only constant in those line-ups. The expert was to point out that this scenario is one that may induce confusion.

The trial judge ruled that Hunt had no expertise in this case. He decided that jurors should be guided by their common sense in determining the accuracy of the witness's recall.

It was never explained to the jury that scientists know human beings can offer eyewitness identification in good faith and yet, due to unconscious transfer, be mistaken. The psychological principle of unconscious transfer holds that when an individual sees a certain event and subsequently experiences an intervening event, the latter may color recollection of the former. Jennifer unwittingly may have relied on her viewing of the photo line-up, rather than the rape scene itself, for her selection in the physical line-up. With every intention of expressing an honest account, even a determined eyewitness can be dead wrong.

During the trial, Ronald Cotton never testified. His lawyer knew if Cotton took the stand, it would open him up to cross examination. Then prosecutors would be allowed to introduce Cotton's criminal record, a piece of personal history the defense would rather the jury not know.

To some jurors, Cotton's lack of emotion was highly noticeable. For eight days of trial, he never changed expression. Jurors commented how strange this seemed to them. Absent any sort of reaction or visible emotional response, jury members perceived they were sitting in judgment of a guilty man.

On January 17, 1985, Ronald Cotton was convicted based on Jennifer Thompson's testimony. He received a sentence of life in prison at North Carolina's maximum-security facility. Thompson toasted the verdict, calling it the happiest day of her life. She was set to put the ordeal behind her.

For Cotton, life took a terrible turn. "I would work out maybe three to four hours on the speed bag to relieve frustration and tension that was building up in me from being incarcerated," Ronald recalled. "I would be mad sometimes during the day. By going down and beating this bag, it helped me a lot. I prefer to do that than fight the other inmates."

Ronald passed most prison nights by writing. He sent letters to his lawyer, to newspapers, to anyone else he thought might be helpful. In one such correspondence, dated December 1, 1985, he wrote, "Mr. Moseley, I've been waiting patiently to hear from you before now, but I assume, being an attorney, you've been extremely busy. Well, it's going on a year that I've been incarcerated at Central Prison and I haven't received any documents concerning my case or much less know how things look on my behalf." Cotton concluded, "... it's hell living here."[12]

In addition to pounding a punching bag and pouring out his feelings in correspondence, Ronald joined the prison choir and read the Bible. Above all, he tried to keep faith with what his father told him—someday justice would prevail.

In a September 8, 1986, letter to his attorney, Ronald wrote, "Sir, I'll agree I have indeed been highly frustrated by the fact of how things have been going in my case. It's as though I'm left without anything to look forward to. I'm lost and don't know what's happening."[13]

About a year into his sentence, Cotton was joined by another prisoner assigned to kitchen detail. The coworker's name was Bobby Poole. He had been sentenced to consecutive life terms for a series of vicious sexual assaults. He was boasting to inmates that Cotton was serving his time. Cotton's hatred for Poole intensified. Ronald recalls getting a piece of metal and crafting a blade out of it, to kill Poole.

Cotton's father pleaded against that. His father advised him to put his faith in God. Killing Poole, he cautioned, would only mean Ronald really did belong behind bars.

So Cotton discarded his weapon and put his faith in a Higher Authority. Ronald directed an eye-opening correspondence to his attorney. Cotton described discovering the true perpetrator of the rapes. In a letter dated September 30, 1986, he wrote his lawyer, "There is no doubt in my mind that Bobby Poole did the crime I'm serving time for. I work in the kitchen with him, as well as sleep in the same dorm. Mr. Moseley, as I've said before, Poole is the one. I've enclosed a picture of Poole and me that was taken October 31st, 1985. Maybe you could use it." With a renewed sense of purpose, Cotton closed, "I say the truth will come to light and the Lord knows I'm an innocent man. Some day, somewhere, the truth is going to come out in my case. Thank you."[14]

Other prisoners were willing to support Ronald's assertion. Dennis Bass, former inmate, talking with a reporter, said, "Yeah, I knew Bobby Poole in the street, okay. I went to jail and we was in the same cell together. We got to talking and he was telling me about the crimes they had Ronald Cotton charged with and he said he didn't do them. I'm saying, 'Well, how do you know he didn't do them?' And he said, 'Because I did.' And I'm saying, 'Well, why don't you say something?' He's the type of guy didn't care either-or. He was just waiting for a break."[15]

After serving two years, Cotton was granted a new trial on grounds that the jury should have been allowed to hear evidence relating to the second rape. When he learned he'd won a retrial, his hope was restored. Another woman had been raped an hour after Jennifer Thompson. The second crime occurred in the same neighborhood and was a similar assault. Police were certain it was the same culprit.

At new proceedings, Cotton believed, the victims would get a good look at Poole, who would be subpoenaed by the defense. At last, he'd be free, thought Ronald. But, once again, circumstances in the courtroom conspired against him.

The second woman changed her mind, saying now she would identify Ronald as her assailant. The defense remained confident of Cotton's exoneration. That was, until Bobby Poole offered testimony.

Under oath, Poole testified that he did not commit the two rapes. He denied making statements to the prison informants. Making matters worse for the defense, Jennifer Thompson again took the stand.

During proceedings prior to retrial, Thompson learned that another inmate had claimed to be her attacker. This man had been boasting of the assault in the same prison wing where Ronald Cotton was being held. This man was Bobby Poole.

Poole was brought into court. Jennifer was asked, "Ms. Thompson, have you ever seen this man?" She replied: "I have never seen him in my life. I have no idea who he is."[16]

The second victim then entered the court. From a distance of fifteen feet, as Jennifer had previously, the second woman got a clear look at Bobby Poole. Independently, she testified that Poole was not her rapist. Each woman insisted Ronald Cotton was.

"I never remember looking at Bobby Poole, thinking, 'Oh, I've got the wrong person! I've made a huge mistake,'" Jennifer recalled. "Now I remember that never entered my head." Quite disenchanted, she added, "Again, I thought, 'Oh, this is just a game. This is just a game they're playing.'"[17]

Jennifer told herself for so long that Ronald Cotton was her rapist, she made herself believe it. She had taken the witness stand and sworn on the Bible that the man who raped her was Ronald Cotton. She was certain. By the time she set eyes on Poole, she was not about to change her mind. She was deeply invested in her eyewitness identification. She wasn't likely to reverse herself and admit making a mistake. Whatever impression was burnished in her mind of the rapist, that image was Ronald Cotton.

During the second trial, the judge ruled that the evidence that Poole committed the sexual assaults did not meet the standard in North Carolina for direct evidence. The reasoning followed that the defense was not allowed to present his testimony. Nor was the defense permitted to present any evidence that Poole committed these offenses.

At the conclusion, the judge turned to Cotton, asking if he had anything he'd like to add to counsel's comments. Ronald offered an unusual response, requesting permission to sing a song he had composed. The courtroom became ghostly quiet. No one was accustomed to singing in the courtroom.

Ronald issued his lyrical, legal lament: "Decisions I could no longer make because my future's so unknown to me/ And then I could no longer take/ Because during the day I wonder/ At night I hurt with fear/ Call out Your name so much till suddenly tears appear/ Until God came in my life, until God came in my life./ Until God come in my life."[18]

"By singing in the choir when I was incarcerated," Ronald explained, "it helped me to be joyful and happy with myself. It helped me deal with what I was going through."

As Ronald sang, rage was welling within Jennifer Thompson. "How dare you try to receive sympathy from people in this courtroom when you've done this horrible crime," Jennifer thought. But she also was conflicted. If Ronald had found religion, more power to him was her inclination. She would recall, "There was such a mixed feeling that it was sickening. It was nauseating. I wanted to throw up. I wanted to cry. I can remember my face feeling hot, my heart racing. And it was ... one of the moments that I lost it."

Cotton was convicted on both rape charges. He was returned to prison to serve two life sentences. As far as Jennifer was concerned, Ronald Cotton was never going to see the light of day; he was never going to get out; he was never going to hurt any body; he was never going to rape another woman.

For eight years, the status quo held in Cotton's case. Then, purely by accident, in the summer of 1985, Ronald's plight caught the attention of law professor Rich Rosen. Routinely, Rosen is asked by attorneys to review cases of inmates seeking guidance. A lack of time, generally, causes the professor to turn down these requests.

This time something was different. Once on Rosen's radar screen, the case impressed him by how little evidence there was. Aside from eyewitness identifications, the state offered nothing of substance. Even one of the eyewitness identifications was weak. Given the amount of time the perpetrator spent in the victims' homes and given the nature of the attacks, one would have expected more physical evidence to implicate Cotton. That it just wasn't there surprised the professor.

By this point a new forensic technique had emerged that Rosen could utilize, possibly to Cotton's benefit. DNA testing of semen samples had become a standard tool in the investigation of rape cases. In this instance, DNA results might help overturn Cotton's convictions. The process was not without risks.

Cotton's supporters believed there was a solid claim upon which to base the request for DNA testing. They felt they had a good shot to win such a claim and earn Ronald a new trial. Risk remained that if DNA testing were conducted and results showed Ronald committed the crimes, his fate would be sealed. When this was brought to Cotton's attention, he insisted the testing be done. His legal team discussed the ramifications with him. After thoughtful deliberation, it was decided to proceed with the request.

DNA testing requires something upon which to be tested. Was old evidence from the case preserved? Authorities are not mandated to maintain evidence once a case is over. Such material is usually destroyed. But to the surprise of Cotton's advocates, the medical evidence from the investigation was still in the police's custody. It had been saved by Detective Gauldin.

Gauldin suspected this would be a case that would linger. The matter was heavily litigated starting in 1984. Following the conviction in '87, a state supreme court review seemed likely. So Gauldin continued to sign off on the evidence and instruct the appropriate police personnel to preserve it.

Even with evidence maintained, a new DNA examination required the willingness of prosecutors to open an old case. Why would they consider having two hard-won convictions, litigated in front of separate juries, overturned?

Prosecutor Rob Johnson knew well what was at stake. He didn't want to be the one responsible for setting a serial rapist loose on his fellow Alamance County citizens. Nor did he wish to be liable for holding an innocent man behind bars.

Since the last round of proceedings, Jennifer Thompson had had little interaction with the authorities. Then, as if from the blue, a call came from Detective Gauldin.

"It was Spring 1995," Jennifer remembered. "I was happy where I was at in my life. And I received a phone call from Mike Gauldin. He told me that they needed to see me. When he and Rob Johnson came over, they began to tell me about DNA."

"I was asked to provide a blood sample so DNA tests could be run on evidence from the rape," said Jennifer. "I agreed because I knew that Ronald Cotton had raped me and DNA was only going to confirm that. The test would allow me to move on once and for all."

Following preliminary DNA investigation, an awkward conversation ensued. The detective and the prosecuting attorney informed Jennifer that DNA testing raised questions as to Cotton's guilt. Although the results of the examination were not yet conclusive, it was clear that serious concerns of wrongful conviction had been flagged. As the discussion advanced, Johnson and Gauldin knew they were dredging up events Jennifer would rather not recall. They knew she had already publicly relived the awful assault of 1984, once at trial in 1985, and again during the retrial in 1987.

"I will never forget the day I learned about the DNA results," states Jennifer sadly. "I was standing in my kitchen when the detective and the district attorney visited. They were good and decent people who were trying to do their jobs—as I had done mine."

Jennifer recalls, "They told me: 'Ronald Cotton didn't rape you. It was Bobby Poole.'"

"The man I was so sure I had never seen in my life was the man who was inches from my throat, who raped me, who hurt me, who took my spirit away, who robbed me of my soul." Swallowing hard, Jennifer adds, "And the man I identified so emphatically on so many occasions was absolutely innocent."

Ronald Cotton would be released after serving eleven years in prison. Bobby Poole would plead guilty to raping Jennifer Thompson.

Cotton's conviction could be considered the result of a systemwide breakdown. But, the tragic error was about to be corrected. An exceptional chain of events was about to undo a grave injustice: the defendant's doggedly maintaining his innocence; a law professor's intervention; the fact that sophisticated scientific testing, not available all those years ago, could now be applied.

UNC professor Richard Rosen had accepted the case concerned that a man was sentenced to life in prison entirely on the basis of eyewitness testimony. "In so many cases, eyewitnesses can be unreliable," Rosen said. "I had no idea how compelling Thompson was. I'm not sure any jury would have acquitted him in the face of her testimony."[19] Rosen's insistence led to closer examination of DNA samples from Cotton and Poole. By a fortunate fluke, authorities had saved evidence from the crime scenes.

In the end, Gauldin consoled Thompson, justice prevailed for the wrongly accused. An innocent individual was set free. Ronald Cotton, noted the detective, was a lucky man.

When word finally came that DNA tests could be conducted and their results excluded Ronald as the perpetrator, a whirlwind of emotions was unleashed. The exhilarating liberation experienced by Ronald and his supporters was balanced by an intense uneasiness on Jennifer's part. While Cotton expressed that he brought no bitterness with him out of prison, Jennifer felt "an overwhelming sense of guilt" that she had made the mistake responsible for taking away such a large chunk of a man's life.

"How do I give someone back eleven years?" cried Jennifer.[20]

The question remained: If Ronald didn't commit the crimes, who did? The authorities revisited the DNA lab, this time to nab the real rapist. Locked in a freezer were samples from 20,000 violent offenders. Police pulled a blood-soaked card from the freezer. This particular card was labeled with Bobby Poole's name. When confronted with the DNA evidence, Poole admitted committing both rapes.

Ronald Cotton was just one in a long line of inmates exonerated because DNA disproved the state's case. At the time of his release, Ronald joined more than three dozen convicted rapists freed by DNA during the previous four years.

Janet Reno, U.S. Attorney General during the latter years of Cotton's prison time, told *Frontline*, "When you look at the cases of people who've been wrongfully convicted, it's a recognition that mistakes can be made, that we've got to renew our efforts to make sure innocent people aren't charged in the first place, but that once a prosecution is instituted, it is important prosecutors, detectives, participants in the criminal justice system keep their eyes and ears open for any sign, that we may be on the wrong track."[21]

Many of the situations that have been turned around thanks to DNA evidence started with an inquiry letter sent from a prisoner to The Innocence Project at Cardozo Law School in New York. There, law students review and research pleas from inmates all over the country hoping to overturn convictions.

When one analyzes the volume of postconviction exonerations, one is led to believe these cases are the tip of the iceberg. Perhaps there are thousands of individuals who are actually, factually innocent. They are the proverbial "wrong guy," the person who didn't do it, didn't commit the crime. No one knows how many people are rotting in prisons or sitting on death rows waiting to be executed for crimes they didn't commit. These cases confirm other studies that have concluded mistaken identification is the single greatest reason for wrongful conviction. Previous suspicions that mistaken eyewitness identifications have led to convicting the innocent are supported to a high degree of certainty by DNA testing. What's being revealed is that the issue of wrongful convictions may be a bigger problem than previously thought.

Back in North Carolina, those responsible for Ronald Cotton's conviction still wrestle to comprehend the case's twists and turns. Mike Gauldin recalls that early in his career he heard there were people in prison that ought not be there. He didn't see how that could be true. He believed that if the authorities conducted a good investigation, and the suspect was found guilty, then he deserved to be behind bars. Gauldin reflected that the Cotton case is a reminder that regardless of police intentions or procedures, there are those—like Ronald—who should not be in prison.

As for the state's star witness, "In my mind, I was sure of what I saw." Jennifer said, "Thinking back on it, I don't know that I would have done anything different."

Elizabeth Loftus is a professor at the University of Washington, specializing in human memory. Often called upon in legal matters to offer expert testimony regarding the recollections of an eyewitness, Loftus has these insights. "One of the things that we know about memory is that when you experience something extremely upsetting or traumatic, you don't just record the event, like a videotape machine. The process is more complex. What's happening is you're taking in bits and pieces of the experience. You're storing some information about the experience. But it's not some indelible image that you're going to dig out and replay later on."

Loftus points out that eyewitnesses are more prone to mistakes when they identify an individual of another race. One of the things learned from a number of studies is that "people do have more trouble identifying faces of strangers of a different race than strangers of their own race," according to Loftus. "It doesn't have to do with how much prejudice you feel. Even people who are relatively free of prejudice still have the cross-racial identification problem. It may be that we are scanning those faces differently, processing them differently and, ultimately, this affects our ability to recognize."

In response to Gauldin's constant self-scrutiny, searching for the answer to what the police might have done differently, Professor Loftus advises the detective to revisit the initial opportunity that Jennifer Thompson had to select Cotton as the suspect. "When a victim goes to a photo spread, one of the things that would be natural is for that victim to think, 'The police must have a suspect or they wouldn't have brought me here,'" Loftus notes. "So if they've got a suspect in mind, and they communicate that idea to the victim, even unwittingly, she may be more sensitive to picking up that communication."[22]

As if to reinforce the point, Jennifer observed, "After I picked [Cotton's photo] out, they looked at me and they said, 'We thought this might be the one.'"

This is the sort of authoritative feedback that can generate false confidence on the victim's part. This off-handed "attaboy" can artificially boost the witness's sense of certainty. Running through the victim's mind is the idea that "if the police believe there's something to this identification, I must be on to something." This creates a situation where the victim may be more persuasive than her memory merits.

"I felt a lot of pressure because I knew that my testimony was going to be a lot of what the jury was going to take in," Jennifer said. "A lot of their decision would be based on my strength as an eyewitness."

"We're finding out that, yes, mistakes have been made even in cases where people were really close to each other, as in a rape case." Loftus raises more questions. "But the implications for all the other cases out there—if this can happen in a rape case, what about assaults? What about car-jackings? What about other robberies, where two people see each other briefly and later there's some identification? What is it saying about all those cases?"[23]

Following exoneration, Ronald Cotton hired on with the employer most apt to be sympathetic and never doubt his innocence, the laboratory that examined his DNA. He savors the life he has carved out with his wife and young daughter. He appears to harbor no bitterness about the eleven years

lost in prison. Cotton directs no ill will toward anyone who had a hand in his wrongful conviction. In fact, he and Jennifer Thompson have reconciled past differences and forged a relationship bordering on the miraculous.

"Our story transcends the legal system," Jennifer states emphatically.

For two years after Detective Gauldin broke the news that she had identified the wrong man, Jennifer never stopped feeling ashamed. Gauldin had no answer for her anguished plea, "How do I restore eleven years in a person's life?" Then, one day it came to her. The answer that turned off her tears. She knew what she must do. Gauldin knew, too, as soon as Jennifer phoned.

"You want to meet Ronald Cotton, don't you?" the detective anticipated.[24]

"Ronald Cotton and I are the same age," Jennifer reflects. "So I knew what he had missed during those 11 years. My life had gone on." She had gotten married, graduated from college, gotten a job, had kids. "Ronald Cotton hadn't gotten to do any of that," lamented Jennifer.

Together with her husband and pastor, Jennifer drove 50 miles to the college town where she'd been raped. They pulled up to the church that was the prearranged location for her meeting with Ronald Cotton. She drew a deep breath and turned to the two men who had accompanied her. She asked them to leave so she might be on her own.

Her hands shook as she twisted the knob to the church door. She had prayed for courage to confront this moment. She had prayed for strength to face this man.

Ronald Cotton was about to get answers to questions that had hounded him in prison. "Why did this woman never come see me all the years I was incarcerated?" And, "I wonder what she'll say to me when she sees me." Jennifer cried out, "I'm sorry. If I spent every day the rest of my life telling you how sorry I am, it wouldn't come close to what I feel." Cotton was quiet and calm. He took in the impact of their interaction before breaking his silence. "I'm not mad at you," he reflected softly. "I've never been mad at you. I just want you to have a good life."[25] With these words, Jennifer's spirits began to climb, supported by an overwhelming sense of relief.

For two hours, these two individuals, linked originally by a horrible summer's night in 1984, talked and talked. Their families paced nervously outside the church. She asked him about prison life. He asked her how she could have been so sure. All she could say was, "I don't know." They talked about the shortcomings of memory, the power of faith, the amazing turn of events triggered by DNA. They discussed the strange life journey that had pulled them together. They shared opinions about Bobby Poole. 'We were both victims,' Cotton offered, and Thompson agreed.

The afternoon was fading as they left the church. Their families sobbed. Jennifer Thompson and Ronald Cotton engaged in a heartfelt hug. They shared a long embrace.

Buoyed by this encounter, Jennifer was determined to confront all the demons from her traumatic attack. Jennifer wrote to Bobby Poole. She asked him to meet with her. "I faced you with courage and bravery on that July night," she wrote. "You never asked my permission. Now I ask you to face me."[26] If she could receive Cotton's forgiveness, Jennifer reasoned, she could grant Poole hers. Poole never answered her letter. He died in prison, felled by cancer, in 2000.

As Jennifer reflects on the strange journey she's traveled with Ronald Cotton, she says, "Mr. Cotton and I have crossed the boundaries of both the terrible way we came together and our racial difference and have become friends. Although he is now moving on with his life, I live with constant anguish that my profound mistake cost him so dearly." She adds, "I cannot begin to imagine what would have happened had my mistaken identification occurred in a capital case."

Jennifer Thompson is an effective spokesperson against capital punishment. She leverages her experience and the notoriety it brings, to convince others of the unreliability of eyewitness identification. Sometimes on the speaking circuit she shares a podium with an exonerated death row inmate like Kirk Bloodsworth. The aptly named Bloodsworth was convicted for the rape of a little girl. His was the first death sentence overturned by DNA testing. As Thompson and Bloodsworth retell their stories, they persuasively cover a lot of anti–death penalty ground.

Thompson and Cotton frequently talk. Ronald will call to check in with Jennifer, to make sure she's OK. "He is an amazing human being," in Jennifer's estimation. "He has been a good teacher for me." He's taught her the meaning of reconciliation. He's opened insights on forgiveness, healing, and faith. Ronald's guided her through the process of not feeling like a victim anymore.

Jennifer has helped him, too, reciprocating in many ways. She has lobbied to amend legislation so Cotton would receive more than the $5,000 originally offered by North Carolina as compensation. She corresponded with state representatives. Tirelessly, she subjected herself to media interviews. Her diligence paid off as Ronald received a settlement of approximately $110,000.

Cotton's first postexoneration work was with the DNA lab that conducted the tests that freed him. Now, he works for an insulation company. He owns a house in Mebane, sixty miles from Jennifer's home in Winston-Salem. Ronald married a coworker. Together they have a nine-year-old daughter. Some day the girl will hear about her father's eleven lost years in prison. Someday, she may meet Jennifer Thompson so that the miraculous connection based on compassion, understanding, and love might be strengthened.

As Jennifer ponders her history with Ronald, she states, "If anything good can come out of what Ronald Cotton suffered because of my limitations, let it be an awareness that eyewitnesses make mistakes. I have had occasion to study this subject and realize that eyewitness error has been recognized as the leading cause of wrongful convictions."

Jennifer adds, "One witness is not enough, especially when her story is contradicted by other good people." Jennifer Thompson knows well that even an eyewitness who is absolutely certain of what she saw may be dead wrong.

The Thompson–Cotton story raises significant issues. How reliable are eyewitness identifications? Jennifer was inches away from her attacker, yet wasn't able to identify Bobby Poole as her rapist. What role does stress play in affecting eyewitness identification? Jennifer surely experienced a high degree of emotional and physical trauma as a result of her rape; could that trauma have influenced misidentification? Does the construction of police lineups and photo spreads affect eyewitness identification? Jennifer chose Ronald Cotton from a set of police photos as well as from a lineup; were there safeguards that the authorities could have used to protect him from misidentification? Is there a correlation between the confidence of an eyewitness and the accuracy of that witness's testimony? Jennifer was very confident about her identification until DNA testing exonerated Ronald Cotton. Should the police and the jury have accepted her word? How do juries make decisions regarding guilt and innocence, and what factors influence those decisions? The jurors in both trials appeared to give Jennifer's account more credence than Ronald's. Why? Is discrimination a problem in the legal system? Might race have influenced the verdict?

Instances of mistaken eyewitness identification may not be unusual occurrences. Social psychologists believe eyewitness error causes thousands of convictions of innocent individuals.[27] Substantial research demonstrates that eyewitness identifications frequently are mistaken.[28] One such study involved two researchers posing as customers who visited 63 convenience stores. So the clerks would notice them, the two pseudo customers acted oddly. One of the role-playing researchers bought cigarettes entirely with pennies, then asked the clerk for directions to a distant location. The researchers allowed two hours to pass. Then they sent into the store two young men dressed in suits who introduced themselves as law interns. The two asked the clerks to pick out each of the confederate customers from a group of six photographs. The clerks made an accurate identification only 34.2 percent of the time.[29]

Why are eyewitness identifications so unreliable? Scholars distinguish between two types of factors that influence eyewitness identification. The two factors have been classified as estimator variables and system variables.[30] Estimator variables are those associated with the eyewitness and/or the situation in which an event was witnessed. The distance from which the witness observed the event, the amount of fear experienced by the witness, and the race of the witness and of the suspect are examples of estimator variables.

System variables are factors that are under the control of the criminal justice system. Biases in police lineups and suggestive questioning by police or prosecutors are examples of system variables.

Furthermore, it is instructive to consider three psychological processes involved in eyewitness identifications. They are acquisition, storage, and retrieval. Acquisition is the process of perceiving and interpreting information. To provide a reliable account, a witness must notice significant aspects of an event, such as physical characteristics of the perpetrator and specific sequences of behaviors. The witness also must interpret these acts accurately. Picture a witness observing a man with his hands around the neck of another individual who is stretched out on the street. There is a big difference whether that witness interprets the behavior as strangling the other person or checking whether the downed individual has a pulse. Storage is the process of maintaining acquired information in memory. Prosecutions often progress gradually. So a great deal of time may pass between an observed event, police questioning, and trial testimony. It therefore is critical that witnesses keep the information they have acquired. Lastly, retrieval is the process of recalling information that witnesses have stored in memory. Witnesses may have to retrieve the information they know at several points in time, including questioning by authorities, lineup identification, and courtroom testimony. It is important to keep these processes in mind as one sorts through estimator and system variables, determining which process is influenced by each variable.

ESTIMATOR VARIABLES

Viewing Opportunity

So that a witness may acquire accurate information about an event, he or she needs to be able to see and/or hear it clearly. A person who witnesses an event that occurs twenty yards away under clear conditions will be able to offer a better account than a person who observes an act one hundred yards away on a foggy night. The Supreme Court has held that a witness's opportunity to view an event and his or her degree of attention to that event are elements that should be considered when evaluating eyewitness testimony.[31] An analysis of more than one hundred studies of eyewitness identification and facial recognition confirms this point. Witnesses are more apt to correctly identify faces when they are able to look at them longer and when they are able to direct greater concentration to the faces during the acquisition stage.[32] Witnesses often fail to recognize the effects of poor viewing conditions. One study found that individuals who witnessed an event under poor viewing conditions were as likely to make an identification as were individuals who observed an event under better viewing conditions.[33]

Stress and Arousal

People who witness crimes often experience negative emotions. Witnesses may be angry that an offense is taking place, worried about the person who is being victimized, and fearful that they may be in danger themselves. Considerable research has shown that these negative emotions affect eyewitnesses' memories. Individuals who observe a negative emotional event tend to have accurate recall of the event, but less accurate memories of what transpired before and after the event.[34] One who witnesses a mugging is likely to have accurate memories of the attack, but less reliable memories of what the assailant did following the assault.

Weapon Focus

Imagine this situation. You are standing in line at your bank. The person behind you pulls out a gun, aims it directly at your face, and threatens to use it if he's not given all the teller's cash. Odds are, you will keep your eyes fixed on the gun while the teller gets the money. You may wind up remembering more about the gun than about the actual bank robber. Studies have underscored this phenomenon, known as the weapon focus effect.[35] The weapon focus effect may occur because witnesses who are trying to assess the degree of the danger they are in find it helpful to lock their eyes on any weapons. The novelty of weapons for most people may attract their attention.

An interesting observation was detected by Kramer, Buckhout, and Eugenio.[36] The weapon focus effect occurs whether or not a witness is in physical danger. This research was conducted with participants watching a slide presentation in which a person walked through a room carrying either a bloody meat cleaver or a rolled-up magazine. Even in this nonthreatening situation, the participants who saw the meat cleaver remembered fewer details about the walker than did the participants who saw the magazine.

Own-Race Bias

Witnesses tend to be more accurate when identifying individuals of their own race.[37] Own-race bias is an example of the outgroup homogeneity effect. People are able to distinguish between members of their own racial group, but may experience individuals of other racial groups as "all looking alike." This effect tends to be stronger in whites than in blacks.[38] Studies suggest that cross-racial interaction can diminish the own-race bias.[39] The finding helps explain why black individuals are more accurate at identifying whites. Blacks tend to have more exposure to white individuals, directly and indirectly through media. Thus blacks may develop a better ability to distinguish between white people.

Retention Interval

Retention interval is the amount of time that passes between witnessing an event and making an identification. The accuracy of testimony diminishes with time. The longer the interval between witnessing an event and making an identification, the less reliable the identification.[40]

One reason that accuracy decreases over time has to do with forgetting. As time passes, people forget details that could help them make accurate identifications. The relationship between time and forgetting is not linear. Just as there is a "learning curve," there seems to be a pattern for forgetting. In the "forgetting curve," accuracy tails off dramatically soon after an event, then drops much more gradually thereafter.[41] Imagine you witness a robbery. You will recall the most information right after the event. After twenty-four hours, the amount of information you will be able to remember decreases significantly. The decline in your memory will soon level off. A year later, the passage of twenty-four hours will not make much difference. Another reason why accuracy diminishes over time is because, as time goes by, people are more exposed to things that influence their memory. Witnesses can contaminate each other's recollections by talking with each other. If one witness says she remembers a certain detail, such as eye color, other witnesses may claim to "remember" that detail as well.[42]

SYSTEM VARIABLES

Suggestive Questioning

System variables are those that are under the control of the criminal justice system. A critical way the legal system affects eyewitness identification involves questioning techniques. Considerable research shows that the way witnesses are questioned influences not only their responses, but also their long-term recollections of events.[43]

Some questions are suggestive even though they are not deliberately misleading. Minor modifications in wording can influence the way people respond. In a classic study, participants watched a video of an automobile accident. They were then asked to estimate the speed at which the cars were traveling at the moment of impact. The key variable was the word used to describe the accident. Specifically, participants estimated the speed at which the vehicles "contacted," "hit," "bumped," collided," or "smashed." Participants who were asked about the speed at which the cars "contacted" gave estimates that were nine miles per hour lower than participants who were asked about the rate at which the automobiles "smashed." These findings indicate that witnesses' interpretations of what they have seen are influenced by the way an event is labeled or described.[44]

Some questions, on the other hand, are deliberately misleading. People may ask witnesses questions about nonexistent details or events that didn't actually occur. In another Loftus study, participants watched a similar video of a car accident. Afterwards, participants were asked one of two questions. "How fast was the white sports car going while traveling along the country road?" or "How fast was the white sports car going *when it passed the barn* while traveling along the country road?" In reality, there was no barn in the footage viewed. However, 17.3 percent of those asked the second question reported seeing a barn, compared with only 2.7 percent of participants who were asked the first question. So, questions including postevent information can make us believe we remember something that did not exist—even something as sizeable as a barn.[45]

There are three leading theories about how postevent information influences memory. One is the overwriting hypothesis. This position holds that postevent information replaces the information witnesses originally encode about an experience, permanently altering existing memories.[46] This hypothesis suggests that memory operates similarly to writing something on a blackboard. It can be erased and replaced with something new. An alternative theory involves forgetting. People simply forget details from a witnessed event. When they are questioned about material they've forgotten, they resort to other available information, including postevent information, to answer those questions. According to the forgetting hypothesis, postevent information does not alter existing memories; rather it plugs gaps left by forgetting.[47] A third theory is known as source monitoring. This hypothesis suggests people retain memories for both initial event and postevent information. The problem is that people frequently have difficulty distinguishing where a piece of information originated. Consequently, people mistakenly conclude that pieces of postevent information came from their observations of the event.[48]

Source monitoring theory suggests that eyewitnesses can identify their original memories and separate them from postevent information if they are helped to pinpoint the sources of their knowledge. There is support that this prediction is valid, at least for adult witnesses. In research conducted by Lindsay and Johnson, subjects scrutinized a picture of an office that had many appropriately placed objects. They then read a misleading description of the office that included objects not actually in the picture. Finally, the participants were asked to identify which objects they had actually seen. The study found that subjects who were asked yes–no questions (e.g., "Did you see a coffee cup?") made a large number of mistakes. They claimed they had seen items that were only described in writing. By contrast, participants who were asked source-monitoring questions (e.g., "Did you see a coffee cup in the picture or did you read about it in the text?") were able to identify where they learned about the object with greater accuracy.[49]

That subjects can report both original and postevent information when specifically prompted indicates that the overwriting hypothesis is not the best explanation for errors in eyewitness testimony. Although memory change and forgetting undoubtedly influences testimony in specific instances, source monitoring theory offers the best explanation for eyewitness suggestibility effects.

LINEUP BIASES

A crucial phase of police investigations involves identification procedures in which witnesses are asked to identify a particular suspect. Generally these identifications are made from a photo spread or from an in-person lineup.

There are several ways to configure a lineup. The particular method used in a case can impact the accuracy of eyewitness identifications. "Show-ups" are the name for the procedure when a single suspect is presented to a witness who is supposed to report whether that person is the perpetrator. A police officer who nabs someone sprinting away from a crime scene may return that individual to a witness and pose the question, "Is this the fellow who snatched your purse?" Show-up identifications often are incorrect as there is an overbearing suggestion that the person is the actual culprit. Lineups are not so suggestive when more than one suspect is included.

Simultaneous lineups take place when several suspects are presented next to each other and the witness is asked to choose the perpetrator. Identifications from simultaneous lineups may be problematic because of the logic processes witnesses use in making identifications. Simultaneous lineups, in particular, foster relative judgments. Simultaneous lineups encourage witnesses to make decisions about which person looks most like the perpetrator rather than judgments about whether the culprit actually is present.[50]

Sequential lineups, on the other hand, seem to produce the most reliable eyewitness identifications.[51] In these procedures, potential perpetrators are presented one at a time, and witnesses decide whether one person is the perpetrator before viewing the next. This sort of lineup generates closer attention to each person and more thoughtful decision making. It diminishes reliance on relative judgments.

Another aspect of constructing a lineup deals with choosing foils. Foils are the individuals other than the suspect who comprise the lineup. Lineups can be created so that a particular member sticks out noticeably. An example might be a situation where the suspect is the only individual who stands taller than 6 feet 5 inches, while all his lineup mates are 6 feet tall or shorter. It is important to select appropriate foils. Studies show that identifications are more reliable when all foils resemble the witness's original description of the perpetrator, and none stand out from each other.[52]

The instructions given to witnesses during lineups are critical. Some lineup instructions can be suggestive. If a police officer asks a witness, "Which person is the one who attacked you?" he may be implying that the real perpetrator actually is present in the lineup, making it more likely that the witness will venture an identification.[53] Identifications are more accurate when witnesses are told explicitly that the perpetrator may or may not be part of the current lineup.

It is noteworthy that research on the social psychological dimensions of eyewitness identification is being employed by significant policy makers. In the autumn of 1999, the U.S. Department of Justice issued guidelines for law enforcement authorities to use when working with eyewitnesses. Included in the government's taskforce that developed the guidelines were six cognitive and social psychology researchers who conducted analyses of eyewitness identification.[54] The guidelines were based in large part on the social psychological research previously reported. The guidelines recommend that police officers use open-ended questions (e.g., "Tell me what you saw") instead of leading questions. They recommend that authorities explicitly tell eyewitnesses the perpetrator may or may not be part of the lineup. By influencing national guidelines for police procedures, social psychological research may play a vital part in improving eyewitness identification.

Despite the inaccuracies of such testimony and the misconceptions of jurors, the legal system can neither afford to exclude eyewitness testimony nor ignore it. Sometimes it is the only evidence available, and it can be correct. The questions remain, what can attorneys do to provide jurors a clearer understanding of the use and pitfalls of eyewitness testimony? What can lawyers do to manage problematic eyewitness accounts?

Often in capital cases, the principle evidence presented by the prosecution connecting defendants to crimes is the testimony of an eyewitness who either identified the accused in a lineup or from a photo spread. According to The Innocence Project, of the seventy-seven men whose convictions were reversed after DNA testing proved them innocent, sixty-five had been convicted on the basis of faulty eyewitness statements. Of roughly 2,000,000 people incarcerated in the United States in 2001, it is estimated that 8,000 to 10,000 were wrongly convicted owing to inaccurate eyewitness identification.[55] DNA testing has demonstrated that eyewitnesses have been wrong and has established that such testimony is extremely fallible.

Eyewitness error remains a significant cause of wrongful convictions. Experts believe the two most frequent causes of erroneous convictions are perjury by prosecution witnesses and mistaken eyewitness testimony.[56] Cases of proven wrongful convictions consistently show that mistaken eyewitness identification is responsible for more of these wrongful convictions than all other causes combined.

An insightful suggestion to minimize the deleterious effects of mistaken eyewitness identification is found in an article written by Monika Jain, published in the *Journal of Criminal Law and Criminology*.[57] "With the fallibility of eyewitness testimony being so high, capital cases that rely on such testimony should require a quantitative evidentiary standard.... If the prosecution wishes to offer eyewitness testimony as evidence in a capital case, a constitutionally based federal corroboration requirement must be instated." The article further proposes that the next time the Supreme Court reviews a capital case in which eyewitness testimony is offered, the Court should rule that unless the testimony is corroborated, the defendant's conviction, if based largely on such testimony, must be overturned. Such a conviction should be declared a violation of the accuser's Eighth Amendment rights.

This approach does not imply that a prosecutor could not try a defendant if there were no eyewitnesses. The position merely requires that if a prosecutor plans on using an eyewitness account, he must provide some corroboration for the testimony because of the likelihood of its fallibility. If no such corroboration is available, the prosecution may circumvent the quantitative requirement either by foregoing the eyewitness testimony or by seeking a lesser sentence than death.

Requiring corroboration as a condition to obtaining a capital conviction has precedence in the criminal justice system. The law pertaining to treason requires corroboration and is explicitly stated in the Constitution.[58] The prerequisite is more commonly referred to as the two-witness rule. Its objectives are protecting those who are innocent and increasing reliability. The rule mandates that an individual may not be found guilty of treason unless at least two witnesses testify to the same act.

The Innocence Project's finding that 84 percent of the seventy-seven DNA exonerations they examined involved mistaken eyewitness identification as the primary cause for the wrongful convictions was not the first such study. Yale law professor Edwin Borchard, in 1932, published a collection of sixty-five cases in which an innocent individual was convicted. Borchard's book, *Convicting the Innocent: Errors of Criminal Justice*, cites eyewitness error as the major cause of these mistakes. Faulty eyewitness testimony was responsible for twenty-nine of the sixty-five miscarriages of justice. The author offered this insight:

These cases illustrate that the emotional balance of the victim or eyewitness is so disturbed by his extraordinary experience that his powers of perception become distorted and his identification is frequently most untrustworthy. Into the identification enter other motives, not necessarily stimulated originally by the accused personally— the desire to requite a crime, to exact vengeance upon the person believed guilty, to find a scapegoat, to support an identification already made by another. How valueless are these identifications by the victim of a crime is indicated by the fact that in eight of these cases the wrongfully accused person and the really guilty criminal bore not the slightest resemblance to each other, whereas in twelve other cases, the resemblance, while fair, was still not at all close.

Even in 1932, Borchard recognized the various risks inherent in eyewitness testimony, including the general distortion of a witness's perception and the prospect that a witness's identification could be encouraged by inappropriate motives.

Psychologists and legal scholars have long tried to understand the phenomenon of inaccurate eyewitness testimony. Some assume a scientific approach and contend that what is seen by a witness goes through a complex process before being fully comprehended and retained. These psychologists claim that what transpires in front of one's eyes is transformed inside the head, and is refined, revisited, restored, and embellished. Elizabeth Loftus believes that many faulty identifications result from "unconscious transference." This is the phenomenon in which a person seen in one situation is confused with a person seen in a second setting.[59]

Studies have been conducted concerning the correlation between strength of a witness's confidence in his identification and accuracy of that testimony. The research revealed that witnesses who were highly confident in their identifications were more likely to be correct as compared to witnesses who showed little confidence. Researcher Gary Wells emphasizes, however, that "more likely" does not mean "always."

In a videotape produced in January 2001, "Wrongful Convictions: Causes and Remedies," Wells describes the concept of "false certainty." This notion, whereby an eyewitness is both highly certain of her identification and is in fact wrong, was central to Ronald Cotton's situation. Jennifer Thompson was face to face with her assailant, worked hard to study his features during their encounter, and still did not make an accurate identification. The are ample examples of cases where eyewitnesses made observations from a distance and were similarly incorrect in their identifications. Such situations highlight the risk that innocent lives may be taken on the basis of fallible evidence.

Because of the strong possibility of inaccurate eyewitness accounting, a corroboration requirement should be introduced whenever such testimony is presented in a capital case. There are no such federal evidentiary requirements governing capital crimes. The three federal offenses for which a death sentence may be imposed are murder, espionage, and treason. Each pertinent statute states that a possible punishment for the crime may be death. The laws do not delineate an evidentiary requirement before a capital sentence may be imposed.

The guidelines provided by the United States Code concerning imposition of the death penalty are a list of aggravating and mitigating factors to be weighed when assessing whether death is warranted.[60] Impaired capacity, minor participation, duress, and no prior criminal record are among the mitigating factors to be considered. The corresponding list of aggravating factors includes previous convictions, death during the commission of another crime, and grave risk of death to additional persons. These considerations, however, have nothing to do with the quantity of evidence that must be presented by the prosecution before obtaining a capital conviction.

Similarly, the Model Penal Code neglects to establish a mandate for the quantitative evidence necessary in a matter that qualifies for the death penalty.[61] While the Code spells out what may constitute evidence in a murder case, it does not address the quantity of evidence.

Because of the highly fallable nature of eyewitness testimony, some sort of standard controlling this form of evidence should be instated. Absent such authoritative guidelines, the door is open for the kind of avoidable, legal tragedy that befell Ronald Cotton.

The law of treason may prove instructive for dealing with capital cases in general.[62] This law consists of two elements: a two-witness rule and an overt act requirement.

Treason is "the breach of the allegiance which a person owes to the state under whose protection he lives, and the most serious crime known to the law." The U.S. Constitution's Treason Clause was drafted by patriots whose notions were rooted in English law. The phrasing of Article III, Section 3, is drawn from the Statute of 25 Edward III—a British treason law enacted in 1350. The statute split the allegiance that every English subject owed his sovereign into two categories, petit treason and high treason. Petit treason, later to be considered as murder, included the killing of master by servant and the killing of husband by wife. High treason was tantamount to offences against the sovereign. There were seven transgressions that constituted this category. The seven included planning the death of the king, his wife, or their heir, or raping the king's wife or eldest daughter.

The two-witness mandate of the Treason Clause of the Constitution was woven into some of the laws of the colonies as early as the late seventeenth century. The Clause was premised on the Statute of 7 William III.[63] According to this law, witnesses must testify to the same treasonable offense. One witness to each of two separate treasonable acts would not be sufficient.

The earliest colonial legislation requiring two or more eyewitnesses for capital crimes is the Law of the New Haven Colony, which was adopted in 1656. The act reads:

That no man shall be put to death, for any offense, or misdemeanour in any case, without the testimony of two witnesses at least, or that which is Equivalent thereunto, provided, and to prevent, or suppresse much inconvenience, which may grow, either to the publick, or to particular Persons, by a mistake herein, it is Ordered, and declared, by the Authority aforesaid, that two, or three single witnesses, being of competent age, of sound understanding, and of good Reputation, and witnessing to the case in question (whither it concerne the publick peace, and welfare, or any one, and the same particular person) shall be accounted (the party concerned having no just exception against them) sufficient proofe, though they did not together see, or hear, and so witness to the same individual, any particular Act, in reference to those circumstances of time, and place.

New Jersey in 1668 and the New Plymouth Colony in 1671 enacted similar legislation, requiring at least two witnesses before a sentence of death could be imposed.

During the American Revolution, new treason legislation was enacted. These laws bore a strong resemblance to the statutes of Edward III and of William III. Mosaic law also was influential in the new American legislation. "One witness shall not rise up against a man for any inquity, or for any sin, in any sin that he sinneth: at the mouth of two witnesses, or at the mouth of three witnesses, shall the matter be established."[64] Another Biblical passage states, "At the mouth of two witnesses, or three witnesses, shall he that is worthy of death be put to death; but at the mouth of one witness he shall not be put to death."[65]

During the Revolutionary period, nearly all basic treason statutes required the testimony of two lawful, credible witnesses. When America achieved independence in 1776, retaining the two-witness requirement was a priority of the Constitution's framers.

The founding fathers decided to narrowly define treason. History had shown that those in power might falsely charge their opponents with treason. Thus, they denied Congress authority to modify the offense. James Madison, writing in Number 43 of *The Federalist*, described the goal of ensuring a protection in the law of treason against the "peculiar danger" of corruptly motivated accusations aimed at the innocent.

In treason trials, presentation of two witnesses is not, on its face, sufficient to convict. The two witnesses must each testify to the same overt act. In the Federal Convention debates of 1787, the delegates discussed the wording of Article III, Section 3, and moved to insert the words "to the same overt act" after "two witnesses." Pennsylvania delegate Benjamin Franklin pushed for this amendment because "prosecutions for treason were generally virulent; and perjury too easily [was] made use of against innocence."[66]

In *Cramer* v. *United States*, the first Supreme Court treason conviction review, Justice Jackson explained what dangers concerned the founding fathers when they drafted the Treason Clause. Wrote Jackson:

Historical materials aid interpretations chiefly in that they show two kinds of dangers against which the framers were concerned to guard the treason offense: (1) Perversion by established authority to repress peaceful political opposition; and (2) conviction of the innocent as a result of perjury, passion, or inadequate evidence. The first danger could be diminished by closely circumscribing the kind of conduct which should be treason. ... The second danger lay in the manner of trial and was one which would be diminished mainly by procedural requirements.[67]

In drafting Article III, Section 3, of the Constitution, the founding fathers joined English law, French philosophy, and religious thought, and agreed upon the requirement of two witnesses to the same overt act. The framers wanted to ensure that an individual would not be tried for treason unless he or she committed an act that violated allegiance to the United States. What the Constitution's authors did not clarify, and thus left to the Courts, was what constituted an overt act.

The Supreme Court defined an overt act as that which manifested a criminal intent and tended toward the commission of treason.[68] The Court determined that while two witnesses had to testify to the same act, the witness's accounts did not have to be identical. The Court stated witnesses did not have to prove the defendant's intent. Intent could be inferred from circumstances surrounding the overt act.

The framers decided to keep the overt act requirement in the Constitution because they wanted to make sure people would not face prosecution for their thoughts. While the threat of prosecution based solely on one's thoughts is not inherent in homicide, imposing the two-witness rule and the overt act requirement could be useful in minimizing the risk of faulty eyewitness testimony.

Broadening the interpretation of the two-witness rule means that another witness need not be the only form of acceptable corroboration. As long as some form of corroboration is offered to support each witness's testimony, the conviction can be secured. To corroborate an eyewitness account, the prosecution might present proof such as DNA or fingerprint evidence, or even an audio- or videotape of what the witness saw.

Connecticut imposes a similar requirement. Concerning testimony required in capital cases, the law states, "No person shall be convicted of any crime punishable by death without the testimony of at least two witnesses, or that which is equilvalent thereto."[69] Connecticut's statute, enacted in 1672, was based not on treason law, but on the Mosaic code of Deuteronomy. The Connecticut Supreme Court later stated the statute was designed "to prevent a person from being put to death by the unsupported testimony of one witness."[70] The court explained, "A single witness, however positive, however credible, will not warrant a conviction, where life is in question."

The D.C. circuit reasoned that treason's two-witness rule is applicable to other crimes as well. In 1952, the circuit justified imposing the two-witness rule in a sex crime prosecution.[71] The issue was whether a sex offense conviction could be sustained, as in the Cotton case, upon the testimony of one witness, without corroboration. The bench noted that courts are skeptical of accusations about sexual offenses. The court conjectured that such skepticism stems from fear of the stigma attached to an unjustly convicted defendant. The court cautioned that while one of the statute's functions is to deter the commission of crime, if the crime is perpetrated, another purpose is to safeguard irreparable ruin of one's reputation resulting from an unwarranted accusation.

The D.C. circuit recognized that problems of quantitative requirements of evidence in criminal matters are not new. The court justified the two-witness rule for treason by explaining that a quantitative measure of proof in such cases is warranted "because the likelihood of false accusations is enormous and the harm done by failure to convict is relatively small."[72] The court also acknowledged that the problem with a rigid corroboration requirement is that it may not be possible for the requirement to be met.

In her journal article, Monika Jain suggests a balanced approach.[73] If the prosecution wishes to present eyewitness evidence in a capital case, the prosecutor must also offer corroboration. If no such corroboration is available, the prosecutor may circumvent the requirement by either not presenting eyewitness testimony or by offering the uncorroborated evidence and pursuing a sentence of life imprisonment rather than death. The corroboration mandate would only come into play when the prosecution chooses to use an eyewitness account as evidence in a capital conviction.

Certain analogies may be drawn with regard to prosecutions for treason and homicide. These analogies support applying treason's two-witness rule to homicide. While the opportunities for false accusations differ between the crimes, the motives behind the unjust accusations do not. As for treason, false accusations were largely driven by political motivations—people in power were apt to accuse their opponents of treason for personal advantage. Similarly, with respect to homicide, false accusations often are triggered by political pressures. The public places great demand on law enforcement to apprehend the perpetrators of violent crime and restore security to the community. Particularly with heinous homicide cases—those likely to attract great public interest—police and prosecutors are under tremendous pressures to obtain convictions. These pressures may result in perjured eyewitness identification.

Justice Brennan, in *U.S. v. Wade*, addressed prosecutorial influence upon eyewitness testimony.

The vagaries of eyewitness identification are well known; the annals of criminal law are rife with instances of mistaken identification. Mr. Justice Frankfurter once said: "What is the worth of identification testimony even when uncontradicted? The identification of strangers is proverbially untrustworthy. The hazards of such testimony are established by a formidable number of instances in the records of English and American trials. . . ." A major factor contributing to the high incidence of miscarriage of justice from mistaken identification has been the degree of suggestion inherent in the manner in which the prosecution presents the suspect to witnesses for pretrial identification. A commentator has observed that "the influence of improper suggestion upon identifying witnesses probably accounts for more miscarriages of justice than any other single factor—perhaps it is responsible for more such errors than all other factors combined."[74]

Brennan articulates the dangers inherent in eyewitness testimony. Further support is found in Wigmore's Treatise on Evidence. Wigmore wrote that the purpose of the two-witness rule is to "secure the subject from being sacrificed to fictitious conspiracies, which have been the engines of profligate and crafty politicians in all ages."[75]

To safeguard innocent citizens from being unjustly accused of treason owing to improper political motivations, the framers decided to include England's two-witness rule in the U.S. Constitution. To protect innocents from being wrongly accused of murder because of political pressures, the Supreme Court should consider a mandate that if a prosecutor intends to offer eyewitness testimony that could produce a death sentence, unless the prosecution can provide corroboration, the testimony ought to be inadmissible.

While motives behind the commission of treason and homicide may be different, the resulting injury to the wrongly accused is much the same. It is this result that the two-witness rule was meant to prevent. The D.C. circuit acknowledged this when it applied the rule to a sex prosecution case. The court wanted to protect an unjustly accused defendant from the stigma that attaches owing to the nature of the crime. Just as the two-witness rule was implemented to prevent citizens from unjustifiably being tried for treason, similar corroboration could prevent people from being unjustifiably tried for any capital offense.

False accusations are made and perjured testimony presented whatever the crime may be. The results of those accusations may be damaging, even deadly. Even in situations where evil motives are not involved, the reality is that innocent people are being convicted for crimes they did not commit. Often the culprit causing these miscarriages of justice is a fallible form of evidence—eyewitness identification. Mistaken identification is the single largest factor accounting for wrongful convictions.

It may be impossible to eliminate the dangers of capital convictions based on eyewitness testimony. But mitigating such risks is possible by requiring corroboration in capital cases. Permitting a defendant to be sentenced to death when his conviction is based largely on evidence historically proven fallible violates the defendant's Eighth Amendment right to be free from cruel and unusual punishment. To prevent such a situation, when next given the opportunity to review a capital case relying on eyewitness testimony, the Supreme Court should rule that unless testimony is corroborated, the conviction should be reversed and declared a violation of the defendant's Eighth Amendment rights.

4

Systemic Corruption

As he weaves through the packed reception of the National Legal Aid and Defenders Association, hobnobbing with fellow board members, you marvel at the ease with which he works the crowd. Freddie Pitts carries himself with celebrity self-assurance. Truth be told, he bears a striking resemblance to blues legend B.B. King. Freddie takes his look-alike status so far as to joke that frequently he gets offered the hotel room keys of strange women mistaking him for the musical superstar. In this crowd of powerful Washington lawyers, legislators, and lobbyists, Freddie is well known in his own right. Conference attendees are buzzing about the anticipated keynote speech to be delivered later by former Illinois governor George Ryan. For now they are drawn to Freddie Pitts, as much for his charismatic smile and hearty handshake as for the tragic miscarriage of justice his life represents.

Freddie's entanglement with the law begins in the steamy summer heat of Florida's panhandle in 1963. In the dark of night, on August 1st, a double murder was committed at a gas station in Highland View, Florida. Over the next several days, Freddie Pitts and codefendant Wilbert Lee would confess to committing the crimes. Both men soon recanted, claiming their confessions were beaten out of them. Both men wound up serving twelve years in prison for crimes they didn't commit.

The biggest news of the day was breaking from Birmingham, Alabama. The U.S. Department of Justice filed the nation's largest voter discrimination suit. Months before, on Good Friday, Dr. Martin Luther King, Jr., was jailed

Having served a decade on Florida's Death Row, Freddie Pitts now serves on the Board of Directors of the National Legal Aid & Defenders Association. Photo credit: Cristina Villaraos, student in the School of Communication at American University, Washington, DC.

for deliberately disobeying a law prohibiting parading without a permit. His civil disobedience was aimed at Alabama's segregation.

King explained that those who violate unjust laws must do so "openly, lovingly, and with a will to accept the penalty." One who breaks a law that his conscience deems unjust and who willingly accepts imprisonment to alert the community's conscience to the law's injustice is "expressing the highest respect for the law." King further observed, "We who engage in non-violent action are not the creators of tension. We merely bring to the surface the hidden tensions that are already alive."[1]

On August 28, history was made in the U.S. civil rights movement. Before the largest assemblage of protesters ever gathered in the nation's capital, standing on the steps of the Lincoln Memorial, Dr. King, proclaimed, "I have a dream that one day this nation will rise up and live out the true meaning of its creed: 'We hold these truths to be self-evident, that all men are created equal.'" He continued, "I have a dream that one day on the red hills of Georgia the sons of former slaves and the sons of former slave owners will sit down together at the table of brotherhood."

Building to a powerful crescendo, King cried out, "I have a dream that my four little children will one day live in a nation where they will not be judged by the color of their skin but by the content of their character. This is our hope."[2]

Ironically, on the very day King was delivering his moving oratory, the gavel came down on Freddie Pitts and Wilbert Lee. In an unprecedented proceeding, a Gulf County, Florida, magistrate seated a jury for the sole purpose of assessing the issue of mercy. Should Pitts and Lee be executed, or sentenced to life imprisonment? That was the only consideration. The codefendants had confessed to committing a heinous crime. They pleaded guilty to first-degree murder.

The mercy hearing was adjudicated in Wewahitchka in an old-fashioned, leaky courthouse. The proceedings lasted less than a day. The men were sentenced to die in Florida's electric chair. The content of their character had little to do with how they were judged. The men were condemned on the color of their skin.

In the predawn hours of August 1, 1963, a newspaper delivery man made his routine stop at an all-night Mo-Jo gas station. The driver, normally, exchanged banter with the two service station attendants. On this occasion, he found the place deserted. Sensing trouble, he phoned police. The authorities who responded found an empty cash register. They searched further and discovered a gun was missing. The two Mo-Jo employees, Grover Floyd and Jessie Burkett, were nowhere to be found.

For three days speculation swirled around the men's disappearance. Had they been abducted? Did they run away in fear? Or, did they abscond with company cash? No one knew what happened.

Since he'd been at the Mo-Jo on the night of July 31st, twenty-eight-year-old Wilbert Lee became the first target of police questioning. Lee's initial exchange with authorities went well enough. The police followed up, however, with a visit to Lee's home the next morning. About 5:00 A.M., Lee answered a knock at the door. The police wanted to take him to the station. Insisting he needn't bother to brush his teeth as he'd be coming right back, police escorted Lee into the patrol car.

At the station, Lee was greeted with this cold line: "Nigger, I'm locking your ass up for first degree murder."[3] The frightened, confused suspect was taken upstairs. Lee was subject to interrogation. Hours passed. He was hooked to a polygraph machine, where several tests were administered.

Wilbert recounts how the lie detector was explained to him as the measurement of movements of the polygraph needle. When the subject tells a little lie the needle moves just a little. When it's a big lie, there's a lot of movement. Lee responded to the polygraph operator by insisting he was reporting the truth, regardless of what the machine said.

Lee's story began with his hosting a party at his small house in Port St. Joe. Needing to make a call, and not having a telephone, Lee left the party with a few friends. Those accompanying Wilbert piled into Freddie Pitts' car and went to the Mo-Jo station, in search of a phone.

Before departing the service station, one of the women asked to use the restroom. She was denied access based on race. "We've only got an all-white bathroom," the woman was told, with the implication that the facilities were off-limits to her. A heated argument ensued, although Lee, Pitts, and party were to find no relief at the Mo-Jo.

The group got back into Pitts' car and went looking for something to eat. After driving a short way, they turned around and headed back to the party. Once home, Wilbert claims he climbed into bed and went to sleep.

His story was backed up by Willie Mae Lee, a family friend but no relation to Wilbert. Willie Mae, who also goes by Billie, joined the group at the Mo-Jo station. She told police she was a witness to the gas station attendants' murders. She informed authorities the killers were two army soldiers who had attended Wilbert's party. One she identified was a nineteen-year-old native of New Orleans, Freddie Pitts.

Pitts was taken into custody and subjected to polygraph tests. He had no objections to lie detector tests. In his mind, he had nothing to hide.

While at the jail, Pitts recalls, "they started searching the car. I mean, didn't say anything to me, they just started searching the car. And, from that point on, it was down hill."[4]

For their own safety, to protect the suspects from potential mob action, authorities escorted Lee and Pitts out of Port St. Joe. The two were transported to a holding facility in neighboring Panama City.

Ella Mae Lee, Wilbert's wife, also was taken into custody. She confirmed that her husband had been home in bed when the murders occurred. The couple was released.

The next day, August 3rd, the bodies of Jessie Burkett and Grover Floyd were found in a secluded area 12 miles from the Mo-Jo station. The bodies lay next to a canal owned by the paper mill on the outskirts of Port St. Joe. Two local women were fishing in the canal when they came across the corpses.

Authorities determined, from the angle of bullet wounds, that both men had been shot in the head after being forced to lie down. Police continued to investigate. They questioned anyone who might have information. This included Billie Mae Lee, who had evolved into the case's lead witness. She continued to finger Freddie Pitts. She changed her story to substitute Wilbert Lee as the other killer. It would surface later that she had been threatened by the Sheriff. If Billie didn't deliver testimony to the Sheriff's liking, he would have her little girl taken away. Billie believed she'd be locked up for fifteen years.

So, Wilbert Lee was arrested again. He was subjected to another round of interrogation and polygraph exams. This time, before questioning was concluded, Pitts confessed to committing the crimes.

Pitts' recollection of the confession is fuzzy. For good reason. He was taken to various locations for questioning. He was grilled as to where the murder victims' bodies were. The heated interrogation often crossed the line of physical intimidation. Pitts would black out from being beaten only to regain consciousness in a different location. He was not able to supply the police with the bodies' whereabouts, as this was information he didn't know.

On top of the physical abuse heaped upon Pitts, the two suspects were given a court-appointed attorney who turned out to be a family member of one of the murder victims. The dazed young Pitts was given the impression he wouldn't have legal representation if he didn't go along with what everyone wanted him to say. So Pitts broke. He made a generalized confession in line with what those hounding him wanted to hear. Lee confessed the next day.

Later, Pitts and Lee would tell military investigators they were innocent. But, at their arraignment hearing within the month, the two pleaded guilty.

In an unusual move, the judge impaneled a jury for the single purpose of determining the fate of Lee and Pitts. The atmosphere at the hearing was tense and emotionally charged. That the courtroom was segregated with blacks in the back didn't ehnance the defendants' comfort level, either.

Pitts and Lee threw themselves on the court's mercy. The all-white, male jury did not respond kindly. Their verdict was that the defendants should die. From suspects to convicts in twenty-eight days. Life had changed so much so fast that when Lee and Pitts found themselves on death row, their heads were still spinning.

Off they were whisked, from the courthouse to the Florida State prison. Here they would spend the next decade, tilting at the legal system's windmills, wondering when their date with the executioner may arrive.

Freddie Pitts describes confinement in terms nonconvicts might understand. "About the closest experience I can think of is locking yourself in a bathroom with a bunk. Basically that's what it is. The cell is as big as your average bathroom."[5]

When asked about the emotional adjustment to death row, Pitts says it was "aggravating, frustrating, depressing."[6] He experienced "anger which I had to learn to control." For Pitts "it came down to understanding the situation and controlling the anger and frustration enough to do that." When one is able to gain such control, according to Pitts, "you can learn what you are capable of doing for yourself."

Asked how he maintained his sanity on death row, Pitts talks about influential authors whose works he devoured. Was Martin Luther King, Jr., among those who influenced him? "Not really," Pitts replies. "I didn't find what Dr. King was doing in society relevant to me, while I was wallowing in prison."

While in prison, Pitts said, "Depression is not the word to describe my feelings. At times I was flatly angry. For a person who is locked behind bars 24 hours a day, 7 days a week, 52 weeks a year, every triviality becomes a source of tension, hate, anger or depression."[7]

Nothing in their lives prepared them for the aching isolation or gnawing anxiety they endured in their six-by-nine-foot cells. When the ordeal began, they barely knew each other. They met for the first time at a party the night before the murders. Freddie Pitts was a nineteen-year-old army private from Mobile, Alabama, who had come to Florida's Panhandle with his company to refuel army rigs. Wilbert Lee, twenty-eight years old, was an uneducated laborer raised in black southern poverty.

The prison profile of Pitts listed him as a quiet, average, nontroublemaker. In fact, he was a member of the church choir and led Bible studies.

Pitts noted that the frustrations of prison often became unbearable. It wasn't easy listening to people telling him to be patient. Such advice wasn't appreciated even coming from his mother. She answered Freddie's letters saying that God was looking after him, that He would provide. She urged him to keep praying and keep faith. In answering her Freddie wanted to ask where was God when those policemen were beating him? Where was God when this whole mess was transpiring?

What puzzled prison evaluators was Pitts' insistence of innocence. Officials noted his claims of innocence even though he pled guilty.

Pitts also complained to the Federal Bureau of Investigation. In October 1963, two months after conviction, two FBI agents responded. The agents came to Raiford Prison to take Pitts' statement. To the FBI, he maintained innocence. He told them his confession was false and had been coerced.

Pitts stuck to his story: Deputy Sheriffs George Kittrell and Wayne White took him out in a squad car. Two white employees of Skipper's Mo-Jo station were missing after the robbery, during the early morning hours of 8/1/63. Kittrell and White kept asking where the bodies were. Pitts kept telling them he didn't know. Pitts was sitting on the right hand side in the back seat with Kittrell next to him. When Pitts denied knowledge of the robbery or the bodies, Kittrell thumped his head with a blackjack. The blow knocked Pitts unconscious. When he regained consciousness the authorities began questioning Pitts again.

Kittrell kept hitting him. The night became a blur. Freddie remembers being at Skipper's station and Skipper asking, 'Nigger, what did you do with those white boys?' Kittrell answered, 'He hasn't told us yet but he will before the night's over. . . ."[8]

The investigators learned that Pitts had been in the army at the time of the murders. He was a soldier on maneuvers near Port St. Joe. Pitts informed them that no one from the Army attended the trial. He explained that while in custody he had been questioned only once by Army Criminal Investigation Department agents. Pitts told these agents he was innocent. They examined the wounds he had received from the beating by Kittrell.

A perfunctory investigation was performed by Tullis Easterling. Easterling was an FBI agent with political aspirations. He had been assigned to Panama City. He would become Bay County's sheriff. His investigation was deemed "inconclusive."

George Kittrell also offered a statement. He said he did not remember ever being alone with either Pitts or Lee. Nor did he recall their being struck. Bay County Sheriff M.J. "Doc" Daffin, who had taken the men's confessions, claimed he didn't know about any beatings. Judge Warren Fitzpatrick and defense attorney Fred Turner said they didn't either.

Army investigator Sergeant Bruce Potts conducted an interview outside the panhandle that could have shaken things up. Unfortunately, it didn't. Potts reported that when he saw Freddie Pitts he noticed a swollen right jaw, loose teeth, and three lumps on his head, in addition to bloodshot eyes. Complaints to the FBI went for naught. An attorney in the Civil Rights Division of the Justice Department in Washington closed the case in December 1963. The official government position was there was no corroboration of the death row recantations.

Pitts's assertion to Judge Fitzpatrick that his lawyer, Fred Turner, "is satisfied with the judgment of this honorable court" led the Judge to direct counsel to file an appeal. Complaining that he lacked grounds for appeal, Turner reluctantly complied in November 1963.

Turner's appeal would forestall any immediate execution. No death warrant could be signed until the state Supreme Court reviewed the convictions.

The following spring, a Key West justice was sentencing Curtis Adams, Jr., to twenty years for the armed robbery of a loan company's office. A few days later, contemplating jailbreak, Adams asked to speak with a detective, Lieutenant Terry Jones. Adams was a shrewd, calculating fellow who did not look forward to his transfer to the Florida State Prison at Raiford.

Jones summoned the prisoner and listened to his disconcerting story. Adams spoke of a double murder in Port St. Joe the previous summer. He claimed knowledge of the two service station attendants who had been shot. Initially skeptical, Jones sought details. Adams responded, saying he knew how to clear the murders. He knew where the weapon was and how the crime happened. Adams stopped short of confessing. But he was eager to exchange information for a sentencing deal.

Adams asked the lieutenant to phone Byrd Parker, the Gulf County sheriff. Adams wanted to be returned to Port St. Joe, claiming he wanted to see his dying mother before starting his sentence. Jones placed the call to the Wewahitchka sheriff. After identifying himself, he explained Adams' Key West incarceration. Jones then handed the phone to the prisoner.

Years later, under oath Parker would say he didn't recall the conversation well. Parker remembered Adams wanting to come home. He mentioned the Mo-Jo murders, according to the sheriff. But Parker told Adams he didn't care to talk about that.

Turns out Sheriff Parker knew Adams well. He had previously jailed him and knew Adams to be quite the scoundrel. Parker would be content never to see Curtis Adams again. Adams returned the phone to Jones. Parker cautioned the lieutenant not to believe Adams and concluded the conversation bluntly. "I already got two niggers waiting for the chair in Raiford for those murders."[9]

From death row, Private Freddie Pitts begged the Army for assistance. He repeatedly proclaimed his innocence. On Valentines' Day, 1964, the Army replied. Indifferent to Pitts' plight, the communiqué notified the soldier he owed the government $61.98 in withholding tax.

Half a year after his conviction, the office of the staff judge advocate in New Orleans finally dispatched a first lieutenant-lawyer to talk to Pitts. Lieutenant Winick had specific orders to limit advice to the prisoner's constitutional rights. The merits of Pitts' case were not subject for discussion. Military personnel, by law, are subject to civil jurisdiction when accused of crime by civil authorities. Consequently, Fred Turner had been appointed civil counsel for Private Pitts.

Lieutenant Winick tried making an appointment with the local lawyer. Turner was not available. Winick stopped by Turner's office anyway, and a secretary let him peruse Pitts' file. Winick grew disturbed as he read the case. He noted that a guilty plea was an extremely questionable strategy for a charge of first-degree murder. He followed the visit to Turner's office with a face-to-face interview of Private Pitts. Freddie continued insisting he was innocent. Jack Winick believed him.

Papers filed with the court reveal a long memorandum written by Lieutenant Winick to his superiors:

Private Pitts contends he initially told Mr. Turner he was not guilty. Later he was called into the sheriff's office to listen to a recording of Willie Mae Lee's story and Wilbert Lee's confession. After playing the recording, the sheriff and his deputies strongly urged Private Pitts to confess. The private claims that Mr. Turner told him to plead guilty and that if he pleaded guilty Mr. Turner would ask the court for mercy. Private Pitts explained to me that he relied heavily on his legal counsel. ... I asked him how he could confess and explain in detail a series of events he was never involved in. He explained that he restated the story that Willie Mae Lee told. He strongly contends he is innocent.[10]

In September 1964, Pitts received a letter from the Civil Rights Division of the Justice Department: "We have given careful consideration to the information you furnished. Since it does not disclose the violation of a federal criminal statute, this department has no authority to take action."[11]

Lieutenant Winick wouldn't give up. Even after his military discharge, while working as a prosecutor in Minneapolis, he wrote to the executive director of Miami's American Civil Liberties Union. Wasn't there anything the ACLU could do to help Freddie Pitts?

Freddie's prison years were full of upheavals. He was married and lost contact with his wife. He had two kids, but lost touch with them as well. Pitts was isolated from everything except attorneys.

When reminded of the ease with which he now jokes with casual acquaintances, Freddie claims always to have had a light touch. Although his transition to penitentiary life was full of frustration, he learned to cope with his powerful, negative feelings through reading and calm contemplation.

One of the authors who influenced Pitts most was Viktor Frankl. Frankl's work *Man's Search for Meaning* had a profound impact on the inmate. Frankl, too, had been held captive, a victim of the Nazi regime. While in concentration camps, he was subjected to cruel, psychological experimentation. Stripped, interrogated, and tortured, Frankl built an inner reserve of strength that helped him endure tribulations.

He distinguished between liberty and freedom. His captors enjoyed more liberty than he did; liberty being a function of external factors. The opportunity to choose where to go, when, and with whom were external issues. In these matters Frankl's captors had the better of him. But freedom, Frankl found, was a higher order of liberty. Because it was internal, freedom was within one's control. Freedom encompasses the choices one makes independent of external considerations. Starting small and exercising this sense of choice gradually, Frankl discovered an inner power. Yes, the Nazis had more liberty than he. And yes, they could abuse their liberty to harm his body, the outward manifestation of Frankl's self. But through his internal discipline, Viktor Frankl had more freedom than his tormentors. And he steeled himself to the point where they could not hurt him inside. He had risen above that.

Similarly, Freddie Pitts tells of accompanying a guard on his rounds to patrol the cell block. Freddie's good behavior earned him more mobility than other convicts, so he was assigned a roving cleaning detail. Pitts happened to walk by the room that housed "old sparky," the electric chair. He couldn't pass up the chance to poke his head in the death chamber. Flexing his comedic muscle, Pitts struck poses in the electric chair.

"How can you make fun of that contraption?" asked the exasperated guard. "That thing threatens your life."

"What you don't understand is," Pitts explained with enlightenment that would have made Frankl proud, "you may have my body, but you don't have me."[12]

To endure the hardships of the penitentiary Pitts had to muster all the serenity he could, for he and Lee would learn that segregation didn't cease at the prison gates. The small, bathroom-sized cubicles would be home for the next decade. Here, they'd be isolated from white inmates.

Pitts discovered that death row was segregated. There was a white side and a black side.

Lee and Pitts spent four miserable months adjusting to death row when law enforcement authorities offered a reward in exchange for information about a Fort Lauderdale robbery and murder. An inmate in Raiford responded. He claimed fellow inmate Curtis Adams had boasted of committing that crime. Still under questioning, the inmate told police that Adams was the guilty party in the Port St. Joe homicides. The incriminating evidence came through Adams' careless bragging.

The police followed their leads. Deputies visited Adams' girlfriend, Mary Jean Aikens. Mary Jean was living with Adams in 1963. She said he left the house one evening about nine o'clock, with the intent of holding up a place. He returned around three in the morning, with about one hundred dollars. She noticed Adams had mud on his shoes and appeared nervous. Upon entering the house he went to the bathroom to scrape mud from his shoes. Aikens asked him what was wrong. He told her, "I had to kill them."[13]

She pressed him on what he meant by that. She demanded to know. Adams explained that he had to kill the Mo-Jo station attendents because they knew who he was. Adams could not leave any witnesses.

Adams was taken by authorities to Port St. Joe. There, he led the state attorney to the site where the bodies of Jesse Burkett and Grover Floyd were found. Adams revealed information that no one else could have known, a point certainly not lost on Freddie Pitts. Pitts noted that Adams took investigators from Broward County to Port St. Joe and told them things no one could have heard anywhere, from anybody else.[14]

The light shed on the case by Curtis Adams should have ended the nightmare for Pitts and Lee. According to Pitts, had authorities been on the ball from the beginning, the two men wouldn't have spent a single day behind bars. In his estimation, authorities should have known about Curtis Adams long before. Given a competent investigation, Lee and Pitts should not have been sent to prison. The state chief deputy testified that once he discovered a possible crime had been committed, he looked for ex-convicts living in the area who had a history of armed robbery. Curtis Adams' name came up. The deputy went to look for him. He had disappeared. He didn't pursue it. If he had, Pitts and Lee never would have gone to prison. Pitts concluded that the authorities let racism drive the investigation.[15]

As racism is intertwined with capital punishment, Pitts' observation provides an opportunity to explore the subject. In his study of slavery,

They Came in Chains, J. Saunders Redding writes about the foreboding arrival of a mysterious ship into a Virginia harbor in 1619:

Sails furled, flag drooping at her rounded stern, she rode the tide in from the sea. She was a strange ship, indeed, by all accounts, a frightening ship. Whether she was trader, privateer, or man-of-war no one knows. Through her bulwarks black-mouthed cannon yawned. The flag she flew was Dutch; her crew a motley. Her port of call, an English settlement, Jamestown, in the colony of Virginia. She came, she traded, and shortly afterwards was gone. Probably no ship in modern history has carried a more portentous freight. Her cargo? Twenty slaves.[16]

Not a country in the world has made racism such a critical issue, for so long, as the United States. In the context of reforming the criminal justice system, it is appropriate to ask how racism started and, more important, how can it end? Is it possible for people of different racial backgrounds to live together harmoniously, without hatred?

Seeking answers to these questions, the history of North American slavery may prove instructive. After all, on this continent can be traced the arrival of the original whites and blacks.

Scholars believe the first blacks in Virginia were considered servants, similar to the white indentured servants imported from Europe. But it is likely that they were seen as being different than white servants. They were treated differently. They were, in fact, slaves.

Slavery developed rapidly into a regular institution. It became the standard labor practice between blacks and whites in the New World. Associated with it was an inherent racial feeling—hatred, contempt, patronization, or pity. This accompanied the inferior social standing of blacks in America for the next 350 years. Inferior status and derogatory thought add up to racism.

The totality of experience for the early white settlers was the catalyst for enslavement of blacks. The Virginians of 1619 were desperate for labor. They needed it to grow food for survival. Some of them could recall the "starving time," the winter ten years previously, when, crazed by lack of food, they went scavenging the woods for berries and nuts, dug up graves to eat corpses, and died in large numbers. Five hundred colonists were reduced to sixty.

Virginians required labor to raise corn for subsistence and to cultivate tobacco for export. They had learned how to grow tobacco and, in 1617, they shipped the first cargo to England. Discovering that, as with all pleasurable things tinged with moral disapproval, it fetched a good price, the growers were not about to betray their religious hypocrisy and knock a crop so profitable.

Unlike Columbus, colonists could not compel native American Indians to work for them. The settlers were outnumbered. Although they possessed superior fire power and were capable of mass Indian kills, they knew they could face massacre in return. The colonists could not capture them and keep them enslaved. The natives were tough, defiant, and resourceful in a way the English were not. The woods were the Indians' natural habitat and provided them a real home field advantage.

Virginians may have suffered humiliating frustration at their own ineptitude. Their inferiority to the Indians at taking care of themselves may have made the transplanted Englishmen ready to become slave owners. Writing in *American Slavery, American Freedom: The Ordeal of Colonial Virginia*, Edmund Morgan conjures the attitude of the early settler:

If you were a colonist, you knew that your technology was superior to the Indians'. You knew that you were civilized, and they were savages. ... But your superior technology had proved insufficient to extract anything. The Indians, keeping to themselves, laughed at your superior methods and lived from the land more abundantly and with less labor than you did ... and when your own people started deserting in order to live with them, it was too much. ... So you killed the Indians, tortured them, burned their villages, burned their cornfields. It proved your superiority, in spite of your failures. And you gave similar treatment to any of your own people who succumbed to their savage ways of life. But you still did not grow much corn.[17]

Black slaves solved the matter. It was customary to consider imported blacks as slaves, even if slavery would not be institutionalized for decades. By 1619, a million blacks had been forced from Africa to South America and the Caribbean, to the Portuguese and Spanish colonies, to labor as slaves. The Portuguese, fifty years before Columbus, brought ten African blacks to Lisbon. This began a slave trade. African blacks had been subjected to slave labor for a hundred years. So it would have been typical of the times to consider as slaves those twenty blacks, forcibly taken to Jamestown, and auctioned as objects to Englishmen anxious for a reliable labor supply.

Their vulnerability made enslavement easier. The Indians were in their own environment. The whites enjoyed their own European culture. The blacks had been ripped from their land and culture, pushed into a situation where the heritage of family, custom, language, and dress was gradually destroyed, except for the remnants blacks could cling to through extraordinary persistence.

Was their culture inferior and so prone to obliteration? Inferior in military strength, perhaps—helpless against whites' guns and ships. But in no other way. Cultures that are different often are seen as inferior, particularly when such a conclusion is profitable. Even in a military context, while the Westerners could secure forts on the coast of Africa, they were not able to overtake the interior. They had to settle for negotiating with tribal chiefs.

African society was as advanced in its own way as was European civilization. In some ways it may have been more admirable, although it also entailed cruelties, hierarchical privileges, and the willingness to offer human sacrifices for religion or profit. It was a civilization 100,000 million strong. The people used iron implements and were skilled farmers. Society encompassed impressive urban centers. Noteworthy achievements were recorded in sculpture, ceramics, and weaving.

European travelers in the sixteenth century admired the African kingdoms of Mali and Timbuktu, already well organized at a time when European states were only starting to develop into the modern nation. Ramusio, secretary to the Venetian rulers, wrote to the Italian merchants in 1563: "Let them go and do business with the King of Timbuktu and Mali and there is no doubt they will be well-received there with their ships and their goods and treated well, and granted the favors that they ask."[18]

African governance was a feudalism, akin to Europe's, based on agriculture, with hierarchies of lords and vassals. But feudalism as practiced in Africa did not arise, as Europe's did, from slave societies of Rome and Greece, which had wiped out ancient tribal life. In Africa, tribal life was still important. Some of its better aspects—a communal spirit, a kinder and gentler legal system—remained powerful. Since the lords did not posses the weaponry available to European lords, the African hierarchy could not command obedience as readily.

Comparing sixteenth-century Congolese law with that of Portugal and England reveals significant philosophical differences. In the European nations, where the notion of private property was beginning to flourish, theft was punished severely. As late as 1740, in England, a child could be hanged for stealing a rag of cotton. In the Congo, where communal life remained powerful and the concept of private property was strange, thefts were punished with fines of various degrees of servitude.

Slavery was practiced in Africa. That fact was used by Europeans to rationalize their own slave trade. But the "slaves" of Africa more closely resembled European serfs, who accounted for most of Europe's population. It was a demanding servitude, but they did have rights that were denied to slaves who were brought to America. It was an entirely different existence from the human chattel carried on slave ships. An African slave could marry, own property, himself own a slave, swear a legal oath, serve as a competent witness, and ultimately become heir to his master. Nine times out of ten, such a slave might be adopted as a member of the family. His descendants were likely to intermarry with the owner's clan, with the result that few might even know their origin.

Slavery in Africa is hardly praiseworthy. But it was vastly different from forced plantation or mining labor in the Americas. The New World version of slavery was lifelong, morally debilitating, and destructive of family ties. It crushed hope for the future. African slavery lacked two key components that made American slavery the cruelest form of servitude in history. One was the insatiable craving for profit inherent in capitalistic agriculture. The other was the reduction of the slave to subhuman status through racial hatred. With its relentless clarity based on color, racism was inescapable. White was master, black was slave.

That they derived from a settled culture, rich in communal life, family bonds, and traditional customs made the adjustment even harder when these supports were removed. A typical pattern involved being captured in the continent's interior, often by a fellow black engaged in the slave trade, being sold on the coast, then being herded into pens with people of other tribes. Compounding the chaos was the language barrier between the blacks packed together.

The crushing conditions of capture reinforced the exasperation of helplessness felt by the black Africans. Marches to the coast could be a thousand miles. These journeys were made with chains around the people's necks and under constant threat of violence. Two of every five blacks did not survive these death marches. Once on the coast, slaves were caged until they were selected and sold.

Then they were crammed into coffin-sized spaces. They were shackled together in the dark, dank slime of the ship's holds. The stench of their own excrement caused insufferable choking. Contemporary reports describe the conditions:

The height, sometimes, between decks was only eighteen inches; so the unfortunate human beings could not turn around, or even on their sides, the elevation being less than the breadth of their shoulders; and here they are usually chained to the decks by the neck and legs. In such a place the misery and suffocation is so great, the Negroes ... are driven to frenzy.[19]

Peering below deck where slaves were chained together, one could see various stages of suffocation. Some killed others out of desperation to breathe. Others opted to jump overboard and drown rather than prolong their suffering. Observers noted that the blood and mucus covering the slave deck gave it a resemblance to a slaughterhouse.

Under such brutal conditions, one in three slaves would not survive the trans-Atlantic crossing. But the profits were so great, often twice the investment of one trip, that the slave traders pressed on, packing blacks sardinelike into the holds of ships.

The slave trade was dominated first by the Dutch, then the English. By 1795, Liverpool had more than a hundred vessels transporting slaves and accounting for half of such European commerce. New Englanders entered the business in 1637, with the first North American slave ship, the Desire, setting sail from Marblehead, Massachusetts. It was a customized frigate with specially partitioned, two-feet-by-six-feet racks, equipped with bars and leg irons.

By 1800, 10 to 15 million blacks had been taken as slaves to the Americas. This represented perhaps one-third of those originally seized from the continent. Africa lost roughly 50 million people to slavery and slavery-related deaths in those centuries deemed the dawn of modern Western civilization. This human havoc was wreaked by slave traders and plantation owners in Western Europe and America, countries considered the most advanced in the world.

In 1610, Father Sandoval, a Catholic priest serving in the Americas wrote to a religious functionary in Europe, asking if the capture, transport, and enslavement of African blacks was in accord with church doctrine. A letter from Brother Luis Brandaon supplied the response:

Your Reverence writes me that you would like to know whether the Negroes who are sent to your parts have been legally captured. To this I reply that I think your Reverence should have no scruples on this point, because this is a matter which has been questioned by the Board of Conscience in Lisbon, and all its members are learned and conscientious men. Nor did the bishops who were in Sao Thome, Cape Verde, and here in Loando—all learned and virtuous men—find fault with it. We have been here ourselves for forty years and there have been among us very learned Fathers ... never did they consider the trade as illicit. Therefore we and the Fathers of Brazil buy these slaves for our service without any scruple.[20]

All the building blocks of slavery were in place. The early settlers were desperate for labor. Harnessing Indians for plantation tasks proved impossible. It was difficult to exploit whites to the extent necessary. Meanwhile, blacks were being made available in greater numbers by profit-driven traders. On top of that, these blacks were controllable because of the vulnerable psychic and physical state they were in after enduring the ordeal to reach America. Such blacks were ripe for enslavement.

Under the circumstances, even if some blacks were considered servants, it wasn't likely they would be treated the same as white servants.

According to court records of colonial Virginia, one Hugh Davis was "to be soundly whipt ... for abusing himself ... by defiling his body in lying down with a Negro." In 1640, six servants and "a negro of Mr. Reynolds" started to run away. While the white offenders received lighter sentences, "Emmanuel the Negro to receive thirty stripes and to be burnt in the cheek with the letter R, and to work in shackle one year or more as his master shall see cause."[21]

Although slavery was not yet legalized in those early years, the lists of servants indicate blacks were named separately. A law enacted in 1639 mandated "all persons except Negroes" were to get arms and ammunition—to ward off Indians. The following year, when three servants tried to escape, the two whites were punished with an extension of their service. But the third, as the court stated, "being a Negro named John Punch shall serve his master or his assigns for the time of his natural life."[22] Examination of these edicts reveals the roots of racial double standards in the U.S. judicial system.

This unequal treatment, this intertwining of contempt and oppression referred to as racism—was this the outgrowth of a "natural" antipathy of white against black? The question is significant, not just to zero in on historical accuracy, but because an emphasis on "natural" racism lessens the responsibility of the social system. If racism can't be proven natural, it must be the consequence of certain conditions. Society is impelled to ameliorate such conditions.

There is no way of testing behavior of whites and blacks toward one another under favorable conditions—with no history of subordination, no financial incentive compelling exploitation and enslavement, no desperation for survival necessitating forced labor. All the social elements for black and white in seventeenth-century America were just the opposite. All the conditions were pointed toward antagonism and mistreatment. Under such a scenario, the subtlest display of humanity between races might be construed as evidence of a basic human drive toward community.

Even before 1600, when commerce in slaves had just begun, before Africans were branded by it—figuratively and literally—the color black was considered distasteful. According to the Oxford English Dictionary, "black" in pre-1600 England meant: "Deeply stained with dirt; soiled, dirty, foul. Having dark or deadly purposes, malignant; pertaining to or involving death, deadly; baneful disastrous, sinister. Foul, iniquitous, atrocious, horribly wicked. Indicating disgrace, censure, liability to punishment, etc." By contrast, Elizabethan poetry used white to signify purity and beauty.

Absent other overriding factors, darkness and blackness, associated as they are with night and the unknown, might take on those meanings. But the presence of another human being is a significant fact, and the conditions of that presence are critical in assessing whether an initial prejudice, against mere color, isolated from humanity, is transformed into brutality and hatred.

In spite of preconceived notions about blackness and subordination of black people in seventeenth-century America, there is evidence that when whites and blacks found themselves with common dilemmas, common work, common enemy in their master, they behaved toward one another as equals. Historian Kenneth Stamp wrote that black and white servants of the seventeenth century were "remarkably unconcerned about the visible physical differences."[23]

White and black worked together. People of both races fraternized together. That governments felt it necessary to forbid such relations reflects the strength of that tendency. Virginia passed a law in 1661 that "in case any English servant shall run away in company of any Negroes" he would have to give special service for additional years to the master of the runaway Negro. In 1691, Virginia decreed banishment of any "white man or woman being free who shall intermarry with a Negro, mulatto, or Indian man or woman bond or free."[24]

There is tremendous difference between a sensation of racial strangeness, perhaps fear, and the mass enslavement of millions of black people that transpired in the Americas. The transformation from one to the other cannot be explained by "natural" tendencies. It is easier to understand as the result of historical conditions.

Slavery grew with the expansion of the plantation system. The cause is traceable to something other than natural racial repugnance. The number of whites coming to the colonies, whether free or indentured servants (obligated for four to seven years' duty), was insufficient to meet the labor needs of the plantations. By 1700, in Virginia, there were 6,000 slaves, one-twelfth of the population. By 1763, there were 170,000 slaves, accounting for half the population.

Blacks may have been easier to exploit than Indians or whites, but nonetheless were not easy to enslave. From the beginning, transplanted black men and women resisted enslavement. Eventually their resistance was quelled, institutionalizing slavery for 3 million blacks in the South. Still, under the harshest conditions, under pain of mutilation and death, throughout two hundred years of North American enslavement, Afro-Americans rebelled. Occasionally there was an organized insurrection. More often they evidenced refusal to submit by running away. Even more frequently, they engaged in sabotage, work slowdowns, and subtle forms of resistance that affirmed, if only to each other, their human dignity.

The refusal began in Africa. Slave traders reported that blacks were so loathe to leave their homeland, some leaped from slave vessels into the sea, holding their last breaths long enough to drown.

A Virginia law passed in 1669 referred to "the obstinacy of many of them." In 1680, the assembly noted slave meetings "under pretense of feasts and brawls," which they considered of "dangerous consequence."[25] In 1687, in the colony's Northern Neck, a plot was discovered in which slaves planned to kill all whites in the vicinity and escape during a mass funeral.

Slaves recently arrived from Africa, still clinging to their communal heritage, would run away in groups. Once escaped, they'd establish villages of runaways on the wilderness frontier. Slaves who were born in America, on the other hand, were more apt to escape on their own. With skills acquired on the plantation, they would try to pass as free men.

Some scholars believe—on the basis of the infrequency of organized rebellions and the ability of the South to maintain slavery for two hundred years—that the slave population was made submissive by their condition. With their African heritage obliterated, they were reduced to "Sambos," "a society of helpless dependents." So noted Stanley Elkins.[26] Historian Ulrich Phillips describes the slave's diminished status "by racial quality submissive."[27] Examining the totality of slave behavior, at the resistance of everyday life, from subtle noncooperation in work to running away, the story is different.

In 1710, Governor Alexander Spotswood cautioned the General Assembly:

[F]reedom wears a cap which can without tongue, call together all those who long to shake off the fetters of slavery and as such an Insurrection would surely be attended with most dreadful consequences so I think we cannot be too early in providing against it, both by putting ourselves in a better posture of defense and by making a law to prevent the consultations of those Negroes.[28]

Considering the severity of punishment for running away, that so many blacks tried is an indicator of a powerful rebellious drive. Throughout the 1700s, Virginia's slave code decreed:

Whereas many times slaves run away and lie hid and lurking in swamps, woods, and other obscure places, killing hogs, and committing other injuries to the inhabitants ... if the slave does not immediately return, anyone whatsoever may kill or destroy such slaves by such ways and means as he ... [s]hall think fit. ... If the slave is apprehended ... it shall ... [b]e lawful for the county court, to order such punishment for the said slave, either by dismembering or in any other way ... as they in their discretion shall think fit, for the reclaiming any such incorrigible slave, and terrifying others from the like practices ...[29]

In this passage is found the traces of the devaluation of black life by the judicial system and the derivation of the deterrence rationale for imposing capital punishment.

Gerald Mullin, who studied slave resistance in eighteenth-century Virginia in *Flight and Rebellion*, found newspaper advertisements between 1736 and 1801 for 1,138 male runaways and 141 female. One consistent reason for running away was to find members of one's family—showing that despite slavery's intention to break family bonds by not permitting marriages and by separating loved ones, slaves would risk mutilation and death to reunite.

In Maryland, where slaves made up one-third of the population in the mid-1700s, slavery had been written into law since the 1660s. Statutes for containing rebellions had been enacted. There were cases where slave women killed their masters, sometimes by poison, sometimes by arson. Punishments ranged from whipping and branding to execution, but trouble persisted. In 1742, seven slaves were put to death for murdering their master.

Fear of slave revolt seems to have been a permanent fact of plantation life. It was a powerful and intricate system of control that slave owners developed to maintain their labor supply and way of life. The system was subtle and cruel, involving every device that social orders utilize to keep the status quo.

Kenneth Stamp notes:

A wise master did not take seriously the belief that Negroes were natural-born slaves. He knew better. He knew that Negroes freshly imported from Africa had to be broken into bondage; that each succeeding generation had to be carefully trained. This was no easy task, for the bondsman rarely submitted willingly. Moreover, he rarely submitted completely. There was no end to the need for control—at least not until old age reduced the slave to a condition of helplessness.[30]

The system was physical and psychological. Slaves were taught discipline, were impressed repeatedly with the idea of their own inferiority and to "know their place," to see blackness as subordination, to be awed by the master and to merge their interest with his, forsaking their own needs. To achieve this there was the discipline of hard labor, the destruction of the slave family, the numbing effects of religion, and the intentional deunifying of slaves by dividing them into field slaves and the more privileged house slaves. Further force subordinating the slave was the power of law and the immediate authority of the overseer to invoke whipping, burning, branding, mutilation, and death. Dismemberment was written into Virginia Code in 1705. Maryland enacted legislation in 1723 allowing the cutting off of ears of blacks who struck whites. The statute directed that for certain serious offenses, slaves be hanged and the body quartered and exposed.

And still, rebellions took place. There were not many insurrections, but enough to instill fear in white settlers. The first sizeable revolt in the North American colonies took place in 1712 in New York. Slaves accounted for 10 percent of New York's population, the highest proportion in the northern states, where the conditions of commerce usually did not require large numbers of field slaves. Twenty-five blacks and two Indians set a building ablaze, then killed nine white people. They were captured by soldiers and tried. Twenty-one were executed. The Governor reported to England: "Some were burnt, others were hanged, one broke on the wheel, and one hung alive in chains in the town."[31] One had been burned over a slow fire for eight to ten hours. All this was to serve notice to fellow slaves.

Around 1720, there were a number of fires in New Haven and Boston. Negro slaves were the suspected arsonists. One Negro was executed in Boston. Subsequently, Boston's Council enacted a ruling that slaves who on their own assembled in groups of two or more were to be punished by whipping.

In 1739, at Stono, South Carolina, twenty slaves rebelled. They killed two warehouse guards, stole guns and ammunition, and headed south. Along their way, they killed people and burned property. They were joined by others, until they were eighty strong. According to one account, "they called out Liberty, marched on with Colours displayed, and two Drums beating." The militia attacked them. Fifty slaves and twenty-five whites were killed before the uprising was crushed. Researcher Herbert Aptheker, found about 250 instances where a minimum of ten slaves united in revolt or conspiracy.[32]

Occasionally, whites got involved in slave resistance. As early as 1663, indentured white servants and black slaves in Gloucester county, Virginia, formed a conspiracy to rebel and gain freedom. Their plot was betrayed and ended in executions. Gerald Mullin reports that newspaper notices of Virginia runaways often warned "ill-disposed" whites about harboring fugitives. Sometimes slaves and freemen ran off together, or cooperated in crimes. Sometimes black male slaves ran off and joined white women. Occasionally, white ship captains and watermen incorporated runaways into the crew.[33]

Ten thousand whites lived in New York city in 1741. Two thousand blacks lived there also. It had been a difficult winter and the poor—black and white—suffered considerably. When unexplained fires broke out, whites and blacks were accused of conspiring together. Hysteria erupted against the accused. After a trial full of lurid accusations by informers, coupled with coerced confessions, two white men and two white women were executed, eighteen slaves were hanged, and thirteen slaves were burned alive.

The concern greater than black rebellion in American colonies was the fear that discontented whites would join black slaves to overthrow the status quo. In slavery's early years, particularly before racist attitudes became ingrained, when white indentured servants were likely to be treated as badly as black slaves, there was a chance of cooperation. Edmund Morgan's observations are insightful:

There are hints that the two despised groups initially saw each other as sharing the same predicament. It was common, for servants and slaves to run away together, steal hogs, get drunk. It was not uncommon for them to make love together. In Bacon's Rebellion, one of the last groups to surrender was a mixed band of eighty Negroes and twenty English servants.[34]

Morgan notes that masters "initially perceived slaves the same way they had always perceived servants ... shiftless, irresponsible, unfaithful, un-grateful, dishonest." And "if freemen with disappointed hopes should make common cause with slaves of desperate hope, the results might be worse than anything Bacon had done."

Consequently, measures were taken. About the time that slave codes, dealing with discipline and punishment, were being enacted by the Virginia Assembly,

Virginia's ruling class, having proclaimed all white men were superior to black, went on to offer their social (but white) inferiors a number of benefits previously denied them. In 1705 a law was passed requiring masters to provide white servants whose indenture time was up with ten bushels of corn, thirty shillings, and a gun, while women servants were to get 15 bushels of corn and forty shillings. Also, newly freed servants were to get 50 acres of land.

Morgan adds: "Once the small planter felt less exploited by taxation and began to prosper a little, he became less turbulent, less dangerous, more respectable. He could see his big neighbor not as an extortionist but as a powerful protector of their common interests."[35]

The picture of those times that emerges is a complex web of historical threads entrapping blacks for slavery in America: the desperation of starving settlers, the helplessness of displaced Africans, the powerful profit incentive for slave trader and plantation owner, the lure of superior status for downcast whites, the elaborate controls against rebellion and escape, and the legal and social punishment of black and white collaboration.

The point to remember is that the threads of this web are historical, not "natural." This does not imply that they are easily disentangled. It means that there is a possibility for something else, under historical conditions not yet realized. One of these conditions is elimination of the class exploitation that has made poor whites desperate for small tokens of status, and has prevented the unity of black and white necessary for joint rebellion and reconstruction.

An unfortunate example of black and white collaboration, tinged with racism, befell Pitts and Lee. Curtis Adams offered his confession to the authorities. This triggered another change of heart for Billie Mae Lee. This time she claimed to have no idea who killed Jessie Burkett and Grover Floyd.

Warren Holmes had conducted an extraordinary interrogation of Curtis Adams. The exchange was documented on an audiotape that ran ninety-eight minutes. In it, Adams raised numerous critical points that could be corroborated, if only the authorities cared. Had the Mo-Jo owner kept a revolver in the desk? Had one of Curtis Adams' guns been put in the desk? In what position were the bodies discovered? What did the autopsies reveal? Could the weapon be found?

Perhaps most significantly, why did Pitts and Lee confess? Were they at imminent risk of execution? Holmes didn't have the answers. He could only raise the questions. But local officials weren't listening. Broward County had closed the case. Authorities in the Panhandle repeatedly said they were convinced they had the Port St. Joe murderers. The army's investigation was closed.

Holmes sought the attorney representing Lee and Pitts. He found Maurice Rosen, the ACLU volunteer lawyer. Rosen had visited his clients on death row the previous spring. He believed in their innocence. Seeking assistance, Rosen went to Phillip Hubbart, a respected appellate lawyer and an assistant Miami public defender. Hubbart decided to attack the Gulf County practice of precluding blacks from grand juries in an attempt to overturn the verdict.

Hubbart's research revealed that in 1963, 14.4 percent of all registered voters in Gulf County were black. Yet not one black person served on a grand jury. He termed this "systematic exclusion" by race, long disallowed by the Supreme Court. If two innocent people were awaiting execution, Hubbart's legal fine point hardly addressed the case's merits. Yet the legal wrangling served a purpose. With an appeal pending, death warrants could not be signed.

Now, five years into their sentences, another lie detector test was administered to Lee and Pitts. Warren Holmes was their polygraph operator. An independent contractor, Holmes worked for neither the state nor the defense. As a result of his examination, Holmes drew this conclusion, which he shared with Florida Public Television: "These two men are either innocent, or the two biggest con men in the history of the United States."

In Holmes' opinion both Lee and Pitts "ran good tests." He believed it conclusive that Pitts and Lee did not kill the gas station attendants. After testing them separately, Holmes brought them together in the examining room to inform them that another man had confessed to the murders for which they were serving time.

Holmes had been in the polygraph business for 43 years. He characterized his exchange with Lee and Pitts as "the most dramatic moment in my career." Holmes also noted the irony that though the men anticipated their release that very day, it would be another nine years before Pitts and Lee were set free.

In the dead of night, August 28, 1963, Panhandle police delivered the condemned murderers to the Florida State Prison in Raiford. Lee and Pitts were taken to death row to await electrocution. Freddie Pitts was to begin his struggle for survival.

"I never thought I was going to die in the electric chair. Never. I knew somehow, some way, the truth was going to come out."[36]

For a year Pitts heard from no one. The FBI had come. The Army sent a lawyer. The ACLU sent a representative. They carried encouragement and faint hope: a death warrant could not be signed while litigation was pending. What these supporters could not establish was grounds for an innocence claim. That did not surface until December 22, 1966. Nearly three and a half years after the death sentence was pronounced, Warren Holmes told them a convict named Curtis Adams, Jr., had confessed to the murders.

ACLU lawyer Maurice Rosen took Adams' taped confession to the Panhandle in January 1967, three weeks after Holmes recorded it. He met prosecutor J. Frank Adams and implored him to listen to the tape.

The prosecutor was cordial, though aloof, to Rosen. He professed no interest in the Curtis Adams confession. He didn't want to hear it. Unbeknownst to the ACLU attorney, he had chatted privately in a car with Curtis Adams just two months before.

Another key Bay County figure, and undisputed leader of local politics, was Sheriff M.J. "Doc" Daffin. This man confidently maintained his opinions. "I don't *think* they did it, I *know* they did it," he bellowed. His campaign slogan simultaneously established his bedrock credibility and betrayed his vulnerable investment in the present case: "Not a major crime unsolved." He claimed he'd never heard of Curtis Adams, Jr. He certainly didn't buy Adams' confession.

Chief Deputy Louie Wayne White was cautious around strangers, and not too subtle. When informed that Freddie Pitts had claimed to have been beaten, Deputy White proclaimed if anyone said White had beaten him, he'd resign long enough to settle the matter mano-a-mano.

In Tallahassee, Warren Holmes visited Reeves Bowen, chief of the criminal appellate division. Bowen was impatient. He didn't have time to listen to much of Adams' confession tape. To this state official, guilt or innocence wasn't the issue. What mattered to Bowen was whether the defendants had received a fair trial.

Capturing the essence of the tragic injustice, Holmes blurted out, "You mean it doesn't make any difference if they are innocent?" Barely containing his anger, he asked, "You go ahead and electrocute them anyway if they received a fair trial?"[37]

Bowen felt sure they would receive competent representation on appeal. That was the only aspect of the case he was willing to discuss. He didn't want to be troubled.

The *Miami Herald* printed its first two major articles on the Pitts–Lee case in February 1967. The *Panama City News-Herald* ran a full-page spread the following Sunday. The coverage emphasized the media's role in the matter. Under the headline "All Say Pitts, Lee Guilty," the subhead read: "Blame Newspapers for Starting Furor." The lead stated:

Two Florida newspapers have retried one of the Panhandle's most bizarre murder cases in their news pages, and in so doing have thrown the entire area into a furor. Serving as prosecutor, defense attorney, judge and jury, the newspapers have rejected the original verdict rendered by neighboring Gulf County's highest court. They find innocent two men who freely confessed to the crime and now are sweating out electrocution on Death Row at Raiford State Penitentiary ...[38]

The newspaper quoted the judge, prosecuting attorney, defense counsel, court clerk, court stenographer, two sheriffs, and Curtis Adams's father. They agreed Lee and Pitts confessed freely and were guilty.

Mrs. Jewel Poole, a citizen who lived near the Mo-Jo in Gulf County, offered her two cents to the newspaper. "The Adams fellow knew Burkett and Floyd. He knew not to mess with them both. He just couldn't have done it. ... Maybe somebody has put him up to this. Like some member of something like NAACP. He's probably mad with everybody up here and figures he don't have nothing to lose and can make the folks up here look like fools."

The *Panama City News-Herald* wrote, "One of Parker's close associates said a brash reporter from the giant Miami newspaper visited Parker and during the interview asked the old-time lawman why he had beaten the confession out of Pitts and Lee."

The Panama City paper denounced the *Miami Herald* and "its Northwest Florida satellite," the *Tallahassee Democrat*, for "impugning the integrity of the five-county 14th Judicial Circuit."

A piece in the *Panama City News-Herald* reported:

Spread out over several pages during a two-day period, the Miami newspaper depicted the people of this area as a bunch of red necked half-wits. . . . Even the courts were held up to ridicule, law enforcement officers were pictured as dim-witted clods with the inability to track an elephant across a snow bank. Written in fiction style similar to that used by detective magazines, the articles have drawn criticism from officials, responsible members of the working press and the public in general.

On March 27, 1967, the Supreme Court denied a writ of certiorari on whether blacks had been systematically excluded from the 1963 Gulf County grand jury. Attorney Phillip Hubbart, representing Lee and Pitts on appeal, had filed the writ before Curtis Adams confessed. The court's action was not unexpected. Hubbart knew that by law the matter should have been raised at trial in 1963. Defense failed to do so. The denial meant the Supreme Court, which during that term reviewed only seven of every hundred writs filed, simply did not want to hear the case.

Hubbart met with prosecutor J. Frank Adams, telling him he was disturbed about the Pitts and Lee case. In Hubbart's opinion, the men were innocent. Attorney Adams replied he was strongly convinced they were guilty and that Curtis Adams and Mary Jean Akins were lying. The prosecutor stated he was thinking about instituting a grand jury investigation of Warren Holmes for contempt of court and tampering with a witness. Hubbart asked what evidence Adams had for such a charge. The prosecutor responded that Willie Mae Lee told him Holmes had been trying to intimidate her. Hubbart suggested she was lying. Adams offered no reply. Hubbart emphasized that he believed Holmes was guilty of nothing.

The two lawyers spoke at length. Hubbart found Adams to be cordial. Casually he asked him if he had photographs of the bodies and a statement by Willie Mae Lee pointing blame at someone other than Lee and Pitts. Adams conceded he had both, but refused Hubbart's request to see them.

This exchange prompted Hubbart to note that the community was very closed-minded about the Pitts and Lee case. The community regarded it as a racial incident instigated by radicals in Miami—mainly the *Miami Herald*. None of the people Hubbart encountered were aware of the new facts which had been uncovered since December 1963. It seemed no one read the newspaper articles other than J. Frank Adams.

After the Supreme Court's denial, representatives for Lee and Pitts decided upon a more direct appeal. Washington power attorney Edward Bennett Williams had joined Hubbart and ACLU counsel Rosen. Williams grasped the situation quickly. His major concern was Curtis Adams, Jr. What assurance was there that Curtis Adams would testify that he was the Port St. Joe murderer? There was none.

Attorneys Hubbart and Williams concurred on a basic strategic approach—get the Pitts–Lee case out of the politically sensitive state courts in the Panhandle. To seek relief there, they conjectured, would be time consuming and likely futile.

The Pitts–Lee legal team filed a petition in the U.S. district court for the Middle District of Florida, requesting a federal judge in Jacksonville take jurisdiction and conduct a hearing. Judge William Mcrae left the case idle for two months while he recovered from cataract surgery. He transferred the petition to the federal court for the Northern District of Florida.

There, by happenstance, the petition went to the chambers of a federal judge in Tallahassee who had an exceptionally dismal record in habeas corpus petitions. He had repeatedly turned them down without hearings. His reputation was that of a mediocre judge with severe antagonism toward civil rights.

The judge, G. Harrold Carswell, in a political stump speech years earlier, emphatically stated: "I am a southerner. I believe segregation is the only correct way of life. I shall be the last to submit to any attempt to weaken this established policy. ... I yield to no man in the vigorous belief in white supremacy, and I shall always be so governed."[39]

Judge Carswell would live to regret these words, dubbing them "obnoxious and abhorrent," after President Richard M. Nixon nominated him to the United States Supreme Court in January 1970. The following spring, the U.S. Senate roundly rejected the nomination.

In the summer of '67, three years before Carswell's moment in the national spotlight, a Florida assistant attorney general argued that Lee and Pitts hadn't exhausted state remedies. Judge Carswell was quick to agree, denying their petition. If, as he maintained in 1970, Carswell no longer supported white supremacy, he blew an opportunity to show it.

Another key player working against Pitts and Lee, unfortunately, was the trial lawyer who was supposed to be representing them. The right of an indigent defendant to have an attorney appointed for him implicitly means an effective attorney. Nowhere is that concept more crucial than in a capital case. In February 1968, Phillip Hubbart questioned W. Fred Turner about the defense he prepared on behalf of Lee and Pitts in 1963. Shortly after his interaction with Turner, Hubbart filed a motion charging defense counsel with being incompetent. Hubbart believed Turner's conduct to be a reprehensible breach of duty. Hubbart's view was that the service provided to the defendants turned the proceedings into a farce. Turner abdicated his professional responsibilities, according to Hubbart. Defense counsel left his clients to fend for themselves, with disastrous results. Hubbart charged Turner, in a thirty-two-page motion, of failing to prepare his case. Turner's omissions and gross mistakes constituted a failure to properly represent the petitioners, according to Hubbart.

In a meandering, revealing deposition, Turner defended his conduct. He spoke of the alleged eagerness of his clients to plead guilty in 1963. He didn't dwell on his own guilty plea and incarceration at the Federal Correctional Institution at Tallahassee thirteen years earlier. Turner had been sentenced to one year after pleading guilty to two counts of willful failure to file income tax returns. The brush with the law didn't keep him from his legal practice for long. In Florida's Panhandle his five-year suspension was made probationary after his release. He kept practicing in the state courts. When he became involved in a federal case, three circuit judges in the Panhandle, including Warren Fitzpatrick, the judge in the Pitts–Lee trial, recommended his reinstatement in the federal tribunals. Federal Judge G. Harrold Carswell obliged.

This was ancient history in Turner's life by 1963. These troubling episodes were rarely mentioned. Turner was highly regarded for his courtroom skills at the time of the mercy hearing.

Hubbart asked Turner directly, "What did you decide to do in the way of putting on a case for mercy?"

"Well, mercy is an ethereal quality," answered Turner. "Our lives are built on quid for quo. Mercy is not like that at all," he explained. "We decided to put on these boys—give the jury some biographical history of their lives, and see if the jury would grant them mercy. . . . Mercy is something you can't buy or barter. They understood that."[40]

Turner told his clients their appearance on the witness stand would be most important. He spoke with Pitts about putting on evidence of his marital situation. That became problematic with the presence of a girlfriend, who supposedly benefited from the loot of the robbery. Turner abandoned that approach.

Turner noted the daunting challenge of presenting his clients in a context that would resonate with the jury. He wasn't up to the challenge.

In his brief, Hubbart listed the damaging admissions and incriminating facts that Turner had elicited from his clients on the witness stand. One statement Turner extracted casting his clients in the worst possible light was— "The older victim allegedly begged the petitioners not to kill the younger victim because the latter had a family."[41]

Turner testified that his knowledge of the case was based on pretrial discovery. This statement took Hubbart by surprise. For, under oath, Turner had represented that he was not aware that Willie Mae Lee had fingered someone other than Lee and Pitts. He was not aware that the Florida Sheriff's

Bureau had conducted an investigation and discovered no physical evidence connecting the defendants to the crime. He was unaware two Army investigators had found Pitts beaten and had a written retraction. Turner wasn't aware his clients had made statements to police. He had no recollection of talking to witnesses who could have told him they were in the room with Wilbert Lee about the time of the crime.

Turner testified he had interviewed key witnesses, including Wilbert's wife Ella Mae. He pinpointed dates and places where exchanges occurred. But in at least two cases, the person Turner claimed to have interviewed could prove him wrong. In Ella Mae's case she could document she was miles removed from the interview scene.

The most egregious of Turner's incompetencies concerned whether he had extracted a confession from his clients in the presence of Sheriff Daffin and Chief Barron when confronted by Willie Mae Lee. He insisted he hadn't.

That the Willie Mae confrontation took place was not in question. By Turner's account, Pitts had demanded it. Willie Mae retold her version of the events in Pitts' presence. According to Turner, Pitts concurred.

Were Daffin and Barron there for this interaction? Hubbart wanted to know.

Turner denied ever discussing the case with his clients in the presence of law enforcement. Turner carefully parsed his words.

Hubbart offered to refresh Turner's memory by showing him the transcript of Daffin's testimony from the 1963 mercy hearing. Turner began reading the testimony and grew embarrassed. He read the portion of the transcript in which Daffin recounted the confrontation in his jail where Lee and Pitts confessed:

Q. Was the conversation between you and these two boys and Willie Mae free and voluntary?

A. Yes, sir. And after they had been appointed an attorney.

Q. And was this conversation in the presence of several witnesses?

A. Yes, sir.

Q. . . . you say they had been appointed an attorney?

A. Yes, sir.

Q. Was he present when the conversation was held?

A. Yes, sir. He was.[42]

Attorney Turner insisted he did not recall any such occasion.

Hubbart covered the same ground the next day with Sheriff Daffin under oath. Daffin assured Hubbart Turner was present for the critical exchange.

Hubbart later recalled that he could scarcely imagine a more egregious breach of professional responsibility.

So, where was the truth? With two indigent defendants who'd been convicted of murder? Or with their attorney, W. Fred Turner?

Turner claimed Pitts told him he had a police record. Pitts said he did not tell him that. In fact, Pitts did not have a record.

Turner said he never recommended Pitts and Lee plead guilty. They say differently, that he did.

Turner said he informed his clients the court would appoint a different lawyer if they had different pleas. Pitts said he believed he'd be denied counsel if he pleaded not guilty.

Turner insists his clients never told him they were beaten. They claim they did.

Turner said Pitts never mentioned the Army investigation and his retraction. Pitts begs to differ.

Turner said his clients did not tell him they had confessed when he initially interviewed them. Both said they informed Turner they did.

During the deposition of February 1968, Turner expressed sympathy for Wilbert Lee. He said, even years after abandoning the case, he had gone to the state house to persuade the governor to spare Lee's life. The governor refused to intervene.

For Freddie Pitts, Turner had no sympathy. He felt no obligation to sympathize with someone he believed was a merciless, ruthless murderer. Turner found Pitts remorseless. Turner said he asked Pitts if he shot one of the victims behind the head with his hands tied behind his back? He says his client replied that, in fact, he shot twice.

Pitts denied such a conversation. Hubbart commented it never occurred to Turner that Freddie might have no remorse because he was innocent.

The Pitts–Lee case is unique in the history of Florida law: Never had a judge seated a jury solely to determine mercy following a guilty plea. Who conceived this legal machination?

According to defense counsel Turner, the idea originated with Private Freddie Pitts. Turner said Pitts had asked if a jury could pass judgment as to mercy. Turner called the maneuver highly unusual. He'd have to make a special request of the court. Judge Fitzpatrick agreed the move was unorthodox. He told counsel, if it would get Turner out of a jam, he'd consider it.

Judge Fitzpatrick later testified that Turner did inquire about that. Fitzpatrick commented he had long been bothered that the state placed the awful power of pronouncing a death sentence in one man's hands. He had wished that Florida allowed juries to pass on the question of mercy, believing that a single individual should not be in a position of determining life and death for another person. He was receptive to Turner's unprecedented request.

The procedure was a source of embarrassment for Turner in his 1963 appeal to the Florida Supreme Court. He did not want to pursue the appeal. He did so under orders from Judge Fitzpatrick.

He felt foolish arguing the illegality of the mercy hearing because it was done at his request. His motion was brief. In ten paragraphs he laid out case statement, argument, and conclusion.

Turner made his stance at the outset of proceedings, declaring to the court that he was directed by the circuit judge to institute and perfect the appeal. In his brief Turner underscored the word "directed," asserting that he could find no evidence that the defendants had been mistreated at any stage of the proceedings. He added that the pleas of Pitts and Lee were freely and voluntarily entered.

Wanting to confirm that counsel was expressing himself independently, Hubbart asked Turner if either defendant had authorized him to make such statements?

Turner replied that they had not. At the time, in fact, Lee and Pitts were in prison.

Hubbart handed Turner the document and asked if there were any legal authorities cited in his brief?

Turner answered the question with a question: "I'm pretty sure there is at least one case, is there not?" There wasn't.

Hubbart continued his probe, asking if counsel had ever written an appellate brief with no legal authorities in it? Turner admitted that this was the only one. Shoddy defense cost Pitts and Lee death verdicts that were upheld by the Florida Supreme Court on May 29, 1964.

The Pitts–Lee defense team, in Fall 1968, filed for a new trial. The five-day proceeding commenced on September 23, in the courtroom of Circuit Judge Charles R. Holley. Holley had run for governor a few years earlier on a platform to the right of Barry Goldwater, the 1964 Republican presidential nominee. Holley took over the case when Judge Fitzpatrick, anticipating a subpoena to be a witness, recused himself.

Irwin J. Block, an outstanding defense lawyer who occasionally volunteered with the American Civil Liberties Union, joined forces with Philip Hubbart. They attacked the conviction of Lee and Pitts on five grounds: innocence, suppression of evidence, coerced confessions, incompetency of counsel, and prejudicial venue. As petitioners, they carried the burden of proof. Their witnesses opened the testimony.

For the state's part, attorneys tried to keep out of the record the tape-recorded confession of Curtis Adams. They tried to keep the Army's investigations of the beatings out of the record. They tried to keep out the Lee and Pitts complaints to the FBI of police brutality. They tried to keep out autopsy reports. They even tried to prevent Pitts and Lee from testifying.

After a lengthy legal tussle, Judge Holley decided he would listen to the Curtis Adams confessions. Adams' tape-recorded voice echoed in the quiet courtroom. "Grover Floyd, he laid down. You see, I had my back to the canal and I was facing the tree. He laid down to my right and Jesse Burkett laid down to my left. . . . Their feet was about three foot apart, I imagine."

"Did you tie them up?" the tape-recorded voice of polygraph operator Warren Holmes asked.
"No, sir."
"Who did you shoot first?"
"Grover Floyd."
"In what part of his body did you shoot him?"
"In the head . . ."[43]

Detective Elihu Phares testified about the Broward County murder investigation of Floyd McFarland. He told of Curtis Adams' confession, the trip he made with Adams to Port St. Joe, and how Adams had led him to the location where the Mo-Jo attendants had been killed. Following Phares' testimony, attorney Block depicted the racially charged atmosphere in Florida's Panhandle in 1963. He pointed to the disturbing fact that these defendants had been arrested, tried, convicted, and on their way to Raiford within thirty days.

Conservative Judge Holley considered such expediency a matter of pride.

On the second day of hearings, Curtis Adams, Jr., came forward to testify. The defense had no idea what he would say. They felt they had no choice but to ask the judge to call Adams as a witness. Without him, how could they prove innocence? Hubbart believed the taped confession was insurance, a fallback to be used to impeach Adams' testimony if need be.

Hubbart began his examination of the witness. Adams said he lived in Port St. Joe at the time of the homicides. He acknowledged having seen Pitts and Lee on the streets and in prison.

The ensuing line of questions produced a curve ball the defense did not anticipate. "You say you went to Skipper's Mo-Jo station on the night of July 31st, 1963?" Adams concurred.

"Did you go into the bathroom?" Again, yes.

"Did you open the door at any time and look out?" Another yes.

"Did you see a man making a telephone call at that time in a phone booth?" The bombshell: "No, sir. The last thing I saw when I looked out the door was two men walking off with Jesse Burkett and Grover Floyd."[44]

This response knocked the defense for a loop. Incredibly, Curtis Adams, Jr., had transformed himself into an innocent bystander.

A flabbergasted Hubbart shouted, "[didn't] you yourself kidnap Jesse Burkett and Grover Floyd, Jr., and take them out in the country road and murder them?"

"No," the witness calmly responded.

"State whether or not you told Officer Terry Jones of the Monroe County sheriff's office in the spring of 1964 that you knew something about the Floyd–Burkett murders in Port St. Joe?" Hubbart demanded.

Adams replied, "Refuse to answer on the grounds it might tend to incriminate me."

This response set off legal wrangling as to whether Adams could invoke Fifth Amendment privileges. Judge Holley ruled in his favor.

Hubbart took another tack. "State whether or not you told Lieutenant Elihu Phares on January 17, 1967, at the Broward County Jail that you committed the murders of Grover Floyd and Jesse Burkett?"

"Against my wishes, yes," answered Adams. Hubbart asked the witness to explain himself. "I was doped, threatened, hung up on the bars and beat and full of liquor." Hubbart wanted to know who had done all this to Adams.

"Sergeant Eugene Sullivan, the head jailer, had sixteen niggers to put me in a cell and threaten me, hang me on the bars, and beat me with a sheet wrapped up in my kidneys," Adams angrily replied.

Hubbart sought to have Adams identify his own voice on the taped 1966 confession. The judge permitted him to play a small portion.

"I'd went to Panama City that night that we discussed Skipper's place. I'd went over there to rob a liquor store and didn't. I came back. . . . It was too much traffic, too many people. I couldn't rob it by myself."

Did that voice belong to Curtis Adams? "I refuse to answer on the grounds it might tend to incriminate me," he declared, his voice more harsh than the subdued tone on tape. Thus ended the day's courtroom battle.[45]

The following day, Curtis Adams sought an audience with Judge Holley. The judge had Adams brought into the courtroom. He stood humbly before the bench. That he resurfaced on the second day of the hearing was a surprise. The courtroom was abuzz.

Adams admitted to the judge that what he wanted to discuss related to his previous testimony. Holley would have no part of it unless Adams' attorney was present. Defense counsel Block, sensing a major turnaround in Adams' demeanor, interjected his opinion. He was of the mind to strike while the iron was hot. Delaying discussion would risk Adams' changing his mind. The judge insisted that any interaction not involving Adams' lawyer would be improper.

Adams' court-appointed counsel would not be available for another day. In the meantime, Curtis did change his mind. He notified the judge that he no longer had anything to say.

Hubbart took some consolation from Adams' repudiating his confession. In his latest testimony, Adams placed himself at the crime scene at the time of the offence. Hubbart reasoned, Adams' contention that two black women—not just Willie Mae Lee—took part in the crime refuted every known detail.

The hearing's second day produced one of the most bizarre pieces of courtroom show business in the history of U.S. jurisprudence. Judge Holley called Willie Mae Lee as a witness. He requested the state arrange for a competent psychiatrist to appear before the court when Willie Mae Lee would be interrogated. The psychiatrist was to see if, through hypnosis, he could get Willie Mae to revisit the night of the murders.

These moves caught Block and Hubbart off guard and left the defense dumbfounded. Was the judge actually going to have a psychiatrist put a witness under hypnosis in the courtroom?

As if by psychic coincidence, the state's attorney just happened to have scheduled a hypnotist for the next morning's proceedings. Joe McCawley, a licensed ethical hypnotist, was on his way.

Befuddled, Block and Hubbart wondered what was happening. A hypnotic séance was being requested by the judge and the state already had a hypnotist scheduled to arrive. What sort of setup was this?

Willie Mae Lee had undergone two previous practice séances in secret in Orlando in the spring. Both had been conducted by Joe McCawley. Upon learning this, Block objected that this was not the independent professional he imagined the judge intended. The judge didn't agree, overruling the objection.

Judge Holley was determined there'd be a public demonstration. Three times Hubbart rose to object. Hubbart pressed the point that the state had already indoctrinated Willie Mae through two prior hypnotic episodes. He contended the state had biased her thinking and implanted in her mind the story it wanted her to recite. Hubbart believed the hypnotic sessions to be a due process violation under the Fourteenth Amendment. He argued that Pitts and Lee were being denied a fair trial because the witness could not be properly cross-examined. Hubbart noted that defendents' Sixth and Fourteenth Amendment protections were being violated as they could not confront the witness. Hubbart also objected that his clients' right to effective counsel was being compromised.

Holley thanked defense counsel, saying he'd take these objections under advisement. He already proclaimed that he had faith in hypnosis and regression. Perhaps as a slight concession, he instructed the state to bring a psychiatrist to court to accompany Joe McCawley.

Although Block's cross-examination was overshadowed by the drama of the séance to follow, Willie Mae Lee fared poorly as a witness. She hid behind a self-proclaimed bad memory. On the stand she had forgotten the police held her in jail three weeks. She failed to remember that she'd supposedly seen Freddie Pitts with a car jack and a gun. She couldn't recall that Pitts supposedly pistol-whipped a man and blood ran down the victim's shirt. She forgot she had testified to seeing Pitts in the Mo-Jo office. She didn't remember she supposedly saw him carrying out a sack of cash.

She replied, "I don't remember," to thirty-three questions. "I don't know" was her answer on thirty-six occasions. Fourteen times she didn't answer at all. She couldn't recall that when deposed she'd admitted to telling "a heap of lies." Seven times Block got her to admit she had previously lied under oath.

McCawley sensed he was about to make history. His séance would merit status as one of the most eccentric exhibitions to take place in a courtroom in the annals of American law. Until that afternoon in 1968, there had been only one recorded instance of hypnotism in a U.S. legal proceeding.[46]

McCawley, whose academic achievement consisted of graduating from a junior college in Orlando, identified himself as the nation's first "ethical hypnotist." He claims to have been licensed. It turns out he paid thirty-five dollars for his occupational certification, no examination required.

Block laid into McCawley, asking if it were true that a hypnotist couldn't get anybody to lie under hypnosis against their will. He continued this line of questioning, wondering if a hypnotist could get subjects to lie under hypnosis with their will?

McCawley explained that a person's hypnotic behavior was determined by his non-hypnotic behavior. This meant that if someone normally would lie out of hypnosis, he also could lie in hypnosis.

That's all the questioning Block wanted to do. Soon Judge Holley was ready to proceed. Hubbart asserted one final, futile objection.

Willie Mae Lee took the witness stand again. With a little hocus-pocus, Joe McCawley made her "relive" the shootings of Burkett and Floyd. Judge Holley prefaced the unusual procedure by asking the witness if anybody had discussed with her being hypnotized in the courtroom? She indicated no by shaking her head. Obviously, this wasn't the right answer.

Undeterred, the judge continued. He explained that he had written instructions from the bailiff to the effect that Willie Mae, wanted assurance that only Mr. McCawley or Judge Holley would ask questions under hypnosis. To this she nodded yes.

The hypnotist proceeded to transport Willie Mae back to July 31, 1963, to the party at Wilbert Lee's house on the eve of the crime. Her head slumping over her arm, the witness' regression included enough swigs of moonshine to become inebriated. She began to tell of her trip to the Mo-Jo. As much of her testimony was mumbled, Willie Mae required frequent reminders to speak up and speak clearly.

Although her commentary was sprinkled with screams and screeches, blubbers and sobs, it was not the incomprehensible nature of Willie Mae's testimony that left the lasting impression. Her message was unmistakable.

"No, no, don't do this!" Willie Mae shouted in her trance.

"Don't do what," McCawley probed.

"Oh, don't do it. Just don't do it. Lord have mercy. Don't do this."

Again the hypnotist sought clarification.

"Got mans in the car," said Willie Mae.

"Got who in the car?"

"That fat man and that old man ... Mr. Burkett and Floyd ..." The witness continued, "Don't beg that damn nigger."

"Who's saying that?"

"The fat man." Willie Mae tearfully shrieked, "No! No! Don't do it."

"Don't do what?"

"Let me go! Let them go! Oh, no! Don't ... Oh, God ... Let me go ... Talking with Freddie, I'm talking to him. 'Shut up your mouth.' ... Freddie told me to shut up. ... They're getting out. ... 'Hand me my gun, you ain't got no damn nerve.'"

"Who's saying that?"

"Freddie. ... He telling Wilbert ... No, no! No, don't do it, please!" Willie Mae wept full force.

"Lord have mercy, don't do it! Don't kill men! Don't carry men down there. I'm sorry I ran away. So scared, so scared ... I'm running."

"Where are you running?"

"Down the side of the road ... Coming back, nowhere to go. 'Freddie, what you all did? What you did! What you did? Take me home, I won't tell. I ain't going to tell. I swear I won't. I won't ... carry me home, please. I just want sleep. Ain't nothing wrong with me. I won't stay out this late any more.'"[47]

As Joe McCawley concluded his interrogation, Judge Holley turned to the defense to ask if they had any questions to put to Willie Mae through the hypnotist. Irwin Block replied, "On the basis of our prior objection, we cannot present questions, your honor."

Later that day, Dr. Michael Gilbert, psychiatric expert for the defense, cast doubt on the intensity of Willie Mae's hypnotic state. Attorney Block noticed that Willie Mae referred to the victims by name, facts not known by her when she issued her statements back in 1963. Block wondered, would she be able to recall under regression what she didn't know at the time?

"Not ordinarily," Gilbert replied. When Dr. Gilbert pricked her hand twice while Willie Mae was under hypnosis, he said he detected a reaction. He explained that an individual in a trance needn't be sleepy nor dopey. Such a person can be alert, articulate, and act out anything the hypnotist suggests. Gilbert's opinion was that Willie Mae was play-acting.

The state's expert on hypnosis, Dr. Israel Hanenson, carried little clout as he admitted he didn't know a lot about the subject. He had never observed regression.

An independent opinion was voiced by Dr. Harold Rosen, professor of psychiatry at Johns Hopkins University. He served as chair of the American Medical Association's Committee on Hypnosis. He characterized the Port

St. Joe séance as "dangerous, degrading claptrap"[48] as far as a truth-finding venture. He offered that hypnotized individuals might confess to crimes they only fantasized or to offences their hypnotists think they've done. Such subjects may falsify testimony. They may be induced to believing they recall perpetrating crimes that were never committed. Dr. Rosen could document 203 occasions in which he served as psychiatric consultant where hypnosis caused dangerous adverse results. Ethical hypnotist McCawley claimed there could be no adverse complications.

Dr. Rosen noted that the risks of hypnosis arise from its injudicious use by psychiatrically naïve practitioners. Data from hypnotic sessions can be misleading. A hypnotized individual is in a state of clouded consciousness. In Rosen's view, hypnosis did not belong in the courtroom. In regression, a subject may "relive" an experience he never had.

Anyone of normal intelligence, according to Dr. Rosen, can learn hypnotic techniques in thirty minutes. A person can be hypnotized with or without his consent. Controlled experiments at Johns Hopkins and Harvard revealed that an individual pretending to be hypnotized can fool experts. Rosen referred to a case where, in hypnotic trance, a man confessed to murdering his sister. Problem was, he didn't have a sister.

Judge Holley did not issue an opinion concerning a new trial for seven months. On April 21, 1969, Holley announced he wanted additional testimony before ruling. Freddie Pitts, Wilbert Lee, Willie Mae Lee, Sheriff Daffin, and Fred Turner received subpoenas. To the defense team, it was apparent the judge wanted to review Pitts' and Lee's 1963 confessions to the sheriff in the presence of their own attorney. Judge Holley set the hearing date for April 28. The proceeding would be conducted in his Clearwater courtroom.

With a couple of key participants unable to attend, Judge Holley changed his mind about additional testimony. On the morning the hearing had been scheduled, a new character entered the cast. Into the courtroom came Terry Furnell, a criminal lawyer who had just been appointed appellate counsel for Curtis Adams. Furnell had seen Adams in prison. Adams asked him the question he had previously posed, a question he'd wanted to ask Judge Holley in Port St. Joe the day after his repudiation: Could he be granted immunity?

Furnell had the rapt attention of the courtroom as he proposed the following motion: "Curtis Adams, Jr., is possessed of information which will demonstrate conclusively the innocence of Freddie Pitts and Wilbert Lee. . . . Such evidence is prejudicial to and incriminating of Curtis Adams, Jr., as to the homicides attributed to Pitts and Lee."

Furnell sought immunity for Adams. "If not granted he will be precluded from testifying in order to protect himself from prosecution, which may result in the wrongful execution or continued wrongful confinement of two innocent individuals."[49]

At this dramatic moment, Judge Holley required a recess. He retreated to chambers and drafted a brief, pointed opinion. It was eleven powerful paragraphs. He returned to the courtroom and read:

"This court finds for Pitts and Lee on the issues of knowingly or negligently withholding evidence by the state—and innocence." At this, the defendants could hardly contain their joy. There was more to come.

"This court finds against Pitts and Lee on the issues of incompetent counsel and coerced confession," Judge Holley proclaimed. "With respect to the coerced confession, this court does find ... the guilty pleas reasonably may have been the result of fear. ... The death sentences imposed upon defendants ... are set aside, vacated, declared naught."[50]

The judge's findings made moot Curtis Adam's immunity request. It was not within Holley's purview to grant immunity. But as he proved with the Port St. Joe séance, Holley was a jurist who did things his own way.

J. Frank Adams stormed out of the courtroom, displeased with what just transpired. He decided that even though the verdict had been reversed, the 1963 indictment was still intact. Because of J. Frank Adams's unwillingness to see them go free, Lee and Pitts remained behind bars.

With the defendants still in jail under the 1963 indictment, attorneys for the state took their sweet time. Adams delayed filing an appeal until the thirtieth and final day after Holley's decision. After ten days, a colleague sought ten additional days to file "an assignment of errors." Then the court clerk required another fifty days to index the record. The prosecution claimed it needed another thirty days. The pattern became painfully obvious to the defendants.

"It was nothing more than I'd learned to expect," Pitts commented philosophically.[51] It was exasperating to the defendants, as they were certain the prosecution recognized their innocence.

The prosecution's dawdling appeal stalled proceedings for a year and a half. Hubbart crafted the brief on Pitts' and Lee's behalf. Defense counsel contended Judge Holley ruled properly and the innocent men should be released. Hubbart concluded that the enormity of the injustice was beyond belief. He observed that no evasions, rationalizations or eloquent legal arguments could obscure the plain truth that the oppressed of this country must turn to the courts for protection against injustice.

Despite the evidence in their favor, Lee and Pitts did not receive a new trial until 1971. That second proceeding was relocated to Marianna, Florida, about sixty miles north of Port St. Joe.

Events conspired against Pitts and Lee. Key testimony that could have checkmated the prosecution was never forthcoming. Curtis Adams, who had confessed to committing the murders, agreed to testify on one condition. Since he was already serving a life sentence for past offenses, he sought immunity from prosecution for crimes presently being adjudicated.

The state wasn't willing to deal. There would be no immunity exchanged for confession. As a result, when he testified, Adams pled the Fifth Amendment, refusing to incriminate himself.

Next, defense called Mary Jean Aikens, Adams' former girlfriend. She traveled to the second trial and made statements. However, her comments were not uttered before the jury. The judge deemed her testimony inadmissible. It was considered hearsay. Her knowledge of the crime amounted to what she'd been told, not what she'd actually seen.

The defense absorbed another blow when Billie Mae Lee resurfaced as prosecution witness. The state's story centered on how Billie Mae had been hypnotized during the 1968 hearing. While under hypnosis, she claimed Lee and Pitts forced her to go to the canal where they shot the gas station employees.

Recalling Billie Mae's testimony, Bobby Burkett, nephew of one of the victims, told Florida Public Television, "What convinced me most was in 1968, when they hypnotized Willie Mae Lee and carried her back to that time and place, she lived it just like she was living it then. That was impressive." When asked what it was like to witness that testimony, Bobby Burkett said, "It was not pleasant. She was emotionally upset, crying and telling what they were saying and doing. She recounted the whole thing."[52]

To this characterization of that testimony, Pitts countered, "That was a joke, if they really examined that. At one point, she said in the hypnosis, 'What do I say now?'" That gaff left such an impression Pitts repeated it. "That was the one thing she said in that hypnosis. 'What do I say now?'"[53]

The hypnotism, apparently, was sufficient to persuade the jurors. They again voted to convict. Again, the men were given death sentences.

However, fate, in the form of a Supreme Court decision, intervened on the condemned's behalf. In 1972, the Court ruled the death penalty, as drafted in the various jurisdictions, arbitrary and capricious. The Justices ruled capital punishment unconstitutional. So, after nearly ten years on death row, the sentences of Wilbert Lee and Freddie Pitts were commuted to life in prison.

It took another three years, however, for the miracle Pitts and Lee had longed for to occur. Florida Governor Reubin Askew pardoned both men. At the exoneration proceedings the Governor first referred to Grover Floyd and Jesse Burkett. "My heart and prayers will remain with the families of those two men." Then Governor Askew went about setting the record straight. "I have decided though, that substantial doubt exists as to the guilt of Pitts and Lee."[54]

5

Reasonable Doubt at
a Reasonable Price

"The surest way to avoid the death penalty" is for defendants to "get good defense lawyers."[1] So said Jamie Fellner, director of the U.S. Program at Human Rights Watch. She was commenting on the World Court's March, 2004, order that the government review the cases of fifty-one Mexicans facing death sentences. The International Court of Justice determined these Mexican nationals had been denied access to consular officials, who could have aided their defense. Mexican officials and human rights activists applauded the ruling as vindication of Mexico's claim that the United States systematically violated prisoners' rights.

The plight of Gregory Ralph Wilhoit unfolded along similar lines. The surest way Greg could have avoided spending eight years shuttling between the courts and Oklahoma's death row would have been for him to have had decent defense counsel. If mistaken eyewitness identification is the leading cause of wrongful convictions, ineffective legal defense may be the most frustrating. If systemic corruption manifest in police misconduct or prosecutorial overreaching—often motivated by racism—is the most insidious element in the miscarriage of justice, incompetent lawyering may be the most exasperating. An innocent person sits in court, certain of his disassociation from the crime but helpless as his mouthpiece bumbles away his case.

"Equal Justice Under the Law" are the reassuring words greeting visitors as they enter the United States Supreme Court building. This phrase

Greg Wilhoit has become a leading advocate in
the fight against the death penalty. Photo credit:
Mark Zimmerman/*The Edmond (OK) Sun.*

forms the foundation of the Sixth Amendment to the U.S. Constitution.
That amendment reads:

In all criminal prosecutions, the accused shall enjoy the right to a speedy and public
trial, by an impartial jury of the State and district wherein the crime shall have
been committed, which district shall have been previously ascertained by law, and
to be informed of the nature and cause of the accusation; to be confronted with
the witnesses against him; to have compulsory process for obtaining witnesses in his
favor, and to *have the assistance of counsel for his defense.*[2] [emphasis added]

Supreme Court cases decided over the past eight decades have modified
the Sixth Amendment. Various interpretations of the law have intended to
protect indigent individuals who have been accused of crime. Special attention has been paid to the final point enumerated in the Sixth Amendment—
the right of the accused to assistance of counsel. To ensure a fair trial is
administered for all defendants, the right to a court-appointed attorney was

extended to those who qualified on the basis of low income. To add teeth to this Amendment, not only is one entitled to counsel but counsel must be effective. Attorneys must be trained, have sufficient resources, and be appropriately applying their skills to represent clients competently.

Greg Wilhoit's nightmare began June 1, 1985, with the murder of his wife, Kathy. When Greg retells his tale, listeners are struck by his openness. He keeps no secrets. He refers to his life as an "open book." Perhaps it is easier to be candid when your life is on the public record.

It also is remarkable that Greg speaks without bitterness. He betrays none of the animosity one expects from someone who'd been dealt a terrible fate. When he presents himself, Greg alternates between a matter-of-fact tone and an easygoing, joking style. Whether his demeanor is the result of so much time passing since his life's tragedies or having recited his story so often, is hard to say. Whatever shapes his delivery, Greg comes across as someone who has accepted the hardships that have befallen him. Not only does Greg not let his unfortunate past weigh him down, he draws strength from enlightening others.

As Greg says, "A sense of humor will take you a long way."[3]

Greg exhibits a folksy eloquence. He is thoughtful and articulate. There is inspiration to be drawn from one forced to confront his mortality by such cruel circumstances. One ponders, even if Greg does not, how his life might have turned out differently. It is understandable for one to feel awestruck thinking about how close Greg came to being executed; that, had Oklahoma followed through on this miscarriage of justice, the listener would be deprived of sharing moments with this gentle soul.

Greg and his wife had been separated three weeks by the time of the crime. Kathy had moved several miles from the family's home. She took with her the couple's two baby girls, four months and fourteen months old. While Kathy's apartment was within Tulsa's city limits, it was in the part of town that spilled into Osage County. Greg would learn that this jurisdictional quirk made a difference in the persistence with which prosecutors would pursue the case.

The nonstop crying of the babies alerted a neighbor that something was wrong. Failing to arouse anyone in the apartment, the neighbor phoned police. When authorities arrived, they entered the apartment to discover Kathy's body downstairs and the girls in their cribs upstairs. Following a preliminary inspection, police determined rape and murder had been committed.

Law enforcement officials requested Greg come to the police station and make a statement. They wanted to know his whereabouts the previous night. Greg offered his statement voluntarily. As evidence was pieced together by the medical examiner, it was estimated that Kathy's killing occurred sometime between 1:00 A.M. and 6:00 A.M. Greg, living alone, could establish no alibi for where he was in the middle of the night.

Suspicions in such situations naturally revolve around a separated spouse. On the advice of a family friend, Greg retained counsel to monitor the investigation and keep apprised of developments. Greg's family engaged the services of Gullekson, Thompson & Daniels, a firm recommended by a friend who happened to be a lawyer.

As details unfolded, it was discovered that the perpetrator left a bite mark on the body. This bite mark would become the critical piece of evidence in the prosecution's case.

A few months after the homicide, police asked Greg's permission to make an impression of his teeth. Following advice of counsel, Greg refused to submit to the process voluntarily. Subsequently, he was subpoenaed to have his teeth examined.

From Summer 1985 through the following January, Greg had no contact with authorities. In January that would change. Police arrived at Greg's house with a warrant for his arrest. He was booked and charged with first-degree murder. Until this devastating turn of events, Greg worked full-time as a journeyman ironworker. With assistance from family members, he'd been taking care of his little daughters. He spent three days in the Osage County jail before being released on a $50,000 bond.

Shortly after Greg's arrest, he and his parents met with attorneys Pat Thompson and Larry Gullekson. The family was informed the fee for representing Greg would be $25,000. The Preliminary Hearing was held in July of 1986. Greg was bound over for trial on July 16. For more than a year, Thompson and Gullekson told Greg's family they'd been informed by the Osage County District Attorney that Greg's files were open for counsels' inspection and that they could access all evidence in the prosecution's possession. The lawyers told the family they were going to have Greg examined by a psychologist, they were going to hire a private investigator, and they would find a dentist who could testify as an expert for the defense. The attorneys told Greg's parents they were going to Oklahoma City to review the forensic dental evidence that was the basis of the first-degree murder charge.

Greg continued working until early in the summer of 1986. The stress of being charged with murdering his wife began to wear on him. Bouts of anxiety were turning him into a nervous wreck. He was seeing a psychiatrist regularly. A couple of times, Greg was hospitalized for depression. Although his wife had been murdered a year earlier, Greg was still out on bond.

When Kathy was alive, she stayed home with their daughters while Greg went to work. After Kathy's murder, Greg took care of his girls for eighteen months. "I didn't have much experience changing diapers. I learned really quick."[4]

Came the fall and Greg realized he could no longer provide for his kids. He could barely tend his own needs. Since his parents worked full-time and were deeply involved in his case, Greg decided his girls would be better off with someone outside the family. Through church, Greg found a family willing to take his children while allowing Greg and his parents to play an active role in the girls' lives. "Everything considered, it worked out good," says Greg.[5]

The new family was to provide a foster home until Greg's legal woes were resolved. In October 1986, Greg sent his daughters to live with their new foster family. This was "the hardest decision I ever had to make," said Greg.[6]

When he reflects on what he missed most in prison, there is no hesitation. His relationship with his daughters meant everything to him. Not getting to watch them grow up was his biggest loss.

During five years in prison, Greg didn't see his daughters once. He explains, "I wasn't going to let them have a memory of visiting Daddy on death row."[7] The girls were told their dad was in the Navy. Contact with the girls was via phone and mail. Even though inmates were permitted visitors a couple of times a week, since his parents were a three-hour drive from McAlester, they only made it every other week.

On January 29, 1987, the hammer came down. The State of Oklahoma filed its Notice of Intent to Ask the Death Penalty. Greg believed the prosecution's strategy in seeking a death sentence was to intimidate him into plea bargaining. Greg does not scare easily. He did, though, grow despondent.

On January 31, the family met with Thompson and Gulleckson again. The lawyers said they had not yet traveled to Oklahoma City to meet with the State's forensic dentist, Dr. Glass. The legal team said they were going to go the following week and look at the work Dr. Glass had done on the case. The family again was told of the attorneys' intentions to have Greg examined by a psychologist, to hire an investigator, and to locate a dentist to review bite mark evidence. Greg's parents assured counsel they supported these plans and were willing to pay necessary expenses. In a pleading filed in the appeal of Greg's murder conviction, however, the Osage County District Attorney said Pat Thompson told him "that appellant and his parents would not or were having difficulty obtaining funds to engage the services of an expert on bite mark identification."[8]

At the January 31 meeting, Greg and his family expressed concern that in the 18 months since taking the case, his attorney had done little. It appeared to the Wilhoits that the defense hadn't gotten off square one.

In February, the family was introduced to a private investigator, Woody Gates, who showed great interest in Greg's case. Mr. and Mrs. Wilhoit told Woody they wouldn't hire him without the approval of attorney Thompson. The private investigator understood and said he would call the lawyer and give him references. Woody seemed confident he could work with the legal team. In addition to having Mr. Gates do investigative work and interview witnesses, the family wanted him to accompany counsel to Oklahoma City when they visited the forensic dentist.

Following the family's interaction with the investigator, however, Thompson told Gates his services would not be needed. Woody reported to the family that he couldn't get Thompson to return a phone call. This prompted Greg to refer to his attorney as "an arrogant cuss."[9]

On March 17, 1987, an order was entered setting Greg's trial for May 5. On March 18, cocounsel Thompson and Gullekson finally went to Oklahoma City to meet with Dr. Glass. They reviewed the state's forensic dental evidence. Upon Thompson's return, he called Greg's mother, Ida Mae. Mrs. Wilhoit asked the attorney what he'd done about finding a dentist to testify for the defense. He admitted he hadn't even tried, as he thought another dentist would arrive at similar conclusions.

A week later, Greg's parents again met with Thompson. They had lost faith in their chosen counsel. A few days prior, Thompson visited Greg to discuss a plea bargain. Lack of confidence was becoming mutual. The attorney insisted the State's bite mark expert was its "smoking gun," even as Greg maintained Oklahoma had the wrong guy. Thompson's advice was to "cop a plea." He asked Greg if he'd plead guilty if Thompson arranged a ten-year sentence.

That's it. That's the best the expensive legal talent could do. After handling the case for a year and a half, all the attorneys could do was try to convince Greg to plead guilty in exchange for a good offer from the prosecutor. These lawyers "didn't grasp the concept that if you're not guilty, you don't plead guilty."[10]

After this conversation, Greg spoke with his parents. He told them he had informed his lawyer he was not willing to plead guilty to something he didn't do, even if the state offered probation. Weighing on Greg's mind was that someday he would have to face his daughters. He wanted no part of confessing to killing their mother.

Thompson's visit came after he had "sworn" several times he would come and speak with Greg at length—but never showed. Once, Thompson phoned the jail to give Greg the message he would be there the next day. But again he was a "no-show." Not keeping his word was one matter Greg's parents brought up with Thompson. He responded, "If I ever do that again, you can kick my ass."[11]

In the lawyer's office on March 24, Thompson told Mr. and Mrs. Wilhoit that he still had not reviewed the prosecutor's files. He intended to do so in the next few weeks. Thompson said he planned to examine any exculpatory evidence that might get Greg off the hook. Mr. Wilhoit replied he wasn't aware such evidence existed. Thompson retorted, "The police think they know who she had sex with."[12]

The law firm of Gullekson, Thompson & Daniels, by now, had the case for twenty months. Greg had been charged with first-degree murder in January 1986 and on March 24, 1987, six weeks before trial, neither Thompson nor Gullekson had seen the State's files or the exculpatory evidence. Not a single witness had been interviewed. Not only had an investigator not been retained, but the services of one whom the family found were refused. No effort had been extended to secure a forensic odontologist. Greg had not been examined by a psychologist. Thompson failed to confer with his client after promising several times to do so. The only things Gullekson and Thompson had done were file a few motions, make a few trips to Pawhuska for some hearings, and travel to Oklahoma City to see Dr. Glass.

After confronting their son's lawyer, Mr. and Mrs. Wilhoit met with Greg to map strategy. They agreed that Gullekson, Thompson and company were inadequate. Numerous failures to maintain communication, to obtain a dentist to testify as an expert, and to make meaningful preparation for trial, caused the Wilhoits to request the withdrawal of Gullekson, Thompson & Daniels as attorneys of record. This action became effective on April 20, 1987.

The family had to get someone else to represent Greg. An attorney was recommended from Pawhuska, the county seat of Osage County and site of the trial. Greg's family contacted George Briggs. Briggs had been a respected defense lawyer with a reputation for the skillful handling of high-profile cases. Briggs was known as an advocate who served the best interests of his clients while plying his unique style.

Briggs visited the Wilhoit family home to discuss Greg's case. The family told Briggs they wanted to use Woody Gates as an investigator and have him interview prospective witnesses. Briggs agreed to contact Gates and have him obtain statements from prospective witnesses. Briggs added that he would talk with each witness himself, as well. He acknowledged how important it was to keep the client informed and he assured the Wilhoits he would do that. After this meeting, mother, father and son agreed that George Briggs would be hired to defend Greg at trial.

So, two weeks prior to litigating the case, responsibility for representing Greg was transferred to George Briggs. At the hearing held to permit Gullekson, Thompson & Daniels to withdraw and Mr. Briggs to become attorney of record, Larry Stuart, the Osage County prosecutor, asked Briggs if he would be seeking a continuance to prepare for trial. Despite investigator Gates' request of Briggs to file for continuance, Briggs insisted that was not necessary and replied to the prosecutor he would not ask for one.

Reflecting on those times, Greg characterizes his outlook, as well as his parents', as "so naïve. We didn't have a clue about how these things worked. We basically buried our heads in the sand and put all our faith in George." Greg adds, "This would prove to be an almost fatal error."[13]

Perhaps the Wilhoits should have been suspicious when Briggs agreed to take a capital murder trial for a $2,500 retainer, a tenth of the fee of the previous legal team. Unfortunately for Greg, by Spring 1987, George Briggs had become an alcoholic. He mixed drink with prescription drugs. He suffered from brain damage as a result of a 1986 accident in which he slipped on ice. Although unbeknownst to Greg's family, Briggs' physical and mental maladies were matters of which his fellow Osage County attorneys and the Oklahoma Bar Association were aware.

The Wilhoits had been told by Greg's first attorney that it was imperative to have an expert witness assess and refute the testimony of the State's dental experts. The family was told it would be difficult to find such an expert. Investigator Gates located Dr. Thomas Krauss, considered one of the country's foremost bite mark identification experts. Dr. Krauss was a practicing dentist in Philipsburg, Kansas. Even though he knew nothing of Greg's case, Krauss was willing to scramble to Tulsa immediately. He was willing to examine the bite mark and offer an opinion as to whether it matched Greg's. He needed time to conduct a thorough inspection. When advised of this, Briggs still refused to seek a continuance.

From the first discussions with Briggs, six weeks prior to trial, until the weekend before opening arguments, Greg's parents phoned the attorney twenty-seven times. They wound up having only three or four conversations. The other times the Wilhoits called, Briggs was not available. The family left word with Briggs' secretary to return the calls. He never did. Greg's parents told Briggs about Dr. Krauss, a forensic odontologist that Woody Gates had contacted who was willing to examine the bite mark and testify for the defense. The family asked Briggs to call this expert witness, but he never did. The lawyer never contacted Gates as promised. He did not venture to Oklahoma City to look at the State's forensic evidence as he promised. The family learned at trial that Briggs never saw any of the evidence even though it was available. The family also discovered that Briggs failed to keep an appointment in Tulsa with the Osage County prosecutor to go over the State's evidence. His excuse was that a fan belt on his car had broken.

On Thursday, April 30, Mrs. Wilhoit called Briggs and asked if he was really planning to go to trial the following Tuesday. He said that was between him and his client. Briggs had seen Greg twice, and only briefly. He did not see Greg again until they met in the courtroom before proceedings commenced. When Greg was brought into the courtroom, he could be heard asking his lawyer, "Are you really ready to go to trial?"[14] Briggs, responding calmly, told Greg not to worry.

The few times Guy Wilhoit spoke with Briggs, he begged him to see his son. Briggs promised he would, but never did. Prior to trial, Greg was held in the Osage County jail, not five minutes from Briggs' office. But he never did go to visit his client. During trial Greg pointed out errors and inconsistencies in witnesses' testimony. Briggs ignored him.

On Friday, May 1, four days before the trial was to proceed, Greg's father gave up on Briggs' returning phone calls. So he drove to Pawhuska and waited in the lawyer's office until he arrived. Mr. Wilhoit pleaded with him to seek a continuance. Briggs was determined to try the case as scheduled. He told Mr. Wilhoit that, more important, Greg needed to shave his beard and get a haircut. The shaggy look would not sit well with the people of Osage County. It would prejudice the jury against his client. The lawyer told Mr. Wilhoit to leave $20 at the Osage County jail to cover the grooming costs. Briggs said he would see to it that Greg got spruced up the next day. Again, Briggs failed to follow through. As a result, Greg appeared at trial with long hair and a scraggly beard.

May 5, 1987, and the first-degree murder trial of Gregory Ralph Wilhoit begins. Briggs had not looked at the State's evidence nor spoken with witnesses. He had not even talked with Dr. Krauss, the expert witness investigator Gates had located. It shouldn't have been surprising, with such blatant lack of preparation, that Briggs opted to make no opening statement. He said he would reserve it till later. He wound up never offering one at all.

During the proceeding's second day it became apparent to Greg, his family, and lawyer how weak the State's case was. Prosecution was putting enormous weight on the bite mark identification.

None of the physical evidence matched Greg, with the exception that someone with Greg's blood type had sex with Kathy within 48 hours of her death. (At the time, DNA analysis was not available.) None of Greg's hairs or fingerprints were discovered at the scene. There were no eyewitnesses who observed anyone entering or leaving Kathy's apartment the night of the murder. There were, however, two pieces of evidence recovered from the scene that matched neither Kathy nor Greg. Found in a pool of blood beside Kathy's body was a pubic hair. There was a fingerprint found on the telephone that the killer had ripped from the wall and placed next to the victim. These two pieces of evidence remain unidentified.

Sometime during the first day of trial, Greg's mother called Dr. Krauss and asked if he would initiate contact with George Briggs. The dentist said he would. Dr. Krauss phoned Briggs the evening of May 7 but the conversation did not go well. Krauss had a hard time understanding Briggs as the attorney kept slurring his speech. Krauss speculated that Briggs was either drunk or had a speech impediment.

Dr. Krauss informed the Wilhoits that since he had not been able to see any of the evidence, he would not take the stand to testify. He said he would be willing to go to Pawhuska the weekend of May 9 to "educate" attorney Briggs on what questions to ask on cross-examination of the State's forensic dentists. Greg's parents discussed this with his lawyer. Briggs agreed to have Dr. Krauss come to Pawhuska. The family met with the attorney and the doctor at Briggs' office that Saturday afternoon. Dr. Krauss stayed in Pawhuska until Sunday evening going over the technical language with Mr. Briggs. Krauss offered to attend the trial as an advisor to Briggs during the testimony of the dentists. Briggs declined.

On Wednesday, May 13, following a lunch break, trial was to resume at 2:00. Mr. and Mrs. Wilhoit were in Pawhuska at noon because they wanted to give Mr. Briggs some information. The Wilhoits ate lunch with Briggs at a restaurant in Pawhuska. Greg's parents observed Briggs drink two bottles of beer with his meal. This was consistent with the amount of beer they saw him drink with lunch earlier in the week.

Several days into the trial, when Briggs returned from lunch, it became obvious he had been drinking. Greg expressed concern to his mother. He asked her if she thought he should say something to the judge. Because of their inexperience in these matters, Mrs. Wilhoit discouraged Greg from doing so. The witnesses who were seated outside the courtroom told the family later they, too, had noticed that Briggs was unsteady and had difficulty getting through the courtroom doors.

On Thursday, May 14, defense witnesses were to take the stand. Mr. Briggs had Greg's father bring the subpoenas to Tulsa, where Woody Gates served them. Six witnesses were friends of Greg's. Gates had interviewed them earlier. But Briggs had never met them. Gates had transcribed his interviews and furnished copies to Briggs. The lawyer asked Mr. Wilhoit to see that these witnesses were at the courthouse an hour before trial. He wanted to use that hour to talk to the witnesses. They arrived at the requested time. Briggs, however, could not be found. He walked past the group in the hallway just before proceedings began. Greg's father told Briggs the witnesses were waiting to talk with him. As he strolled by he said, "I'll see them soon enough."[15]

During examination of defense witnesses, Briggs read questions directly from the transcriptions of interviews Woody Gates had conducted. Gates informed the family later that he never meant for the questions he asked to be the ones used during trial. Briggs had never seen nor spoken with these people until they took the witness stand.

The murder trial continued this way for ten days. As Greg describes it, it "was just a comedy of errors. If it hadn't been a life or death decision for me, I'd have busted out laughing."[16]

At no point prior to or during trial did counsel suggest that either Greg's mother or father testify. The family was not even aware testimony could be offered during the sentencing phase. Such ineptitude on Briggs' part added to the feelings of frustration and helplessness experienced by the Wilhoits. Learning later they could have played more active roles at trial only fed their feelings of guilt.

After the prosecutor offered his closing argument Briggs made a stab at presenting one. The judge then instructed the jury to deliberate and return a verdict. It took the jurors an hour to zero in on their decision. On May 15, 1987, the verdict of guilty was read to the court. Gregory Wilhoit became the only person in the annals of U.S. jurisprudence to be convicted of first-degree murder solely on the basis of a bite mark.[17]

Following a forty-five-minute recess, during which the judge prepared instructions, the jury was asked to reconvene in their secluded quarters.

This time their task was to determine the sentence. Greg Wilhoit's fate lay in their hands.

After the travesty of trial, Greg had an idea of what to expect from the jury. Greg says he "made a conscious decision right then that I would rather be executed than spend the rest of my life in prison for something I didn't do."[18] Greg insisted that no mitigating evidence be submitted during the penalty phase of the proceedings.

The prosecutor explained why Greg deserved to die, why justice would be served if Oklahoma killed the man the jury deemed perpetrator of a capital crime. The State's Attorney then sat down. He had no more evidence to adduce. The judge turned to George Briggs. Might defense counsel now care to issue his opening statement? Briggs politely declined, waiving that strategic procedure.

The jury retreated to deliberate. About an hour passed. Jurors filed back into the courtroom. The foreman announced they had unanimously agreed on Greg Wilhoit's punishment. That punishment should be death.

On June 9, Greg's father drove to Pawhuska to visit his son. He also dropped by to see George Briggs. When Mr. Wilhoit asked the lawyer why he hadn't visited Greg, Briggs claimed he didn't know Greg was still being held in the local jail. Briggs never did see Greg until the two were briefly reunited in the courtroom on June 16, 1987, the day Greg was formally notified by the State that he must die.

About a year and a half after Guy Wilhoit's encounter with George Briggs in Pawhuska, he received a letter from John E. Douglas, Assistant General Counsel to the Oklahoma Bar Association. The message, dated January 9, 1989, acknowledged receipt of Mr. Wilhoit's grievance filed against George Briggs. Apparently Briggs' incompetence was not confined to Greg's case.

According to Mark Barrett, the Public Defender who wound up handling Greg's legal affairs, Briggs had become known as "the town drunk." It didn't enhance his reputation that Barrister Briggs had urinated on himself in court and had vomitted in the chambers of a local judge.[19]

"On September 16, 1988," wrote Douglas, "George Briggs was indefinitely suspended from the practice of law by the Supreme Court of Oklahoma." The letter informed Mr. Wilhoit that his complaint would be "impounded ... until such time as he [Briggs] applies for reinstatement to the practice of law."[20] If that were to occur, Briggs would be asked to respond to the Wilhoits' grievances and the Bar investigation would proceed.

It was small consolation, but at least Briggs wouldn't be lousing up any other defendant's legal chances. The Assistant General Counsel advised Mr. Wilhoit that he may want to consult another attorney concerning postconviction relief for Greg. Although it wasn't stated in the letter from the Oklahoma Bar, the pursuit of Greg's postconviction relief would be on grounds including ineffective assistance of counsel.

Greg was formally sentenced 30 days after trial. He describes this phase as "the most bizarre experience of my life."[21] The judge told Greg that he had been found guilty by a jury of his peers. Now the judge was about to impose sentence. He informed Greg that he was to be executed by lethal injection.

The judge's account of the sequence of possibilities still rings in Greg's ears. "In the event I could not be lethally injected," Greg recalls, "then I would be electrocuted. If for some reason I could not be electrocuted, I would be hung, and if they could not find a rope, I'd be shot." The memory gives Greg pause. "This was a very sobering experience!"[22]

The judge asked if Greg had funds for an appeal. Greg told the Court he was broke. This proved to be a fortunate twist of fate. Now Greg was afforded use of one of the best Appellate Public Defenders' offices in the country.

The history of U.S. jurisprudence was beginning to align itself with Greg's case. The landmark decision of *Gideon* v. *Wainwright*, in 1963, expanded Sixth Amendment protection.[23] Counsel's role was recognized as indispensable to the administration of justice. When a criminal defendant could not afford an attorney, one would be appointed by the court.

During the colonial period, and for decades after, the government followed England's Common Law. British precedent denied counsel to indigents accused of felonies. Those charged with misdemeanors, meanwhile, were appointed counsel who were subject to restrictions. When the Sixth Amendment was drafted, it was limited to guaranteeing absolute right to counsel for those who could afford representation.

The Supreme Court took a hard look at the Sixth Amendment's application to state capital cases in the 1932 appeal of *Powell* v. *Alabama*.[24] The Court determined that if the defendant in this capital conviction could neither afford counsel nor defend himself, the right to counsel was guaranteed by the Due Process Clause of the Fourteenth Amendment. The Court ruled that Powell was entitled a court-appointed attorney. In that matter the Justices limited their decision to the case in question and made no mention of extending the principle to appoint counsel to all indigent defendants.

Six years after rendering its opinion in *Powell*, the Court was confronted again with the provision of effective, free counsel to poor defendants. In *Johnson* v. *Zerbst*, Justice Black wrote that a person accused of a federal crime is entitled to counsel based on the Sixth Amendment.[25] The 1942 *Betts* v. *Brady* case clarified this right, emphasizing its federal nature.[26] The decision, cloaked in the defense of states rights, determined that indigents charged with state offenses were not entitled the right of counsel. Justice Black dissented. He believed the Sixth Amendment applied to the States as well. He was of the mind that denying a defendant the right to counsel in a capital case was deplorable to the judicial system and violated the country's democratic belief of equal justice for all.[27]

During the next twenty years, the rights of indigent defendants in the federal system were protected by appointment of counsel. Those same rights of poor people in state courts were not necessarily safeguarded.

In 1961, Clarence Earl Gideon was arrested and charged with breaking and entering into a Panama City, Florida, pool hall with intent to commit a misdemeanor. This criminal proceeding was initiated in state court. Judge Robert McCray, Jr., presided over the case in the Circuit Court of Florida's Fourteenth Judicial Circuit. Proceedings commenced on August 4, 1961.

Gideon was not a man of means. He was unable to hire an attorney. He asked the judge to appoint a lawyer for him. The court denied his request. Judge McCray ruled state courts could only appoint counsel to defendants if the individuals were charged with capital crimes. Gideon was forced to represent himself.

Untrained in the law, Gideon lost his case. The Judge sentenced him to five years in prison. While incarcerated, Gideon engaged in some jailhouse lawyering. He filed a handwritten motion with the Supreme Court. Gideon asked the Justices to issue a writ of certiorari to Florida's Supreme Court ordering his conviction overturned because he was not given a fair trial nor granted counsel.

The Court heard Gideon's case in 1962 and appointed Abe Fortas counsel. Fortas, a well-known Washington lawyer, later would serve briefly on the Supreme Court. A few months after hearing arguments, the Court ruled on the case. On March 18, 1963, Justice Black read the decision. Black explained that defendants in State and Federal courts who cannot afford counsel would be denied a fair trial unless courts provide legal representation.

Gideon's determination to prove his right to a fair trial and the necessity of court-appointed counsel to ensure this right were the driving forces behind changing the U.S. court system to be inclusive of these rights for all indigent criminal defendants.[28] The Justices have determined that court-appointed attorneys must provide "effective aid in the preparation and trial of the case."[29]

In July 1987, Greg was taken to the Oklahoma State Penitentiary in McAlester. He spent the next four years on death row. Having never been in prison, Greg braced himself for whatever lay ahead, though he hadn't a clue what survival in the penitentiary meant. Shackled at the hands and feet, with a belly chain connecting the two, Greg was ushered into a giant rotunda of tiered cells four levels high. He was led down a flight of stairs and introduced to the place he would call home for several years to come.

At the top of the entrance was a large sign. Letters two feet high spelled the cold reality, "DEATH ROW." Greg had enjoyed prison movies. Hollywood gave him preconceived notions about death row. The prisoners and guards must have watched the same movies. The characters were well typecast and acted their parts perfectly. The experience couldn't be more authentic.

Ahead of Greg lay a long, dark hallway lined with bleak cells. Just as in the movies, a hand holding a mirror protruded from each cell. Greg was escorted past these cells to the hooting of fellow death row inmates. He was delivered to the end of the corridor, to Cell #13.

While imprisoned, Greg felt physically drained. Fighting to make his voice heard, to convince others to listen to what happened, left him emotionally spent as well. Greg describes the sensation as "screaming in the dark, [with] no one to listen."[30]

Greg came to appreciate death row as "the great equalizer." He observed that "Rich or poor, innocent or guilty, black or white—it doesn't matter. Once you hit the row, you better not be putting on airs. You are just like everybody else."[31]

An avid reader, Greg spent much time with his head buried in books or newspapers. One of the roles played by death row prisoners was that of runner—a sort of puppy dog for the guards—who would bring other inmates books and ice. Many of the men vied for that position. Not Greg. He preferred to be in his cell. He retreated in it and emerged only when necessary.

Greg says that for his entire prison term he was in denial. "I think it was the survival instinct," he explains. He covered the bars with newspapers and would leave only a six-inch hole so the guards could peak in on him. Greg would "watch my TV and read and pretend I was somewhere else."

He noted, "No matter how hard I tried, I couldn't wrap my mind around the reality that I was on death row for the murder of my wife. It was too abstract a concept." With newspapers covering the bars, Greg wouldn't see what was going on outside his cell. "I would stay inside my little pretend world."[32]

To pass time and preserve his sanity, Greg would write. Referring to his predicament in the third person, he mused, "This probably sounds like the plot of a bad movie. Be assured, this is a harsh reality that has confronted Gregory Wilhoit every waking hour for the last four years. He is imprisoned deep within the bowels of the Oklahoma State Penitentiary on 'Death Row' which, steeped in the finest traditions of 'Death Rows,' is at best a hostile non-nurturing environment and at worst will kill you."

The prison-scribe offered this insight. "Gregory Wilhoit thus far has been able to survive in this environment for one reason—he has hope that the truth will set him free and that justice will prevail."[33]

Greg's hope, his truth and justice, lay in forensic odontology, the science of identifying bite marks. The use of this technique had been instrumental in obtaining convictions in some of the most famous cases in the history of criminology. Among those apprehended with the help of accurate bite mark identification were serial killer Ted Bundy, and California's Hillside Strangler, Freeway Strangler, and Night Stalker.

Although odontology can be integral to homicide investigation, and lead to successful prosecution, it is imperative that the consulting odontologist adhere to a strict code of ethics and standards developed by the American Board of Forensic Odontology. This maintains the integrity of the evidence and safeguards accurate interpretation. If one deviates from the guidelines and misrepresents abilities to assess a bite mark, a miscarriage of justice may result. The inexperience of the state's expert against Greg contributed to his wrongful conviction.

The force fueling Greg's hope was Appellate Public Defender Mark Barrett. The two met after Greg arrived at the penitentiary. Little did Greg know that he and Barrett would forge a strong friendship.

It is worth revisiting a bit of criminal justice history, without which the bond between Barrett and his client never could have developed. In 1964, Congress drafted the Criminal Justice Act, which led to the creation of the Federal Public Defender System. This system administers the court-appointed federal representation of indigent criminal defendants. State Bar Associations collaborated with their respective jurisdictions to create individual state-run public defender services. *Gideon* has yet to be completely implemented and applied uniformly to all poor defendants. Efforts to expand Public Defender Offices to more jurisdictions have been stymied by legislatures who skimp on resources and cut back funding.

Defendants may be appointed attorneys, but sometimes those lawyers lack experience or expertise. Low salaries and oppressive caseloads drive quality public defenders out of the system. Many state budgets do not allot sufficient funds to run an effective program.

New York State is one of the jurisdictions that has created a strong Public Defender Backup Center System. This has enabled the Empire State to provide supportive services to public defenders, such as drafting and filing amicus briefs, educating communities about the importance of public defender services, consulting with lawyers during litigation, and administering training courses for attorneys.

New York's Bar Association was founded four years after *Gideon*, and strives to improve the Public Defender services in the state. It is a model for other jurisdictions.[34]

Knowing there was no physical proof (hairs, fingerprints, fibers, fluids, etc.) or eyewitness testimony against his client, attorney Barrett focused on the single piece of evidence used to convict Greg. Barrett gathered names of respected forensic odontologists. He had a list of eleven such experts. Many of these scientists testified exclusively for the prosecution in the past. Some had experience in the most celebrated bite mark cases.

The American Board of Forensic Odontologists (ABFO) is the field's governing body. It is the only recognized organization that certifies forensic odontologists. The requirements for acceptance are stringent. Only after passing a rigorous written exam is one considered board certified.

The odontologists whom Barrett involved in Greg's case were not only board certified, several were members of AFBO's Credentialing Committee. Others served as officers of the ABFO.

All of these experts determined, independently, that Greg's teeth did not match the bite mark found on the victim. These experts had been given copies of the evidence by Dr. Krauss. He had concluded that "Mr. Wilhoit's teeth are drastically different from the bite mark found on the homicide victim, thereby eliminating him as the perpetrator of the bite mark."[35] Krauss, who had been hired by Greg's family as the primary bite mark expert to analyze case evidence, was President of the AFBO.

Krauss's fellow experts arrived at their conclusions after analyzing the evidence, which included casts, molds, and photographs of the bite marks identical to those the State's dentists used. These were compared with casts, molds, and photographs of Greg's teeth.

These experts researched the evidence independently from each other and from Dr. Krauss. The odontologists were not told whether Krauss was working for the prosecution or the defense. All the odontologists were aware that in the past Krauss had worked on cases for both.

All the experts concluded that the bite mark did not match Greg's teeth, without Dr. Krauss guiding them in their analyses or without his expressing opinion concerning his own interpretation of the evidence. Every effort was made to ensure the neutrality and objectivity of the experts' findings.

That eleven recognized experts disagree with the prosecution's dentists regarding the only significant grounds on which a conviction was based is startling. More remarkable is the fact that the discrepancies between Greg's identification and the actual bite mark are numerous and noticeable.

Neither Dr. Keith Montgomery nor Dr. Richard Glass, the State's bite mark experts, were board certified. Dr. Montgomery was the primary bite mark authority for the prosecution. When he got involved in the case, he had been out of dental school less than a year. He has since testified under oath that the Wilhoit case was the first in which he'd testified as a bite mark expert. He also stated that in the years since the Wilhoit case, he has not offered testimony in another bite mark matter.

In addition to the impressive case built by the cumulative analyses of the bite mark experts, there were other strong indicators of Greg's innocence. That a pubic hair found in a pool of blood next to the victim's body matched neither Greg nor Kathy could be considered exculpatory evidence. An identifiable fingerprint left on the telephone found next to the victim matched neither Greg nor Kathy. At trial, the State's fingerprint expert testified that a red substance on the phone appeared to be blood. Despite efforts to collect evidence, none of the hairs nor fingerprints lifted from the crime scene matched Greg's.

As Greg settled into his new life on death row, the task of weaving the various strands of innocence into a strong tapestry was left to appellate counsel Mark Barrett. It was too much for Greg to think he might one day be free.

In his first six months in prison, Greg kept to himself. Although inmates were allowed to go to the yard for an hour a day, five days a week, the time allotment shrunk in half after accounting for the time it took to shackle and unshackle prisoners. Groups of ten to twelve men would go out to the yard. Each person had to sign a waiver that, in Greg's words, signified "you're okay going out in the yard with these other guys, in the event you get killed."[36]

Greg didn't venture out of his cell much at first because he was scared. Gradually, curiosity drew him into the yard. When Greg arrived at prison, inmates were allowed to exercise with free weights. It wasn't long before men started beating each other with the weights. So this privilege was removed. The same thing happened when free weights were replaced with stationary weights.

"Eventually," says Greg, "you went outside and looked at the sky."[37] Greg spent most of his yard time playing cards. With just half an hour to be outside, there was barely enough time to deal a good round.

Early in his confinement, Greg suffered culture shock. Denial of his situation dictated self-imposed isolation. His loss of freedom was too abstract for him to comprehend. When he would awaken some mornings, he'd look around at his surroundings and burst out laughing. The scene was just too unreal.

Sleep became Greg's only escape. He would log twelve to fourteen hours of sleep a day. Greg evolved the philosophy that as long as he was asleep he wasn't doing time. The more he slept, the less time he did.

Next to relationships with loved ones, what Greg missed most was decent food. "I was starving for five years."[38] Although inmates were fed three times a day, the food was horrible. Like the old punch line, not only was the food bad, but worse, the portions were so small.

Because those on death row were the last to be fed, what was supposed to be hot was always cold. Greg says he didn't get a hot meal the entire time he was at McAlester. The food would be cooked elsewhere and brought in on a cart. "While other guys would have pictures of pinups and stuff," Greg joked, "I would have pinned up on my wall pictures of Christmas dinners and turkey dinners."[39]

Greg could speak only with those people placed directly across from him and those adjacent to that cell. Those were the only inmates Greg could see. Thus was the restrictive nature of the architecture.

A year after Greg's arrival in cellblock F, he got a new neighbor. Ron Williamson was placed in the cell directly across from Greg's. Williamson too found it hard to believe he was living among killers. "I've never been so miserable in my life," he would tell reporters.[40]

Like most death row inmates, Wilhoit and Williamson maintained their innocence. Their determination to prove it forged an unusual bond, a powerful force in their drive toward exoneration.

Williamson also had been convicted of a brutal murder. Once a star baseball player, Ron's career ended in injury. He was a promising enough player that he'd been drafted by the Oakland A's.

His path to the penitentiary started in 1982, when Debra Carter, a 22-year-old waitress, was found raped and strangled in her apartment in Ada, Oklahoma. Williamson, a loner, with mental problems and a police record, became the target of the authorities' investigation. Five years following the crime, Ron and a codefendant were convicted. Williamson found himself in McAlester's prison by 1988.

When he first landed on cellblock F, Williamson kept to himself. The threat of violence was constant. Ron and Greg began to chit-chat. From those talks, the fear and suspicion central to prison life gradually lifted.

Their friendship had evolved to the point where they were comfortable enough with each other to go into the yard together. Although their friendship started when they were placed in cells directly across from each other, they were not always so situated. When they were moved around they were forced to seek each other during yard visits.

During their early conversations, Greg and Ron discovered they had a few things in common. Greg mentioned he had been an ironworker for thirteen years. Ron had had three roommates over the years who also were ironworkers. From the initial exchange of small talk, their friendship blossomed. They learned that they shared other similarities, such as that each had two sisters and no brothers.

"Plus, [Ron] was a genuinely decent sort. You don't see that many," observed Greg.[41]

The trust and bond between the two men grew stronger. They hid nothing from each other.

Although Greg became friends with a number of others on death row, Ron was the only one who convinced Greg of his innocence. Greg describes himself as a "really hard sell." Greg pored over Ron's case transcript, all 5,000 pages, and concluded that Ron "had gotten the screws put to him."[42]

As Greg was determining that his friend was being railroaded, time was running out for Ron. The executioner's clock was ticking. The gravity of Ron's situation reached the point where his sister had received a letter from the prison explaining procedures to claim his body. When things appeared bleakest, Williamson caught a break. Mark Barrett, the public defender who came to Greg's rescue, pinpointed crucial errors in Ron's conviction.

The Williamson and Wilhoit cases were similar in that both were influenced by bad scientific evidence and by bad lawyering. Both cases benefitted from better scientific evidence.

For Williamson, stray hairs were the centerpiece of the state's case. Twelve years earlier, a few strands of hair found on the victim had been linked to Williamson and his codefendant by the way they looked under a microscope. But in 1999, the hairs' DNA was examined and Barrett and cocounsel

Barry Scheck proved their clients innocent. With Greg Wilhoit present in the courtroom, Williamson was finally told he was free. He had endured more than a decade behind bars.

When Greg contemplates what friendship meant to him while on death row, he says that having a friend gave him "peace of mind. I wasn't alone." The idea that "someone cares about you" was comforting during the difficulties of confinement.[43] It was encouraging that at least one person was interested in being helpful. It never proved necessary for Greg or Ron to cover for the other physically. Nonetheless, it was good to know they each had someone to "vouch" for the other emotionally and psychologically.

Greg and Ron were still going strong as friends up until Ron's death in 2004. Their relationship was one propelled by adverse forces outside their control. "We went through some extraordinary circumstances and somehow came out on the other end. We were just players in the scheme of things," Greg notes. Even when Greg won his release and Ron was still imprisoned, their friendship grew. Greg couldn't imagine anything coming in the way of that. He considered Ron his best friend.[44]

The former prison pals warmly reunited when both were on the outside. Even though both suffered through years of injustice, they were overwhelmingly thankful—for their friendship and for life. After revisiting McAlester with Williamson and a national news crew, Greg summed up his sentiments. "It's a good feeling to know I can leave whenever I want ."[45] Greg was equally grateful he could leave with his buddy Ron.

Greg tried to persuade Ron to move from Oklahoma to California. Greg believed only heartache happened in Oklahoma. He was suspicious that Ron's sister, his court-appointed sponsor, wanted to keep him there so she could spend his money. Greg considered Ron's sister "no fun." He laughs as he says, "We'd been around her a bunch of times and she was a wet blanket. She knew he'd never come back if he came out [to California]." Greg thought Ron needed to "divest himself of bad memories and start over."[46]

Ron received substantial compensation, which he thought would cure what ailed him. In some ways the money made life worse. Ron's relatives all wanted some of his wealth. Greg believes Ron was "bummed out," disappointed that money did not solve his woes. In Greg's estimation, Ron deserved even more compensation for the twelve years he endured death row.

Attorney Barrett remained active in Ron's life, running interference between Ron and his sister. Barrett also stays involved in Greg's life.

Greg had invited Ron to join him in the abolitionist movement. Ron wasn't interested. He had gone on stage with Greg a few times. He did fine as long as Greg prompted him.

After a while on death row and before solidifying his friendship with Williamson, curiosity got the better of Greg. He took a chance and wandered out to the yard. At this point, he still hadn't made the acquaintance of any of the fellows on death row. Greg figured it might be interesting to interact with his colleagues. What an understatement. The first two inmates he met on the yard were Roger Dale Stafford and Chuck Coleman, cellmates who, between them, were serving thirteen death sentences.

Stafford and Coleman turned out to be "two of the most solid, stand-up convicts" Greg would meet. Greg, recalling his first encounter with the two, said, "They just walked up to me, stuck out their hands, introduced themselves, and welcomed me to what I was sure would be the last home I would ever know." Though these two "committed some of the most horrific crimes to ever stain the State of Oklahoma," within the prison and given the circumstances in which they were thrust, Greg considered them friends. Greg recognizes that although they did some horrible things, they still seemed like "regular guys." Greg found them no different from a lot of inmates. They responded well to a highly structured environment. Incarceration seemed to agree with them.[47]

Greg's opinion was that most of the men he met would have been candidates for a very different sentence—Life in Prison Without Parole. Ironically, at that point in his life, Greg was not so charitable.

For Wilhoit's first three years in prison, he maintained his strong support of capital punishment. The ultimate offense required the ultimate sanction. Just because he was "on the business end of a death sentence" didn't mean he was going to change his tune. Greg was not about to compromise convictions.

Nor did he mind sharing his views with death row inmates. To say they didn't appreciate his perspective was putting it mildly. Greg would candidly chat with the likes of Stafford and Coleman. His death penalty position would trigger a heated discussion. The lines of the debate were clearly drawn; all of death row on one side, Greg on the other.

Greg would comment, "You can't behave the way you have and not expect to pay the price. Are you nuts?" Greg's notions were none too popular.[48]

Greg's outspoken nature and stance on "crime and punishment" dug him a deep hole as far other inmates were concerned. It was not enough to cause anyone to want to harm him. There was an odd tolerance for minority viewpoints.

The volume of Greg's TV was another matter. Overly loud personal entertainment provoked animosity. Death row society was layered among several factions constantly jockeying for power. Leaders of these groups thought they ran the row. The leader of one such group took exception to Greg's late night TV viewing. He claimed the TV kept him awake. That's all it took for some inmates to want to have Greg killed. They informed him that if he wanted to live, Greg would have to pay them monthly rent since they owned the row. Greg told them that wasn't going to happen. For the duration of his stay on death row, he looked over his shoulder. Greg had a few friends who would watch his back. The opportunity to kill Greg never arose. These are the niceties with which one concerns himself while biding time on death row.

Public Defender Mark Barrett and Greg hit it off. Greg let himself believe his persuasive skills won over Barrett. Although he wanted to believe it was his charm that convinced his attorney Oklahoma had the wrong guy, he knew it was the facts and evidence that influenced Barrett. Greg enjoyed thinking he was different than everyone else on death row. He hoped his lawyer could detect the difference. Greg knew deep down that as professional protocol, Barrett had to take anyone's claim of innocence with a grain of salt. In Barrett's initial assessment, Greg was no different than any other inmate. Soon, though, Greg and his attorney built an argument for wrongful conviction. The facts of Greg's case spoke for themselves. The pieces to Greg's puzzle fell perfectly into place.

During their first conversation, Greg made it clear that if his appeal was unsuccessful, he did not want Barrett pursuing other legal remedies. Greg believed it better to let the state execute him. He felt confident about his afterlife. Besides, he had better things to do than rot on death row for years. Compared to the alternative, it was the death penalty that he wanted. There was no way he was going to spend the rest of his life behind bars for something he didn't do.

"I wasn't scared to die," says Greg. He wasn't aware that people actually got off death row. So it never dawned on him that his release was possible. "I wanted to end my anguish as quickly as I could."[49]

Fortunately for Greg, Barrett took his client seriously. Barrett told his team of lawyers and investigators they had one shot and they better get it right the first time. They did.

Greg and the defense team started at square one—destroying the credibility of the state's bite mark experts. That was the easy part. At trial, Dr. Krauss, bite mark expert from Kansas, was the sitting President of the American Board of Forensic Odontologists. That his credentials were unsurpassed made Krauss's credibility impeccable.

Barrett came to Greg's cell and asked if he was sure he wanted Dr. Krauss to evaluate the bite mark. Barrett informed Greg that the case could blow up in his face if Krauss discovered that Greg's bite mark matched that on Kathy's body. Barrett told his client that such an outcome would leave the appeal dead in the water. Greg assured his lawyer that whoever's bite mark that was, it wasn't Greg's.

Dr. Krauss, with corroboration of eleven well-respected experts, backed up Greg's assurances. The forensic odontologists agreed that Greg's teeth were not the match for the mark on Kathy's body.

Things were looking up for Wilhoit. He could sense light at the end of his tunnel. Chuck Coleman would not be so lucky. His death sentences had been affirmed, and he was scheduled to be executed. He was to be the first Oklahoman executed in nearly thirty years. Chuck's anxiety was palpable.

At this point, Greg still supported capital punishment. He didn't think he'd be phased by Chuck Coleman's execution, even though Greg considered Chuck a friend. Greg was dead wrong. Alone in his cell, not far from where Chuck was preparing to die, Greg watched TV. Most of the guards and inmates were doing the same. Television commentators were counting down the minutes until Coleman's execution. When the news reported that Charles Troy Coleman was announced dead at 12:14 A.M., Greg was overcome by grief. Greg had an epiphany. His position concerning capital punishment pirouetted 180 degrees. Reflecting on his moment of enlightenment, Greg refers to it as "practically a religious experience."[50]

"In the Big Picture," Greg believed, "executing Chuck hadn't solved anything. The world was not safer. All it accomplished basically was nothing—except to put the fear of God in everyone else on death row." Reiterating the philosophy of punishment that came to him later in life, "I think life without parole would have been a viable alternative."[51]

Greg believes that it was only by the Grace of God and the skill of his lawyer that he escaped the executioner's needle. In Greg's faith, there is no room for State-sanctioned murder.

At last, in July 1990—three years after Greg landed on death row—the Court of Criminal Appeals remanded the case to the District Court of Osage County to conduct an evidentiary hearing to determine whether a new trial should be ordered. This hearing was held two days in August, three days in October, and resolved on December 10, 1990.

In March 1991, the Osage County Judge submitted his Findings of Fact and Conclusions of Law to the Court of Criminal Appeals. On April 16 of that year the court reversed Greg's sentence and granted him a new trial. In recommending Greg be retried, Osage County District Judge J.R. Pearlman said, "There is a reasonable probability that the result of Mr. Wilhoit's trial would have been different" if Briggs had used the forensic odontologist who was ready to refute the testimony of prosecution experts.[52]

Briggs quit practicing law shortly after botching Greg's case. He said he had no reason—legal or strategic—not to use the odontologist. The witness, along with eleven other forensic experts, testified that the bite mark found on Kathy Wilhoit was not inflicted by her former husband.

While Briggs lamented he had no reason to act as he did, Pearlman had a good idea. Without hesitation, the judge noted that Briggs suffered from habitual use of alcoholic beverages and prescription medications, compounding the brain damage he endured.

"Wilhoit," observed Pearlman, "was represented by a person who, though licensed to practice law, was not capable (and thus) Wilhoit was not really represented."

Some of the Court's other findings:

- "Since defense did not have the bite mark evidence examined by an expert, defense counsel did not exercise reasonable professional judgment. The representation afforded Mr. Wilhoit was not in accord with standards for reasonableness and diligence."
- "Because of evidence, confirmed by an Oklahoma Bar Association finding, that Mr. Briggs' abilities as an attorney were thwarted during the time Mr. Briggs was representing Mr. Wilhoit, Mr. Wilhoit in effect was not represented by counsel in his homicide case."
- "Evidentiary hearing affidavits and testimony established alcoholism, mental illness and brain damage on the part of defense counsel George Briggs."
- "George Briggs was suffering from the habitual use of alcoholic beverages or liquids of alcoholic content in conjunction with prescription drugs to the extent which impaired or tended to impair his ability to conduct properly the affairs undertaken for a client in the practice of law. The Bar Association records establish that this use of intoxicants continued thereafter and caused Mr. Briggs to be unfit to practice law."
- "Although Mr. Briggs was on the roll of attorneys at the time he represented Mr. Wilhoit, he did not meet the requirements to be a member in good standing of the Oklahoma Bar Association."
- "The law is established that when a person is represented by counsel only in theory, but not also in substance, the situation is the equivalent of not being represented by counsel at all."[53]

The point is that without effective assistance of counsel, defendant does not receive a just and fair trial. In capital cases this means that people are in jeopardy of losing their lives. Capital punishment law is so nuanced and complex that the accused deserve highly qualified attorneys.

The annals of U.S. jurisprudence, unfortunately, are replete with cases in which incompetent lawyers let their clients down. To cite a few:

Aden Harrison, Jr., a black man, appointed James Venable, an 83-year-old who had worked with the Ku Klux Klan for years. A judge in Georgia said Venable deserted Harrison and displayed "advanced age, and numerous lapses of judgment." The lawyer later was disbarred.[54]

Judy Haney was appointed an attorney who came to court so intoxicated that he was held in contempt and arrested. This lawyer failed to show Haney's hospital records that depicted the abuse she endured repeatedly from her husband. As that mistreatment was the critical force motivating Haney to murder her husband, counsel failed to establish an important mitigating element behind the crime.[55]

Jack House was represented by counsel who was so inexperienced he never read the death penalty statute. The attorney failed to collect evidence or visit the defendant to gather his account. Also, he left during the testimony of a key prosecution witness. House was sentenced to death. Counsel requested a new trial but failed to tell the judge that "three credible neighbors had surfaced who claimed to have seen the victim after the State's certified time of death."[56]

In these incidents, it is clear state governments were responsible for appointing incompetent counsel.

Gary Nelson is another example of someone assigned a lawyer not up to the challenge. Nelson's attorney was paid $18 an hour. The lawyer had no experience representing capital defendants. He was aware of his limitations to the extent of asking the court to appoint a cocounsel. He also sought funds to hire an investigator. The state rejected both requests, making it difficult for the attorney to defend Nelson's innocence. Nelson was convicted and sentenced to die. He spent eleven years waiting for his execution.

Subsequently, an Atlanta firm picked up his appeal. The firm conducted a thorough investigation. Ultimately, Nelson was released in 1991. Georgia wasted thousands of tax dollars on the initial trial, Nelson's incarceration, and the inmate's successful appeal. Nelson himself wasted eleven years of life rotting on death row.

Had he been appointed an experienced attorney initially, one with sufficient training and resources, perhaps Nelson would have avoided the tragedy that befell him. Without the intervention of skilled lawyers, Nelson most likely would be dead today.[57]

In criminal proceedings in which defendants enjoy the constitutional right to counsel, they also are deemed to deserve effective assistance of counsel. In the early 1980s, a poor man named Strickland was charged with three murders in Washington State. He had confessed to committing burglaries in the past; otherwise he had no prior convictions.

Strickland told the Court he was struggling to support his family and had become destitute. He was appointed counsel. His lawyer, however, did not request a psychiatric evaluation, which prohibited cross-examination of his mental competency. This weighed heavily against Strickland's receiving a fair trail. Ultimately, he was handed a death sentence.

In prison, Strickland filed habeas corpus petition in Federal District Court on grounds of ineffective assistance of counsel. The Federal District Court held an evidentiary hearing. On the basis of the findings, Strickland was denied a new trial. His death sentence was reaffirmed.

On appeal, the District Court's decision was reversed. The Court of Appeals stated that the Sixth Amendment not only provides defendants with the right to counsel, but that counsel must provide effective assistance. As the 1984 *Strickland* v. *Washington* decision was reviewed, it forced the Supreme Court to develop standards for determining whether defense attorneys render effective counsel. The Supreme Court reversed the ruling of the Court of Appeals and held against Strickland. In so doing, the justices laid out guidelines establishing that the right to counsel meant effective counsel.[58]

Despite the Court's fine-tuning during the decades since *Gideon* v. *Wainwright*, its best efforts to safeguard defendants' rights at the state and federal level do not always prevail. At times, defendants in capital cases still lack competent counsel. The predictable consequences are unfair trials.

Columbia University Professor James S. Liebman conducted a study analyzing error rates in 5,760 capital cases. The time frame covered was 1973 to 1995. Out of 2,370 death sentences studied, Liebman found that 90 percent were overturned at the state level. The most prevalent errors, according to the research, resulted from incompetent counsel failing to show evidence of innocence.[59]

In Greg Wilhoit's case, the Osage County District Judge noted:

• "There exists some evidence which indicated that some person other than Gregory Wilhoit may have committed the murder of Kathryn Wilhoit."[60]

A short time later, Greg was released on a $75,000 bond. It would be nearly two years before his second trial.

Greg had a heady decision to make. The Indigent Defense System had recently been established. Greg's was the system's first case. Capital murder convictions were the exclusive focus of the system. Greg's case met the qualifications for the system's jurisdiction. Greg had the luxury of choice. Because of all the media attention his case generated, several attorneys in private practice expressed interest in handling Greg's case on a pro bono basis. Those most interested were seasoned trial lawyers, experienced litigating capital cases. Greg discussed options with his family and with Public Defender Barrett. Greg and his support team spoke with an attorney from Texas and another in Tulsa. Throughout this process, Barrett was kind enough to assist Greg's family with the interviews. Ultimately, the decision as to who would best represent Greg's interests rested with Greg himself.

Greg's instincts tended toward Barrett. Greg didn't forget that it was Barrett who was with him when Greg needed him most. It was Barrett who was responsible for the reversal of Greg's fate. It was Barrett's effort that resulted in a new trial. Barrett was prepared to quit the Appellate Public Defender's Office and go to work for the Indigent Defense System just so he could handle Greg's retrial. However, although Greg's sentiments screamed out for Barrett, he had a slight hesitation. Greg was aware Barrett had never been a trial lawyer. This would be Barrett's initial experience as first-chair attorney in death penalty litigation. After thorough consideration, Greg chose Mark Barrett to represent him. It proved to be a decision Greg wouldn't regret.

Prior to the second trial, the judge ruled the state's bite mark experts could not testify. The judge cited lack of credibility as grounds for denying their testimony.

The prosecution put on its case. It soon became apparent the state's case lacked substance. The prosecution didn't come close to meeting its burden of proof. When the state rested after four days, Barrett asked the judge for a Directed Verdict of Innocence. At that point, the Court adjourned for lunch.

In never occurred to Greg that the judge would grant the motion. This generally doesn't happen in death penalty matters. When Greg and his counsel returned from lunch, the judge was ready to rule on the motion. To Greg's delight, Barrett's request was granted. With the judge's utterance, "Mr. Wilhoit, you are free to go," Greg's nightmare was over.[61] Greg and his loved ones lived this tragedy for eight years.

When Greg reflects on reuniting with his beloved daughters for the first time following his release, he says it was "quite an emotional moment." Greg's mother, appreciating the special nature of the meeting, told the girls she had a surprise for them. "They didn't know what to think at first," says Greg.[62]

Even with emotions running so high, Greg didn't take his girls back when he was released. He felt unfit to raise two young daughters. His mother agreed.

Greg was strongly encouraged to relocate from Oklahoma. He was told it would be best for him and everyone else. Greg moved to California the day after his release. The tough part of the move was leaving behind his entire family, including his two sisters. Nancy is one year older than Greg and has been very helpful. Greg thinks the world of his older sister. He is not as close with his younger sister, Betsy.

Greg has lived in Sacramento since 1993. He chose the California capital because a friend told him he could find him work as an ironworker. Greg had been a union ironworker for many years before going to prison.

Greg is fond of Northern California. His political views are considered mainstream there. "I wasted 38 years out [in Oklahoma]," Greg says. "I felt like a square peg fitting into a round hole." He describes Oklahoma as "nothing but troubles, heartaches."[63]

Greg says that he is really happy in Sacramento. "It would take a case of dynamite to blow me out of California." There is no mistaking Greg's feelings toward the two states in which he's lived when he says, "I would rather live on the streets of California than in the grandest mansion in Oklahoma." Greg even takes it a step further when he refers to Oklahoma as "the worst place in America."[64]

During Greg's first seven years out of prison he didn't do much. He characterizes himself at that time as " a degenerate gambler." However, in 2001, Greg became involved in the abolitionist movement. This has given Greg a sense of purpose, which has made a huge difference in his life. He derives great satisfaction from educating people. Every time Greg speaks publicly, it validates his experience. He feels that his presentations are therapeutic, part of his healing process.

Greg becomes animated when speaking of his experience in the movement, remarking that through his involvement he helps people understand the realities of capital punishment. He appreciates the chance to take part in fun activities, like attending the Death Penalty Focus fundraiser in Beverly Hills where he spoke to a large audience that included movie stars and TV personalities. Through his involvement in the abolitionist movement, Greg has presented awards to Governor George Ryan and former First Lady, Rosalyn Carter. He has known the thrill of receiving a standing ovation from hundreds of celebrities, which he describes as very humbling.

Greg knows his death row experience was a defining moment in his life. Now he embraces the philosophy that "every day is a new day." He never thinks about death row except when he shares his story. He claims to never have had bad dreams about his experience. He attributes the experience's lack of prominence in his mind to the fact that his prison term was surreal, "too abstract" for him to comprehend. He has to convince himself that his experience really happened.

When Greg thinks about the future, he knows money dictates what he'll be able to do. He lives on disability income, which limits travel and other activities. He wishes to continue contributing to the abolitionist movement. He plans to remain in Northern California, where he has made wonderful friends.

His girls are young adults now, in their twenties. They reside in Oklahoma. Owing to his meager wages, Greg can't afford to see them much. He is very close to his older daughter. She is married and has presented Greg with a granddaughter. Greg approves of his elder daughter's spouse, describing him as someone with a strong work ethic.

Greg characterizes his relationship with his younger daughter as not very close. "She doesn't dislike me but we're like strangers passing through the night."[65] She is a bit of a drifter by her father's account. Greg hopes she will find herself soon. He hopes that he will be able to cultivate a better relationship with his younger girl.

Greg has pivoted positions on the death penalty. He had been a lifelong proponent of capital punishment. During his first three years on death row he was an outspoken advocate of executions. He freely spoke his mind, expressing his unpopular opinions in a most hostile environment. As he thinks back on it, his viewpoint was partially propelled by not being saddled with a guilty conscience.

Greg was raised in the church and, like many others, believed in the tenets of his faith. However, he did not place religion as a priority in his life. Greg believes that when everything's going okay in someone's life, that person tends to put faith on a back burner. However, when people get in difficult spots, they either move toward God or turn their backs on Him. "There's not much middle ground on death row." He chose to embrace God.

Greg believes in divine intervention. His religious convictions play an important role in his attitude toward the death penalty. He feels that it is God's decision whether someone should live or die. "It's presumptuous for us to play God. He would take a dim view of us usurping His authority."[66]

While on death row, Greg made the acquaintance of a chaplain who has ministered to prisoners for some time. Greg remains friends with the chaplain and visits him whenever possible. While incarcerated, Greg asked the chaplain to pray the truth would come out and justice would be served. During his time administering to prisoners, the chaplain witnessed nearly 50 executions and counseled numerous death row inmates. Yet, of all the prisoners the chaplain had come to know, Greg Wilhoit and Ron Williamson were the only ones to convince him of their innocence.

Greg thinks many people are on the periphery of involvement. They are on death row by "virtue of circumstances. I'm not saying that some of these guys don't deserve [to die] for their heinous crimes. . . . But if most of us got what we deserved, most of us would be screwed."[67]

Greg now believes the ultimate sanction is strictly punitive. He believes the death penalty is not a deterrent to crime and offers numerous anecdotes to support his contention. "I personally knew over 100 death row inmates, and not one stopped to think before murdering someone, 'Will I get the death penalty or will I only get life in prison?'" Greg's critique of capital punishment includes these observations: "The death penalty is applied with no rhyme or reason and is especially slanted toward the poor and minorities. If you are a person of color or financially embarrassed, you don't have a chance."[68]

As Greg recalls his courtroom experience, he recognizes one of the saddest things about his trial was that the judge and every lawyer in Pawhuska knew George Briggs had a serious drinking problem, and was inebriated during Greg's trial. The Oklahoma Bar officially notified Briggs he was to take no more cases because of alcoholism. In his meager defense, Briggs claimed he never opened his mail. In addition, he was addicted to pain killers and suffered brain damage.

Greg reflects on an old legal adage, "you either want the best lawyer in town or you want the worst." This philosophy held in Greg's case. If he hadn't fired his original attorneys, they would have provided him with marginally acceptable representation. Their defense of Greg would have been just good enough so that he would not have had grounds for claiming ineffective assistance of counsel. Greg would not have received relief from the court. However, if Greg had had the means to engage the best lawyer in town, he would not have been convicted in the first place.

Yet another bit of irony was that after Greg was vindicated, a childhood pal who later became the head Public Defender for Tulsa County told Greg that if Kathy's murder had been committed 200 yards further south, in Tulsa County rather than Osage, there never would have been a trial. Tulsa County prosecutors were not about to try the matter only on the basis of bite mark evidence. They had determined the State's case too weak.

When Greg was released in 1993, no one knew what to do. The President of the Oklahoma State Senate represented him in a wrongful conviction suit but "promptly sold me out," according to Greg.[69] The statute of limitations expired and Greg was out of luck. He feels that if he were released today, he would receive compensation similar to Ron's. As it was, Greg had to pay out of pocket and even had to sell his house, to cover legal costs. Greg expresses this matter-of-factly, with some irritation, but without the anger one might expect. Greg remarked that Ron deserved even more than the settlement he received after being exonerated. Greg says this without a hint of jealousy.

As for his wife's murder, there were no suspects but Greg. There is a perfect thumbprint and ample DNA evidence with which to track another suspect. But, Greg points out, "To this day, they won't do it." When asked why he thinks that's so, Greg says he believes those responsible are "saving face."[70]

Rulings in Greg's case raise larger questions than his wrongful conviction. The legal community must ask whose responsibility, professionally and ethically, it was to challenge George Briggs' taking this case in the first place. That same responsibility extends to any case Briggs may have accepted during the period of his chemical dependence.

The answer glares through the legal fog: everyone who knew of his condition.

The trial judge, the late Associate District Judge Mermon Potter, should have known since, as Osage County District Judge Pearlman pointed out, Briggs' drinking was no secret. If Potter knew, he was obligated to say something when Wilhoit and his parents engaged Briggs' services.

The Oklahoma Bar Association knew. It had been receiving complaints against Briggs for some time—including one filed the month Briggs was hired to defend Greg.

Bar association investigations are secret. Briggs' voluntary resignation in 1987 effectively sealed the matter. The full extent of Briggs' substance abuse, as well as complaints unrelated to the Wilhoit prosecution, did not become public until a series of court hearings in 1990 prompted by the work of Appellate Public Defender Mark Barrett.

The Oklahoma Supreme Court and the State Bar have made strides in encouraging attorneys and judges to report substance abuse in their ranks. No longer is it an issue of which to be embarrassed or ashamed. Most people acknowledge substance abuse to be the disease that it is. The common conception no longer is that it is simply a voluntary crawl into a bottle.

One can only wonder what might have happened had that sensibility been prevalent when the Wilhoits were looking for a lawyer to represent Greg.

Perhaps it would have made a difference not only to Greg and his family, but to George Briggs as well.

As for Greg's take on his fate, he underscores his affection for his adopted state and his satisfaction with postprison life. "It was worth five years on death row to come to Northern California. It couldn't have worked out differently."[71]

Welcome Home

Although it's been more than ten years since Kirk Bloodsworth was released from death row, the burly waterman still has nights he awakens in a cold sweat. Bloodsworth's recurring nightmare left the Maryland House of Corrections with him on June 28, 1993. In his dream, Kirk is being dragged down a hallway toward his execution. He tries fending off guards who are forcing him forward. His struggle is useless. There is no escape. Looming larger than life, the metallic gas chamber that will asphyxiate his life dominates the dreamscape. The killing machine's vents hiss. Leather restraints squeeze his flesh. The inmate's heart pounds, about to explode.

Just before the fatal dream sequence, Bloodsworth awakens. Body soaked, he's gasping for air.

The events leading to Kirk Bloodsworth's nightmare began in Summer 1984. Bloodsworth was twenty-four years old, with no criminal record nor history of deviance. Dawn Venice Hamilton, a nine-year-old girl walked into the woods by her east Baltimore apartment. She was searching for her younger cousin. The cousin showed up a short time later. Dawn never did.

On July 25th, 10:30 A.M., Dawn was reported missing. Four hours later, her body was found. She was naked from the waist down. Her head had been crushed.

Two boys who had been fishing at the edge of the woods told authorities a stranger had wandered past and offered to help Dawn find her cousin. The boys described the stranger as six foot five inches tall, with curly blond hair and a bushy mustache. They said the man had tan skin and that he was skinny.

When Bloodsworth relates the story of his arrest and gets to the point of the boys' eyewitness identification, he stands straight and tall, stretching to the full extent of his six feet. The height differential is apparent. For emphasis he adds, "And I ain't never been skinny."[1]

The identification offered by the young fishermen was flawed for other reasons, as well. Nonetheless, when a suspect's composite was constructed on the basis of the boys' account, the likeness to Bloodsworth was considerable. A hotline tipster directed police to Bloodsworth. Kirk had been in the area since early July, attempting to save his marriage. He had vanished the week following the slaying, and back home in Cambridge, Maryland, bemoaned "a terrible thing" he had done.

At trial, Bloodsworth explained his "terrible thing" utterance referred to how guilty he felt for abandoning his wife and their debts. But the other possible interpretations of the comment, combined with the eyewitness identification, resulted in a quick jury deliberation.

Following Bloodsworth's conviction, a Baltimore County judge ordered his execution for raping and murdering Dawn Hamilton. He didn't do it, Bloodsworth insisted to the judge and jury. He repeated that refrain relentlessly to the hundreds of people he wrote from prison. Politicians, entertainers, and novelists were on his mailing list. Each letter was signed with the initials A.I.M. This acronym stood for "an innocent man," the essence of his message.

On death row his social circle included multiple murderers. One fellow inmate had bound, gagged, and stabbed to death an elderly couple in their living room. Bloodsworth, though, learned the penitentiary pecking order. One sent to prison for killing a child is the lowest of the low.

Following eight years eleven months and nineteen days of trying to persuade the world of his innocence, the State of Maryland finally agreed. Scientific testing that was merely science fiction at the time of the crime had progressed sufficiently to confirm that a slim semen stain on the victim's clothing was not Bloodworth's. His exoneration established a precedence for scientific evidence. Never in U.S. jurisprudence had DNA cleared someone confined to death row.

The former Marine and Eastern Shore crabber was released to a stretch limousine. This was the vehicle in which he would cruise to his happily-ever-after. Given what he'd endured, he figured he was headed for easy days.

A decade passes. He's not so certain.

"It's a daily struggle," Bloodsworth concedes. "You're fighting with the fact you went through this."[2]

For the longest time, he refused to discuss his past. Ignoring what happened was his way to move on. But after years of silence, he's become one of the most articulate speakers within the exclusive ranks of death row exonerees. While states wrestle with the inequities and emotions of the matter, Bloodsworth is on the stump addressing legislative bodies, legal conferences, and college students. He's a simple, plainspoken waterman-turned-activist who argues against capital punishment on the most basic grounds.

"As long as there's the possibility—no matter how remote—that an innocent person could be killed, nobody should be for the death penalty."[3]

When Kirk Bloodsworth tells his tale there is this uplifting lilt in his march toward freedom. But he wants everyone to know that leaving prison is not where his story ends. No one should downplay the damage done even when the legal system attempts to correct a tragic error. The repercussions of incarceration have long-lasting aftereffects.

He could not ignore when someone smeared graffiti on his car after his release. The statement scrawled on his windshield, "child killer," was painful. Although the governor's pardon exonerated him in a court of law, Bloodsworth's reputation was still contested in the court of public opinion. The anonymous calls left on his answering machine with the vindictive message, "They never should have let you out," served as further evidence that DNA proof of innocence did not equate with societal acceptance.

The aftershocks of confinement manifest still in the claustrophobia Bloodsworth experiences whenever he's in a room without windows. Anxiety that grips him when he's home alone or on the road without someone to witness his whereabouts is another indication of the psychological reverberations of life spent on death row.

The person who eases his anxieties and accompanies him through these tribulations is his wife, Brenda. The two have been married four years. They rent a modest A-frame house outside Cambridge. Kirk phones Brenda at work to let her know he's home.

About the need for checking in he says, "I shouldn't have to feel that way. But that's the byproduct of my imprisonment. My *false* imprisonment."[4]

Bloodsworth is far removed from his early days of liberation. He's been a free man since the summer of 1993. It didn't take long, though, to tumble from the euphoria of emancipation into doubt and depression. The state saw to it that Bloodsworth received compensation for his wrongful conviction. However, much of the $300,000 Maryland gave him went to pay legal bills. What remained was blown on extravagances like a cherry-red Corvette. Once the car of his dreams was repossessed, Kirk was left to figure out how to reassemble his life. Not only did his ride slide, but in the bleakest moments of a desperate winter, he lived in an unheated truck, trapping rodents to survive.

At 46, he has come to grips with who he is. He credits finally embracing his past for helping set a course for his future. The echoing taunts from his early days of release used to make him wish people would simply forget who he was. He is determined now to make sure people know exactly who he is.

"If it could happen to me," he admonishes audiences, "it could happen to you."[5]

Prior to prison, Bloodsworth harbored dreams of competing in the discus. He fared well at track meets. But life on death row is not conducive to athletic training. Smoking cigarettes became an acquired bad habit. When the cell doors slammed shut, all that mattered was survival.

Growing up in the country, Bloodsworth was accustomed to roaming freely, pursuing his love of hunting and fishing. Being confined nearly drove him crazy. To maintain his sanity, Bloodsworth constructed a boat, plank by plank, in his head. He christened his mental model "Jeanett's Pearl," in honor of his grandmother and mother. He kept a calendar for a time, until the advice of a fellow inmate sunk in. It dawned on Bloodsworth that he was counting down days till his own demise.

In 1987, the legal system teased Bloodsworth with a glimmer of hope when it overturned his sentence and ordered a new trial. On retrial, Bloodsworth again was found guilty. This time the sentence was life without parole. This amounted to a torturous confinement of a different nature.

When lawyers analyze this case, they conclude systemic misconduct was not the issue. Neither police nor prosecutors overstepped their bounds. This was not a matter of inadequate defense counsel, nor did the case hinge on tainted evidence.

Robert Morin, Bloodsworth's appellate attorney says, "I think an argument can be made that no one did anything wrong ... this was a situation where there was just a series of human judgments ... that imprisoned the wrong man."[6]

Reflecting on the case, Morin, who serves as a D.C. Superior Court judge, recalls being pressed by colleagues to visit Bloodsworth and pursue an appeal. Morin remembers Bloodsworth's obsession with DNA testing. The inmate spent much of his prison time reading. He came across a Joseph Wambaugh text about two British murders solved through "genetic fingerprinting." The attorney was doubtful. Most likely, the victim's clothing had been destroyed. Even if it were intact, there may be no DNA residue to test.

Things finally began unfolding Bloodsworth's way. Evidence had not been disposed. It was located in a court clerk's office. Prosecutors okayed the testing. As he'd maintained, the results cleared Bloodsworth conclusively. Morin could barely contain himself. He shouted into the phone, "Kirk, it's not you!" Reflecting on that message still chokes up Bloodsworth. He figured his nightmare was over.

He couldn't know how mistaken he was.

What people do not comprehend, Morin comments, is that "Kirk had an incredibly difficult and painful reentry."[7] Most released inmates, exonerated or otherwise, have similarly treacherous transitions. A fairy-tale ending generally does not materialize.

PRISONER REENTRY

The Bureau of Justice Statistics estimates that nearly 600,000 people—approximately 1,600 every day—are released from prisons and returned to their home communities each year.[8] The transition from incarceration to community may not be considered noteworthy. After all, ever since jails were built, individuals have confronted the challenges of going from confinement to liberty.

From several policy perspectives, prisoner reintegration is gathering significance. More inmates are returning home, having lived longer locked up, less prepared for life on the outside, with less support in their reintegration. It is, as Kirk first felt, like they're doomed to fail. They have difficulties reconnecting to work, housing, even family. They may remain plagued by health and substance abuse problems. The majority will be rearrested. Many will be sent back to prison for new crimes or violations of parole conditions. This cycle of removal and return of large numbers of people is increasingly concentrated in a relatively small number of communities that already face daunting economic and social dilemmas.

The costs of this revolving door between prison and community are great. Public safety bears a burden from this cycle. It is anticipated that nearly two-thirds of released inmates will be rearrested within three years of their release. This recidivism results in thousands of new victimizations annually.

The incarceration–release cycle has serious fiscal implications. Large sums of state budgets are tied up in a criminal–industrial complex. Expenditures on corrections increased fivefold from 1982 to 1997. Bureau of Justice Statistics show the fifteen-year jump from $9 billion to $44 billion. These numbers do not include costs of police and court work to capture and sentence perpetrators or the cost to victims.

There are severe social costs. Prisoner reentry has collateral consequences, including public health risks, homelessness, disenfranchisement, and deteriorated ties among families and communities.

The opportunities also are profound. Coordinating reentry to minimize crime would enhance public safety. Managing reentry so there are fewer returns to incarceration would result in significant cost savings. Attaining long-term reintegration would generate benefits for families and communities as well as for former inmates. These interwoven opportunities bring the rewards of reentry into perspective. There is much to be gained.

The costs and opportunities also raise questions about what can be done to prepare both ex-inmates and their communities for their inevitable reunion. How can public resources best be directed to improve overall safety and curtail recidivism? What strategies can be developed that enhance the chances of prisoner reintegration success? What policies can be implemented to make a short-term impact?

SENTENCING AND PAROLE IN CONTEXT

Over the past generation, U.S. sentencing policy has been shaped by three major influences. The first is a dramatic increase in incarceration. Combining the populations of state prisons (about 1,200,000), the federal system (135,000), and local jails (605,000), the United States locks up nearly two million of its citizens. Since the early 1970s, when the level of imprisonment was 110 citizens per 100,000, there has been a fourfold jump to 476 incarcerated individuals per 100,000 residents in the year 2000.[9]

The effect of increased imprisonment on reentry is apparent. The more people are placed in prison, the more eventually will be released. Over the past two decades, the number of inmates released each year has grown nearly four times, from 147,895 in 1977 to an estimated 585,000 in 2000.[10]

During the same period, the overriding philosophy that once guided reentry—the principle of rehabilitation and earned reintegration within a structure of indeterminate sentencing—lost its policy dominance. Under the indeterminate approach, state statutes offered wide latitude in sentences, authorized the release of inmates by parole boards, and emphasized rehabilitation of prisoners as corrections' goal. In the mid-1970s critics from different ideological perspectives started pressing for changes. Civil rights activists and defense lawyers, citing evidence of widespread class and racial disparities in sentencing and correctional administration, called for restricting the discretion of judges and other authorities in sentencing matters. Political conservatives noted increasing crime rates and research findings that doubted the effectiveness of rehabilitation. They advocated sentencing reforms as a way to enforce stricter standards and crackdown on criminals. This shift away from indeterminate sentencing has had a great impact on sentencing policy. Past unifying philosophy has been replaced with a range of experiments, including mandatory minimums, abolition of discretionary parole release, three-strikes statutes, sex offender registration, curtailed judicial discretion, and truth-in-sentencing policies.

Such cornerstones of correctional administration as good-time credits earned through compliance with requirements and successful completion of in-prison training programs and discretionary release through parole board review have been abandoned or reduced in many jurisdictions. Intensive case management, pre- and postrelease, and the accessibility of community support services have not been priorities. Polls of parole officers indicate that more of them give priority to the law enforcement function of parole, rather than its rehabilitation purpose.[11] The level of per capita spending for parole supervision has been reduced while per-officer parole caseloads have increased.[12] New surveillance capabilities—including electronic monitoring and drug testing—have been introduced, providing greater capacity to detect violations and to increase revocation rates.

The rate of parole violations has increased significantly over recent years. In 1985, 70 percent of parolees completed their terms of parole successfully; by 1998, the rate had fallen to 45 percent. Parole revocations now are more than a third of prison admissions, up from 18 percent in 1980.[13] Parole violators are the fastest-growing category of prison admissions.

The burden on the systems that manage reentry has increased while the operational capacity to administer these increases has not kept pace. The increased number of prison releases has placed greater stresses on the communities where prisoner removal and return are most concentrated.

PUBLIC SAFETY AND REENTRY

Releasing prisoners into society poses two interrelated challenges: How to protect the public's safety, and how to facilitate an individual's transition from one living behind bars to a contributing member of the community. Even though these issues are connected, it is helpful to distinguish public safety benefits from the advantages to communities and former inmates that successful reintegration promises.

Some 600,000 prisoners are released annually. The majority under supervision fail while on parole. Key questions arise: To what degree is this population committing new crimes and endangering the community? How much additional safety can be generated by better reentry strategies?

Given the centrality of these issues to the development of policies guiding prisoner reentry, it is remarkable how little research has been conducted. In 1989, the Bureau of Justice Statistics published the largest study on recidivism. The researchers tracked a large segment of prisoners released from eleven states in 1983. They measured recidivism rates over the ensuing three years. The eleven jurisdictions accounted for more than half of all state prison releases (57 percent) in the United States that year. During that time, 63 percent of the 1983 release cohort were rearrested at least once; 47 percent were reconvicted; and 41 percent were reincarcerated. Individuals were most apt to reoffend during their first year out of prison—40 percent were rearrested within that critical first year.

According to the research, approximately 68,000 of the released inmates were arrested and charged with some 327,000 felonies and serious misdemeanors. These included 50,000 violent arrests, 141,000 property offenses, 46,000 drug offenses, and 80,000 public order violations.[14] More than 93,000 of these arrests are classified as Uniform Crime Reports Index crime (i.e., murder and negligent manslaughter, rape, robbery, aggravated assault, burglary, larceny, and motor vehicle theft). The group of inmates released in 1983 accounted for 3.9 percent of all arrests for Index crimes in the eleven jurisdictions over the first six months, and 2.8 percent of all arrests for Index crimes over that three-year period. This 2.8 percent accounts for only the arrests of prisoners released in 1983. It does not factor the extent to which inmates released in 1981 or 1982 added to arrests in 1983. These recidivism rates mark only those offenses that were reported to the police (typically just over one-third of victimizations are reported) and resulted in arrest.[15] Reoffending rates among ex-inmates may be higher than that reported in the research. The contribution of their rates to the overall crime rate is more substantial and their effects on specific communities even more pronounced. It is unclear whether the increase in the country's annual release since 1983 has produced a proportional increase in crimes attributable to this group.

The safety threat posed by returning prisoners can be seen through a community perspective. Inmates leaving incarceration return to a relatively small number of neighborhoods concentrated within the nation's urban centers. This critical mass of individuals at high risk of reoffending offers opportunities, in addition to risks. Development of "place-based" crime reduction strategies, more common among police departments and neighborhood crime prevention coalitions, could benefit from a geographic analysis of the safety threats posed and barriers confronted by returning prisoners. Even small gains realized in individual recidivism could amount to appreciable gains collectively for communities with high inmate reentry rates.

Boston's crime reduction approach, known as "Operation Ceasefire," aimed attention at the behaviors of individuals under supervision in targeted neighborhoods. This strategy generated substantial improvement.[16] Boston is working on adapting the Ceasefire model to address prisoner reentry.

Challenges of reentry and inherent safety concerns should be examined through the eyes of inmates' families. As the number of prison releases grows, the impact of recidivism may be experienced disproportionately by families with histories of domestic violence. Some former prisoners, whether convicted of violent acts against a family member or other criminal offense, may pose risks to the families to which they return. Remarkably little is known about the effects returning inmates have on incidences of domestic violence and child abuse. These matters merit investigation.

How should society respond to the high rates of reoffending? One approach could be continued expansion of incarceration. Those supporting this strategy cite studies concluding national prison growth had an effect on recent declines in crime rates. Applying different approaches, two researchers estimated that prison expansion may account for 25 percent of the fall in crime.[17] One of the researchers suggests that further prison expansion—following the buildup of the last twenty years—would result in only minimal safety gains.[18] Any gains must be balanced against fiscal and social costs, as well as alternate crime control strategies that could produce similar results.

Within state budgets, there is a struggle between spending priorities. Such a tug-of-war exists between higher education and corrections. Cumulatively, state spending on corrections increased 1,200 percent between 1973 and

1993. These expenditures went to construct prisons to house new inmates. Spending on higher education rose only 419 percent, despite a boom in university enrollments.[19]

One provocative study suggests more incarceration is counterproductive—that at some point in some neighborhoods, more imprisonment may increase crime rates. These community-level effects generate crime because massive incarceration practices break down the informal social structures associated with crime prevention. These supports include strong families and workforce participation of men in the community. A tipping point may be reached where crime is less inhibited.[20]

There are ways to manage the public safety risks from returning inmates without expanding the prison population. Research has identified several interventions, such as drug treatment, job training, and educational programs. These have demonstrated their worth as effective methods to reduce reoffending rates. Greater investment in proven interventions is needed. More innovation in the field and evaluation research would produce new approaches matching the reality of the large number of prison releases.

REENTRY PROCESS

More than 95 percent of the nation's state inmates eventually return home. Approximately 40 percent of those in state confinement will be released within the next twelve months.[21] What is known about the processes under which prisoners are released? What are the characteristics of returning prisoners? How are release decisions made? How are inmates prepared for reintegration? What is known about the "moment of release," about postprison supervision, and about the increased frequency of parole revocation?

WHO ARE THE RETURNEES?

Returning inmates are at high risk along several dimensions. Of the nearly 600,000 prisoners returning to communities each year, the majority have not finished high school, have limited employment skills, and have histories of health problems, including substance abuse. About one-third of all inmates are released following a conviction for a drug offense (up from 11 percent in 1985). One-fourth are released following a conviction for a violent crime (down from 32 percent in 1985). Returning prisoners have served longer sentences than in the past, meaning they may be more removed from work, family, and community.

The vast majority of released inmates are male (88 percent), although the percentage of women in the parole population has risen from 8 to 12 percent during the past decade.[22] The median age is 34 and median education is eleventh grade. In 1998, more than half of returning inmates were white

(55 percent) and 44 percent were African American. Twenty-one percent of these returning inmates were Hispanic (perhaps of any race).

One characteristic of returning prisoners that has changed in recent years is the crime for which they were convicted. Examining all releases from state and federal prisons, one sees that the number of returning prisoners convicted of violent crimes has nearly doubled from 1985 to 1998—from about 75,000 to more than 140,000. This increase may continue.

During the same stretch, the number of released prisoners who had been convicted of drug offenses (sales and possession) and their share of the returning population increased substantially. The number of released drug offenders rose from about 25,000 in 1985 to 182,000 in 1998.[23] The proportion of released inmates who were drug offenders increased from 11 percent in 1985 to 32 percent by 1998.

Most prisoners have a criminal history. Nearly half have been convicted of a violent offense at some point in their past. Three-fourths of state prisoners have been sentenced to probation or incarceration at least once. Forty-three percent have been sentenced to probation or incarceration at least three times.[24]

As a result of sentencing reforms of the past twenty years, including mandatory minimums and truth-in-sentencing statutes, individuals released from incarceration have, on average, served longer sentences than past inmates. The amount of time prisoners serve prior to release has risen 27 percent since 1990, from an average of 22 months for those released in 1980 to 28 months for those released in 1998.[25]

The proportion of soon-to-be-released prisoners who reported that they had served five years or more almost doubled between 1991 and 1997—increasing from 12 percent to 21 percent. These longer terms mean further detachment from communities. The share of returning inmates who served between one and five years also increased. The share of prisoners serving one year or less dropped—from 33 percent in 1991 to 16 percent in 1997.[26]

Returning prisoners are released with a range of health problems. Substance abuse and mental illness are common among inmates expecting to be released within 12 months. Three-fourths of this population have a history of substance abuse, and about 16 percent suffer from mental illness. Less than one-third of released prisoners receive substance abuse or mental health treatment while incarcerated.[27]

A disproportionate percentage of the prison population also live with chronic health problems or infectious diseases. In 1997, about one-fourth of the individuals living with HIV or AIDS in the United States had been released from a correctional facility that year. Roughly one-third of those infected with hepatitis C and tuberculosis were released from incarceration in 1999. In terms of prevalence of infectious disease among inmates, between 2 and 3 percent of the prison population are HIV positive or have AIDS; 18 percent are infected with hepatitis C; and 7 percent have a TB infection.

These rates of infection are five to ten times greater than those found in the general U.S. population.[28]

The health, substance abuse, education, housing, and employment dilemmas of returning prisoners present daunting challenges to successful reintegration. One study of California parolees reported that 85 percent of the state's parole population are chronic alcohol or drug abusers; approximately 80 percent are unemployed; half are functionally illiterate; 18 percent suffer psychiatric problems; and 10 percent are homeless.[29] In most cases, individuals enter prison already burdened with these problems. Sometimes, prison may actually improve these conditions. Inmates often have better access to medical treatment than do persons of similar sociodemographic characteristics not in prison. On the other hand, incarceration may create or exacerbate adverse physical or psychological conditions. Some inmates experience serious injuries and/or psychological trauma while incarcerated. More can be done in prison and upon release to address these issues and aid inmates in making a successful transition to community life.

INCARCERATION AND REENTRY: EFFECTS ON AFRICAN AMERICAN FAMILIES AND COMMUNITIES

Young, low-income black males are imprisoned at greater rates than any group, and therefore are most affected by the reentry experience. The Bureau of Justice Statistics estimated that, in 1991, an African American male had a 29 percent lifetime chance of serving at least one year behind bars. This rate is six times higher than that of white males. Hispanic males, who may be of any race, have lifetime odds of incarceration of 16 percent. Nine percent of African American males aged 25 to 29 were in prison in 1999, compared to 3 percent of Hispanic males and 1 percent of white males of the same age group. One estimate calculates more than one-third of young, black male high-school dropouts were in prison in the late 1990s—more than those who held jobs.[30]

The disproportionate percentage of African Americans in the criminal justice system has been made worse by changes in sentencing policy. A 1990 RAND study found that while defendants in California received generally comparable sentences for comparable crimes regardless of race, this was not the case with regard to drug offenses.[31] Sentencing policy changes throughout the 1980s and 1990s requiring mandatory minimum sentences for a range of drug-related offenses produced a substantial increase in drug offenders sentenced to prison and serving longer terms. This had a significant impact on African American prison populations. The number of black drug offenders sentenced to prison rose 707 percent between 1985 and 1995. The number of white drug offenders increased by 306 percent.[32] Drug offenders accounted for 42 percent of the increase in the white prison population during that span.

High rates of incarceration among African Americans have intergenerational ramifications. In a 1996 study of black inmates, nearly half had a family member who had been incarcerated.[33] There is evidence suggesting children of incarcerated parents are at risk of delinquency and/or criminal behavior.[34]

Removal and reentry of African American men have consequences for family stability. In some communities, high rates of incarceration, homicide, and limited job prospects among African American males have resulted in an imbalance of marriageable African American men to women. Researchers contend that severely imbalanced gender ratios are predictors of family disruption and an increased chance of crime and violence.[35] Prison Fellowship calculates that only 15 percent of married couples are able to endure a period of incarceration of one partner. Of the 15 percent who do manage to stay together during the prison term, only about 4 percent remain together one year following release.[36]

INMATE RELEASE DECISIONS

In the past, prisoners were released after parole boards deemed them "ready." An inmate would serve a portion of his sentence, with the remainder being served in the community under parole supervision. The advantages of this approach were that release decisions were based on assessment of individual risk. Inmates had an incentive to behave well and participate in programs while incarcerated.

Shujaa Graham spent thirteen years in a California prison, the final nine on death row, before being exonerated in 1982. He tells of an unfortunate twist to the release decision. "Guys would be sent to solitary confinement as punishment for bad behavior. They'd be given a certain length of time to serve in solitary lockup," Graham noted. "They'd finish their time in solitary, but prison officials would decide they weren't ready to be returned to the general (prison) population. So they'd finish the rest of their sentence in solitary. Now, keep in mind, they weren't ready to be released into the general prison population, but their sentences were up. So, even less prepared than they otherwise might have been, they're released back into society."[37]

In the late 1970s and early 1980s, indeterminate sentencing and parole release fell out of favor among policy makers, giving way to significant policy changes. In the 1980s and 1990s, truth-in-sentencing laws were enacted, essentially eliminating the parole board for certain prisoners. As a result of these changes, there are now fewer inmates released on the basis of parole determination, more prisoners released "automatically" under mandatory release (with subsequent supervision), and more individuals whose sentences expire and are released without any supervision whatsoever.

Under indeterminate sentencing practices, inmates were released from incarceration to parole only after a parole board had considered them "ready"—meaning, at least theoretically, they had been rehabilitated and/or had productive community connections. Release to parole was considered a privilege to be earned. This system came under increasing criticism over the years as arbitrary, racially biased, and a politically expedient way to relieve prison overcrowding. A series of sentencing reforms passed during the past twenty years have reduced the authority of parole boards to make individualized release decisions.

Truth-in-sentencing laws were enacted in the 1980s and 1990s to diminish discrepancies between sentences imposed and time served. Forty states have passed truth-in-sentencing legislation requiring violent offenders to serve at least half of their sentences; of these jurisdictions, twenty-seven plus the District of Columbia require violent offenders to serve at least 85 percent of their time.[38] These laws minimize the role of parole boards in making release decisions. Fewer inmates are released because of parole board rulings.

In 1990, 39 percent of prisoners were released on the basis of a parole board decision. By 1998, the portion dipped to 26 percent. Forty percent of state prisoners are now released mandatorily, up from 29 percent in 1990.[39]

This development has implications for corrections policy. Does the absence of discretionary release remove incentive for good behavior? Does automatic release reduce the inmate's incentive to find a stable residence or employment—factors that traditionally influenced parole board determinations? Does a policy of mandatory release decrease a correctional agency's commitment to developing connections between an individual's life in and outside of prison? Does mandatory release remove the ability of a parole board to rethink risks posed by an individual, once prison behaviors have been observed? For states with policies granting victims' participation in parole hearings, what role do victims have in the process?

More inmates are serving full terms and therefore are released without supervision. Slightly more than 22 percent of prisoners were released "unconditionally" in 1998. The number released unconditionally has doubled since 1990. More than 100,000 inmates are now released unconditionally each year.[40] In most of these situations, inmates have served full sentences and thus face no parole time or community supervision at the end of incarceration.

Generally, inmates are not paroled for one of three reasons: (1) they were convicted of a particularly violent offense; (2) they behaved badly in prison, and forfeited possible good-time that would have enabled an earlier release; and (3) they received relatively short sentences, so an early release may not be an option. For these individuals, there are no further obligations to report to a parole officer or abide by certain conditions. Not much is known about the behavior and recidivism of inmates released who are not under supervision. This matter needs more study.

PREPARATION FOR RELEASE AND REINTEGRATION

Given that nearly all inmates eventually are returned to their communities—40 percent within the next twelve months—prison could be an opportunity to improve individuals' skills, treat addictions, and prepare for life on the outside. Many prisoners have histories of mental and physical problems, addiction and substance abuse, and low levels of education and job skills. There is evidence that in-prison programs are beneficial and cost-effective in preparing prisoners for life after incarceration. Surveys suggest that relatively few individuals receive training or treatment while in prison.

The criminal justice system of the 1970s could be characterized as a period of pessimism. A frustrating "What's the use?" attitude seemed to hold sway. Since those times, experts increasingly, though cautiously, are optimistic about the effectiveness of certain in-prison programs for changing behavior. While the quantity and quality of evidence varies widely according to type of intervention, it appears that certain approaches—including cognitive skills, vocational training, drug treatment, educational, and other prison-based programs—work at reducing recidivism. These interventions are most successful when programs are matched to individual's risks and needs, when they are properly managed, and when the intervention is supported by postrelease supervision. While present analyses report only slight reductions in recidivism rates for participants, even modest reductions can have a significant cumulative effect on criminal behavior in communities with high concentrations of returning inmates.[41]

In addition to individual rehabilitative benefits, programming may be advantageous to the management of correctional facilities. Idle inmates are more prone to trouble than other prisoners. According to research, some level of structured activity (job training, education, prison industry, etc.) is essential to running a safe and humane institution.[42]

Most inmates do not take advantage of prison programs and participation rates have declined during the previous decade. About one-third of soon-to-be released prisoners reported participating in vocational programs or educational offerings. This percentage is down from 1991 figures.[43] These dips in participation are more precipitous than they appear, as smaller percentages of larger populations are involved. This means that significantly greater numbers of inmates are being released without educational or vocational preparation.

Although most individuals enter prison with substance abuse problems, only 10 percent of state inmates in 1997 reported receiving professional treatment. This number is down from 25 percent in 1991. Of the soon-to-be released prisoners, less than one-fifth of those with a substance abuse problem received treatment while incarcerated.[44] An estimated 7 percent of the prison population reported participating in prison industries, while a quarter were idle altogether.[45] Involvement of soon-to-be-released prisoners in activities labeled "pre-release programs" remained stable through the 1990s, although at just 12 percent.[46]

The profile of the prison population reveals deficiencies in human capital that diminish an individual's potential to function in society. Many of these deficits are affiliated with high rates of recidivism. The emerging research concerning successful prison programs indicates that focused investments in these interventions could yield public safety benefits and raise overall social functioning. The research consensus comes when a smaller percentage of prisoners seems to be receiving training and treatment than in the past.

THE MOMENT OF RELEASE

The flashpoint in a prisoner's life, the "moment of release," and the hours and days immediately following, are pivotal in the transition back to community. Many barriers—some logistical—could be cleared relatively smoothly with proper planning. Systematic attention to small but important details, key at the moment of release, such as time of day, whether the inmate has identification, and arranging for family reunification, treatment, work, and housing upon departing prison could ease the transition back to life on the outside.

Following release, prisoners are moved directly from a very controlled environment to a low level of supervision or complete freedom. They may soon confront high-risk persons, places, and situations. Few have developed relapse prevention mechanisms. It may be difficult to resist certain temptations. Inmates facing release often report anxieties about reestablishing family ties, securing employment, and managing finances once they're home.[47] Even though "gate fever"—a syndrome centered on the irritability and anxiety experienced by a prisoner when released—is acknowledged by correctional authorities, little empirical research has been done on the subject. The few studies that have been undertaken conclude that while a small number of prisoners find the experience of release debilitating, the increased stress levels documented at the time of departure reflect real anxieties about coping with the outside world.[48]

Most inmates are released with little more than a bus ticket and a bit of cash. Some jurisdictions provide bus fare to return ex-prisoners to their destination, but just half report making any transportation arrangements. For those states that do provide funds, the amount ranges from about $25 to $200. About one-third of all corrections departments report not offering any financial support upon release.[49]

Inmates often are returned to home communities at odd hours of the night, making it difficult to connect with loved ones and service providers during the crucial first hours of freedom. Prisoners often are returned home without essential pieces of identification needed to get jobs, gain access to substance abuse treatment, or apply for public assistance. Some former inmates suffer delays in entering drug treatment because they lack Medicaid. Those who are released may not completely comprehend the criminal justice system requirements they must fulfill. In an American Correctional Association study of all states, two-thirds reported not providing any documentation or reporting instructions to prisoners upon release.[50]

The moment of release is a "moment of truth" for the inmate's transition process. This critical period presents opportunities for policy innovation—to develop strategies that build a bridge during this time of transition. Released inmates find few resources to assist them in securing work, accessing substance abuse programs, and reestablishing bonds with family and community. Intertwining these pre-release preparations, combined with appropriate follow-up (via parole, nonprofit community agencies, faith institutions, family, or friends), might diminish risk of recidivism or drug relapse and improve chances of successful reintegration following release.

POSTRELEASE SUPERVISION

Although fewer release determinations are being made by parole boards, the majority of returning inmates are subject to some period of postprison supervision. Of more than half-million state prisoners released in 2000, more than three-quarters were released to some sort of postprison supervision, most frequently "parole." Increasing incarceration and release rates during the last two decades have resulted in an expanding parolee population. Resources have not kept pace with the increases. Caseloads are higher, per capita spending is lower, and services have diminished. Little is known about parole effectiveness. What is known suggests that surveillance alone does not work. Supervision strategies that include treatment or rehabilitation in concert with surveillance have been shown to reduce recidivism.

Most inmates are released from incarceration into some type of conditional supervision status. Individuals released to parole supervision serve an average of less than two years in their states.[51] There were more than 700,000 people on parole or its functional equivalent in 1999. This figure is up from 220,000 in 1980.[52] Growth in the prison population has had the effect of increasing the parole population, without proportionate increases in resources. This creates heavier caseloads for parole officers. In the 1970s, the average parole officer managed a caseload of forty-five parolees. Today, most officers supervise about seventy parolees, about twice the number thought ideal.[53] Per capita expenditure per parolee has dropped nationally—from more than $11,000 annually in 1985 to roughly $9,500 in 1998.[54]

Limited resources mean only nominal supervision can be provided. More than 80 percent of parolees are supervised on "regular" caseloads—each meeting with a parole official for about 15 minutes, once or twice a month.[55] Another 8 percent of parolees (about 56,000 in 1998) are classified on "abscond" status at any given time, meaning they cannot be located and have no contact with their parole officer.[56] California's abscond rate is nearly 20 percent.[57] As supervisory offices lose contact with this group of released prisoners, little is known about their behavior.

Conditions of parole vary by jurisdiction. They include avoiding drugs, maintaining employment, observing curfews, and steering clear of high-risk people and places. Enforcement of those conditions differs as well, but it might involve home visits, drug testing, and electronic monitoring. A few states are experimenting with global positioning system satellites, whereby parolees' movements are tracked twenty-four hours a day. Innovative surveillance technologies such as these have made the monitoring aspect of supervision more efficient. They raise significant questions concerning civil liberties.

Little research exists examining the connection between parole supervision and deterrence or rehabilitation. It is not known whether case management approaches that simply crank up the level of supervision, such as intensive community oversight, increased drug testing, and home confinement, have reduced recidivism. Enhanced supervision entails greater surveillance, which increases the chances of catching technical violations.[58] If noncompliance with technical conditions of release indicated patterns of criminal behavior among parolees, then returning them to prison might prevent future crime. Studies suggest no support for the argument that terminating parole on the basis of technical violations suppresses new arrests.[59] Evidence is lacking to conclude that solely increasing parole supervision will result in less crime.

Parole approaches that include some degree of treatment or rehabilitation in conjunction with surveillance have been shown to lessen reoffending. According to the research, a treatment component is vital to modifying behavior and reducing crime.[60]

Social services for parolees have diminished. More resources have been invested in building new prison beds, leaving fewer funds available for services. There is a gap between needs and availability of services addressing concerns such as housing, mental health, and substance abuse.

Given high rates of recidivism, there is opportunity to supervise parolees—especially individuals at high risk—by combining treatment and surveillance to prevent future crimes.

PAROLE VIOLATIONS

More individuals than ever are returning to prison, both for technical violations and for committing new offenses. In 1980, parole violators accounted for 18 percent of prison admissions. Parole violators now constitute one-third of prison admissions. Of those returned to incarceration, nearly one-third were returned for a new conviction and two-thirds for a technical violation. There has been little study of the nature of technical violations or the parole revocation process. Not much is known about the effect of the growing numbers of parole revocations and reincarceration on public safety.

In 1984, 70 percent of parolees successfully completed their term. By 1998, that figure dropped to 45 percent. Some 206,000 parole violators were reincarcerated that year. Another 9 percent of adults failed to finish parole because they had absconded.[61] Parole violators as a percentage of prison admissions have doubled since the 1980s.[62]

The administrative documentation of parole violations does not reveal much about parolees' underlying behavior. Although many violations are registered as "technical," they may not be entirely crime-free. Often technical violators may be arrested, but not tried, for a new crime while under parole supervision. Forty-three percent of the "technical" violators of 1991 reported having been arrested for a new crime at least once while on parole.[63] For policy and practice, a better understanding is needed of the actual reasons behind parole violations and revocations.

It is not apparent why parole failures are higher now. It may be attributable to better monitoring techniques that make it easier to detect violations. It may be that technical violations are being used as a method for managing ever-expanding caseloads. Parole revocation may represent a tough-on-crime philosophy in some jurisdictions. Perhaps more individuals actually are committing crime while on parole. This failure rate also may reflect cutbacks in preparation for reentry, such as in-prison and community-based treatment, education, and job training programs. It is unclear whether supervision agencies are effectively identifying the highest-risk parolees and preventing new offenses or inefficiently returning individuals to the correctional system—at high cost to taxpayers without clear safety benefits.

A few states, as an alternative to reincarceration, employ intermediate sanctions for violations. Such measures include residential treatment, community service, curfew, electronic monitoring, increased level of supervision and counseling, loss of travel privileges, stepped up alcohol/drug testing, and reprimand by parole supervisor. Structured sanctions offer a graduated response, with return to incarceration as the ultimate penalty. Immediate, intermediate measures heighten the certainty of punishment, while preserving prison space for violent individuals. Limited evidence indicates that graduated sanctions may be more effective in reducing recidivism than merely returning parole violators to confinement. Certainty of sanctions appears to carry a high correlation with positive changes in individual behavior. This certainty is based on consistent application of a punishment schedule and close monitoring of behaviors, whereby individuals are not able to have infractions go undetected, thus reinforcing the misbehavior.

Despite the fiscal and crime control implications, parole has received little attention from researchers, policy makers, or practitioners. Research studies could uncover the social costs associated with the increasing number of parole violators, the nature of technical violations, the parole revocation process, and the effect of parole policies on preventing new crimes. A rational analysis of a process little understood even by those in the system could produce significant benefits. Prison expenditures on the increasing admissions of technical violators could be put toward improving community corrections systems.

EMPLOYABILITY AND PARTICIPATION IN THE WORKFORCE

An emphasis on employment and housing may prove instructive in developing programmatic and policy strategies to reduce the likelihood of reoffending. There is a complex relationship between employment and crime. Having a real job diminishes the odds of reoffending following release from incarceration. The better the pay, the less likely it is that released prisoners will fall back on their criminal ways.[64] Research reveals that released inmates face a lowered prospect for stable employment and decent wages throughout their lifetimes. Job training and placement programs suggest promise in connecting ex-prisoners with work, lessening the likelihood of further offending. Fewer individuals are receiving in-prison vocational training than in the past and fewer still have access to transitional programs that assist in linking them to jobs in the community.

The ability to secure a steady, sufficient source of income upon release is a critical factor in an individual's successful transition from prison to life on the outside. Decent wages are associated with lower rates of reoffending. Declines in wages are likely to lead to increases in illegal earnings and criminal activity. According to one estimate, a 10 percent decrease in an individual's pay is linked with a 10 to 20 percent increase in his criminal activity and likelihood of incarceration.[65]

Many offenders were connected to legitimate work prior to prison and presumably want to find stable employment following release. Three-quarters of state inmates reportedly held a job just before imprisonment. Of those, slightly more than half were employed full-time.[66] They must have had some skills and connections to mainstream employment. It is not surprising that released inmates face a diminished prospect for steady work and decent pay throughout their lives.

Several reasons help explain why incarceration lowers the employability and subsequent earning power of released individuals. First, the stigma attached to incarceration makes it hard for ex-prisoners to be hired. Employers are reluctant to hire people with criminal records. Such histories are a red flag that the individual may not be trustworthy.[67] A survey of employers in five U.S. urban markets revealed that two-thirds of respondents would not knowingly hire an ex-offender and at least one-third checked the criminal histories of their most recent hires.[68]

Released offenders are prohibited from working in certain fields. At least six states (Alabama, Delaware, Iowa, Mississippi, Rhode Island, and South Carolina) ban former inmates from public employment.[69] Most jurisdictions impose restrictions on hiring ex-offenders for certain professions, including law, medicine, nursing, education, and physical therapy.

Time out of the labor market interrupts one's job experience and keeps individuals from building employment skills. During incarceration, people become exposed to a prison culture that frequently serves to strengthen links to gangs and the underground world.[70]

Advancing in the job market results from learning through new experiences and opportunities. The same holds true for involvement in criminal enterprises. Research examining the impact of incarceration on prospective employment concludes that as time spent in prison increases, the likelihood of participating in the legal economy decreases.[71]

While there are no national statistics concerning unemployment and underemployment among parolees, data from California are instructive. In the early 1990s, only 21 percent of California's parolees had full-time jobs.[72] When returning inmates land work, they earn less than individuals with similar backgrounds who have not been imprisoned. One researcher estimates the "wage penalty" of confinement to be 10 to 20 percent.[73] Ex-inmates, on average, experience no real wage increases through their twenties and thirties, in contrast to never-incarcerated young men, whose wages rise rapidly through this period.[74]

Confinement could be seen as an opportunity to build skills and prepare for placement at a prospective job. However, research presents mixed reviews of the effectiveness of job training programs for offenders. Some studies conclude that it is difficult to improve an individual's employment chances and earnings, especially if that person has become "embedded in criminal activity."[75]

A more recent analysis of in-prison work and vocational programs provides some optimism. There is evidence that participation in job training and placement programs can lead to employment and reduced recidivism. On average, individuals in vocational programs were more apt to be employed following release and to have a recidivism rate 20 percent lower than nonparticipants.[76] Although current research does not provide enough evidence to support a definitive assertion that these programs "work," it does suggest that vocational programs may lower recidivism for motivated individuals.

The most successful programs are those targeted at released inmates in their midtwenties or older. An analysis of several studies suggests that work programs had a significant effect on the employment outcomes and recidivism rates of males who were at least 26 years old.[77] These individuals may be more motivated than younger offenders to change lifestyles and break connections to crime. That 80 percent of the prison population is 25 or older speaks to the need for more training for more prisoners.

Few approaches have proven effective for younger ex-inmates. Ensuring a successful postprison adjustment for this population remains challenging.

Research indicates that it is not sufficient to try to improve an individual's human capital. It also is critical to address changes in motivation and lifestyle away from criminal activity to positive involvement in the community. It is more complicated than teaching marketable skills. It may mean reestablishing links with community institutions. What results from these efforts is an individual not only committed to self-improvement, but also deeply invested in his environment.

One reason vocational training has not been more effective in lowering recidivism is the lack of job placement assistance and other follow-up after release. Successful programs not only strive to improve individuals' job skills, but also attempt to improve job readiness, provide case management for other social services, place former inmates in jobs, and continue to work with them for a follow-up period. Follow-up may be especially significant for employers, who indicate a willingness to hire ex-offenders if a third-party intermediary is available to intervene on the new hire's behalf.[78] These programs, operating within departments of correction or functioning as community-based agencies, offer promise in connecting ex-inmates to full-time employment and reducing levels of criminal activity.

IN-PRISON EDUCATIONAL PROGRAMS

In the 1870s, American prisons started experimenting with programs to improve the literacy and communication skills of inmates. By the 1930s, prison rehabilitation efforts centered around educational programs, which had grown enormously. Today, most U.S. prison systems offer a broad range of educational opportunities, from vocational training to postsecondary education courses. These diverse programs improve prisoners' behavior, by nurturing the maturation and conscientiousness of the inmate, and reduce recidivism, by enhancing employment prospects and providing a greater frame of reference within which to make decisions.[79]

Prison educational programs would benefit from closer scrutiny as to effectiveness. A recent study sponsored by the Virginia Department of Correctional Education tracked reincarceration rates among Virginia offenders over a fifteen-year period. The analysis revealed recidivism rates nearly 60 percent lower for those inmates who had completed prison educational programs compared to those who had not.[80] Preliminary findings from the largest, most comprehensive correctional education and recidivism study to date also indicate lower rates of recidivism among prisoners who participated in these programs, although results are not as dramatic as those for

Virginia. In this study of more than 3,000 inmates, reincarceration rates for offenders who participated in education programs were 20 percent less than for prisoners who did not.[81] Certain studies that have tried to gauge the impact prison education programs have on postrelease employment also demonstrate positive results. A 1994 overview revealed in three of the four studies, in-prison education programs significantly increased prospects for obtaining employment following release.[82]

Despite such findings, funding for these programs has not kept pace with expansion of the prison population. During the "get tough on crime" philosophy that dominated the 1990s, many jurisdictions cut existing prison educational programs, often to underwrite new prison construction. In California the number of prison teachers dropped by 200 during the past 15 years, while prison population expanded more than fivefold, from 30,000 to 160,000.[83] Also, in 1994 prisoners were declared ineligible for college Pell grants, leaving inmates without funds to pursue college degrees during their prison terms.

REENTRY AND HOUSING

Sometimes overlooked, housing may pose challenges for released offenders. Finding a place to stay is one of the first orders of business for an individual leaving prison and it is problematic. Inmates rarely have the financial wherewithal or personal references required to secure a unit in the private housing market. Furthermore, federal laws prohibit many ex-convicts from public housing and federally assisted housing programs. Lastly, a percentage of prisoners are not welcome back in their family homes. As a result, some returnees wind up homeless, with all the inherent risks.

Returning inmates need a place to live when they depart prison. The initial obstacles to securing affordable housing are similar to those for finding work. Most people leave prison without sufficient funds for a security deposit on an apartment. Landlords generally ask prospective tenants to list employment and previous housing references and disclose financial and criminal history information. On the basis of these requirements, ex-inmates are often left out of the private housing market. Public housing also may be out of reach for prisoners returning to the community. Federal housing policies allow—and sometimes require—public housing authorities, Section 8 providers, and other federally supported housing programs to deny housing to individuals who have been convicted of certain offenses.[84] The guidelines for denying housing are broad and may include those who have engaged in drug-related activity, violent crime, or other criminal conduct that would adversely affect the health and safety of other residents. Housing authorities have the right to obtain criminal records on tenants and applicants.

Individuals who have been evicted from public housing because of drug-related criminal activity cannot reapply for such housing for three years.

Housing providers have discretion to shorten the three-year ban for individuals who demonstrate they are getting help for their drug problem through participation in a rehabilitation or treatment program. Similarly, anyone found to be abusing illegal drugs or alcohol is ineligible for public housing benefits. Here, as well, providers can make exceptions for individuals who are involved in treatment programs. Convicted sex offenders who are subject to a lifetime registration requirement are ineligible for all public, Section 8, and other federally assisted housing programs.

One possibility for ex-offenders is to stay with family members upon release. Evidence suggests, however, that among the many who do reside with relatives, these arrangements often amount to short-lived solutions. One reason is that family members living in public housing may not welcome a returning inmate home when doing so may imperil their own housing situation. These familial relationships may also be so severely strained that staying with family members is not a viable option.

Given restrictions of the private housing market, policies of public housing, and other difficulties returning prisoners confront, it is not surprising that many wind up living on the streets. One study from the late 1980s estimated that as many as one-fourth of all homeless people had spent time in prison.[85] California's Department of Corrections reports that 10 percent of the state's parolees are homeless. The rate is greater in California's cities, where 30 to 50 percent of parolees are estimated to be homeless.[86]

Although homeless shelters serve as a last resort for former inmates in dire need of housing, they are not always available. Federally funded shelters require individuals be homeless for at least 24 hours before being eligible for a bed. Shelters with limited space may be hesitant to house offenders. The period immediately following release, when a returning prisoner is most tempted to revert to old habits, is crucial. Access to affordable housing that assists transition to community life is important in preventing relapse.

LOSS OF CIVIL LIBERTIES

On top of health, housing, and employment challenges, released ex-offenders experience a series of collateral consequences resulting from felony convictions. In many jurisdictions, ex-felons are barred from voting, holding political office, serving on juries, or holding certain jobs. They may temporarily or permanently forfeit eligibility for certain public health benefits.[87]

VOTING RIGHTS

Denial of the right to vote has significant implications for individual offenders and for certain communities in the United States. For that matter, might the razor-thin margin of difference in the 2000 presidential election have been altered had a sizeable block of ex-felons in Florida not been disenfranchised? Nearly all jurisdictions restrict voting rights of convicted individuals in some way.[88] The laws of forty-six states and the District of Columbia stipulate that convicted offenders cannot cast ballots while behind bars, and thirty-two states prevent offenders on probation or parole from voting. In more than a dozen states, a convicted felon forfeits the right to vote for life. Nearly 4 million Americans—one in fifty adults—are either presently or permanently prohibited from voting due to a felony conviction. Of these, 1.4 million are African American, accounting for 13 percent of the adult black male population. In jurisdictions imposing lifetime voting sanctions, the aggregate ramifications in African American communities are profound. One in every four African American men have forfeited the right to vote for life in Alabama, Florida, Iowa, Mississippi, New Mexico, Virginia, and Wyoming.[89] From a community standpoint, these restrictions have severe implications for democratic participation and political influence.

CRIMINAL REGISTRATION REQUIREMENTS

During the past fifteen years, the trend has been to extend punishment beyond an individual's probation, prison, and parole sentence. This has been the case particularly for sex offenders. Just eight states in 1986 required released offenders to register with a local police department. A series of high-profile, violent crimes committed by released offenders resulted in legislative initiatives making it mandatory for offenders to register with law enforcement agencies upon their release. By 1998, convicted sex offenders in every state were subject to a registration requirement. These requirements vary widely. While most jurisdictions mandate sex offender registration for those convicted after the effective date of the legislation, several states made the requirement retroactive. Eight states require registration of all eligible offenders convicted before 1980. The durations of offender requirements range from 10 years to life. A dozen states mandate lifetime registration for everyone in the registry. As of 1998, there were almost 280,000 sex offenders listed in state sex offender registries across the nation.[90]

IMPLICATIONS OF PRISONER REENTRY FOR FAMILIES AND COMMUNITIES

One distinct consequence of confinement is that relationships with families and communities are disrupted. Most prisoners are parents—about half of male inmates and two-thirds of female offenders leave at least one child behind when they are incarcerated. In 1999, more than 1.5 million minor children had a parent in prison, an increase of more than a half-million since 1991. The removal of a family member may prove beneficial for those left behind—especially someone who has been violent at home or draining financial resources to support a drug habit. But in many circumstances it is traumatic for families, with ramifications that reverberate well beyond an individual's release from confinement. For communities with high rates of removal and return of offenders, these consequences have far-reaching implications.

THE EFFECT OF REENTRY ON FAMILIES AND CHILDREN OF FORMER INMATES

The increase in incarceration during the previous two decades has major consequences for the loved ones of former prisoners. More than 50 percent of all state inmates had children below the age of 18.[91] The increase in the number of female inmates in recent years—the female population of prisoners has more than doubled since 1990—contributes significantly to the total inmates with children. This is an important point, because incarcerated mothers and fathers typically have a different level of involvement with their children before imprisonment, which affects the subsequent caregiving arrangement, ongoing contact during confinement, and reunification upon release.

Although removing certain individuals can be advantageous for some families—resulting in greater attention to children, more resources available, fewer distractions from home life, and less fear or violence in the household—evidence indicates many families suffer when a parent is removed from the home.

Jailed males are fathers to 1.2 million children. Although only 44 percent of these fathers lived with their children prior to prison, most contributed income, child care, and social support.[92] Studies document the desire of nonresident fathers to stay involved with their kids through visits and financial support.

Prison life strains relationships between fathers and their children. Only 40 percent of incarcerated fathers report having weekly contact with their kids, mainly by phone and mail.[93] The frequency of contact decreases in reverse proportion to the length of time served.[94] Given that 60 percent of state inmates are confined in institutions more than 100 miles from their homes, it is no surprise that most fathers (57 percent) report never having a personal visit from their children once admitted to prison.[95]

Although women make up a smaller share of the prison population, the female inmate total is growing faster than that of men. From the child's perspective, imprisonment of a mother has different consequences than that of a father. Because mothers are more likely to be the primary caregivers, a child's placement after a mother is imprisoned is more uncertain than when the father is incarcerated. Less than one-third of children with an incarcerated mother remain with their fathers. Most are taken care of by extended family—53 percent of children with a mother in confinement live with a grandparent and 26 percent stay with other relatives. Some children become part of the foster care system. Ten percent of incarcerated mothers and 2 percent of incarcerated fathers report they have a child in foster care.[96]

Mothers tend to stay in closer touch with their children while incarcerated. Nearly 80 percent reported monthly contact and 60 percent reported contact on a weekly basis. Personal visits are even harder for incarcerated mothers, who, owing to the paucity of women's prisons, tend to be an average of 160 miles farther from their families than are incarcerated fathers.[97] Despite this separation, most mothers expect to be reunited with their children upon release.

According to research conducted by Denise Johnston at the Center for Children of Incarcerated Parents, the family configurations of imprisoned parents and their children can be very complicated.[98] It is not uncommon for both incarcerated mothers and fathers to have offspring by more than one partner. This means that while 44 percent of fathers and 64 percent of mothers report living with their children prior to confinement, they may have only lived with some of their children.[99] Although a parent may have been living with his or her children before being sent to prison, that does not mean the parent was the primary caregiver. These families may include extended family members who have assumed the role of primary caregiver. In Johnston's most recent research of female inmates living in mother–child correctional facilities, fewer than one-third of the women had been living with all of their children prior to incarceration and even fewer were their children's primary care provider.

Incarceration of a parent is a factor in many children's lives. Two percent of all minor children in the United States, in 1999, had a parent in prison. About 7 percent of all African American children had an incarcerated parent. This translates into one in every fourteen African American kids with a mother or father locked up. How is the experience of having a parent incarcerated felt by these children? What are the long-term ramifications? Such questions have received little empirical attention. Existing research does little to parse out the causal connection between imprisonment of a parent and child outcomes.[100] What is known is that children whose parents have been incarcerated experience a range of negative consequences. Conclusions cannot be drawn as to the extent to which consequences are a direct result of a parent being imprisoned or the nature of family life in that household.[101] Several studies have found that children of incarcerated parents are more prone to exhibit low self-esteem, depression, emotional withdrawal from family and friends, and disruptive or other inappropriate behavior. Evidence suggests that children of incarcerated parents are at high risk of future delinquency and/or criminal behavior. Two studies have found that children of offenders are substantially more likely than other kids to be arrested or jailed.[102]

Comprehending the effect of parental incarceration on children is complicated because these consequences may be related to any number of factors—the parent–child separation, the crime and arrest that preceded imprisonment, or the general instability and inadequacy of care at home. The extent to which a child is affected by confinement of a parent depends on several variables, including the age of the child at time of separation, the length of the separation, the level of disruption, the number and result of previous separations, and the availability of family or community support.[103]

The role parents play in the development of their kids' lives and the potential impact of a parent–child separation resulting from incarceration underscore the need to find ways to help families stay in touch during imprisonment and reunite upon release. Maintaining these relationships—between the parents and between the parent and child—during times of confinement can be hard. Hurdles identified by the Women's Prison Association include inadequate information on visiting procedures, little assistance from correctional institutions about visiting arrangements, time involved covering vast distances to reach the facility, visiting procedures that are uncomfortable or humiliating, and concerns about children's reactions to in-prison visits.[104] These circumstances can strain parent–child relationships.[105]

Struggling families can provide some "protective" support that may result in lower recidivism among released prisoners. One study found that inmates with family ties during confinement do better when released than do those without such bonds.[106] A study by the Vera Institute of Justice noted that supportive families were an indicator of success, correlating with lower drug use, greater likelihood of landing work, and reduced criminal activity.[107]

There are situations in which families are better served without an abusive parent or partner in their lives. Some individuals may have been convicted of a violent act in the home, while others exhibit patterns of abuse. Some individuals are better off not returning to a family environment conducive to substance abuse, criminal activity, and other negative influences that could stimulate past behaviors.

There are many committed, caring mothers and fathers in prison who expect to resume their parenting role upon release. Recent legislative initiatives have made it harder for incarcerated parents—especially mothers—to reunite with their kids. The 1997 Adoption and Safe Families Act, which replaces the 1980 Adoption Assistance and Child Welfare Act, mandates termination of parental rights once a child has been in foster care for fifteen or more of the previous twenty-two months. Incarcerated women, on average, serve sentences of eighteen months.[108] The result is that the average incarcerated female whose children are put in foster care could lose the right to reunite with her kids.

Welfare reform legislation could make it harder for parents to rebuild a life with their kids. Returning inmates are at a disadvantage in finding work for several reasons. Access to public benefits that could assist families in securing a stable situation following release has been undercut. Individuals violating parole or probation can be prohibited from receiving federal welfare benefits, food stamps, Supplemental Security Income, and access to public housing.[109] Individuals convicted of a drug felony are permanently barred from receiving federal welfare or food stamps. This could have devastating consequences for incarcerated mothers, as 35 percent are jailed for a drug charge.[110]

Incarceration and reintegration had significant effects on a large and expanding number of families—ranging from loss of financial and emotional support to the social stigma attached to having a loved one behind bars. These complex relationships, added to the great distances between most prisons and their home communities, require creative management on the part of families, government agencies, and community support systems to minimize damage to children and families.

THE IMPACT OF REENTRY ON COMMUNITIES

Returning inmates are concentrated in a few states, a few core urban counties within those jurisdictions, and a handful of neighborhoods within those counties. In 1998, five states accounted for half of all releases, and sixteen states accounted for three-quarters.[111] Within these states, inmates typically return to a relatively few neighborhoods. Compounding problems, these communities generally are already experiencing significant disadvantage. Research has found that high concentrations of prisoner removal and return can further destabilize these communities. Studies conclude that, under certain conditions, high incarceration rates can result in even greater rates of crime. Attempts are being made to leverage these concentrations— where community, corrections, service providers, and the private sector are developing partnerships to anticipate and address the prisoner population returning home.

Most inmates are released into counties containing city centers of metropolitan areas. In 1996, roughly two-thirds of state offenders were released into these "core counties"—an increase from 50 percent in 1984.[112] This translates into a greater percentage of prisoners being returned to a relatively few metropolitan areas. Typically, central cities are poorer than neighboring areas, and confront different challenges, such as loss of labor market share to suburban sectors.

Research indicates that large numbers of inmates come from a relatively small number of neighborhoods within the urban centers of the core counties. In some Brooklyn neighborhoods, one of eight parenting-age males is admitted to prison in a single year.[113] The six police precincts with the highest number of residents on parole account for only a quarter of the total population of Brooklyn, but are home to 55 percent of all Brooklyn's paroleees.[114]

Reviewing data on Ohio state inmates from Cuyahoga County reveals that two-thirds of the county's prisoners come from Cleveland. Concentrations are such that less than 1 percent of neighborhoods in the county account for approximately 20 percent of the county's offenders. In such "high-rate" pockets, somewhere between 8 and 15 percent of the young black males are incarcerated on a given day.[115] Similar conclusions are drawn from Baltimore, where 15 percent of the neighborhoods accounted for 56 percent of inmate releases.[116]

The revolving door of inmate removal and return may further destabilize disadvantaged neighborhoods. Research by Todd Clear and Dina Rose suggests that high rates of imprisonment may disrupt a community's social network, affecting family formation, reducing informal control of children and income to families, and weakening bonds between residents. The investigators believe that when removal and return rates reach a certain tipping point, they may produce greater crime rates, as the neighborhood becomes increasingly unstable and less coercive means of social control are undermined.[117]

Community concentrations are important because the social, economic, and emotional impact of reintegration on individuals and their loved ones becomes compounded. These communities may lack the ability to address needs of residents and offenders, such as work opportunities, health care, substance abuse treatment, housing, and counseling. A California study found considerable gaps between the needs of parolees and available services: There are more than 10,000 homeless parolees and only 200 shelter beds; four mental health clinics must service 18,000 psychiatric cases; and 85,000 released substance abusers must make do with 750 treatment beds.[118] Proximity to services in the high-rate neighborhoods also is a problem. Researchers examined where ex-offenders in Tallahassee, Florida, lived in relation to social services and supervision offices. They discovered that services and supervision offices often were quite a distance from the high-concentration neighborhoods that housed clients.

The disconnect between community needs and expenditures was highlighted by the Wisconsin Sentencing Commission. It found that $2 million in criminal justice funds were spent in one year on arrest, prosecution, and incarceration of drug offenders in one Milwaukee neighborhood that experienced a high crime rate. Police reportedly made 94 arrests at one heavily drug-trafficked intersection within three months. Despite high conviction rates and relatively harsh sentences, crime conditions on that corner did not change. The Sentencing Commission posed strategic questions: Could those government resources have been put to better use? Might redirecting state expenditures produce improved safety results?[119]

This community-level examination of removal and return has sparked new inquiry about effective methods to address reintegration. Would place-based strategies that entail a small team of parole officials partnering with local services be a better way to manage this population? Or might community-based social service providers, employers, faith institutions, neighborhood associations, and families collaborate with corrections and paroling authorities to prepare for prisoner returns, deter misconduct, and improve prospects for reintegration?

New approaches are being explored that focus on problem solving, community partnerships, and public safety. Building on community policing models, the community supervision effort involves place-based management strategies and partnerships between law enforcement agencies and individual residents. Such endeavors entail diverse entities—from prospective employers, to social service providers, to family members, to community corrections organizations, to faith-based institutions. Each component has a unique role to play in anticipating and preparing inmate reintegration. A number of small-scale reentry experiments are being conducted to test some of these proactive approaches. The goal of such projects is improving risk management of released offenders by strengthening individual and community support systems, enhancing monitoring and surveillance, and healing damage done to victims.

A community-based philosophy on prisoner reintegration underscores ideas concerning the public's role in the justice system. In the mid-1990s, the Vermont Department of Corrections commissioned a study to learn what the public expects from the criminal justice system and from offenders.[120] They discovered that citizens desire safety, accountability for the crime, treatment for the returning individual, and involvement in decision making. They want ex-convicts to accept responsibility, acknowledge misconduct, and repair damage inflicted on victims and on the community. Citizens indicated willingness to be involved in planning to promote justice, believing they could be instrumental in assisting correctional authorities to create a safe, just community. This "community justice" strategy opens possibilities for the individual, the community, and the corrections system.

ENHANCING THE CHANCES OF SUCCESSFUL REENTRY

Communities may take many actions to ease offenders' transitions to life after prison. These steps include the following:

Start working with inmates and corrections departments before prisoners are released, to arrange work, housing, health care, and treatment programs.

Meet offenders immediately upon release, providing guidance through the first trying hours and days of freedom.

Create or leverage neighborhood-based networks of workforce development partners and local businesses who will focus on preparation and employment of parolees.

Involve local community-based entities that can assist family members in supporting parolees to overcome substance abuse issues, remain employed, and satisfy mandates of supervision and reintegration plans.

Engage local faith institutions that can facilitate mentoring support in the neighborhood to parolees and their families.

Offer parolees opportunities to participate in community service and demonstrate that they can be assets to the community.

Develop coalitions of local leaders who will oversee reintegration efforts and ensure accountability for community and offender obligations.

The phenomenon of prisoner reentry is not new. Ever since individuals have been locked away, society has had to deal with implications of the moment when the sentence was complete and the inmate returned home. What are the mutual obligations of the ex-offender, his or her family, the victim, the community, and the state? What are the conditions under which reintegration can be achieved? What social goals are to be pursued following the prisoner's return home, and who is responsible for them? How are success and failure defined? How does society respond if failure occurs?

For generations, scholars, philosophers, practitioners, and concerned citizens have wrestled with these basic questions. The reality of inmate reentry leads to the conclusion that prisoner reintegration has yet to receive adequate attention. It is difficult not to conclude that attention focused on prison construction and the frenetic pace of sentencing reform over the past decades have been at the expense of solid thinking about prisoner reentry. The reductions in per capita funding for parole supervision—at a time of considerable increases in underwriting for prison expansion—present a persuasive example of the policy tradeoff. Increasing the size of the prison population does not reduce the problems associated with prisoner reentry. Those difficulties are compounded as more people depart prison.

The shift from indeterminate to determinate sentencing—and the related movement from discretionary to mandatory prison terms—has far-reaching repercussions for the process of reintegration. Even if prison populations had not increased, this change in sentencing philosophy would necessitate a fresh examination of expectations for prisoner reentry. If release from incarceration is automatic, does that alter inmate incentives and correctional authority obligations to prepare for the prisoner's release? If the offender leaves prison having completed his sentence, is there no societal interest in his reintegration?

The dimensions of prisoner reentry demand a closer look at the nexus among the jurisprudence of sentencing, the mission of corrections agencies, the availability and quality of services for prisoners and their families, and the overarching goal of society concerning prisoner reintegration.

An emphasis on reentry highlights new ways to approach these issues. Focusing on the moment of release, with its attendant risks and opportunities, suggests that correctional institutions and community organizations could develop new connections to ease the transition from prison to freedom. Ensuring the inmate has proper identification, a roof over his or her head, and a community agency to report to the next day may avert pitfalls of the immediate transitional stage. Significant links could be created when the health and substance abuse needs of returning inmates are contemplated. Ties to health care providers, drug treatment, transitional work environments, family counseling, and faith institutions should be considered. This strategy encourages moving the reentry planning process into the penitentiary so that these connections may be established in advance of the moment of release.

While prisoner reentry is felt at the community level, state agencies are responsible for the management of the reintegration process. By deploying conditional supervision and graduated sanctions, criminal justice agencies could play an enhanced role in deterring criminal conduct and diminishing drug abuse.[121] But government cannot manage reentry alone. There are opportunities for supervision agencies to collaborate with treatment providers, law enforcement, and the community to engage problem-solving approaches that address risks of reoffending. Such temptations include high-risk places, drug relapse, and reunification with the criminal element. These methodologies do not require a shift in jurisprudence so much as the articulation of a new vision—to enhance the chances of successful return to the community.

Prisoner reentry raises questions concerning ultimate goals of the process. Public safety remains an essential objective. Renewed attention to inmate reintegration could improve the safety of communities and families most affected by the returnees. This perspective of the impact of reentry underscores the range of related possibilities. Could improvements in prisoner reentry generate gains in public health? Might ramifications include reduced levels of drug abuse in a community? Could increased worker output be a by-product? Might measurable improvement in child development and parent–child relationships be expected to follow? Would an emphasis on prisoner reentry spawn a new sense of civic attachment on the part of both the returning inmates and those involved in their transition to communal life?

The broader view of prisoner reentry suggests the goal is best conceptualized as social reintegration, not merely reduction in recidivism. This philosophy envisions a new partnership of public and private entities that have a stake in improving those outcomes, not only out of concern for former inmates, but also out of concern for those whose well-being is affected by their transition. This perspective should pump new energy into age-old debates over the purposes of criminal law and the goals of sentencing.

BLOODSWORTH'S RETURN

During Kirk Bloodworth's first night of freedom, he stayed at his father's home. In the middle of the night, he got up to relieve himself. Thinking he was still in his maximum security cell, standing in front of his old urinal, he left a puddle in the corner of the bedroom. He phoned his lawyer at 3:00 A.M. to share the excitement that he was making toast. It had been nine years since he held a knife in his hands.

The first few months of his emancipation were an absurd roller-coaster ride. The next few years got worse. His mother had died just before the DNA verdict was returned. She never got to hear the official confirmation that her son was innocent. He mourned deeply for his mother. His shattered life seemed to be overwhelming him increasingly each day. His father, Curtis, stood behind him through the entire ordeal, to the point of depleting retirement savings to cover costs of Kirk's legal fees. Curtis knew his son had so much to deal with that he couldn't think clearly.

Regardless of the economy, landing work was a daunting mission. He faced every job application with two strikes against him. "Have you ever been convicted of a crime?" was part of the exchange with every prospective employer. Even if he could clear that hurdle by presenting his official pardon papers, there was an aura of suspicion that hounded him. His past caught up with him in Ocean City when he briefly worked as a prep cook in a restaurant and again in Baltimore when he had a one-day stint representing an environmental concern. Wherever Kirk went, he carried with him a certain notoriety. The people he encountered recognized him and let it be known that Bloodsworth's kind was not welcome.

Before a congressional subcommittee, in June 2000, Bloodsworth offered observations as an expert on the wrongly accused. "I'm having great difficulty putting my life together," he told them.[122]

The tragedy that befell Bloodsworth's victim continued to snowball. Six months after Kirk's Capitol Hill appearance, Dawn Hamilton's father was convicted and sentenced five years for arson. He set ablaze a Baltimore bar where his girlfriend worked. She was on the verge of breaking up with him. He confessed to his attorney that he could not bear the idea of losing another person in his life.

To a situation already tragically overburdened add yet another horror.

Dawn Hamilton's murderer still is not behind bars. Baltimore County prosecutors say the matter is under investigation. They will not disclose whether evidence has been further examined for DNA or if any discoveries have been placed in the national law enforcement databank.

Prosecutors even express doubt as to Bloodsworth's innocence. They do acknowledge they would not convict him on the basis of what is known now.

Bloodsworth's supporters are infuriated by such equivocation. His supporters include many influential people in the criminal justice reform movement. Among those who stand with the ex-inmate are Barry Scheck, civil rights lawyer and cofounder of the Innocence Project, Wayne Smith, Executive Director of the Justice Project, and John Rago, Dean of Duquesne University's Law School in Pittsburgh. Rago considers Bloodsworth a historic figure in American jurisprudence. He has asked Bloodsworth to consult as the school develops its own initiative to assist Pennsylvania inmates claiming innocence.

Rago asserts that Bloodsworth is making a critical difference in the lives of others. He is far from being a token footnote in the history of death penalty abolitionism.

Bloodsworth's ardent supporters have heard him speak publicly. They admire his ability to talk calmly, without bitterness. His delivery is natural, unpretentious, from the heart. His allies appreciate not only the impact he has on an audience, but also the cathartic effect public disclosure has on him. Bloodsworth is fortunate. He finds solace in telling his story.

This deep involvement has given direction to Bloodsworth's life. He has accepted such activism as the rationalization for all he endured. To let everyone know the tragic pitfalls that line the criminal justice system must be the reason he was sent to hell and back.

Bloodsworth's anti–death penalty message is well honed. It doesn't square neatly with arguments over racial bias and geographic disparity frequently cited by capital punishment opponents. Although these factors skew who gets hammered with a death sentence, these points are not the essence of Bloodsworth's teachings. Nor does he sympathize with certain death row residents he left behind. Steven H. Oken, a triple murderer, is one Bloodsworth mentions specifically.

"I'm not weeping for Steven Oken. It's not for him that I want the death penalty abolished," Bloodsworth states emphatically. "But we have to save these people in order to save people like me."[123]

Bloodsworth's healing process is slow but steady. He's written a book on his experience, *Bloodsworth: The True Story of the First Death Row Inmate Exonerated by DNA*.[124] He reads letters from inmates imploring him to look into their cases, correspondence similar to the notes he signed "A.I.M." He still pursues his waterman's passion, having purchased the thirty-eight-foot craft he'd dreamed of and christened Jeanett's Pearl.

COMPENSATION

Like Kirk Bloodsworth, others are being exonerated for crimes they did not commit. Well over a hundred prisoners have been set free who had been scheduled to die for something they did not do. The exonerated have not gained freedom through some legal loophole or technicality. Their innocence has been proven a variety of ways: DNA evidence, another admitting guilt, verified misconduct on the part of law enforcement, etc. They are innocent people who landed in prison because the system failed them. They paid a heavy price—with their freedom, careers, relationships, and dignity.

The topic of compensating the exonerated is not new. The notion dates back to the early 1900s. The movement to compensate the wrongfully convicted has been unable to gain momentum—until now. With more victims being released from jail, the issue of compensating those who have been wrongfully convicted is more relevant than ever before.

One might think the issue of providing compensation to those who have spent time in prison for a crime they did not commit is clearly defined and obvious. However, there is debate among scholars and lawmakers as to the best way to compensate those who have been exonerated without further compromising the justice system. Those who have been wronged by our justice system often are reluctant to initiate civil litigation, which can be painful and time consuming.

A handful of advocates are working to achieve mandatory compensation for the exonerated. A few states have passed laws entitling those wrongfully convicted to receive monetary compensation from the government. The number of jurisdictions adhering to such a policy remains small.

BRIEF HISTORY OF THE INDEMNIFICATION MOVEMENT

Concern for the wrongfully convicted is not a recent phenomenon, but it has been slow to develop. The inception of such research is credited to Edwin M. Borchard. Borchard's interest in the innocent dates to 1913 when he published an article in the *Journal of Criminal Law and Criminology*.[125] According to Borchard, no attempt had been made in the United States to indemnify the wrongfully convicted.

His research culminated in *Convicting the Innocent*, in which he detailed the stories of sixty-five wrongly convicted and punished individuals.[126] *Convicting the Innocent* led to passage of the first federal statute providing limited compensation for those wrongfully convicted of federal crimes.[127]

One of the first documented cases relating to wrongful conviction and compensation is that of Andrew Toth.[128] Toth was sentenced to death on April 8, 1891, for a murder he didn't commit. Toth, a man of Hungarian descent living in Pennsylvania, was eventually exonerated, but upon release, he had no funds for passage back to Hungary. Seeing this, Andrew Carnegie was moved to provide him a pension of $40 a month, enabling him to go home. Carnegie, a wealthy private citizen, was the only person to step forward and attempt to provide Toth with compensation.

The Toth case gave rise to a movement led by John Henry Wigmore, the distinguished dean of the Northwestern University Law School. He explained his thoughts in a 1913 editorial in the *Journal of Law and Criminology*: "to deprive a man of liberty, put him into heavy expense in defending himself, and to cut his power to earn a living—these are the sacrifices which the state imposes on him for the public purpose of punishing crime. And when it is found that he incurred these sacrifices through no fault of his own, that he was innocent, then should not the state at least compensate him, so far as money can do so?"[129]

THE CASE FOR COMPENSATION

Wrongfully convicted individuals have suffered severe harm as a consequence of their imprisonment: they have lost jobs and reputations, often have spent large sums on legal services, have been deprived of liberty, and have suffered detrimental psychological consequences.

Defense lawyer Bryan Stevenson, director of the Equal Justice Initiative of Alabama, says that "the presumption should be, if you were exonerated, the state should compensate you for the time you were in prison and to help make your transition easier into the real world."[130]

Some scholars believe a legislative remedy is the logical answer for issues regarding exoneration and compensation. In his piece, "Tort Reform and the Erroneously Convicted," Craig M. Cooley writes,

While traditional tort law actions (i.e., malicious prosecution, etc) provide the erroneously convicted with at least some avenues of legal redress, simply bringing such action does not guarantee that he or she will adequately be redressed for his or her injuries or whether they will be compensated at all. Compensation for the incorrectly incarcerated should be guaranteed, not a crapshoot. A legislative remedy is the only reliable and fair response to the inevitable mistakes that occur as a by-product of the operation of a criminal justice system as large as ours. States should finally acknowledge their responsibility to provide fair compensation for innocent citizens who have been wrongfully convicted.[131]

Compensating people who have been wrongfully convicted seems like a natural step in curing some of the ills in our criminal justice system. It is important to define the reasons for compensating the wrongfully convicted. It is equally important to craft thoughtful legislation for compensating the wrongfully convicted. Neither the justice system nor the wrongfully convicted will benefit from legislation that merely aims to compensate a victim for lost time. Effective legislation must consider the reasons and ramifications for how the wrongful conviction happened in the first place.

The Life After Exoneration project was founded in 2003 as a collaboration between The Innocence Project and the DNA Identification Technology and Human Rights Center of Berkeley, California. Under the guidance of Peter Neufeld and Barry Scheck of The Innocence Project and Dr. Laurie Lola Vollen of the University of California, the organization provides social services, mentoring, exoneree networking, and state and federal policy development. The project, supported by the Tides Foundation, concluded that legal expenses incurred in pleading their cases and the absence of income during imprisonment deprived the majority of the wrongfully convicted of their assets. The project found that nearly half of wrongfully convicted individuals earned less after release than they did before conviction.

Howard Master detailed the rationales for compensation in his article "Revisiting the Takings-based Argument for Compensating the Wrongfully Convicted."[132] He lists these arguments in defense of compensation:

1. Compensation motivates the government to protect the innocent from wrongful conviction. If governmental entities know they will be liable for damages if they convict an innocent individual, they may be more diligent in the process. Many innocent people are imprisoned because of racism, subpar legal representation, unethical law enforcement, etc. If government officials know there is a hefty price tag for putting the wrong person behind bars, they may pay more attention to the case itself.

2. Compensation provides social insurance. Having a policy that compensates people wrongfully imprisoned reduces the risk of harm from a socially beneficial but still dangerous criminal justice system.

3. It is fair to compensate those who have been wrongfully convicted by a system put in place to protect the innocent, especially if these individuals did nothing to contribute to their own conviction. While this is more a moral argument, it still is valid.

4. Provide equal treatment for those in similar situations. Putting in place a definitive value for time served, etc., and compensating the exonerated equally will ensure equitable compensation for those wrongfully convicted.

Although placing a dollar amount on loss of liberty seems arbitrary, measuring damages in wrongful conviction has proved no more difficult than in any other category of personal injury case. Freedom is valuable and its loss can be measured, if imperfectly, and compensated.

ROADBLOCKS AND BARRIERS

Although a few states offer compensation, that award is not automatic upon release from prison. As journalist Craig Savoye observes, "When a judge vacates a conviction because of DNA evidence, it is not necessarily the legal equivalent of innocence."[133] Some cases of indemnification may depend on getting a pardon by the state's governor, which can be a time-consuming, tedious hurdle to overcome. Such statutes, requiring an unjustly convicted person to first win a full pardon on grounds of innocence in order to bring claim, can be prohibitively discouraging.

Most compensation statutes require wrongfully convicted individuals to take the initiative to surmount onerous procedural obstacles to be eligible for compensation. Even if the procedural and substantive hurdles are overcome, these statutes often provide awards inadequate to fully compensate the exonerated person for legal fees, lost wages while incarcerated, and medical and psychological expenses associated with the trauma of wrongful imprisonment. Placing arbitrary and unjustified limits on compensation guarantees that the wrongfully convicted will be undercompensated. Other statutes limit damage awards to such an extent that filing a claim becomes pointless.

To collect, exonerees must reside in a state that provides for compensation. Only 16 jurisdictions have such legislation. If a former inmate is not lucky, that individual is forced to file a private tort action claiming malicious prosecution, false imprisonment, or legal malpractice. Exonerees may bring suit under the Civil Rights Act of 1871 if their constitutional rights were violated. Besides private and civil rights actions, the mistakenly convicted may turn to their legislature for compensation. While it appears the wrongfully convicted have options to seek relief, each alternative presents difficulties. Prosecutorial and law enforcement immunity routinely shield the state from liability.

The decision to seek compensation is not easily made. Typically, wrongful convictions stem from more than one factor. Once one element is introduced, this may adversely affect a whole host of other considerations. As a result, many wrongfully convicted individuals never seek compensation because legal hurdles discourage them from doing so.

These hurdles include police immunity from prosecution. This makes proving malice difficult. The standard of proof is set so high for someone to establish malicious prosecution and/or false imprisonment that it deters people from bringing suit.

As if the dispiriting hurdles of the common law were not enough, legislative enactments also have demoralizing requirements. These statutes provide little incentive for the unjustly convicted to seek compensation.

CURRENT COMPENSATION STATUTES

According to analyst Timothy W. Maier,

Some say state laws make it all but impossible for the innocent to file lawsuits seeking compensation for the years spent behind bars. Of some 88 inmates who have been exonerated and released because of the work of the New York-based Innocence Project, nearly two-thirds did not receive a dime.... A review by the Associated Press indicates that 43 out of the 110 men exonerated received compensation. The compensation ranged from $25,000 in a Texas case to a $36 million civil judgment shared by the Fordam Heights Four (Chicago, Illinois), who were incarcerated for a combined 65 years. Just 13 of the 110 collected $1 million or more from civil lawsuits.[134]

Vehicles for compensating the wrongfully convicted under common law and constitutional tort doctrines, or, alternatively, through legislative action by special bills or statutory compensation schemes, have not proven capable of providing meaningful remedies to most wrongfully convicted individuals. Most state and federal legislatures have failed to adopt statutory compensation schemes to supplement common-law remedies, and even those jurisdictions that have done so tend to shortchange those who qualify.

Federal law states that a wrongfully imprisoned person can receive a maximum of $5,000 in compensation after exoneration.[135] This figure holds regardless of how many years the individual spent incarcerated.

Only fifteen states and the District of Columbia have laws providing compensation for the wrongfully convicted. These laws are diverse in terms of monetary compensation and requirements to be deemed innocent once wrongfully convicted. More than two-thirds of prisoners exonerated in the past decade have received nothing.

In terms of compensation, some states have minimum awards, some have maximums, some do not provide for punitive damages, and a few even provide for mental health care. Alabama has a minimum of $50,000 for each year of incarceration. California provides merely a maximum of $100 per day of wrongful imprisonment. The District of Columbia has no limit on compensation, but punitive damages are not allowed. Texas allows $25,000 per year up to a maximum of $500,000, plus one year of counseling. New York and West Virginia do not have monetary limits. Perhaps the most open-ended law is that of Tennessee, which states that the court "shall hear claims for compensation by persons wrongfully imprisoned and granted exoneration of unconditional pardon due to innocence."[136]

States also have different requirements for proving one's innocence. While Wisconsin, New Jersey, New York, Maine, and Iowa adhere to "clear and convincing" standards of proof, Texas requires claimants to prove they "did not by his or her act or failure to act contribute to bring about the conviction or imprisonment for which he or she seeks compensation." This means no false confessions, regardless how that confession came about, whether through trickery or coercion. Only Maryland, New York, the District of Columbia, Ohio, West Virginia, and Tennessee do not limit recovery for wages lost during imprisonment. Just a few states make recovery for other damages suffered freely available.[137]

Among scholars, New York's laws regarding compensating the wrongfully convicted are deemed most fair. Statutes enacted by the Empire State comprise model legislation for victims of wrongful convictions. New York requires plaintiffs to establish that (1) their conviction was reversed or, if a new trail was ordered, they were found not guilty; and (2) the reversal or vacation of conviction was made on one or more specific Criminal Procedure Law grounds. If plaintiff can establish these issues, then a claimant can be awarded as much money as a jury sees fit because New York does not limit compensation.[138]

Maier notes that "Lawsuits filed by the exonerated are difficult to win because they must prove misconduct on the part of the police or prosecutor—especially difficult when state laws provide prosecutors and police immunity." If the exonerated are to collect damages, they must rely on individual states for compensation. "Making matters worse is that prosecutors and law enforcement officials often are immune from lawsuits under both state and federal law as long as they were doing their jobs."[139]

The roadblocks to obtaining compensation generally outweigh the desire to seek compensation for time unjustly spent in prison. In the few states where seeking compensation is allowed, many find it just too difficult and cumbersome to devote precious resources to seeking indemnification. For many of the jurisdictions that have compensation statutes, standards are set so high that the law dissuades the same people whom the law was meant to protect.

OPPOSITION TO COMPENSATION

Those opposed to compensation cite various reasons for their beliefs. Among reasons stated are the belief that the state should not be held liable for mistakes of private citizens serving as jurors and the opinion that legislation supporting compensation would open floodgates to others who simply "got off" on a technicality. Others believe that wrongful convictions are part of an imperfect system. They even float the notion that wrongful convictions do not exist, that it's virtually impossible for people to be convicted of crimes they did not commit. Some don't believe the justice system can fail defendants.

"We don't have a perfect system," says Oklahoma legislator William Graves (R), who voted against a compensation bill. "Does that mean the state has to pay every time a jury finds the wrong person guilty?"[140]

Some states fear legislation of this sort would bring forth a slew of plaintiffs who are not truly innocent, but simply not found guilty. We are a litigious society. The impact of monetary awards for those who have not truly been wrongfully convicted could have a significant impact on a state's budget. The best answer to those concerns lies in a study of statutes, which proves the fears unfounded. Evidence that such opportunities are not abused lies in the experience with crime victims compensation statutes, which were enacted to assist a similarly situated class of innocent injured people.

A core value of American criminal jurisprudence is that with all its safe-guards, the system appears to bend over backwards to protect defendants against the power of a police state. This principle is embodied in the maxim "it is far worse to convict an innocent man than to let a guilty man go free." More honest feelings, perhaps, are betrayed by Americans' outrage at O.J. Simpson's not guilty verdict contrasted with the apathy felt by most for the time spent in prison by Kirk Bloodsworth for a crime he did not commit.

There are those who do not believe that wrongful convictions happen. Huff, Rattner, and Sagarin polled participants in the Ohio criminal justice system—judges, prosecutors, public defenders, and police—and asked each to estimate how often they believe wrongful convictions occur. Respondents estimated that 99.5 percent of all guilty verdicts in felony cases are correct.[141]

NATIONAL MOVEMENT

Adele Bernhard, a professor at Pace Law School in White Plains, New York, and a leading authority on compensation of exonerated prisoners says, "We can't seem to get the energy going nationally. There is no constituency to support legislation." She adds, "Some believe because there are so few prisoners exonerated compared to the general prison population, legislators do not see urgency."[142] The matter becomes more a political issue than a legislative one. If voters do not feel a need, then lawmakers do not place this issue on their legislative agenda.

Attitudes toward the exonerated may be a factor in why this issue has not gained momentum. Attitudes toward the wrongfully convicted have been studied since 1932. Professor Borchard argued that the wrongfully convicted were undercompensated because those subject to erroneous conviction were "a weak social group."[143] He suggests those affected by wrongful arrest and conviction continue to be a "weak social group" for two reasons: (1) mi-norities being disproportionately subject to imprisonment and (2) public stigmatization of those who obtain redress through the political process. Be-cause many of the exonerated are from a "socially weak group," the public does not recognize their need for compensation.

Wrongful conviction does not affect enough people for lawmakers to consider it important. And those who are generally affected by wrongful convictions are not considered as important as others. Finally, opponents to compensation have a strong voice and some valid argument. These factors work to prevent compensation of the wrongfully convicted from achieving front-page status.

To overcome these obstacles, more outreach toward media organizations is essential. The media find wrongful conviction stories riveting and news-worthy. What is missing is a call to action. Simply reporting what happened to a particular wrongfully convicted individual and how he or she was released is not enough. Emphasis should be placed on preventing wrongful convictions and the importance of compensating wrongfully convicted individuals.

Traditional tort actions, such as malicious prosecution, may provide the erroneously convicted with some legal redress. However, merely bringing an action does not guarantee the wronged individual will be adequately redressed or compensated at all. This is not acceptable for the erroneously convicted, since that person has already established the wrong levied against him—the mistaken incarceration at the hands of the state. Compensation should not be a crapshoot. It should be guaranteed. Accordingly, a legislative remedy may be the most reliable and fair response to the inevitable mistakes that happen as a by-product of such a large criminal justice system. With mounting evidence of our criminal justice system's susceptibility to error, jurisdictions should admit responsibility to provide fair compensation for innocent citizens who have been wrongly convicted and erroneously incarcerated.

Local coalitions must be encouraged to take on state legislatures. Action is more likely to happen if legislators are confronted personally. Direct lobbying will be more productive than simply hoping legislators passively take notice of this important issue.

With a carefully conceived public communication plan, the awareness of legislators of the need for compensation statutes will be raised. The consequences of heightened consciousness could be state-by-state passage of compensation bills. Local legislatures must not harbor the misconception that wrongful convictions only happen in someone else's backyard. They must be proactive in crafting compensation legislation. Well-considered law allowing for compensation for the wrongfully convicted is an important step in ensuring that our justice system is as fair and equitable as possible.

Reasons and Remedies for Wrongful Convictions

A district attorney in Worcester County, Massachusetts, once asserted, "Innocent men are never convicted. Don't worry about it, it never happens in the [real] world. It is a physical impossibility."[1] The attorney was influenced by the leading legal scholar of the day, the Honorable Learned Hand. Hand believed the "ghost of the innocent man convicted" remains an "unreal dream."[2] With such sentiments, it is not surprising that "One of the most common American myths is the belief that innocent people are not convicted for crimes they have not committed."[3] Unfortunately, the "physically impossible" is possible and the "unreal dream" has repeatedly revealed itself in the daily "reality" of the criminal justice system. Thanks to developments in forensic science—notably DNA technology—the American public is seeing Judge Hand's "unreal dream." It is a common occurrence to read about an erroneously convicted individual being exonerated by DNA evidence.

While recognizing that "America's criminal justice system creates significant risk that innocent people will be systematically convicted"[4] and that "the criminal justice system is not fallible"[5] is one thing, compelling the state and federal government to accept responsibility for their parts in producing wrongful conviction is another matter. Just sixteen jurisdictions have passed indemnification statutes to compensate the wrongly convicted. Thirty-six states have not enacted indemnification legislation. Only 37 percent of wrongfully convicted individuals are offered relief.[6] This being so,

Edwin M. Borchard's insights of 1913 are still an accurate assessment of
the state of legislative affairs: "When social justice is the watchword of legislative reform, it is strange that society utterly disregards the plight of the
innocent victim of unjust conviction."[7]

WRONGLY CONVICTED: PAST AND PRESENT

The public may be hardened to the notion of criminals harming innocent
individuals, but everyone cringes when the judicial system dishes out injustice
to innocent people. American jurisprudence prides itself on the promise of
due process enunciated in the Constitution. These pledges were enacted
to ensure only those guilty beyond a reasonable doubt are convicted. The
President's Commission on Law Enforcement and Administration of Justice
issued a report in 1967 entitled, "The Challenge of Crime in a Free Society."
The Commission noted, "What distinguishes the [criminal justice] system of
one country from another is the extent of protections it offers individuals
in the process of determining guilt and imposing punishment." Moreover,
the Commission stated, "Our system of justice deliberately sacrifices much
in efficiency and effectiveness to ... protect the individual."

During the twentieth century, the due process clause of the Fourteenth
Amendment began to flex its muscle. At times, the Supreme Court had
appeared more concerned with the criminal process than crime. As legal
scholars point out, "Never had the term due process been more rigorously
implemented in all phases of justice—from arrest to final release from state
control. Such phrases as Miranda warnings, the exclusionary rule, equity and
fairness, arbitrary and capricious decisions, fair trial, and inmate rights ...
[were] forced on the system by federal and higher state courts."[8] These
safeguards are meant to protect the innocent from unintentional mistakes
and intentional abuses of police, prosecutors, and judges.

Ironically, even though the American judicial system emphasizes the need
for due process, an unprecedented number of errors are being recognized.

EDWIN M. BORCHARD—ONE OF THE FIRST TO SOUND THE ALARM

Concern for the innocent and wrongly convicted is not new. Edwin M.
Borchard pioneered such research. Borchard's interest for the wrongly convicted dates to 1913, when, triggered by his study of governmental liability,
or lack thereof, he wrote an article for the *Journal of Criminal Law and
Criminology*. According to his findings, "No attempt seems to have been
made in the United States to indemnify [the wrongly convicted] ... although
cases of shocking injustices are not infrequent occurrences."[9] During the
next two decades, Borchard investigated the plight of the erroneously convicted. Borchard's work culminated in the groundbreaking book *Convicting*

the Innocent, in which he tells the stories of sixty-five wrongly convicted and punished individuals. From Borchard's perspective,

Among the most shocking ... [and] glaring of injustices are erroneous convictions of innocent persons. The State must prosecute persons legitimately suspected of crime; but when it is discovered after conviction that the wrong man was condemned, the least the State can do to right his irreparable injury is to reimburse the innocent man, by an appropriate indemnity, for the damage suffered.[10]

Borchard's research revealed that wrongful convictions were not limited to any jurisdiction as miscarriages of justice occurred in both federal and state systems. While wrongful convictions most often stemmed from murder trials (twenty-nine of sixty-five), such injustices were also reported in robbery cases (twenty-three), forgery (five), criminal assaults (four), obscenity cases (two), accepting bribes (one), and prostitution (one). The primary causes of these erroneous convictions included "misidentification, circumstantial evidence, frame-ups, overzealous police or prosecutors, prior convictions or unsavory records, community opinion demanding a conviction, and unreliability of expert evidence. Erroneous convictions result from guilty pleas and confessions by innocent persons, or from the use of a false alibi by an innocent accused."[11] Many of these variables still affect the justice system, causing numerous wrongful convictions. As Borchard noted in 1941, "The accidents ... of the criminal law happen through an unfortunate concurrence of circumstances."[12] According to Bernhard, "Borchard's portraits convince us that anyone could be both wrongly accused and unable to prove innocence.[13]

Following Borchard's trailblazing efforts, Erle Stanley Gardner contributed to the literature on wrongful convictions. In his 1954 work, *The Court of Last Resort*, Gardner tells the stories of eight innocent people convicted of murder. Gardner's publication parallels Borchard's, both being more descriptive than normative. Gardner details eight tragic instances of wrongful convictions. Though Gardner underscored the various causal dynamics resulting in the injustices, he offered little constructive guidance about what needed to be done to diminish erroneous convictions.

Jerome Frank, a Second Circuit Court of Appeals judge, and his daughter Barbara published an important work twenty-five years after Borchard's research. The father–daughter team's book *Not Guilty* depicted the misfortune of a different set of wrongly convicted individuals.[14] The Franks articulated the causes of erroneous convictions. They suggested remedies to eliminate these injustices. On the heels of the Franks' work, Edward Radin published another significant text on the topic.[15] In outlining the despair of wrongly convicted individuals, Radin's manuscript dispelled "one of the most common American myths: the belief that innocent people are not convicted for crimes they have not committed."[16] He exposed the notion that "wearing a detective's badge does not automatically make that man diligent or competent. He may conduct an inept investigation, jump to conclusion rather than let facts lead the way, be too lazy to check out information thoroughly, or ignore facts which tend to support the story told by a suspect."[17] Radin questioned the competence of law enforcement agencies responsible for collecting evidence that sent an innocent individual to prison.

Christine Davies and Ruth Brandon, in 1972, wrote *Wrongful Imprisonment: Mistaken Convictions and Their Consequences*. While the authors focused on the English criminal justice system, they provided comparisons with the French and American judicial systems as well. For three years, Brandon and Davies gathered material from newspapers, trial transcripts, books, attorneys, and interviews with exonerees. Borchard's investigation asserted that "serendipity accounted for the discovery of many of the mistakes."[18] Brandon and Davies echoed the sentiment noting, "In a large proportion of the cases, the new evidence which got the case reopened only came to light as a result of some completely chance occurrence."[19] Davies and Brandon believed the wrongful convictions they identified "looked more like the tip of a much larger iceberg."[20] Davies and Brandon identified key causal factors as misidentification, confessions made under duress or without adequate mental competence, withholding of exculpatory evidence, perjury, ineffective assistance of counsel, and jailhouse snitches. Preceding the 1990s, the decade of DNA exonerations, Martin Yant published *Presumed Guilty: When Innocent People Are Wrongly Convicted*. This work underscored more wrongful convictions and their causes. According to the author, "The American criminal justice system is too often a source of injustice for the innocent rather than of justice for the guilty."[21]

WRONGFUL CONVICTIONS AND CAPITAL PUNISHMENT

Death penalty opponents have written extensively on the subject of executing the innocent. The earliest effort was published in 1912 by the American Prison Congress.[22] The Prison Congress stated that it would "carefully investigate every reported case of unjust conviction and try to discover if the death penalty has ever been inflicted upon an innocent man."[23] After reviewing these cases for a year, the Congress concluded that no innocent person had been put to death. Subsequent higher-quality research has debunked the Congress's finding.[24]

Executing the innocent is the strongest argument against capital punishment. As Professor MacNamara noted in 1969, while such sentiment has "frequently been sneered at as 'unAmerican' or unlearned in the law,"[25] it must be perceived as credible since research suggests "innocent lives have been executed."[26]

Past and present Supreme Court Justices have touched on the topic. In *Furman* v. *Georgia*, Justice Thurgood Marshall asserted grave concern about executing the innocent.[27] According to Marshall, "There is evidence that innocent people have been executed before their innocence [could] be proved."[28] Longtime capital punishment proponent, Justice Sandra Day O'Connor, speaking to the Minnesota Women Lawyers Association in Summer 2001, commented, "If statistics are any indication, the system may well be allowing innocent defendants to be executed."[29] O'Connor took her concerns a step further at a subsequent meeting of the Nebraska Bar Association when she warned that "innocent people may well continue to receive the death penalty if lawyers don't . . . start doing more pro bono work for indigent defendants."[30] Justice William J. Brennan expressed the "bleakest fact of all is that the death penalty is imposed not only in a freakish and discriminatory manner, but also in some cases upon defendants who are *actually innocent*."[31]

Congress has spoken to the point: "Judging by past experience, a substantial number of death row inmates are indeed innocent and there is a high risk that some of them will be executed. The danger is inherent in the punishment itself and the fallibility of human nature."[32]

That a growing number of influential individuals is acknowledging the vulnerability of the capital punishment system is a tribute to the investigation of Hugo Bedau and Michael Radelet. In the authors' words, "Few errors made by government officials can compare with the horror of executing a person wrongly convicted of a capital crime."[33] In their groundbreaking work, Radalet and Bedau outlined 350 twentieth-century cases in which convicted capital (or potential capital) defendants subsequently were found innocent. The researchers identified twenty-three cases in which defendants who were probably innocent were nonetheless executed.[34] Following their probe, Bedau and Radelet, along with Boston-based writer Constance Putnam, published results of their continued research in a 1992 text, *In Spite of Innocence*. While this book identified sixty-six more wrongful murder convictions, bringing the researcher's total to 416, the authors were unable to pinpoint any more cases where a presumably innocent individual was executed. Following this work, Bedau and Radelet teamed with William Lofquist to conduct further studies on the fallibility of capital convictions.[35] Their research unearthed seventy cases where death row inmates were later released because of doubts about their guilt.

The unprecedented number of exonerations prompted the authors to calculate that, "With 313 executions in the U.S. between 1970 and 1985, one death row inmate is released because of innocence for every five inmates executed."[36] Another study revealed that twenty-one condemned prisoners were released from death row between 1993 and 1997.[37] By mid-2004, 115 individuals had been freed from death row after their innocence was established. From these numbers, it appears that "miscarriages of justice are far more likely to occur in capital cases than in other felony prosecutions."[38]

In 1988, Arye Rattner published the most comprehensive synopsis of information on known injustices in the United States, regardless of offense or cause—205 erroneous convictions from 1900 on. In 45 percent of Rattner's cases the crime was murder, and in 12 percent the penalty was death.[39] Although this research establishes a heightened risk of executing the innocent, the U.S. Congress nonetheless enacted legislation making federal habeas corpus remedies for actual innocence more difficult to secure.[40]

That thirteen death row inmates were exonerated in Illinois over the past quarter century prompted Governor George Ryan to impose a moratorium on executions in January 2000.[41] Three years later, believing the state legislature was not fixing the system, Ryan commuted the sentences of all those on death row. In May 2002, Maryland Governor Parris Glendening imposed a similar moratorium. This decree held until Glendening's successor, Robert Ehrlich, allowed Steven Oken's execution in June 2004.

Fearing execution of the innocent, two federal judges ruled the federal death penalty unconstitutional. In *U.S. v. Quinones*, Judge Rakoff held the 1994 Federal Death Penalty Act (18 U.S.C. sections 3591–3598) unconstitutional.[42] That September, Vermont Chief Judge William K. Sessions III followed Rakoff's reasoning and ruled the federal death penalty statute violates the due process clause because of "relaxed evidentiary standards" in the penalty phase of capital cases.[43]

Two Virginia cases—Joseph O'Dell and Roger Keith Coleman—gained notoriety for their focus on whether the innocent have already been executed. Both men were convicted with circumstantial evidence and both cases involved questionable forensic science testimony. O'Dell's case involved a suspect DNA analysis,[44] while Coleman's involved an overexaggerated hair identification.[45] Supporters for both wanted certain pieces of biological evidence retested, postexecution, to determine innocence. The Virginia Supreme Court rejected both requests concluding the Commonwealth was not legally obligated to reexamine evidence to establish whether an innocent man had been executed.[46] Outgoing Governor Mark Warner ordered DNA testing in Coleman's case in January, 2006. Unfortunately for Coleman, the unprecedented procedure confirmed guilt.[47]

PROVING ACTUAL INNOCENCE THROUGH DNA

When DNA testing came onto the criminal justice scene it was touted as the "greatest advance in crime fighting technology since fingerprints."[48] While its initial purpose was to identify "bad guys," DNA evidence has had the greatest impact in the struggle against wrongful convictions. "The introduction of DNA evidence and its acceptance as a forensic tool to identify the guilty and exonerate the innocent has revealed that the innocent as well as the guilty are convicted and punished."[49] The number of postconviction DNA exonerations exceeds 115.[50] The growing awareness of postconviction DNA exonerations was made possible by a 1996 Department of Justice publication that catalogued postconviction exonerations between 1989 and 1996.[51] Beginning with the exoneration of Gary Dotson, the document detailed twenty-seven other wrongly convicted individuals who achieved freedom through DNA analysis. Cases originated in fifteen jurisdictions between 1979 and 1991. The convicted men, on average, spent seven years in prison.[52]

Many argue that more inmates could establish innocence if not for DNA backlogs. While nearly half the states have enacted postconviction DNA statutes, many of these laws were enacted without consideration for how they will interact with "traditional" postconviction remedies, which are governed by strict procedural rules, often serving to deny petitioners substantive review. While improvements have been implemented concerning postconviction DNA examination, other barriers still exist for the wrongly convicted. Crime labs across the country are severely backlogged. "At least 180,000 rape kits containing physical evidence sit in storage, waiting for technicians to pinpoint genetic clues."[53] Even though the FBI launched a national DNA data bank in 1998, samples from 600,000 convicts await processing.[54] Backlogs have been identified in more than a dozen jurisdictions. In an effort to reduce the nationwide backlog, then–Attorney General John Ashcroft directed $30 million from the Justice Department to help states hire more DNA technicians and upgrade technology.[55] Rectifying the logjam will identify the wrongly convicted and help track true perpetrators.[56] Despite these backlogs, "DNA testing has demonstrated far more wrongful convictions occur than the most cynical scholars had suspected."[57]

AS MATTERS STAND

Innocent people are convicted of offenses they never committed. As noted by Givelber, "Judging from the media, convictions of innocent parties represent a pressing problem for this country's criminal justice system."[58] Scholars have intensified their examination of wrongful convictions over the past two decades. Sociologists have conducted studies to assess how the socially constructed criminal justice system cranks out wrongful convictions.[59] Huff, Rattner, and Sagarin surveyed criminal justice practitioners in Ohio (judges, prosecutors, defense attorneys, police officers, etc.), asking them to estimate how often innocent citizens are wrongly convicted. Huff and his colleagues chose Ohio because of its population base (seventh largest in the United States), its demographic mix, and its representative criminal justice system.

According to their findings, respondents anticipated that 99.5 percent of all guilty verdicts in felony cases are correct. Assuming this figure's accuracy,

Huff and colleagues ventured that such a percentage would result in considerable questionable verdicts every year. For instance, if 70 percent of those charged with felonies are convicted[60] and if 99.5 percent of the convictions are accurate, the researchers concluded that almost 10,000 people were erroneously convicted in 1993 on the basis of approximately 2,848,000 arrests that year.[61]

Other researchers have put the number of wrongful convictions between 0.8 and 4 percent.[62] This percentage will increase, as will be seen in the many states that have enacted postconviction DNA statutes. How many postconviction DNA exonerations will there be? As Scheck and Neufeld note, "It is impossible to answer this question precisely, but one can confidently identify certain trends. ... In little more than four years, [eighty seven] more have come to light." In short, "the pace of exonerations is accelerating."[63] Despite DNA and innocence research over the past decade, scholars have yet to design a method that accurately gauges how many cases of false positives actually occur in a year.

Although determining the precise percentage of wrongful convictions is an essential objective for the legal community, identifying and combating the causes of such convictions is of equal significance. Once identified, appropriate measures can be implemented to help remedy the causes.

The Role of Innocence Commissions: Identifying Reasons and Remedies for Wrongful Convictions

"The vigilant search for the truth is the hallmark of our criminal justice system. Our methods of investigation, rules of criminal procedure, and appellate process are designed to ensure that the guilty are apprehended and convicted while the innocent are protected," according to former U.S. Attorney General Janet Reno.[64] The Supreme Court has reinforced Reno's notion by stating, "The central purpose of any system of criminal justice is to convict the guilty and free the innocent."[65]

"At least twenty-seven states and the District of Columbia presently have at least one case in which a wrongly convicted person has been exonerated by DNA testing. Those cases present a powerful argument for examining the systems that produced those errors."[66] Americans are afforded more legal protections against wrongful convictions than the citizens of any other country. The Constitution's first ten Amendments alone provide nineteen individual rights for alleged criminal defendants. Even with these safeguards, erroneous convictions still permeate the justice system. Wrongful convictions threaten the integrity of the entire process. They challenge the validity of the system's verdicts.

When such mistakes happen it seems logical to ascertain why and how the wrongful conviction came to be. Drawing a parallel from the world of medicine, when a young, healthy individual dies unexpectedly, the medical community does not simply bury the deceased. Endeavoring to understand why such an anomaly occurred, the medical community engages in probing inquiry to determine the precise cause of death. Such investigations not only shed light on medical irregularities exhibited by the deceased, but also may identify a more pervasive problem for an entire class of people. An autopsy conducted on a female, for example, may supply breast cancer researchers with information on how to safeguard the female population from the disease. Similarly, "by studying the details of wrongful conviction cases and following the trail of misinformation from its origin ... we can gain insight into how wrongful convictions occur."[67]

Proponents of our present system disregard wrongful convictions as mere aberrations, unavoidable in any judicial system. They refuse to acknowledge that the American criminal justice system may have certain structural and legal impediments prone to generate mistakes. So strong is their conviction they refuse to test whether their "anomaly" theory carries water. To examine this hypothesis and learn more about the causal mechanisms that produce erroneous convictions, our justice system needs to institute innocence commissions to study the causes and cures of wrongful convictions. Martin Yant's *Presumed Guilty* calls for establishing a quasi-judicial "Court of Last Resort" as an adjunct to state supreme courts to consider the innocence of those claiming to have been wrongfully convicted. In addition to identifying trends and causes of erroneous convictions and suggesting remedial actions, such innocence commissions "would offer convicted defendants with viable claims of actual innocence a state-funded mechanism to consider and investigate their claims after their convictions and unsuccessful appeals, instead of relegating such defendants to attempts to make a disfavored and often restricted or even procedurally prohibited successive petition for post-conviction relief."[68]

Most states lack the machinery to conduct extensive postconviction investigations. Jurisdictions have little interest in making available the tools to implement such a time consuming reexamination of a wrongful conviction. This is surprising considering the exhaustive inquiries conducted following various mishaps. Think: Exxon Valdez. As Neufeld and Scheck observe, "In the United States, there are grave consequences when an airplane falls from the sky; an automobile has a defective part; a patient is the victim of malpractice, a bad drug, or an erroneous laboratory report. Serious inquiries are made: What went wrong? Was it systemic breakdown? An individual's mistake? Was there official misconduct? Can anything be done to correct the problem and prevent it from happening again?"[69]

This is not the case with the criminal justice system. "Only the criminal justice system exempts itself from self-examination. Wrongful convictions are seen not as catastrophes but topics to be avoided."[70] Even though an erroneous conviction and prolonged prison sentence, or worse, a death sentence, "is a human catastrophe of almost unparalleled proportion, ordinarily no inquiry is made into the causes of the error. The order setting aside conviction is a one-line order entered in trial court. Occasionally, an appellate decision addresses the errors. But almost never is there a searching inquiry to determine what led to the errors, and how they can be prevented in the future."[71]

While the American criminal justice system ignores examining the causal dynamics of wrongful convictions, other countries have stepped forward. Not only have they accepted responsibility for erroneous convictions, they have endeavored to make certain such injustices do not recur.

THE CANADIAN EXPERIENCE

Canadian officials have had their share of wrongful convictions. Unlike the United States, Canadian authorities have taken the matter of wrongful convictions head-on, viewing such injustices as a manifestation of a flawed system instead of inconsequential anomalies. The Canadian government has made substantial progress toward alleviating the crisis of wrongful convictions. The cases of Guy Paul Morin and Thomas Sophonow were two of the more notorious examples of Canadian wrongful convictions.

Morin's erroneous conviction stemmed from the 1984 murder of nine-year-old Christine Jessop.[72] Although originally acquitted, Morin's favorable verdict was overturned on appeal. Unlike most jurisdictions, Canadian law allows prosecution to appeal jury acquittals when errors of law exist.[73] The appellate prosecutors argued that the judge mistakenly instructed the jury they should acquit if they had a reasonable doubt about any individual piece of evidence, and that psychiatric testimony was not relevant to the question of guilt. Prosecutors won the appeal. Morin was convicted after his second trial. Following conviction, Morin appealed. On January 23, 1995, on the basis of fresh evidence, Morin was acquitted again.

After exoneration, the Lieutenant Governor in Council insisted a Public Inquiry be conducted since the "course of events ... had raised certain questions about the administration of justice in Ontario."[74] The Province of Ontario ordered an unprecedented comprehensive review of its criminal justice system. The Lieutenant Governor, in 1996, appointed a Commission on the Proceedings Involving Guy Paul Morin that was led by a former judge of the Quebec Court of Appeal. The mission of the Commission was threefold: (1) determine why and how an innocent individual was convicted; (2) make recommendations that would prevent future miscarriages of justice; and (3) enlighten the citizenry about the criminal justice system in general and the action against Morin specifically.

After five months of hearings, the commission produced a two-volume, 1,400-page report detailing 119 recommendations for improving the Canadian criminal justice system. The commission's advice centered on issues of questionable forensic science, dubious police tactics, jailhouse snitch and informant testimony, prosecutorial overreaching, defense counsel training and competence, jury instructions, and the case law and rules governing postconviction review. American authorities would do well to heed Judge Kaufman's concluding comment, "The challenge for all participants in the administration of justice in Ontario will be to draw upon this experience and learn from it."[75]

While Guy Paul Morin tolerated two trials, Thomas Sophonow was forced to endure three. Following his third adjudication, Sophonow was convicted of the 1981 strangulation of sixteen-year-old Barbara Stoppel.[76] However, in 1985, the Manitoba Court of Appeal acquitted Sophonow. Although acquitted, Sophonow spent thirteen years trying to gain a full pardon. Responding to external pressure, Winnipeg Police reopened the case in 1998. On June 8, 2002, two years after the investigation was reopened, Winnipeg officials finally acknowledged that Sophonow was factually innocent while also declaring they identified another suspect. Accepting responsibility for the injustice, Manitoba government personnel publicly apologized to Sophonow and announced a Commission of Inquiry would be established to investigate the police work and court proceedings to assess errors and determine compensation. As in Morin's review, the Sophonow Commission generated an in-depth report outlining the circumstances, oversights, and errors that resulted in the system's disservice to Sophonow. The Commission detailed suggestions that if implemented would improve the administration of justice in Canada. Recommendations pertained to coerced confessions, improved eyewitness identification procedures, and restrictions on jailhouse informants.

Similarly, when Donald Marshall, Jr., was exonerated of a 1971 murder, Nova Scotia authorities launched a "searching inquiry" to determine why and how an innocent man was convicted.[77] The provinces of Newfoundland and Labrador also have conducted "searching inquiries" following Greg Parsons' exoneration by DNA evidence. Parsons, a Newfoundland bodybuilder, had been erroneously convicted of murdering his mother. Following the exoneration, Newfoundland Justice Minister Kelvin Parsons (no relation to Greg) promised a thorough, independent, public investigation of the proceedings.[78]

THE ENGLISH EXPERIENCE

England's Criminal Cases Review Commission (CCRC) is similar to the postexoneration Commissions of Canada. The CCRC's mandate "is to review applications of convicted defendants who claim they have been wrongfully convicted and to refer cases to the court of appeal for review where there is a 'real possibility that the conviction, verdict, finding or sentence would not be upheld were the reference to be made.'"[79] During its first three years, the CCRC received more than 3,500 applications for assessment. The CCRC evaluated nearly 2,400 of those. Of the cases reviewed, 203 (or 4.3 percent) were referred for appellate consideration. Of the 203 appellate-reviewed cases, 49 have been fully adjudicated. The court quashed the conviction in thirty-eight of the fully reviewed cases.[80] The CCRC is on pace to receive 850 cases annually, of which 500 are deemed review eligible. Of those, roughly thirty-five are referred to the Court of Appeal. In 68 percent of the referred matters, the convictions are quashed; while in 80 percent, the sentences are quashed.[81]

THE ILLINOIS EXPERIENCE

While no U.S. jurisdiction has comprehensively reinvestigated a specific injustice to recommend improvements in its criminal justice system, there are commissions examining clusters of wrongful convictions. These studies are conducted to identify remedial actions that could be taken to ensure such injustices do not recur. As there have been an unacceptable number of exonerations in capital cases, commissions have been developed in various states to study the effectiveness of the capital justice system. Leading the way was just such a commission in Illinois. As discussed in Chapter 2, Illinois had exonerated more death row inmates than it had executed since 1977, by thirteen to twelve. On the heels of Anthony Porter's 1999 release came a Chicago Tribune investigative series on the death penalty which ran in November of that year. The newspaper exposé revealed that "capital punishment in Illinois [was] a system so riddled with faulty evidence, unscrupulous trial tactics and legal incompetence that justice had been forsaken."[82] Mills and Armstrong unearthed the fact that more than two-thirds of the 285 Illinois capital convictions since 1977 had been reversed because of "fundamental error." These revelations led Governor Ryan to declare a moratorium on executions on January 31, 2000.

Following his moratorium, Ryan appointed a multidisciplinary, blue-ribbon Commission on Capital Punishment. The panel was to review Illinois' capital system and suggest reforms to rehabilitate the state's death sentence. Frank McGarr, a former federal judge, chaired the Commission. Its fourteen members included prosecutors, defense lawyers, former U.S. Senator Paul Simon, novelist Scott Turow, and the chief of staff to the Chicago police superintendent. The Commission examined every capital case in Illinois dating back twenty years. The Commission assessed the state's capital punishment system—from initial police involvement through trial and sentencing, appeals, and postconviction and clemency proceedings. After two years of hearings, the Commission submitted its final report in April 2002. The Commission issued eighty-five recommendations and stated that, "if implemented . . . [these recommendations would] enhance the fairness, justice and accuracy of capital punishment in Illinois."[83] The fourteen-chapter document discussed a range of substantive and procedural issues, including pretrial investigations by law enforcement officials, DNA and forensic testing, capital punishment eligibility criteria, prosecutorial functions in capital matters, the role of defense counsel and trial judge, pretrial proceedings, the guilt–innocence phase, the sentencing phase, imposing the sentence of death, and postconviction proceedings. The legislature's failure to act on the Commission's recommendations prompted Governor Ryan, just before vacating office, to commute the sentences of all those on Illinois' death row.

Following Illinois' self-examination, other jurisdictions have formed study commissions to guage whether their state's system of capital justice is effective. Recognizing the need for such a study, Arizona's Attorney General Janet Napolitano formed the . . . Capital Case Commission to make recommendations to ensure that the death penalty process is fair to defendants and victims."[84] Its objective is to assess Arizona's capital process and ensure that it functions in a fair, timely, and orderly fashion. The Commission intends to assess how methodically claims of innocence are handled. Indiana, Nebraska, Virginia, and North Carolina are among the jurisdictions that are reevaluating the dynamics and complexities of their capital systems. Ensuring adequate safeguards to protect the innocent is at the core of these self-examinations.[85]

Universities and law schools have independently undertaken to "identify the causes of false convictions . . . and to develop a comprehensive set of criminal justice reforms to prevent the perpetuation of these flaws, which, if left uncorrected, will continue to produce false convictions."[86] Influenced by the outbreak of DNA exonerations, students at Arizona State University College of Law set about identifying the systemic weaknesses in the criminal justice system. In a seminar setting, students sought remedies for those flaws.[87] Their goal was to create a "Model Act embodying a comprehensive set of criminal justice system reforms."[88] After examining numerous studies probing various aspects of the criminal justice system that contributed to false convictions, the students discussed their findings. They debated reforms and policy considerations. By the conclusion of the seminar, the students transformed chosen policies into statutory language. The intent of the Model Act was to minimize the chance of erroneous convictions without lowering the probability of accurate verdicts. Each reform was designed to prevent innocent people from being convicted while preserving the system's ability to correctly identify and convict guilty culprits. Reforms were suggested in the areas of witness interviewing, lineups and photo-spreads, interrogation of suspects, admissibility of confessions, indigent legal representation, underwriting, forensic science, discovery, preservation of evidence, postconviction procedures, and postrelease compensation.

Georgetown University Law Center's Constitution Project assembled a thirty-member committee of former judges, prosecutors, defense lawyers, journalists, and scholars to "address the deeply disturbing risk that

Americans are being wrongly convicted in capital crimes."[89] By examining the complexities of the capital system, the Project attempted to create bipartisan approaches to contemporary constitutional issues. The members of the Project published their findings in 2001. The members advanced eighteen recommendations, such as establishing a minimum standard for capital counsel, making the mentally retarded ineligible for a death sentence, devising mechanisms to ensure the death penalty is not imposed in a racially biased way, requiring jurisdictions to preserve DNA evidence, mandating that prosecuting attorneys provide "open-file discovery," and requiring judges to instruct juries that lingering doubt about guilt may be considered a mitigating circumstance. One major objective of the recommendations was to establish safeguards against the tendency of decision making in the criminal justice system to "pass the buck."

CAUSES OF WRONGFUL CONVICTIONS

Although the United States has not undertaken an all-inclusive examination of a high-profile erroneous conviction, the previously mentioned studies supply information concerning causes of false convictions. Whether sincere or not, the leading causes of wrongful convictions are eyewitness misidentification, fraudulent and flawed forensic science, false confessions, jailhouse snitches, and prosecutorial misconduct.[90] The Innocence Project Web site notes that wrongful convictions have occurred because prosecutors knowingly used false testimony; coerced witnesses; used improper closing arguments; entered into evidence knowingly false statements; and fabricated the content and character of evidence, perjury,[91] and ineffective assistance of counsel. "Since Illinois reinstated capital punishment in 1977, 26 Death Row inmates have received a new trial or sentencing because their attorneys' incompetence rendered the verdict or sentence unfair. And 33 defendants sentenced to death were represented by an attorney who had been, or was later, disbarred or suspended—disciplinary sanctions reserved for conduct so incompetent, unethical or criminal that the state believes an attorney's license should be taken away."[92]

When an innocent person is convicted, the media and judicial system typically attribute the miscarriage of justice to an isolated cause. When such injustices are thoughtfully investigated, however, it becomes clear that injustices do not emerge simply because one person made an error. As Castelle and Loftus note, "Much of the current research into wrongful conviction cases focuses on one mistake or one part of the criminal justice process in which a mistake occurred. While these studies are important because they detail how such mistakes happen, they do not explain how failures in one part of the process can shape the development of the case."[93]

Loftus and Castelle continue, "Rarely is someone innocent for one reason alone; on the contrary, a person who is innocent for one reason should be innocent for many reasons." The authors observe, "When an error in identification is made other evidence should conflict with this identification. If the wrong face has been identified, the person with the wrong face will also have the wrong fingerprints and will likely be the wrong height, wrong weight, and wrong age and have the wrong DNA, wrong hair, wrong clothes, wrong jewelry, wrong scars, wrong tatoos. The person with the wrong face will have been somewhere else at the time of the crime."[94] Once an initial cause enters the scene the entire picture is distorted, leading to the injustice. Most false convictions contain numerous errors acting in concert to produce unjust results.

REMEDIES TO REDUCE THE INCIDENCE OF WRONGFUL CONVICTIONS

The following subsections illuminate policies meant to minimize miscarriages of justice. The subsections are organized in approximate chronological order in which they occur during crime investigation and litigation.

Eyewitness Identification Procedures: Interviewing Witnesses

Police officers get little training in how to elicit accurate information from witnesses. These authorities rarely are instructed in modern and empirically tested techniques of interviewing. Researcher Gary Wells observed that errors routinely committed by police officers while conducting interviews included asking closed-ended questions, interrupting witnesses midnarrative, and asking questions in a rigid, predetermined sequence.[95] Accordingly, good practice should require that police departments provide initial and ongoing training of all staff in effective interviewing techniques. Such instruction should be tailored to an employee's role in relation to witnesses and to the circumstances in which the officer interacts with witnesses. Training should be offered so the employee acquires appropriate skills to handle such encounters. In interviewing witnesses, officers should engage in no prompting and should ask only open-ended questions. Witnesses must refrain from guessing.

Examples of how not to conduct an interview abound in sports journalism. When the star athlete–turned TV commentator thrusts his microphone in the face of today's hero, the protocol for enlightened interviewing gets mangled. The open-ended "Explain how you got open to score the game-winning jump shot?" becomes the leading "Must've felt good to hit that last jumper, especially after having such a disappointing fourth quarter?" That second question isn't even a question. It certainly won't elicit any worthwhile information. Why bother the interviewee, when the interviewer is answering his own question?

All interviews concerning felony investigations should be audio or video recorded. The method of documentation will depend upon available technology. Recordings should be preserved by investigators, prosecutors, defense lawyers, and, in certain circumstances, by judges and juries as well, to assist in reconstructing events and the individuals involved. Whether a witness's recollections are accurate or not is critical to the quality of the investigation that is influenced by those statements. To some degree, the taped comments themselves will indicate the internal consistency, clarity, and validity of a witness's testimony. It would be helpful to seek a statement of certainty from witnesses about components of their statement, such as descriptions of the perpetrator. Such an inquiry would ensure that investigators relying on the statements would be less apt to concentrate on weak leads or incorrect suspects. Another advantage to videotaping the process is that such scrutiny is a safeguard against coerced testimony.

Eyewitness Identification Procedures: Lineups and Photo Spreads

Procedures for maximizing accurate identifications and minimizing erroneous convictions have been extensively examined by cognitive and social psychologists who have reviewed the process of eyewitness identification.[96] Such procedures have been more scientifically and comprehensively studied than any aspect of the criminal justice process. This goes for much of forensic science.[97] Eyewitness error in DNA exonerations compelled the Department of Justice (DOJ) to establish a working group to formulate guidelines on the basis of research results. The guidelines are intended to reduce wrongful convictions attributable to eyewitness error. Most of the findings regarding construction of accurate eyewitness identification procedures have already been incorporated into the Guidelines promulgated by the DOJ.[98]

In accordance with the best available research, photo spreads should have a functional size that includes at least five foils and the suspect. Live lineups should have at least four. Each foil should resemble the description of the perpetrator. Each lineup or photo spread should contain a single suspect. Photo spreads or lineups should be sequential; that is, instead of presenting all lineup members at once, they should be shown one at a time. Each candidate is then judged to be or not to be the perpetrator. All candidates chosen for the lineup or photo spread should be presented, even if the witness selects one early in the sequence. Information given to eyewitnesses as they approach the task holds significant sway on the accuracy of their decisions. They must be properly prepared for the job. Photo spreads and lineups should be preceded by offering witnesses instructions which explain that previous advice should be disregarded, that the perpetrator may or may not be in the lineup, that excluding the innocent is as crucial as pinpointing the guilty, and that if the perpetrator is not in the lineup the investigation will proceed in an effort to locate that actual culprit. The witness must be reassured that accuracy trumps speed.

Information given eyewitnesses following their lineup or photo spread selections has repercussions on their beliefs about subsequent testimony concerning identifications they made. Regardless of whom the witness chooses, a statement of certainty should be taken immediately after the selection and without feedback being given to the witness. The statement of certainty should be given in the witness's own words, and ought to be audio or video recorded, or written by and signed by the witness. The witness should receive no information about suspects (or the responses of other witnesses) prior to identification procedure. Minimal feedback should be offered the witness afterwards. Although there is no prohibition on informing witnesses, especially victims, about the progress of an investigation, good practice mandates that prospective trial witnesses be contaminated as little as possible by such input.

The official conducting the lineup or photo spread should be blind as to who the suspect is or, alternatively, the procedure should be videotaped. Blind administration ensures that the officer does not inadvertently give cues as to who the suspect is. This ensures that the selection of a suspect is clearly the witness's choice. If properly conducted blind, there is no need for videotaping because cues cannot be given. If not administered blind, the procedure needs to be video recorded to preserve opportunity to review whether cues were tipped. At trial, witnesses who are asked to identify the perpetrator should be sequestered from each other.

Interrogation of Suspects

Much of the training regarding how to conduct an interrogation is meant to elicit confessions from suspects. Some of that process involves chicanery.[99] Such interrogations, which have become standard for law enforcement agencies, need not be prohibited. Videotaping, however, should be required of interviews in their entirety. The documentation should be time- and date-stamped. The video recording should prevent the most coercive methods. Such coercion includes physical abuse, threats of harm, threats to implicate innocent relatives, and other unlawful promises. Because anything done during interrogation will be accessible to attorneys and judges, the videotaped documentation guarantees that the validity of the interrogation and any consequent confession can be evaluated. The admissibility of any confession would be subject to assessment of reliability. Upon contesting admissibility of a confession, or upon the court's own motion, burden of proof falls on the proponent of admission to verify the confession's reliability. This should be in addition to the constitutional requirement of voluntaries. In determining admissibility of a confession, the court should exercise the duty to consider whether the confession is internally consistent, whether the questioners fed information to the suspect by using leading questions or otherwise, and whether the testimony is corroborated by independent evidence, taking into account the totality of circumstances.

Given the reliability test of admissibility and the significance of the video-tape in that assessment, the absence of documentation creates difficulties for the judge's evaluation. For police station interrogations, the absence of a videotape should render that confession inadmissible. Several state supreme courts, with Alaska[100] and Minnesota[101] leading the way, have made elec-tronic recording of interrogations a precondition for admissibility. Confes-sions made "on the street" in the aftermath of a felony and which have been audiotaped according to guidelines should also be admissible.

Since it is difficult to enforce specific rules regarding humane treatment of suspects, and since there is justifiable concern about coercion of innocent suspects, a good way to prevent the worst coercive treatment is to require videotaping the entire interrogation. Requiring videotaped interrogations also protects the police; such documentation supplies evidence defending against claims of brutality and unlawful conduct.

Even the infamous Miranda warnings, promulgated in 1966 to ensure that police caution suspects of their right to legal representation and their right to remain silent, have been vulnerable to attempts to undermine their intent. The law enforcement tactic of interrogating suspects twice—once before reading them their rights, once after—was struck down by the Supreme Court. Justice David Souter wrote that a suspect's statements about her involvement in a murder plot were inadmissible because police had arrested her at 3:00 A.M., elicited confession, and only then advised her of her rights. "The reason that question-first is catching on is as obvious as its manifest purpose, which is to get a confession the suspect would not make if he understood his rights," Souter noted.[102] The court closed the door on police strategies meant to induce improper confessions.

Similar to training requirements for interviewing witnesses, requirements must be established for training those who interrogate suspects. Given lim-ited research on effective and noncoercive methods for interrogating sus-pects, allowance should be made for the state to support studies on these issues. The findings should be integrated into subsequent training.

Forensic Science

Faulty forensic science is another leading cause of wrongful convictions. A growing body of literature documents tendencies of crime laboratory employees to improperly and unethically see themselves as advocates for one party to litigation and invoke measures that distort their "scientific" findings.[103] In a 1984 study, Joseph Peterson and colleagues found that of the laboratories reviewed, less than 10 percent of laboratory reports disas-sociated a suspect from the crime.[104] In another analysis, Andre Moenssens explains that "all [forensic science] experts are tempted, during their careers, to report positive results when their inquiries come up inconclusive, or indeed to report a negative result as positive."[105]

Another astonishing development is the awareness that some forensic sciences lack solid scientific foundations. It has been highlighted that

[t]he uniqueness of friction ridge patterns, fingerprints, palm prints, or bare footprints, has long been accepted by the scientific community and the courts. The reason for this acceptance perhaps lies in the fact that fingerprints were introduced at a time in history when society was less demanding of proof and more trusting of authority. As a result of recent challenges that friction ridge identification, as well as other forms of identification evidence, lack a proven scientific foundation, efforts have been ongoing to supply today's demands of validation and verification that is ... required by ... *Daubert v. Merrel Dow Pharmaceuticals.*[106]

Little data has been collected supporting claims made in the fields of forensic individualization science. That became apparent as challenges have been brought, in federal courts. Proponents of some of these fields have not been able to meet the rule's requirement of validity or, as expressed by the *Daubert* court, "evidentiary reliability."[107] When traditional forensic identification sciences and their inferential methodologies are contrasted with DNA typing, the flaws of the traditional "sciences" become obvious.[108] Crime laboratory reform should ensure that forensic science contributes to ascertaining the truth in a given situation employing sound scientific techniques. To accomplish that intention, the organizational structure of forensic laboratories needs to be redesigned. The culture of these operations must be reoriented.

Laboratories should be uncoupled from police departments. Such arrangements should be replaced with independent labs. Management of these facilities should be in the control of real scientists with authentic scientific training. The loyalty of these individuals should be to conducting reliable scientific work. These independent labs should be underwritten by the state. Their budgets should be separate from those of police and prosecuting authorities. Records and personnel should be equally accessible and responsive to prosecution and defense attorneys, consistent with the laboratories' independent nature. This would address problems of discovery and defense counsel's need for forensic science consultation.

A Forensic Laboratory Commission should be established with supervisory, policy-making, and rule-making authority for states' forensic laboratory systems. The Commission should consist of a majority of scientists who are not forensic professionals, but from industry, academia, medical backgrounds, and other government laboratories. Other members should provide balance among prosecution, defense, and judiciary. Its powers should include devising standards for hiring, workload, resources, and quality control methods, including rules for certifying examiners, accrediting laboratories, blind proficiency testing, and external scientific audits of the laboratories' work. Results of quality control testing should be on file with the Commission and available as a matter of public record.

The Forensic Laboratory Commission should guarantee that the states' laboratories formulate and adhere to validated protocols. Specialties that cannot supply adequately validated protocols may be relegated to an investigatory role; these specialties may be used to produce leads, which may not be submitted as proof at trial. The Commission should represent the states' forensic labs to legislatures for all purposes, including budgetary matters. Misconduct by laboratory staff, such as fabrication, falsification, or fudging, should be subject to administrative penalties set by the Commission. When warranted, criminal charges should be brought against such personnel for perjury, obstruction of justice, and the like.

Federal Rules of Evidence address admission of expert testimony at trial. The governing principles are as follows:

If scientific, technical, or other specialized knowledge will assist the trier of fact to understand the evidence or to determine a fact in issue, a witness qualified as an expert by knowledge, skill, experience, training, or education, may testify thereto in the form of an opinion or otherwise, if (1) the testimony is sufficiently based upon reliable facts or data, (2) the testimony is the product of reliable principles and methods, and (3) the witness has applied the principles and methods reliably to the facts of the case.[109]

Indigent Legal Representation

In many jurisdictions, legal representation of the poor is too often characterized by inadequacy: too few lawyers for the caseload, insufficient skill level, and inadequate resources. An important judicial review of death penalty cases revealed that 37 percent of the reversals of convictions resulted from inadequate assistance of counsel.[110]

Indigent legal representation should be achieved through the formation of a centralized, statewide public defender system. Such an organization should be empowered to structure itself into subunits for effective operation. This could be done by geographic units, by trial and appellate units, or by specialized subject matter divisions. In situations where a problem of geographic remoteness, seasonal caseload fluctuations, or conflicts of interest exist, the statewide public defender should be authorized to employ temporary assistants or contract private attorneys, who meet the same standards as permanent public defenders. To deal with matters of conflicts of interest, two approaches have emerged. Kentucky law provides that lawyers from separate offices of the same statewide public defender agency are sufficient to avoid conflict.[111] Colorado established an alternate defense counsel, which supplies legal representation in cases where the state public defender runs into a conflict of interest. A nine-member commission appointed by the Supreme Court of Colorado designates those who serve as alternate counsel.[112]

Public defender offices should adhere to certain mimimum standards, including caseload restrictions. Caseload maximums recommended by the American Bar Association include: "400 misdemeanors per attorney per year, or 200 juvenile cases per attorney per year, or 200 mental commitment cases per attorney per year, or 25 appeals per attorney per year."[113] The office of the public defender should have resources commensurate with those of prosecutors, such as support personnel, investigators, and experts. The necessity for experts depends upon the nature of the state's crime laboratories. Where laboratories are independent and equally available to prosecutors and defenders, there is less need for supplemental support services.

A permanent commission at the state level should oversee the state's public defender system. Such a commission should be within the judicial branch and would determine what sort of system should be implemented in each county. The commission should develop necessary standards for supplying effective representation for all offices within the state, including qualifications and performance evaluations. Its responsibilities should extend to representing the public defenders' interests to the legislature on all issues, including budget. It should have authority to disburse funds targeted to support public defender services.

Prosecutorial Misconduct

Prosecutorial misconduct consists primarily of the suppression of exculpatory evidence or the presentation of false evidence—either of which might be committed inadvertently or deliberately. Most cases of prosecutorial overreaching are not investigated. Rather than pushing for mandatory sanctions to punish offenders after the fact, it would be best to seek an "open file" discovery policy. The rule should be that evidence, and other relevant information, in the government's control should be shared with the defense. Although several jurisdictions already impose broad criminal discovery obligations on prosecutors, these rules often make distinctions between evidence that is to be disclosed and that which may be withheld. Such distinctions should be eliminated. An open-file policy, however, should preclude attorney work product, which would remain nondiscoverable according to normal rules of criminal procedure.[114]

Notwithstanding the open-file policy, any party believing circumstances warrant exclusion of mandatory disclosure may seek a protective order. These conditions may include an unacceptable risk of harm to a witness or an ongoing investigation with multiple defendants when not all have been arrested. Whenever the court grants a protective order, it should issue an order ensuring the defense has appropriate opportunity to collect any exculpatory evidence. The court and parties should find a satisfactory way to meet the goals of the protective order while not defeating the purposes of the mandatory disclosure. When violations of open-file discovery occur, substantial penalties should be incurred by the offending persons, regardless of whether evidence withheld had or would have affected the underlying legal matter. Such penalties should not include overturning the verdict and ordering a new trial unless prosecutorial misconduct is found to have caused actual prejudice.

Postconviction Procedures

The emphasis on finality in existing law has meant that even the most convincing evidence of innocence could not be considered by the courts of many states following conviction. While there is reason not to allow endless appeals on ultra-fine legal points, the law should encourage interventions that can radically alter a case's factual conclusions. There should be provision for the filing of a petition alleging "actual innocence," to be submitted to the state's intermediate court of appeals. If merited, the court should have authority to set aside the conviction and order a new trial. These petitions should be permitted without a time limit and without restriction as to the number of such petitions. They should specify new evidence, or new analyses of old evidence, that would substantially support a claim of actual innocence. The action allowed under this provision should be limited to factual evidence bearing on claims of actual innocence. There should be no requirement to show constitutional violation. Submission of such petitions should not interfere with other substantive or procedural rights that may be available.

Since this rule could create a surplus of filings, courts should be empowered to implement a two-stage review. This process would allow a judge to study a petition and determine whether it ought to be dismissed summarily or whether additional proceedings should be scheduled to more thoroughly examine facts alleged by the petitioner. The aim is to achieve a balance between the value of finality and the societal and individual interest in freeing an innocent person from wrongful punishment. There should be rules requiring preservation of evidence for periods long enough to permit DNA—or other innovations—to be utilized.

Postrelease Rights

When a judicial order is entered vacating a conviction on grounds of actual innocence, the postrelease process should encompass a claim for compensation initiated either by the erroneously convicted individual or by the court. Filing of such motion should be allowed at any time within two years after the order vacating conviction.[115] Damages should be supplemental to any tort or civil rights actions. Compensation should be granted if the claimant establishes innocence by clear, convincing evidence. Such a high standard ensures that compensation is awarded only to the actually innocent, and not to those released only on technical grounds. The elements of damages should include general damages (pain, suffering, loss of enjoyment of life, etc.), taking into consideration the duration and conditions of the unjust confinement, lost earnings and vocational services, costs of rehabilitation or counseling needed to support reintegration into society and taking into account family circumstances, and attorney's fees. Punitive or exemplary damages already covered under 42 U.S.C.A. section 1983 (1994) needn't be supplemented. There exists no cap on these damages. The court may order structured payments instead of one lump sum transaction. These damages should be available even if the state were without fault. The court may expunge the erroneously convicted individual's criminal records resulting from unjust conviction.

Sanctions for Violations

Provision should be made for a schedule of penalties for violating these guidelines. Such penalties might range from reprimands to fines and imprisonment. Such sanctions promote compliance with these principles. The way to achieve benefits of this thinking is for the policies to be taken seriously. That will happen only if these principles have teeth.

Afterword

In discussions of the moral, legal, and political aspects of the death penalty, it can be easy to forget that there would be no need for discussion about the appropriate fate of an offender had there not first been a victim of murder. Prior to the suffering of the innocent defendant wrongly sentenced to death, or the guilty defendant waiting out his last hours in the death house, there was the suffering of the murder victim and then the shock and grief of the victim's surviving family.

It is clear that the effect of a murder on the victim's family is enormous. Many people assume that anyone who has suffered a loss this devastating will want the perpetrator put to death, or will at least not object to that punishment if the state imposes it. "How would you feel if someone in your family were murdered?" is thought to be the toughest question a death penalty proponent can ask of an abolitionist.

If victims can be assumed to favor capital punishment, then invoking the suffering of victims should trump any abolitionist's arguments and give serious pause to those who are trying to figure out where they stand on the issue. But in fact victims are as varied in their beliefs and feelings about the death penalty as they are in race, geographic location, religion, and socioeconomic class. Even after they have been personally devastated by a murder in the family, plenty of survivors agree that the death penalty is *dead wrong*.

Such survivors challenge the assumption that executions are the way to achieve justice for victims—an assumption so culturally entrenched that people often invoke the death penalty as a way of comforting the grieving family. "I hope they fry those people so your family can get some peace," a friend said to Renny Cushing upon learning that his father's murderers had been arrested. "We will honor your sister by proposing to lower the age of eligibility for the death penalty in Illinois," a staffer in the district attorney's office told Jennifer Bishop after her sister had been murdered by a sixteen-year-old.

That Renny Cushing found his friend's remark vastly more hurtful than helpful and that Jennifer Bishop believed expanding the death penalty in her home state would not honor her sister seem inexplicable to many who hear of them. It is not correct to say that since grief and outrage are assumed to engender a desire for revenge and retaliation, anyone who *doesn't* possess that desire must not be grieving as fully as a survivor who wants the perpetrator executed. "After hearing that I oppose the death penalty in spite of my sister's murder, persons have asked me if I loved her," observes North Carolinian Pat McCoy. In such conversations, Pat has to explain that "being against the death penalty doesn't mean that I forget for a minute the suffering that my sister, our family, and all victims of murder and their families and loved ones experienced."

Survivors who oppose the death penalty have heard their views dismissed as "saintly," as though no ordinary, vengeful human could forego a belief in the death penalty after having been a victim of violence. But when you talk with such survivors, you discover quickly that they don't view themselves as more saintly—or less angry at their loved one's murder—than anyone else. "When the prosecutor first asked me how I felt about the death penalty," Virginian David Knight recalls, "I said, 'You just tell me the day and I'll come over and pull the switch if you need me to." David's son, twenty-one-year-old Jamie Knight, had been shot and killed while working the evening shift at a Friendly's restaurant.

No one listening to David Knight could say that he and his wife Jeannie and their three surviving sons have not suffered a full measure after Jamie's murder. For quite some time, that suffering led David to feel about the death penalty the way most people expect a victim's father to feel. "I felt such primitive emotions, such a desire to kill them," he says as he looks back on that time, "and I felt that I had every right to feel that way and no one was going to change my mind. I held on to that feeling with tenacity for three years. It took a long time for me to realize that holding on to a belief in the death penalty was creating a violence within my own soul—it was doing harm to *me*. Now I believe the death penalty only perpetuates the violence that has already taken place, and I don't believe the state has the right to take a life."

Two crucial points emerge from David Knight's story: that a survivor's beliefs about the death penalty are not fixed but changeable, and that the death penalty affects not only the offenders on death row but the survivors in the aftermath of the murder—which includes not only the victim's family but, in some sense, the rest of society as well. Just as David Knight felt himself to be harmed by his wish for another person's death and his willingness to carry out that execution himself if that were possible, so, perhaps, is a society harmed by its readiness to kill its own citizens and its willingness to plan and carry out such killings.

Joy Sojoodi underwent a change of heart similar to David Knight's. In 1993, Joy Sojoodi's parents, Lynn and Richard Ehlenfeldt, owners of Brown's Chicken and Pasta Restaurant in Palatine, Illinois, were killed along with five people who were working with them that night. The killing became known as the "Brown's Chicken Massacre" and remained unsolved for nine years. During the first few of those years, Joy, as she tells it now, believed "that the ultimate punishment of death was exactly what these people deserved. Why should the very people who brutally and systematically took my parents' lives have their lives spared?"

Like David Knight, Joy clung to her belief in the death penalty for quite a while. "I held on to these beliefs in the first few years when my emotions were still raw and visceral," she remembers.

What changed things for Joy? "As time went on," she says, "no arrests were made, so I had no faces to blame. The intensity of my hatred and need for vengeance began to lessen, which allowed me to look at the death penalty with a new perspective." About four years after the murders, Joy felt that she "began to truly comprehend the result of the death penalty. I remember thinking, 'What if the person who killed Mom and Dad had a daughter?' If the killer was then executed, his daughter was going to have to be in the same situation I was now. Some people may say, 'Who cares? Her dad brought it upon himself and his family.' But for some reason I did care. I didn't want more needless suffering of innocent people. Her grief would not lessen mine. You can't pass along the pain, you can only spread it. Advocates of the death penalty would like you to think the result is justice for the victims and for the victims' families. But I realized the true result is more grief, more innocent family members having to cope with a loved one's premeditated, and in this instance, state-sanctioned murder. I do not wish the anguish, sorrow, and pain that I went through on another human being."

Realizing that the death penalty creates another grieving family and—equally important—believing that her own pain would not be lessened by the pain of others, Joy felt her first stirrings of discomfort with the death penalty. Those stirrings coalesced into solid opposition when Joy "began to emulate some of my parents' values. At first I adopted some of their beliefs to honor them and then I came to realize that I believed in their values." Joy's parents' values included an opposition to the death penalty.

Nine years after the murder of Richard and Lynn Ehlenfeldt, the police had exhausted all their leads, and Joy, along with other members of her family, had essentially come to terms with the fact that the case might remain unsolved forever. And then, as Joy tells it, "After nine years of not knowing, nine years of unanswered questions, two men were arrested in 2002 and charged with the murders of my mom and dad and their five employees. Now that there were real people to blame I wondered if the hatred would once again return. Would feelings of vengeance overcome the value system I now held? I had a choice to make: focus on the tragedy or continue to deal with the pain and move forward while being thankful for the eighteen years I did have with my parents. But it turned out there wasn't a choice to make. As painful as it was to come face-to-face with the people accused of shooting my parents, I was not going to change my value system because of their actions; I was not going to let their behavior dictate mine. Going back to being consumed by hatred was not an option."

David Knight and Joy Sojoodi are typical of victims' family members who are initially in favor of the death penalty and come to change their minds a few years after the murder. Joy's determination not to let the murderers' actions alter her own value system as well is typical of many members who have maintained the opposition to the death penalty that they felt before the murder. In many ways, this effort to maintain one's values despite the trauma of a murder requires as much introspection as the process of coming to change one's mind. As a professor of law, Michael Avery had had plenty of occasion to think about the death penalty as an academic and legal issue, but the issue became more than academic for him when murder claimed two members of his own family. The murder of Michael Avery's sister and her daughter was shocking not only to the Avery family but to all those who read about the crime in the newspapers: twenty-three-year-old Martha Vance and her three-year-old daughter Jennifer were killed, along with three other people, when a man entered a Tampa, Florida, supermarket, doused a cashier and several customers with gasoline, and set them on fire.

"My sister's murder did not change my views about the death penalty," Michael explains, "but I had to get past my personal desire for vengeance. For a long time I wanted her killer to die, but I realized that primordial feeling on my part could not justify a deliberate social decision. As a civilized society, our collective morality cannot sanction the taking of life as a punishment." Michael speaks for many similarly minded survivors who say, essentially, "I may sometimes *feel* a desire for vengeance, but I don't want that desire codified into law and I don't want to live in a society that says killing is an acceptable way to redress a wrong."

When Attorney General John Ashcroft decided that family members of the Oklahoma City bombing victims should be allowed to witness the execution of Timothy McVeigh on closed-circuit television, his argument was that the experience would "meet their need for closure." The word *closure* is invoked so frequently in discussions of victims and the death penalty that victims' family members jokingly refer to it as "the *c* word."

Was Ashcroft making an effort to meet the needs of victims' families, or was he making an assumption about those needs and then deciding, based on that common but in fact unsubstantiated claim, that viewing the execution was the best the government could offer these grieving families?

It's a complicated question, and while some survivors do report feeling better after an execution, others say that the event brought them less peace than they had imagined or hoped it would. Without empirical evidence about whether executions actually do benefit victims' families, the most we can reliably say is that victims' needs are varied and that *closure* is not a concept survivors universally interpret in the same way. Furthermore, those who do *not* equate *closure* with *execution* resent the suggestion that this is an equation they ought to make. Johnnie Carter, for example, witnessed the execution of the man who murdered her seven-year-old granddaughter, and she said afterward, "I can tell you this—I didn't get closure by watching somebody else get murdered."

In addition, many families resent not only the suggestion that closure must come from the execution of the perpetrator but also the notion that closure is *possible* after a murder. Indeed, others' emphasis on closure can feel, to a survivor, as though society has only limited tolerance for a surviving family's grief before wanting to hear that the family has recovered and the process is complete.

Some survivors insist that closure is not an achievable goal. Tom Mauser, whose son Daniel was killed, along with twelve other people, in the shootings at Columbine High School, says, "I have come to learn that, even with the death of my son's killer, even with the pressure of those in society who rush us to 'reach closure,' there *is* no closure when you lose a child."

Whatever one believes about the concept of closure, there are clearly problems with the argument that the death penalty, in particular, is necessary for victims' family members, since the death penalty is in fact only imposed on 1 percent of convicted murderers. If executing the offender really is necessary for survivors of homicide victims, then 99 percent of them are out of luck.

As well, when the death penalty is described as being reserved for "the most heinous" of crimes, the "worst of the worst," it creates a hierarchy that may correspond to legal guidelines but does not necessarily resonate with survivors' experience.

Bill Pelke, whose grandmother Ruth Pelke was murdered in Indiana in 1986, remembers that part of his initial support for the death penalty came from feeling that his grandmother's murder was as terrible as any other murder. "As long as the death penalty was an option," Bill remembers, "I felt that if they *didn't* give it to [my grandmother's murderer], they were telling me and the rest of my family that my grandmother wasn't as important as a victim whose murderer did get the death penalty. I think people want the ultimate penalty the state has to offer, and so they may say they want the death penalty when, in fact, if the ultimate penalty in that state were life without parole and the death penalty wasn't an option, the family would be just as satisfied with that. It's not always that families want the murderer executed, but they want to know that the most that can be done is being done."

Bill Pelke reminds us that what looks like support for the death penalty may, in some families, simply reflect a desire to have their particular tragedy taken seriously. Yet it's also important to remember that the state's interest will always be somewhat (or very) different from the victim's family's interest. A family who desires that the defendant be sentenced to life without parole may not get that wish either; victims' rights laws do not go so far as to guarantee victims a particular outcome in a case. Defendants have constitutional rights, and the legal system involves processes and results in outcomes that may or may not match what the victims' family members most want or feel they need. This does not suggest that in order to assist victims a society must discard defendants' rights, but rather that there are inherent difficulties with the assumption that the criminal justice system is where victims' needs are best met. As Kate Lowenstein and Michael Avery have written, "Healing and recovery require an intimate focus on the particular needs of an individual survivor, a focus that it is neither appropriate nor practical to expect the legal system to provide."

Another indication that the criminal justice system cannot be counted on to meet the needs of victims is in the potential for wrongful conviction—a potential that *Dead Wrong* has illustrated so vividly. When the wrong person is convicted of and sentenced for a murder, it is not only the innocent defendant who suffers, the family of the murder victim suffers as well.

Jeanette Popp's story makes this clear. For years after her twenty-year-old daughter Nancy DePriest was raped and murdered during a robbery of the Pizza Hut outlet where she worked, Jeanette Popp believed she knew who was responsible: two men named Chris Ochoa and Richard Danziger, who were arrested a couple of months after the crime and eventually sentenced to life in prison. Jeanette had no idea that while Ochoa and Danziger were in one Texas prison, an inmate at another prison, Achim Marino, was writing letters to the county district attorney and to then-governor George W. Bush, saying that he was the one who had robbed the Pizza Hut and killed Nancy DePriest. Marino said that he acted alone and had no idea why two other men had confessed.

Meanwhile, Chris Ochoa was writing to the Innocence Project at the University of Wisconsin–Madison, explaining that he was serving a life sentence for a murder he didn't commit and that the police had coerced him into confessing to the crime and implicating his roommate, Richard Danziger, as well.

DNA evidence eventually exonerated Chris Ochoa and Richard Danziger and confirmed the truth of Achim Marino's confession. Chris Ochoa and Richard Danziger were released after spending twelve years in prison.

Although Ochoa and Danziger were wrongfully sentenced to life in prison, rather than to death, the death penalty apparently figured prominently in the events that led to the wrongful conviction. It has now come out that Ochoa's confession followed two grueling days of police questioning, during which police openly threatened Ochoa by telling him that he would receive the death penalty if he didn't cooperate (and even going so far as to jab his arm with a pen in a gesture mimicking lethal injection).

Jeanette Popp believes the death penalty should be abolished so that it can no longer be used as a threat to coerce confessions from innocent people. But when she first learned that the two men she had believed were guilty might not be guilty after all, her most pressing question was, has the original story been a lie? Everything she thought she knew about her daughter's murder was now called into question.

"Survivors of murder victims want to know the truth," explains Renny Cushing as he reflects on the intersection between the issues of wrongful conviction and victims' needs. "They want to know what happened, they want to know what their loved one's last moments were like, they want to try to understand the story of this terrible event. When you learn that the wrong person was being punished all this time, all the facts you thought you had come to understand, the facts that helped you move forward, have all been stripped away. You have to start all over again—it's as though the murder just took place."

What *can* we ask the criminal justice system to offer victims? The answer can be found in the wording of the federal Victims of Crime Act or in any state victims' rights law: victims want to be treated with fairness and with respect for their dignity, to receive information, to have the opportunity to speak and be heard in the specific—though limited—ways that the law stipulates, to receive the help and support that victims' advocates are mandated to provide.

Given that these are rights stipulated for all victims of crime, there should be nothing noteworthy about a particular group of victims seeking them. What many have found, however, is that fairness and respect, information and help, can be withheld if the victims oppose the death penalty.

The trouble comes when the very people who are charged with enforcing victims' rights—prosecutors and prosecution-based victims' advocate offices—are also those who have the discretion to withhold them. When the prosecution is seeking the death penalty, victims' family members who oppose the death penalty are automatically in conflict with the prosecution's agenda. As Leigh Eason, who was 11 years old when her uncle, Florida State Trooper Ronald Smith, was shot and killed in the line of duty, observes, "Too often, literature given to victims by the prosecution promotes the death penalty because that is what the prosecution wants. Families are under a lot of pressure to support the death penalty and are made to feel they aren't doing enough for their murdered loved one if they want something different."

This conflict of interest becomes especially problematic for victims, because victims' rights offices are linked (and subordinate) to prosecutors' offices. Too often, victims who oppose the death penalty are viewed as "second-class victims" and are denied the information or participation that victims' rights laws are supposed to secure them.

Felicia Floyd offers a particularly stark assessment of the way the criminal justice system views victims who oppose the death penalty: "They expect we want vengeance and death for the murderer, and when we don't, they consider us bad victims." Felicia, as it happens, has a doubly compelling stake in the issue. When she spoke at the pardon board hearing for the man who had murdered her mother years before, she was asking that his sentence be commuted to life in prison for two reasons: because she opposed the death penalty in general, and because the man whose life she was pleading for was her own father. "This family has endured enough pain," Felicia told the Georgia pardon board. "I beg you not to take my father's life too."

There's no question that Felicia and the other members of her family are the surviving relatives of a murder victim, but the official advocate of the victim, who would ordinarily offer assistance and support to a family preparing to address the pardon board, refused to help this family because they were arguing for the defendant's death sentence to be commuted rather than carried out.

Given that domestic violence is a terrible but undeniable reality for some families, and that murders are committed not only by strangers but by intimate family members, the experience of survivors like Felicia Floyd must be reckoned with when we think about the issue of victims and the death penalty. Some people have a personal stake in the fate of both the victim and the perpetrator. Survivors of intrafamilial murder exemplify in an especially vivid way the fact that executions can add to, rather than assuage, survivors' pain.

Another group of survivors who are victimized by the death penalty are the families of the executed. "I don't think people understand what executions do to the families of the executed," says Billie Jean Mayberry, whose brother, Robert Coe, was executed in Tennessee in 2000. "To us, our brother was murdered right in front of our eyes. It changed all of our lives." Discussions of the death penalty seldom include an acknowledgment of the impact of executions on the family members left behind, but these surviving family members are gradually beginning to organize, to speak out, and to call for further research. At a ceremony marking the launch of a new project called "No Silence, No Shame: Organizing Families of the Executed," Robert Meeropol, son of Ethel and Julius Rosenberg, who were executed by the U.S. Government in 1953, pointed out that there have been no studies of how the execution of an immediate family member affects children. "As far as I can tell," Meeropol said, "no one has bothered to study this even though these children are all innocent victims of the state's efforts to kill their loved ones."

Ask Americans to name the people responsible for the Oklahoma City bombing, and most, if not all, will be able to do it. Ask the same people to name one of the victims of the bombing, and many will come up blank. It might be tempting to attribute this to the number of victims compared to the number of perpetrators, or to the magnitude and national significance of the crime. But the death penalty encourages a focus on the offender even in less notorious cases. Because the offender is facing his or her own death, because *this* life now hangs in the balance, people's attention and passion are drawn to the fate of the accused, whether they are urging the impending death or desperately working to prevent it. As Sylvester and Vicki Schieber have written, "One tragedy of the death penalty is that it turns society's perspective away from the victim and creates an outpouring of support for those who have perpetuated a crime." As the Schiebers go on to observe, it is those who are actively working to stop an execution—ardent death penalty opponents, in other words—who are most vulnerable to this imbalance of attention.

How then can we return our focus to victims? It's not surprising that many survivors of homicide victims become passionate advocates of violence prevention, in many cases founding institutes, organizations, and programs named after the murder victim and dedicated to preventing or reducing violence in one way or another.

The death penalty, in the end, is about choosing how to respond. What do we do when something terrible happens, something that cannot be un-done or ever fully made right? For victims' family members, this is an intensely personal question, but in some sense it should be a question—moral, political, personal—for all of us. Tom Lowenstein, whose father, former Congressman Al Lowenstein, was murdered in 1980, sums it up like this: "As a victim's family member, I came to the inevitable realization that how we react to murder does not affect what happened to the victim. It does, however, affect society. Calling for the death penalty serves to socialize our feelings of anger and hatred and spreads their negative effects more widely, perpetuating the cycle of violence. Anger and hatred won't help my father now, and will only hurt the society he worked so hard to improve." Do we want to be a society of hate and violence, or a society striving for healing and repair? Do we want to mimic the actions of those we say we abhor, or do we want, through our policies, our actions, our responses, to demonstrate another way?

Susannah Sheffer

Susannah Sheffer is the author of several books, most recently *In a Dark Time: A Prisoner's Struggle for Healing and Change*. She works as the staff writer for Murder Victims' Families for Human Rights, an organization of family members of victims of murder and state execution working to oppose the death penalty from a human rights perspective. Please visit www.murdervictimsfamilies.org.

Appendix A

Timeline

1800 B.C.—First established death penalty laws.

1100 A.D.—William the Conqueror will not allow persons to be hanged except for murder.

1608—Captain George Kendall happens to undergo the first recorded execution in the new colonies.

1632—Jane Champion becomes the first woman to be executed in the new colonies.

1767—Cesare Beccaria's essay, "On Crimes and Punishment," theorizes there is no justification for the state to take a life.

Late 1700s—United States abolitionist movement begins.

Early 1800s—Many states reduce their number of capital crimes and build state penitentiaries.

1834—Pennsylvania becomes the first state to move executions into correctional facilities.

1838—Discretionary death penalty statutes enacted in Tennessee.

1846—Michigan becomes the first state to abolish the death penalty for all crimes except treason.

1890—William Kemmler becomes first person executed by electrocution.

Early 1900s—Beginning of the "Progressive Period" of reform in the United States.

1907–1917—Nine states abolish the death penalty for all crimes or strictly limit it.

1920s–1940s—American abolition movement loses support.

1924—The use of cyanide gas is introduced as an execution method.

1930s—Executions reach the highest levels in American history—average 167 per year.

1948—United Nations General Assembly adopts Universal Declaration of Human Rights proclaiming a "right to life."

1958—*Trop* v. *Dulles*. Eighth Amendment's meaning contains "evolving standard of decency that marked the progress of a maturing society."

1966—Support of capital punishment reaches all-time low. Gallup poll shows support of death penalty at only 42%.

1968—*Witherspoon* v. *Illinois*. Dismissing potential jurors solely because they express opposition to death penalty held unconstitutional.

1970—*Crampton* v. *Ohio* and *McGautha* v. *California*. The Supreme Court approves of unfettered jury discretion and nonbifurcated trials.

June 1972—*Furman* v. *Georgia*. Supreme Court effectively voids 40 death penalty statutes and suspends the death penalty.

1976—*Gregg* v. *Georgia*. Guided discretion statutes approved. Death penalty reinstated.

January 17, 1977—Ten-year moratorium on executions ends with the execution of Gary Gilmore by firing squad in Utah.

1977—Oklahoma becomes the first state to adopt lethal injection as a means of execution.

1977—*Coker* v. *Georgia*. Held death penalty is an unconstitutional punishment for rape of an adult woman when the victim is not killed.

December 7, 1982—Charles Brooks becomes the first person to be executed by lethal injection.

1984—Velma Barfield becomes the first woman executed since reinstatement of the death penalty.

1986—*Ford* v. *Wainwright*. Execution of insane persons banned.

1986—*Batson* v. *Kentucky*. Prosecutor who strikes disproportionate number of citizens of the same race in selecting a jury is required to rebut inference of discrimination by showing neutral reasons for strikes.

1987—*McCleskey* v. *Kemp*. Racial disparities not recognized as a constitutional violation of "equal protection of the law" unless intentional racial discrimination against the defendant can be shown.

1988—*Thompson* v. *Oklahoma*. Executions of offenders age 15 and younger at the time of their crimes is unconstitutional.

1989—*Stanford* v. *Kentucky* and *Wilkins* v. *Missouri*. Eighth Amendment does not prohibit the death penalty for crimes committed at age 16 or 17.

1989—*Penry* v. *Lynaugh*. Executing persons with mental retardation is not a violation of the Eighth Amendment.

1993—*Herrera* v. *Collins*. In the absence of other constitutional grounds, new evidence of innocence is no reason for federal court to order a new trial.

1994—President Clinton signs the Violent Crime Control and Law Enforcement Act, expanding federal death penalty.

1996—President Clinton signs the Anti-Terrorism and Effective Death Penalty Act, restricting review in federal courts.

1998—Karla Faye Tucker and Judi Buenoano executed. November 1998, Northwestern University holds the first-ever National Conference on Wrongful Convictions and the Death Penalty. The Conference brings together 30 inmates who were freed from death row because they were innocent.

January 1999—Pope John Paul II visits St. Louis, Missouri, and calls for an end to the death penalty.

April 1999—U.N. Human Rights Commission Resolution Supporting Worldwide Moratorium on Executions.

January 2000—Illinois Governor George Ryan declares a Moratorium on executions and appoints a blue ribbon Commission on Capital Punishment to study the issue.

2002—*Ring* v. *Arizona*. A death sentence where the necessary aggravating factors are determined by a judge violates a defendant's constitutional right to a trial by jury.

2002—*Atkins* v. *Virginia*. Execution of mentally retarded defendants violates Eighth Amendment ban on cruel and unusual punishment.

January 2003—Governor George Ryan grants clemency to all of the remaining 167 death row inmates in Illinois because of the flawed process that led to these sentences.

June 2004—New York's death penalty law declared unconstitutional by the state's high court.

Appendix B

Anti-Death Penalty Organizations

I. RELIGIOUS AND INTERFAITH ORGANIZATIONS LISTED ALPHABETICALLY ACCORDING TO FAITH

Interfaith

National Interreligious Task Force
2800 Swiss Avenue
Dallas, TX 75204
Contact: Rev. Holsey Hickman
Phone: 214-824-8680

Baptist

American Baptist Churches
P.O. Box 851
Valley Forge, PA 19482-0851
Contact: Earl Trent
Phone: 610-768-2487
Email: webmaster@abc-usa.org
Web: http://www.abc-usa.org/

Buddhist

Engaged Zen Foundation
P.O. Box 700
Ramsey, NJ 07446-0700
Contact: Rev. Kobutsu Malone
Phone: 201-236-0335
Email: kobutsu@engaged-zen.org
Web: http://www.engaged-zen.org

Catholic

United States Conference of Catholic Bishops
3211 4th Street, NE
Washington, DC 20017
Contact: Andrew Rivas
Phone: 202-541-3190
Email: arivas@usccb.org
Web: www.usccb.org/sdwp/index.htm

Catholics Against Capital Punishment
P.O. Box 3125
Arlington, VA 22203
Contact: Frank McNeirney
Phone: 301-652-1125

Jehova's Witness

United Church of Christ Justice
and Witness Ministries
110 Maryland Ave., NE Ste 207
Washington, DC 20002
Contact: Sandy Sorenson
Phone: 202-543-1517
Email: sorenses@ucc.org

Jewish

Jewish Peace Fellowship
P.O. Box 271
Nyack, NY 10960
Contact: Joyce Bressler
Phone: 845-358-4601
Email: jpf@forusa.org
Web: www.jewishpeacefellowship.org

Synagogue Council of America
4101 Cathedral Ave, NW
Washington, DC 20016
Contact: Dr. Irwin Blank
Phone: 202-364-7336

Lutheran

Evangelical Lutheran Church in America
8765 W. Higgins Rd.
Chicago, IL 60631
Contact: Josselyn Bennet
Phone: 773-380-2700
Email: info@elca.org
Web: www.elca.org

Mennonite

Mennonite Central Committee
Washington Office
110 Maryland Ave NE #502
Washington, DC 20002-5626
Contact: David Whettstone
Phone: 202-544-6564
Email: David_Whettstone@mcc.org
Web: www.mcc.org

Muslim

National Council on Islamic Affairs
P.O. Box 1028
Long Beach, NY 10561
Contact: Ghazi Khan-Kan
Phone: 516-889-0005

Unitarian

Unitarian Universalists for Alternatives
to the Death Penalty
P.O. Box 2337
Chester, VA 23831-844
Contact: Tim Stanton
Phone: 804-748-3265
Email: tim@uuadp.org
Web: www.uuadp.org

II. LEADING ORGANIZATIONS IN THE AREA OF DEATH PENALTY REFORM

(1) American Civil Liberties Union—
    www.aclu.com
(2) Amnesty International—
    www.amnesty.org
(3) Campaign to End the Death
    Penalty—www.nodeathpenalty.org

(4) Center on Wrongful Convictions—www.law.northwestern.edu/wrongfulconvictions
(5) Death Penalty Information Center—www.deathpenaltyinfo.org
(6) Innocence Project— www.innocenceproject.org
(7) Moratorium Now!—www.quixote.org
(8) National Coalition to Abolish the Death Penalty—www.ncadp.org

Please Note: If your state does not appear in the list below, visit the Web site of one of the national organizations to locate the chapter nearest you.

III. STATE ORGANIZATIONS

Alabama

Alabama Committee to Abolish the Death Penalty
P.O. Box 948
Leeds, AL 35094
George H. Jones
hilesjones@aol.com
www.angelfire.com/al4/alajustice/
   news.html

Alaska

Alaskans Against the Death Penalty
P.O. Box 202296
Anchorage, AK 99520
Kathy Harris
907-258-2296
kathyh@gci.net
www.aadp.info

Arizona

Coalition of Arizonans to Abolish the Death Penalty
P.O. Box 42465
Tucson, AZ 85733
Ann Nichols
520-884-5507 x12
520-325-6240
ann.nichols@asu.edu

Arkansas

Arkansas Coalition to Abolish the Death Penalty
904 West 2nd Street, Suite 1
Little Rock, AR 72205
Ernie Oakleaf
501-663-2414
oakleafs@aol.com

California

Death Penalty Focus
870 Market Street, Suite 859
San Francisco, CA 94102
Lance Lindsey
415-243-0143
info@deathpenalty.org
www.deathpenalty.org

Colorado

Coloradans Against the Death Penalty
P.O. Box 1745
Denver, CO 80201
Dan Bounds
303-715-3163
info@coadp.org
www.coadp.org

Connecticut

Connecticut Network to Abolish the Death Penalty
32 Grand Street
Hartford, CT 06106
203-206-9854
info@cnadp.org
www.cnadp.org

Georgia

Prison and Jail Project
P.O. Box 6749
Americus, GA 31709
John Cole-Vodicka
229-928-2080
Fax: 229-924-7080
Team Defense Project
P.O. Box 1728
Atlanta, GA 30301
Millard Farmer
404-688-8116
Fax: 404-577-0643

Hawaii

ACLU of Hawaii
P.O. Box 3410
Honolulu, HI 96801
Vanessa Chong
808-522-5900
ychong@acluhawaii.org
www.acluhawaii.org

Idaho

ACLU of Idaho
P.O. Box 1897
Boise, ID 83701
Jack Van Valkenburgh
208-344-5243
JackVV@ACLUIdaho.org
www.ACLUIdaho.org

Illinois

Center on Wrongful Convictions
357 East Chicago Avenue
Chicago, IL 60611
Rob Warden
312-503-7412
r_warden@law.northwestern.edu

Kentucky

Kentucky Coalition to Abolish the Death Penalty
P.O. Box 3092
Louisville, KY 40201
Pat Delahanty
502-585-2895
kcadp@earthlink.net
www.kcadp.org

Louisiana

Louisiana Association of Criminal Defense Lawyers
(Death Penalty Committee)
830 Main Street
Baton Rouge, LA 70802
Jim Boren 225-387-5796
jimboren@bellsouth.net

Maryland

Maryland Coalition Against State Executions
P.O. Box 39205
Baltimore, MD 21212
Stephanie Gibson
410-243-8020
info@mdcase.org
www.mdcase.org

Massachusetts

Project Hope to Abolish the Death Penalty—MA Chapter
41 White Avenue
Worcester, MA 01605
Tanya Connor
508-757-6387
Fax: 508-756-8315

Michigan

AFSC Michigan Criminal Justice Program
1414 Hill Street
Ann Arbor, MI 48104
Penny Ryder, Natalie Holbrook
734-761-8283
pryder@afsc.org
nholbrook@afsc.org

Michigan Council on Crime and Delinquency
1115 South Pennsylvania Avenue, Suite 201
Lansing, MI 48912
Elizabeth Arnovits
517-482-4161
mail@miccd.org

Minnesota

Minnesota Advocates for Human Rights
650 Third Avenue South 500
Minneapolis, MN 55402
Rose Park
612-341-3302 x100
hrights@mnadvocates.org
www.mnadvocates.org

Mississippi

Mississippians for Alternatives to the Death Penalty
7760 Deerfield CV
Southaven, MS
Ken McGill
662-416-1981 or 901-336 6932
mcgillken1@aol.com

Missouri

Criminal Justice Ministry
1408 South 10th Street
St. Louis, MO 63104
Carleen Reck
314-241-8062
CJM99@earthlink.net
www.welcome.TO/CJMSTLOUIS

Public Interest Litigation Clinic
305 East 63rd Street
Kansas City, MO 64113
Sean O'Brien/Kent Gipson
816-363-2795
pilc@pilc.net

Montana

Montana Coalition to Abolish the Death Penalty
9650 Hyalite Canyon Road
Bozeman, MT 59715
Estella Vilasenor
Fax: 406-585-2408

Nevada

Office of the Special Public Defender
309 South 3rd Street, 4th Floor
Las Vegas, NV 89155
Phil Kohn
702-455-6265
Fax: 702-455-6273

New Jersey

New Jerseyans for Alternatives to the
Death Penalty
22 Oliver Street
Chatham, NJ 07928
Celeste Fitzgerald
973-635-6396
PaxCF@aol.com

New Mexico

Coalition for Prisoners' Rights
P.O. Box 1911
Santa Fe, NM 87504
Mara Taub
505-982-9520
Fax: 505-982-9520

New York

Judicial Process Commission
121 North Fitzhugh Street
Rochester, NY 14614
Clare Regan, Sue Porters
585-325-7727
Fax: 585-325-2165

New York State Defenders
Association
194 Washington Avenue, Suite 500
Albany, NY 12210
Jonathan Gradess
518-465-3524
info@nysda.org
www.nysda.org

Reconciliation Network: Don't Kill
in My Name
1150 Buffalo Road
Rochester, NY 14624
Jan Armantrout
716-328-3210

North Carolina

Carolina Justice Policy Center
P.O. Box 3092
Durham, NC 27702
Lao Rubert
919-682-1149
Fax: 919-688-1723

Center for Death Penalty Litigation
123 West Main Street, Suite 500
Durham, NC 27701
Kenneth Rose
919-956-9545
Fax: 919-956-9547

North Dakota

ACLU of Dakotas
Manchester Building
112 North University Drive, Suite 301
Fargo, ND 58102
Jennifer Ring
701-461-7290
dakaclu@cs.com

Ohio

American Friends Service Committee
915 Salem Avenue
Dayton, OH 45406
Jana Schroader
937-278-4225
Fax: 937-278-2778

Oregon

Oregonians for Alternatives to the
Death Penalty
5300 Parkview Drive, 1102
Lake Oswego, OR 97035
Tena Hoke
503-639-3841
pssr@portland.quik.com
www.members.tripod.com/ocadp

Pennsylvania

**Capital Habeas Unit of the Federal
Court Division**
Defender Association of Philadelphia
Curtis Center Building, Suite 545 West
Independence Square West
Philadelphia, PA 79106
Pamela Tucker
215-928-0520 x7571
pamela_tucker@fd.org

South Carolina

**South Carolina Center for Capital
Litigation**
P.O. Box 11311
Columbia, SC 29211
Teresa Norris
803-765-0650

South Dakota

South Dakota Peace and Justice Center
P.O. Box 40585
Watertown, SD 57201
Jeanne Koster
605-885-2822
sdpjc@dailypost.com

Tennessee

Friends Outside
P.O. Box 321
Murfreesboro, TN 37130
Shirley Dicks

Texas

ACLU of Texas
P.O. Box 12905
Austin, TX 78711
William Harrell
512-478-7300
info@aclutx.org
www.aclutx.org

Utah

Rocky Mountain Defense Fund
175 East 400 South, Suite 400
Salt Lake City, UT 84111
Ronald J. Yengich
801-355-0320
ronaldy333@aol.com

**Salt Lake City Legal Defender
Association**
424 East 500 South, Suite 300
Salt Lake City, UT 84111
Joan Watt
801-532-5444
Fax: 801-532-0330

Vermont

**Vermont Coalition Against the Death
Penalty**
C/O Unitarian Universalist Church
21 Fairground Road
Springfield, VT 05156
Bob Staley-Mays
802-885-3327

Virginia

**Virginia Capital Representation
Resource Center**
2421 Ivy Road, Suite 301
Charlottesville, VA 22903
Rob Lee
804-817-2970
Roblee@vcrrc.org

**Virginians for Alternatives to the Death
Penalty**
P.O. Box 4804
Charlottesville, VA 22905
Jack Payden Travers
888-567-8237
jack@vadp.org
www.vadp.org

Washington

Washington Association of Criminal Defense Lawyers
810 3rd Avenue, Suite 421
Seattle, WA 98104
Teresa Mathis
206-623-1302
ed@wacdl.org
www.wacdl.org

Wyoming

Wyoming Coalition to Abolish the Death Penalty
1800 East Grand Avenue
Laramie, WY 82070
Carl Callinger
307-745-5461
carl@newmancenter.org

Notes

CHAPTER 1: THE DEATH PENALTY IN CONTEXT

1. H.H. Haines, *Against Capital Punishment: The Anti-Death Penalty Movement in America, 1972–1994*, New York: Oxford Univ. Press, 1996.
2. *Furman* v. *Georgia*, 408 U.S. 238 (1972).
3. Burton Wolfe, *Pileup on Death Row*, Garden City, NY: Doubleday, 1973.
4. F. Zimring and G. Hawkins, *Capital Punishment and the American Agenda*, New York: Cambridge Univ. Press, 1986.
5. Hugo Bedau, *Death Is Different: Studies in the Morality, Law and Politics of Capital Punishment*, Boston: Northeastern Univ. Press, 1987.
6. Rupert Barry, "*Furman* to *Gregg*: The Judicial and Legislative History," *Harvard Law Journal*, 22:53–117, 1979.
7. Ibid. at 87–90.
8. *Gregg* v. *Georgia*, 428 U.S. 123 (1976).
9. *McGautha* v. *California*, 402 U.S. 183, 204 (1971).
10. *Fowler* v. *North Carolina*, 428 U.S. 904 (1976).
11. L. Epstein and J. Kobylka, *The Supreme Court and Legal Change: Abortion and the Death Penalty*, Chapel Hill: Univ. of North Carolina Press, 1992.
12. *Woodson* v. *North Carolina*, 428 U.S. 280 (1976).
13. *Roberts* v. *Louisiana*, 428 U.S. 325 (1976).
14. *Proffitt* v. *Florida*, 428 U.S. 242 (1976).
15. *Jurek* v. *Texas 14*, 428 U.S. 262 (1976).
16. R. Woodward and S. Armstrong, *The Brethren: Inside the Supreme Court*, New York: Simon and Schuster, 1979.

17. I. Ehrlich, "The Deterrent Effect of Capital Punishment: A Question of Life and Death," *American Economic Review*, 65:397, 1975.

18. Note 11, 107–109.

19. W. White, *The Death Penalty in the Eighties, An Examination of the Modern System of Capital Punishment*, Ann Arbor: Univ. of Michigan Press, 1987.

20. Note 11, 81.

21. Note 16, 436–437.

22. G.A. Caldeira, "Courts and Public Opinion," in W. Gates and R. Johnson, eds., *The American Courts: A Critical Assessment*, Washington, DC: CQ Press, pp 303–334, 1991.

23. Note 3, 66–67.

24. R. Weisberg, "Deregulating Death," In B. Kurland, G. Casper, and D.J. Hutchinson, eds., *The Supreme Court Review*, Chicago: Univ. of Chicago Press, pp 305–395, 1983.

25. Ibid. at 322.

26. R. Berger, *Death Penalties: The Supreme Court's Obstacle Course*, Cambridge, MA: Harvard Univ. Press, 1982.

27. A. Neier, *Only Judgment: The Limits of Litigation in Social Change*, Middleton, CT: Wesleyan Univ. Press, pp 207–210, 1982.

28. *Roberts v. Louisiana*, 431 U.S. 633 (1978).

29. *Lockett v. Ohio*, 438 U.S. 586 (1978); *Eddings v. Oklahoma*, 455 U.S. 104 (1982).

30. *Coker v. Georgia*, 433 U.S. 584 (1977); *Enmund v. Florida*, 458 U.S. 782 (1982).

31. *Godfrey v. Georgia*, 466 U.S. 420 (1980).

32. *Adams v. Texas*, 448 U.S. 38 (1980).

33. *Bullington v. Missouri*, 451 U.S. 38 (1981).

34. *Estelle v. Smith*, 451 U.S. 454 (1981).

35. J. Nordheimer, "Gilmore Is Executed after Stay Is Upset: 'Let's Do It!' He Said," *New York Times*, p 1, Jan. 18, 1977.

36. W. Turner, "Murderer in Casino Executed in Nevada," *New York Times*, p 1, Oct. 23, 1979.

37. Note 25, 210–211.

38. R. Johnson, *Death Work: A Study of the Modern Execution Process*, Wadsworth Contemporary Issues in Crime and Justice Series, Belmont, CA: Wadsworth, p 4, 1998.

39. *Roper v. Simmons*, U.S. S. Ct., No. 03–0633 (March 1, 2005).

40. *Penry v. Lynaugh*, 492 U.S. 302 (1989).

41. *Atkins v. Virginia*, 536 U.S. 304 (2002).

42. *In Spite of Innocence: Erroneous Convictions in Capital Cases*, Boston: Northeastern Univ. Press, 1992.

43. Conclusion drawn by the Senate Judiciary Subcommittee on Civil and Constitutional Rights (staff report by the 103rd Cong., 1st session, October 21, 1993).

44. S.E. Barkan and S.F. Cohen, "Racial Prejudice and Support for the Death Penalty by Whites," *Journal of Research in Crime and Delinquency*, 1994.

45. D. Oshinsky, *Worse Than Slavery: Parchman Farm and the Ordeal of Jim Crow Justice*, New York: Free Press, p 19, 1996.

46. D.C. Baldus, G. Woodworth, and C.A. Pulaski, *Equal Justice and the Death Penalty*, Boston: Northeastern Univ. Press, 1990.

47. G.E. Goldhammer, *Dead End*, Brunswick, ME: Biddle Publishing Company, 1996.

48. J. Reiman, *The Rich Get Richer and the Poor Get Prison; Ideology, Class, and Criminal Justice*, 4th ed., Boston: Allyn & Bacon, 1995.

49. J. Jackson, Sr., and J. Jackson, Jr., *Legal Lynching: Racism, Injustice and the Death Penalty*, New York: Marlowe & Co., 1996.

50. L. Radzinowicz, *A History of English Criminal Law*, New York: Macmillan, 1948.

51. P. Spierenburg, *The Spectacle of Suffering: Executions and the Evolution of Repression: From a Preindustrial Metropolis to the European Experience*, Cambridge: Cambridge Univ. Press, 1984.

52. L.P. Masur, *Rites of Execution: Capital Punishment and the Transformation of American Culture, 1776–1865*, New York: Oxford Univ. Press, p 39, 1989.

53. G. Ollyffe, "An Essay Humbly Offer'd, for an Act of Parliament to Prevent Capital Crimes," London: J. Downing, pp 6–7, 1731.

54. C. Daniell, *Death and Burial in Medieval England 1066–1550*, London: Routledge, p 106, 1997.

55. S. Banner, *The Death Penalty: An American History*, Cambridge, MA: Harvard Univ. Press, p 71, 2002.

56. V.A.C. Gatrell, *The Hanging Tree: Execution and the English People 1770–1868*, Oxford: Oxford Univ. Press, p 8, 1994.

57. See note 45.

58. S. Tolnay and E. Beck, *A Festival of Violence: An Analysis of Southern Lynchings, 1882–1930*, Urbana: Univ. of Illinois Press, p 90, 1995.

59. W. Marquart, S. Ekland-Olson, and J.R. Sorensen, *The Rope, the Chair, and the Needle: Capital Punishment in Texas, 1923–1990*, Austin: Univ. of Texas Press, p 7, 1993.

60. W. Garrison, preface to F. Douglass, *Narrative of the Life of Frederic Douglass: An American Slave, Written by Himself*, New York: Penguin, p 2, 1968.

61. F. Butterfield, *All God's Children: The Bosket Family and the American Tradition of Violence*, New York: Knopf, 1995.

62. Note 55, 18.

63. Ibid. at 25.

64. R. Ginzburg, *100 Years of Lynching*, Baltimore: Black Classic Press, p 224, 1988.

65. M. Fearnow, "Theatre for an Angry God: Public Burnings and Hangings in Colonial New York, 1741, *The Drama Review*, 40(2):31, 1996.

66. Note 55, 76.

67. Note 56, 56–58.

68. J.G. Miller, *Search and Destroy: African-American Males in the Criminal Justice System*, Cambridge: Cambridge Univ. Press, p 53, 1996.

69. Note 55, 101.

70. Note 55, 171–172.

71. Ibid. at ix.

72. Ibid. at 100.

73. Note 55, 19.

74. D.W. Denno, "Is Electrocution an Unconstitutional Method of Execution? The Engineering of Death over the Century," *William and Mary Law Review*, 35(2):679, 1994.

75. A. Mencken, *By the Neck: A Book of Hangings*, New York: Hastings House, p 34, 1942.

76. Note 55, 146.

77. Ibid. at 207.

78. A. Liptak and R. Blumenthal, "Death Sentences in Texas Try Supreme Court's Patience," *New York Times*, A1 & 27, Dec. 5, 2004.

79. Ibid. at 27.

80. H. Prejean, *Dead Man Walking: An Eyewitness Account of the Death Penalty in the United States*, New York: Random House, p 105, 1993.

81. Note 57, 557.

82. *Glass v. Louisiana*, 471 U.S. 1080, 1985.

83. "Selected Recent Court Decisions," *American Journal of Law and Medicine*, xx(3):334, 1994.

84. *Chaney v. Heckler*, 718 F. 2d 1174, 1983.

85. *Death Works: A Study of the Modern Execution Process*, Wadsworth, p 47, 1998.

86. Quoted in S. Levine, ed., *Death Row: An Affirmation of Life*, New York: Ballantine, p 167, 1972.

87. A. Camus, "Reflections on the Guillotine," in *Resistance, Rebellion, and Death*, New York: Knopf, 1969.

88. I. Barkan, *Capital Punishment and Ancient Greece*, Chicago: Univ. of Chicago Press, pp 75–76, 1936.

CHAPTER 2: DEAD TO RIGHTS

1. G. Ryan, Speech, Northwestern Univ. Law School, Chicago, IL, Jan. 11, 2003.

2. C. Falsani, "Ryan Draws Applause, Jeers: World Reaction," *Chicago Sun-Times*, p 7A, Jan. 12, 2003.

3. B. McClellan, St. Louis (MO), *Post-Dispatch*, op-ed, Jan. 13, 2003.

4. L. Hockstader, "Dead Men Walking," *Washington Post Magazine*, Feb. 23, 2003.

5. Edwards interview, Dec. 14, 2002.

6. R.E. Pierre, "Former Governor Ryan Is Indicted in Illinois," *Washington Post*, A12, Dec. 18, 2003.

7. Note 4, 38.

8. Ibid.

9. D. McKinney, "Ryan's Views Shift," *Chicago (IL) Sun-Times*, 5A, Jan. 12, 2003.

10. Ibid.

11. Note 4, 39.

12. Note 9.

13. *Lifelines*, newsletter of the National Coalition to Abolish the Death Penalty, No. 91, p 1, Spring 2003.

14. J. Liebman, "A Broken System: Error Rates in Capital Cases," Columbia University, 2000.

15. Note 1.

16. Note 9.

17. *The Voice*, newsletter of Murder Victims' Families for Reconciliation, Fall/Winter 2002.

18. Ibid.

19. 391 U.S. 510 (1968).

20. S. Turow, "To Kill or Not to Kill," *The New Yorker*, p 43, Jan. 6, 2003.

21. Y. Husbands-Hankin interview, June 1997.

22. D. Spiegel, A. Freinkel, and C. Koopman; "Effects of Witnessing an Execution," *American Journal of Psychiatry*, 151:1335–1339, 1994.

23. Note 20, 44.

24. Ibid.

25. Ibid at 46.

26. "The Snitch System, A Center on Wrongful Convictions Survey," Northwestern Univ., Winter 2004–2005.

27. Note 20, 47.

28. Note 4, 39.

29. D. Fears, "Justice Dept. to Aid Probe of Till Case," *Washington Post*, sec. A, p 3, May 11, 2004.

30. *The Voice*, newsletter of Murder Victims' Families for Reconciliation, Spring/Summer 2003.

31. Ibid.

32. Note 1.

33. Note 29.

34. A.M. Pallasch, A. Sweeney, and C. Sadovi; "Ryan Empties Death Row of All 167," *Chicago Sun-Times*, 2A, Jan. 12, 2003.

35. Ibid.

36. S. Mills, "Ryan Decides Not to Play God," *Chicago (IL) Tribune*, sec. 1, p 14, Jan. 12, 2003.

37. Ibid.

38. J. Keilman, "Relatives of Victims Feel Cheated," *Chicago Tribune*, sec. 1, p 1, Jan. 12, 2003.

39. Ibid.

40. C. Sadovi, "Relatives Angry Killers Won't Be Put to Death," *Chicago Sun-Times*, 5A, Jan. 12, 2003.

41. Ibid.

42. Note 1.

43. Note 38, 15.

44. Note 1.

45. Note 42.

46. Ibid.

47. Ibid.

48. Note 1.

49. Note 38.

50. Ibid at 3A.

51. Ibid.

52. M. Possley and S. Mills; "Clemency for All," *Chicago Tribune*, sec. 1, p 15, Jan. 12, 2003.

53. Ibid.

54. Ibid.

55. Note 1.

56. Note 57.

57. Note 2.

58. Note 1.

59. Note 57.

60. Ibid.

61. Note 38, 3A.

62. Note 57.

63. Note 38, 3A.

64. Ibid.

65. Note 4, 40.

66. E. Ruder, "Death Row Shut Down in Illinois," *Socialist Worker*, No. 436, p 15, Jan. 17, 2003.

CHAPTER 3: EYEWITNESS TESTIMONY: SEEING ISN'T ALWAYS BELIEVING

1. Phone conversations between Jennifer Thompson and the author, April 4–11, 2003.

2. "What Jennifer Saw," Frontline coproduction with Ben Loeterman Productions, Inc. and WGBH Educational Foundation (1997).

3. Ibid.

4. Note 2.

5. E. Loftus, "Jurors' Beliefs about Eyewitness Testimony," *Eyewitness Testimony: Civil and Criminal*, 1997.

6. Note 2.

7. Note 6.

8. S.M. Kassin and B. Barndollar, "The Psychology of Eyewitness Testimony: A Comparison of Experts and Potential Jurors," *Journal of Applied Social Psychology*, 22:1241, 1992; E. Loftus, "Psychological Aspects of Courtroom Testimony," *Annals of the New York Academy of Sciences*, 347:27, 1980.

9. D. Dieffenbacher and E. Loftus, "Do Jurors Share a Common Understanding of Eyewitness Behavior," *Law and Human Behavior*, 6:15, 1982.

10. W. Seltzer et al., "Juror Ability to Recognize the Limitations of Eyewitness Identifications," *Forensic Reports*, 3:121–137, 1990.

11. Note 3.

12. Ibid.

13. Ibid.

14. Ibid.

15. Ibid.

16. Note 2.

17. Note 3.

18. Ibid.

19. "Perfect Witness Makes Peace with Man She Mistakenly Accused," AP article taken from the *Atlanta Journal-Constitution*, A10, Sunday, Sept. 24, 2000.

20. Ibid.

21. Note 3.

22. Ibid.

23. Ibid.

24. Note 21.

25. Ibid.

26. Ibid.

27. C.R. Huff, A. Rattner, and E. Sagarin, *Convicted but Innocent: Wrongful Conviction and Public Policy*, Thousand Oaks, CA: Sage Publications, 1996.

28. G.L. Wells, "Eyewitness Identifications: Scientific Status," In D.L. Faigman, D.H. Kaye, M.J. Saks, and J. Sanders, eds., *Modern Scientific Evidence: The Law and Science of Expert Testimony*, vol. 1, St. Paul, MN: West Publishing Co., pp 451–479, 1997.

29. J.C. Brigham, A. Maass, L.D. Snyder, and K. Spaulding, "Accuracy of Eyewitness Identifications in a Field Setting," *Journal of Personality and Social Psychology*, 42:673–681, 1982.

30. G.L. Wells, "Applied Eyewitness Testimony Research: System Variables and Estimator Variables," *Journal of Personality and Social Psychology*, 36:1546–1557, 1978.

31. *Neil* v. *Biggers*, 409 U.S. 188 (1972).

32. P.N. Shapiro and S. Penrod, "Meta-analysis of Facial Identification Studies," *Psychological Bulletin*, 100:139–156, 1986.

33. R.C.L. Lindsay, G.L. Wells, and C.M. Rumpel, "Can People Detect Eyewitness Identification Accuracy Within and Between Situations?" *Journal of Applied Psychology*, 66:79–89, 1981.

34. S. Christianson, "Emotional Stress and Eyewitness memory: A Critical Review," *Psychological Bulletin*, 112:284–309, 1992.

35. N.M. Steblay, "A Meta-analytic Review of the Weapon Focus Effect," *Law and Human Behavior*, 16:413–424, 1992.

36. T.H. Kramer, R. Buckhout, and P. Eugenio, "Weapon Focus, Arousal, and Eyewitness Memory: Attention Must Be Paid," *Law and Human Behavior*, 14:167–184, 1990.

37. C.A. Meissner and J.C. Brigham, "Thirty Years of Investigating the Own-Race Bias in Memory for Faces: A Meta-analytic Review," *Psychology, Public Policy, and Law*, 7:3–35, 2001.

38. T. Anthony, C. Copper, and B. Mullen, "Cross-Racial Facial Identification: A Social Cognitive Integration," *Personality and Social Psychology Bulletin*, 18:296–301, 1992.

39. J.E. Chance and A.G. Goldstein, "The Other Race Effect and Eyewitness Identification," in B. Sporer, R.S. Malpass, and A. Koenken, eds., *Psychological Issues in Eyewitness Identification*, Mahwah, NJ: Lawrence Erlbaum Associates, pp 153–176, 1996.

40. Note 31.

41. Ibid.

42. J.S. Shaw III, S. Garvin, and J.M. Wood, "Co-Witness Information Can Have Immediate Effects on Eyewitness Memory Reports," *Law and Human Behavior*, 21:503–523, 1997.

43. C.M. Roebers and W. Schneider, "The Impact of Misleading Questions on Eyewitness Memory in Children and Adults," *Applied Cognitive Psychology*, 14:509–526, 2000.

44. E. Loftus and J.C. Palmer, "Reconstruction of Automobile Destruction: An Example of the Interaction Between Language and Memory," *Journal of Verbal Learning and Verbal Behavior*, 13:585–589, 1974.

45. E. Loftus, "Leading Questions and the Eyewitness Report," *Cognitive Psychology*, 7:560–572, 1975.

46. E. Loftus, *Eyewitness Testimony*, Cambridge, MA: Harvard University Press, 1979.

47. M. McCloskey and M.S. Zaragosa, "Misleading Postevent Information and Memory for Events: Arguments and Evidence against the Memory Impairment Hypothesis," *Journal of Experimental Psychology: General*, 114:1–16, 1985.

48. M.K. Johnson, S. Hashtroudi, and D.S. Lindsay, "Source Monitoring," *Psychological Bulletin*, 114:3–28, 1993.

49. D.S. Lindsay and M.K. Johnson, "The Eyewitness Suggestibility Effect and Memory for Source," *Memory & Cognition*, 17:349–358, 1989.

50. G.L. Wells, "The Psychology of Lineup Identifications," *Journal of Applied Social Psychology*, 66:688–696, 1984.

51. D.S. Lindsay, B. Lea, and T. Fulford, "Sequential Lineup Presentation: Technique Matters," *Journal of Applied Psychology*, 76:741–745, 1991.

52. G.L. Wells, "What Do We Know about Eyewitness Identification?" *American Psychologist*, 48:553–571, 1993.

53. N.M. Steblay, "Social Influence in Eyewitness Recall: A Meta-analytic Review of Lineup Instruction Effects," *Law and Human Behavior*, 21:283–297, 1997.

54. G.L. Wells, R.S. Malpass, R.C.L. Lindsay, R.P. Fisher, J.W. Turtle, and S.M. Fulero, "From the Lab to the Police Station: A Successful Application of Eyewitness Research," *American Psychologist*, 55:581–598, 2000.

55. R. Blummer, "Eyewitness Accounts Often Prove Unreliable," *Chicago Sun-Times*, Jan. 2, 2001, 21.

56. G.L. Wells, R.S. Malpass, M. Small, S. Penrod, S. Fulero, and C. Brimacombe, "Eyewitness Identification Procedures: Recommendations for Lineups and Photospreads," *Law and Human Behavior*, 22:605, 1998.

57. M. Jain, "Mitigating The Dangers of Capital Convictions Based on Eyewitness Testimony Through Treason's Two-Witness Rule," *Journal of Criminal Law and Criminology*, 91(3), 2001.

58. U.S. Constitution, Article III, Section 3 ... No Person shall be convicted of Treason unless on the Testimony of two Witnesses to the same overt Act, or on Confession in open Court.

59. Note 49.

60. 18 U.S.C., section 3592 (2000).

61. Model Penal Code, section 210.6 (1962).

62. U.S. Const., art. III, section 3 (1789).

63. J.W. Hurst, "Treason in the United States," *Harvard Law Review*, 58:395–403, 1945.

64. Deuteronomy 19:15.

65. Deuteronomy 17:6.

66. Note 49.

67. *Cramer* v. *United States*, 325 U.S. 1 (1944).

68. *United States* v. *Robinson*, 259 F. 685, 690 (S.D. N.Y. 1919).

69. Conn. Gen. Stat. Section 54-83 (1960).

70. *State* v. *Schutte*, 117 A. 508, 510 (Conn. 1922).

71. *Kelly* v. *United States*, 194 F.2d 150 (D.C. Cir. 1952).

72. Ibid at 154.

73. Note 60.

74. *United States* v. *Wade*, 388 U.S. 218, 228–229 (1967).

75. 7 Wigmore, Evidence section 2037 (1978), quoting Blackstone, 3 Commentaries 358 (4th ed. 1770).

CHAPTER 4: SYSTEMIC CORRUPTION

1. Martin Luther King, Jr., *Stride Toward Freedom*, New York: Harper & Row/Perennial Library, p 73, 1964.

2. Martin Luther King, Jr., speech, "The March on Washington for Jobs and Freedom," August 28, 1963.

3. Interview with Georgia Davis, "The Price of a Pardon," WFSU-TV.

4. Interview with author, Washington, DC, June 12, 2003.

5. Ibid.

6. Ibid.

7. Ibid.

8. Ibid.

9. http:www.patrickcrusade.org/wrongful.htm

10. Gene Miller, *Invitation to a Lynching*, Garden City, NY: Doubleday & Co., p 18, 1975.

11. Letter from John L. Murphy, acting for Burke Marshall, assistant attorney general, Civil Rights Division, Department of Justice, Washington, DC, September 25, 1964.

12. Note 4.

13. Note 3.

14. Email correspondence with author, throughout Fall 2003.

15. Ibid.

16. J. Saunders Redding, *They Came in Chains*, Philadelphia: Lippincott, 1973.

17. Edmund S. Morgan, *American Slavery, American Freedom: The Ordeal of Colonial Virginia*, New York: W.W. Norton, 1975.

18. Howard Zinn, *A People's History of the United States*, New York: Perennial Classics, p 26, 2001.

19. Ibid at 29.

20. Ibid at 29, 30.

21. Ibid at 30.

22. Ibid.

23. Kenneth M. Stamp, *The Peculiar Institution*, New York: Knopf, 1956.

24. Note 17 at 31.

25. Ibid at 33.

26. Stanley Elkins, *Slavery: A Problem in American Institutional and Intellectual Life*, Chicago: Univ. of Chicago Press, 1976.

27. Ulrich B. Phillips, *American Negro Slavery: A Survey of the Supply, Employment and Control of Negro Labor as Determined by the Plantation Regime*, Baton Rouge: LSU Press, 1966.

28. Note 17 at 34.

29. Ibid.

30. Note 22.

31. Note 17 at 36.

32. Herbert Aptheker, *A Documentary History of the Negro People in the United States*, Secaucus, NJ: Citadel, 1974.

33. Gerald Mullin, *Flight and Rebellion: Slave Resistance in Eighteenth-Century Virginia*, New York: Oxford University Press, 1974.

34. Note 16.

35. Ibid.

36. Note 4.

37. Interview with author, March 18, 2003.

38. M. Darley and G. Middelton, "All Say Pitts, Lee Guilty," *Panama City News-Herald*, Feb. 12, 1967.

39. Note 9 at 161.

40. Ibid at 172.

41. Ibid at 73.

42. Mercy Trial Transcript, August 28, 1963.

43. Buzz Conover, "Pitts and Lee: The Million Dollar Murder," Florida Public Radio Network, October 3, 2002.

44. Ibid.

45. Ibid.

46. June 8, 1962. Murder trial of Arthur Nebb in Columbus, Ohio.

47. Note 9 at 204, 205.

48. Ibid at 207.

49. Ibid at 229, 230.

50. State of Florida Administrative Hearing, Case No. 98-2005.

51. Note 4.

52. Note 3.

53. Note 13.

54. Sydney P. Greenberg, "Freed from Death Row," *St. Petersburg Times*, July 4, 1999.

CHAPTER 5: REASONABLE DOUBT AT A REASONABLE PRICE

1. Kevin Sullivan, "U.S. Told to Review Death Row Cases," *Washington Post*, A22, April 1, 2004.

2. United States Constitution, VI Amendment.

3. Many of Mr. Wilhoit's quotes are drawn from an interview with Rosaline Juan, the author's former graduate assistant, Sacramento, CA, April 10, 2004.

4. Ibid.

5. Ibid.

6. Wilhoit's prepared public speaking comments, sent to the author by Ida Mae Wilhoit, Greg's mother, March 19, 2004.

7. Supra, note 3.

8. First set of notes of Greg's father (concerning Thompson & Gullekson), forwarded to author April 3, 2004.

9. Interview on Flashpoint, National Public Radio, Berkeley, CA, October 3, 2000.

10. Note 3.

11. Note 8.

12. Ibid.

13. Note 6, p 8.

14. Second set of notes from Greg's father (concerning George Briggs), forwarded to author April 3, 2004.

15. Ibid.

16. Note 6, p 12.

17. Introduction to Greg Wilhoit's autobiographical commentary, forwarded to author April 3, 2004.

18. Note 6, p 13.

19. "Through Thick and Then," ABCNews.com, August 19, 2000.

20. Letter from John E. Douglas, Asst. General Counsel of the Oklahoma Bar Association, to Guy Roy Wilhoit, January 9, 1989.

21. Note 6, p 13.

22. Ibid, pp 13–14.

23. *Gideon* v. *Wainwright*, 372 U.S. 335 (1963).

24. *Powell* v. *Alabama*, 287 U.S. 45 (1932).

25. *Johnson* v. *Zerbst*, 304 U.S. 458 (1938).

26. *Betts* v. *Brady*, 316 U.S. 455 (1942).

27. M.M. Reed, "A Constitutional Analysis of Random Vehicle Searches," *American Journal of Trial Advocacy*, 26(3):613, Spring 2003.

28. Ibid.

29. Note 24, at 71–72.

30. Note 3, p 4.

31. Ibid.

32. Ibid, p 5.

33. Note 17.

34. Jonathan E. Gradess, *Public Defense at the Crossroads: Listening to the Voices of Clients*, DMI, NY: 2003.

35. Affidavit of Dr. Thomas C. Krauss, June 21, 1989.

36. Note 3, p 5.

37. Ibid.

38. Ibid.

39. Ibid.

40. Note 19.

41. Note 3, p 2.
42. Note 3, p 2.
43. Note 3, p 2.
44. Ibid.
45. Note 19.
46. Note 3, pp 2–3.
47. Note 6, pp 17–18.
48. Ibid at 19.
49. Note 3, p 8.
50. Note 6, p 27.
51. Ibid.
52. *Wilhoit* v. *Oklahoma*, 809 P.2d 1322 (April 16, 1991).
53. Ibid.
54. P. Marcotte, "Snoozing, Unprepared Lawyer Cited," *ABA Journal*, 14, Feb. 1991.
55. "The Death of Fairness? Counsel Competency and Due Process in Death Penalty Cases," *Houston Law Review*, 31:1105, 1132 (1994).
56. Dieter, Richard, "With Justice for Few: The Growing Crisis in Death Penalty Representation," Death Penalty Information Center, October 1995, p 9.
57. J. Davis and M. Curriden, "Man Condemned for Murder of Girl Is Freed," *The Atlanta Journal-Constitution*, E6, Nov. 7, 1991.
58. *Strickland* v. *Washington*, 80 L. Ed 2nd 674 (1984).
59. J.S. Liebman, "A Broken System: Error Rates in Capital Cases, 1973–1995," Columbia University, New York, 2000.
60. Note 6, p 30.
61. Ibid at 33.
62. Note 3, p 3.
63. Ibid at 6.
64. Ibid.
65. Ibid at 4.
66. Ibid at 6.
67. Ibid at 4.
68. Note 6, p 33.
69. Note 3, p 8.
70. Ibid.
71. Diana G. Erwin, *Sacramento Bee* articles, November 10 & 12, 2002.

CHAPTER 6: WELCOME HOME

1. Kirk Bloodsworth, speech to the annual conference of the National Coalition to Abolish the Death Penalty, Galludet University, Washington, DC, October 9, 2004.
2. Kirk Bloodsworth, address during "Death Penalty Awareness Week," American University, Washington, DC, March 23, 2005.
3. Kirk Bloodsworth, panelist at the Innocence Project regional organizing conference, University of the District of Columbia, Washington, DC, April 1, 2005.
4. Ibid.
5. Note 2.

6. Susan Levine, "MD Man's Exoneration Didn't End Nightmare," *Washington Post*, A 1, Feb. 24, 2003.

7. Ibid at A 8.

8. A.J. Beck, "State and Federal Prisoners Returning to the Community: Findings from the Bureau of Justice Statistics," 2000.

9. Ibid.

10. Bureau of Justice Statistics, "Sentenced Prisoners Released from State or Federal Jurisdiction," 2002.

11. M. Lynch, "Waste Managers? New Penology, Crime Fighting, and the Parole Agent Identity," *Law and Society Review*, 32:839–869, 1998.

12. J. Petersilia, *Parole and Prisoner Reentry in the U.S.*, Chicago: Univ. of Chicago Press, 1999.

13. A. Blumstein and A.J. Beck, "Population Growth in U.S. Prisons, 1980–1996," 1999.

14. A.J. Beck and B.E. Shipley, "Recidivism of Prisoners Released in 1983," Bureau of Justice Statistics Special Report, 1989.

15. M. Rennison, "Criminal Victimization 1999: Changes 1998–1999 with Trends 1993–1999," Bureau of Justice Statistics, 2000.

16. D.M. Kennedy, "Pulling Levers: Chronic Offenders, High Crime Settings, and a Theory of Prevention," *Valparaiso U. Law Review*, 31(2):449–484, Spring 1997.

17. A. Blumstein and J. Wallman, eds., *The Crime Drop in America*, Cambridge, U.K.: Cambridge Univ. Press, 2000.

18. W. Spellman, *The Crime Decline: Why and What's Next*, Washington, DC: Urban Institute, 2002.

19. T.J. Ambrosio and V. Schiraldi, *From Classrooms to Cell Blocks: A National Perspective*, Washington, DC: Justice Policy Institute, 1997.

20. T.R. Clear, D.R. Rose, and J.A. Ryder, "Coercive Mobility and the Community: The Impact of Removing and Returning Offenders," Reentry Roundtable, Washington, DC, 2000.

21. Note 8.

22. T. Bonczar and L. Glaze, "Probation and Parole in the US, 1998." *Bureau of Justice Statistics*, Washington, DC, 1999.

23. Note 11.

24. Bureau of Justice Statistics, *Correctional Populations in the US, 1997*, Washington, DC, 2000.

25. Note 8.

26. Note 11.

27. Note 8.

28. T. Hammett, "Health-Related Issues in Prisoner Reentry to the Community," Reentry Roundtable, Washington, DC, 2000.

29. California Department of Corrections, *Preventing Parolee Failure: An Evaluation*, 1997.

30. B. Western and R. Pettit, "Incarceration and Racial Inequality in Men's Employment," *Industrial and Labor Relations Review*, 54:3–16, 2000.

31. S. Klein, J. Petersilia, and S. Turner, "Race and Imprisonment Decisions in California," *Science*, 247:812–816, Feb. 16, 1990.

32. C. Mumola and A. Beck, *Prisoners in 1996*, Washington, DC: U.S. DOJ, Bureau of Justice Statistics, 1997.

33. Bureau of Justice Statistics, U.S. DOJ, *Correctional Populations in the U.S.*, 1996.

34. D. Johnston and K. Gabel, "Incarcerated Parents." In K. Gabel and D. Johnston, eds., *Children of Incarcerated Parents*, New York: Lexington Books, 1995.

35. D.T. Courtwright, "The Drug War's Hidden Toll," *Issues in Science and Technology*, 13(2):73 W, 1996.

36. M. Dallao, "Coping with Incarceration from the Other Side of the Bars." *Corrections Today*, 59, 1997.

37. Shujaa Graham interviewed after rally to halt Steven Oken's execution, Baltimore, MD, June 12, 2004.

38. P.M. Ditton and D.J. Wilson, "Truth in Sentencing in State Prisons," Bureau of Justice Statistics, Washington, DC, 1999.

39. Note 8.

40. Bureau of Justice Statistics, DOJ, "Prisoners Released Unconditionally from State and Federal Jurisdiction, 1977–98," 2001.

41. G. Gaes, T.J. Flanagan, L. Motuik, and L. Stewart, *Adult Correctional Treatment*, Chicago: Univ. of Chicago Press, 1999.

42. C. Riveland, *Prison Management Trends, 1975–2025*, Chicago: Univ. of Chicago Press, 1999.

43. Note 11.

44. Note 8.

45. J. Austin, M.A. Bruce, L. Carroll, P.L. McCall, and S.C. Richards, *The Use of Incarceration in the U.S.*, San Francisco: American Society of Criminology, 2000.

46. Note 11.

47. I. Waller, *Men Released from Prison*, Univ. of Toronto, 1974.

48. K. Adams, *Adjusting to Prison Life*, Chicago: Univ. of Chicago Press, 1992

49. Research Council of the American Correctional Assoc, *Corrections Compendium*, 25(8):2–25, 2000.

50. American Correctional Association, "A Survey of Correctional Agencies' Research Topics and Interests," 2000.

51. Bureau of Justice Statistics, DOJ, "National Corrections Reporting Program," Washington, DC, various years.

52. Bureau of Justice Statistics, DOJ, "Correctional Populations in the U.S., 1980–1999," 2001.

53. J. Petersilia, "Prisoners Returning to Communities: Political, Economic, and Social Consequences," Reentry Roundtable, Washington, DC, 2000.

54. Note 11.

55. Note 53.

56. T.P. Bonczar and L.E. Glaze, "Probation and Parole in the U.S.," 1998.

57. Note 53.

58. J. Petersilia, "A Decade of Experimenting with Intermediate Sanctions: What Have We Learned?" *Perspectives on Crime and Justice*, Washington, DC, Nat'l Institute of Justice, 1998.

59. J. Petersilia and S. Turner, "Intensive Probation and Parole," *Crime and Justice: A Research Review*, Chicago: Univ. of Chicago Press, 1993.

60. L. Sherman, D. Gottfredson, D. MacKenzie, L. Eck, P. Reuter, and S. Bushway, *Preventing Crime: What Works, What Doesn't, What's Promising*, College Park: Univ. of Maryland, 1997.

61. Note 56.

62. Note 8.

63. R. Cohen, "Probation and Parole Violators in State Prison, 1991," WDC, DOJ, Bureau of Justice Statistics, 1995.

64. J. Kling, D.F. Weiman, and B. Western, "The Labor Market Consequences of 'Mass' Incarceration," Reentry Roundtable, Washington, DC, 2000.

65. Ibid.

66. Bureau of Justice Statistics, *Survey of State Prison Inmates, 1991*, Washington, DC, DOJ, 1993.

67. S. Bushway, "The Stigma of a Criminal History Record in the Labor Market." In J.P. May, ed., *Building Violence: How America's Rush to Incarcerate Creates More Violence*, Thousand Oaks: Sage, 2000.

68. H. Holzer, *What Employers Want: Job Prospects for Less Educated Workers*, New York: Russell Sage, 1996.

69. Note 58.

70. J. Hagan and R. Dinovitzer, "Collateral Consequences of Imprisonment for Children, Communities, and Prisoners," Chicago: Univ. of Chicago Press, 1999.

71. Ibid.

72. J. Irwin and J. Austin, *It's About Time*, Belmont, CA: Wadsworth, 1994.

73. B. Western and R. Pettit, "Incarceration and Racial Inequality in Men's Employment," *Industrial and Labor Relations Review*, 54:3–16, 2000.

74. Ibid.

75. S. Bushway and P. Reuter, *Labor Markets and Crime*, San Francisco, CA: ICS Press, 2002.

76. P. Van Slambrouck, "Push to Expand Book-Learning Behind Bars," *The Christian Science Monitor*, Sept. 15, 2000, p 3.

77. Note 75.

78. The Welfare to Work Partnership, *Member Survey: Taking the Next Step*, 2000 series, No. 1.

79. G.G. Gaes, T.J. Flanagan, L.L. Motuik, and L. Stewart, "Adult Correctional Treatment," *Prisons*, Chicago: Univ. of Chicago Press, 1999.

80. K. Hull, S. Forrester, and A. Brown, "Analysis of Recidivism Rates for Participants of the Academic/Vocational/Transition Education Programs Offered by the Virginia Dept of Correctional Education," *Journal of Correctional Education*, 51(2):256–261, 2000.

81. S.J. Steurer, L.G. Smith, and A. Tracey, Preliminary analysis of the "Office of Correctional Education and Correctional Education Association Three-State Recidivism Study," Washington, DC, 2002.

82. J. Gerber and E.J. Fritsch, "The Effects of Academic and Vocational Program Participation on Inmate Misconduct and Reincarceration," *Prison Education Research Project: Final Report*, Huntsville, TX: Bureau of Prisons, 1994.

83. P. Van Slambrouck, "Push to Expand Book-Learning Behind Bars," *The Christian Science Monitor*, p 3, Sept. 15, 2000.

84. Legal Action Center, "Housing Laws Affecting Individuals with Criminal Convictions," Washington, DC, 2000.

85. P.H. Rossi, *Down and Out in America: Origins of Homelessness*, Chicago: Univ. of Chicago Press, 1989.

86. California Dept of Corrections, *Preventing Parolee Failure Programs: Evaluation*, Sacramento, 1997.

87. M. Love and S. Kuzma, *Civil Disabilities of Convicted Felons: A State-by-State Survey*, Washington, DC: Office of the Pardon Attorney, 1996.

88. M. Mauer, *The Race to Incarcerate*, Washington, DC: The Prison Project, 2000.

89. Ibid.

90. Ibid.

91. C.J. Mumola, "Incarcerated Parents and Their Children," Bureau of Justice Statistics, Special Report, Washington, DC, DOJ, August 2000.

92. Ibid.

93. Ibid.

94. Note 11.

95. Note 91.

96. Ibid.

97. J. Hagan and J.P. Coleman, "Returning Captives of the American War on Drugs: Issues of Community and Family Reentry," Washington, DC: Bureau of Justice Statistics Special Report, 2000.

98. D. Johnston, "Incarceration of Women and Effects on Parenting," Northwestern Univ., 2001.

99. Note 91.

100. Note 70.

101. Note 34.

102. D. Johnston, *Children of Offenders* (1992), *Intergenerational Incarceration* (1993), *Jailed Mothers* (1991), Pasadena, CA: Pacific Oaks Center for Children of Incarcerated Parents.

103. C. Seymour, "Children with Parents in Prison: Child Welfare Policy, Program, and Practice Issues," *Child Welfare*, 77:469–493, 1998.

104. Women's Prison Association, "When a Mother Is Arrested: How the Criminal Justice and Child Welfare Systems Can Work Together More Effectively," A needs assessment initiated by the Maryland Department of Human Resources, 1996.

105. M. Dallao, "Coping with Incarceration from the Other Side of the Bars," 1997.

106. C.F. Hairston, "Family Ties During Imprisonment: Important to Whom and for What?" *Journal of Sociology and Social Welfare*, 18:87–104, 1991.

107. M. Nelson, P. Deess, and C. Allen, *First Month Out: Post-Incarceration Experiences in New York City*, New York: Vera Institute of Justice, 1999.

108. Note 97.

109. Legal Action Ctr, "Public Assistance Laws Affecting Individuals with Criminal Convictions," WDC.

110. Note 91.

111. Note 11.

112. Ibid.

113. Analysis by E. Cadora and C. Swartz for the Community Justice Project at the Center for Alternative Sentencing and Employment Services, 1999.

114. Ibid.

115. Note 11.

116. S. Gottfredson and R. Taylor, "Community Contexts and Criminal Offenders," *Communities and Crimes Reduction*, London, 1988.

117. T.R. Clear, D.R. Rose, and J.A Ryder, "Coercive Mobility and the Community: The Impact of Removing and Returning Offenders," Reentry Roundtable, Washington, DC, 2000.

118. Little Hoover Commission, *Behind Bars: Correctional Reforms to Lower Prison Costs and Reduce Crime*, Sacramento, CA, 1998.

119. M. Smith and W. J. Dickey, "Reforming Sentencing and Corrections for Just Punishment and Public Safety," *Sentencing and Corrections: Issues for the 21st Century, NIJ Research in Brief*, Washington, DC, 1999.

120. J.G. Perry and J.F. Gorczyk, "Restructuring Corrections: Using Market Research in Vermont," *Corrections Management Quarterly*, 1997.

121. D.M. Kennedy, "Pulling Levers: Chronic Offenders, High-Crime Settings, and a Theory of Prevention," *Valparaiso U Law Review*, 31:449–484, 1997.

122. Note 6.

123. Ibid.

124. K. Bloodsworth and J. Junkin, *Bloodsworth: The True Story of the First Death Row Inmate Exonerated by DNA*, Chapel Hill, NC: Algonquin Books, 2004.

125. Edwin Borchard, *European Systems of State Indemnity for Errors of Criminal Justice, Criminal Law and Criminology*, 3:684–695, 1913.

126. Edwin Borchard, *Convicting the Innocent*, 417–421, 1932.

127. 28 U.S.C. sections 1495 & 2513 (2000).

128. *Commonwealth* v. *Toth*, 145 Pa. 308 (1891).

129. John H. Wigmore, "State Indemnity for Errors of Criminal Justice" (Editorial), *Journal of Criminal Law and Criminology*, Jan. 1913.

130. Geraldine Sealy, ABCNews.com, March 17, 2004.

131. Craig Cooley, *Tort Reform and the Erroneously Convicted: Compensating for Lost Time [and Possibly Lost Lives]*, htttp://www.law-forensic.com/tort_reform_wrongly_convicted.htm, March 17, 2004.

132. Howard Master, "Revisiting the Taking-Based Argument for Compensating the Wrongly Convicted," *NYU Annual Survey of American Law*, 60:97, 2004.

133. Craig Savoye, "Putting a Dollar Value on Wrongful Jail Time," *Christian Science Monitor*, July 6, 2001.

134. T. Maier, "Compensation for Injustice," Insight on the News, Oct. 1, 2002.

135. 28 USC 2513.

136. Note 132.

137. Ibid at 109.

138. Ibid.

139. Ibid.

140. Note 133.

141. C.R. Huff, A. Rattner, and E. Sagarin, "Convicted but Innocent: Wrongful Convictions and the Criminal Justice System," *Law and Human Behavior*, 12:203, 1988.

142. PBS Frontline, "Burden of Innocence," interview: Adele Bernhard, May 7, 2004.

143. Note 126.

CHAPTER 7: REASONS AND REMEDIES FOR WRONGFUL CONVICTIONS

1. E.M. Borchard, *Convicting the Innocent*, 1932.
2. *U.S. v Garsson*, 291 F. 646, 649 S.D.N.Y. (1923).
3. E. Radin, *The Innocents*, New York: Tower, 1964.
4. D. Givelber, "Meaningless Acquittals, Meaningful Convictions: Do We Reliably Acquit the Innocent?" *Rutgers Law Review*, 49:1317–1321, 1997.
5. E. Connors, T. Lundregan, N. Miller, and T. McEwan, "Convicted by Juries, Exonerated by Science: Case Studies in the Use of DNA Evidence to Establish Innocence After Trial," U.S. Department of Justice, Washington, DC, 1996; quoting then–Attorney General Janet Reno.
6. B. Scheck, P. Neufeld, and J. Dwyer, *Actual Innocence: Five Days to Execution and Other Dispatches from the Wrongly Convicted*, New York: Doubleday, p 230, 2000.
7. E.M. Borchard, "European Systems of State Indemnity For Errors of Criminal Justice," *Journal of Criminal Law and Criminology*, 3:684, 1913.
8. C.R. Huff, A. Rattner, and E. Sagarin, *Convicted but Innocent: Wrongful Conviction and Public Policy*, Berkeley, CA: Sage, xi–xii, 1996.
9. Supra, note 5.
10. E.M. Borchard, "Convicting the Innocent," v., 1932
11. J.H. King, Jr., "Compensation of Persons Erroneously Confined by the State," *University of Pennsylvania Law Review*, 118:1091, 1970.
12. E.M. Borchard, "State Indemnity for Errors in Criminal Justice," *Boston University Law Review*, 21:201, 1941.
13. A. Bernard, "When Justice Fails: Indemnification for Unjust Conviction," *University of Chicago Law School Roundtable*, 6:77, 1999.
14. J. Frank and B. Frank, *Not Guilty*, New York: Doubleday, 1957.
15. Note 3.
16. Ibid at 7.
17. Ibid.
18. Note 13 at 76.
19. R. Brandon and C. Davies, *Wrongful Imprisonment: Mistaken Convictions and their Consequences*, Bristol, U.K.: Allen & Unwin, p 20, 1973.
20. Ibid.
21. M. Yant, *Presumed Guilty: When Innocent People are Wrongly Convicted*, Amherst, NY: Prometheus, p 12, 1991.
22. R.H. Gault, "Find No Unjust Hangings," *Journal of the American Institute of Criminal Law and Criminology*, 3:131, 1912–1913.
23. Ibid at 131.
24. H. Bedau and M. Radelet, "Miscarriages of Justice in Potentially Capital Cases," *Stanford Law Review*, 40:21, 1987.
25. D. MacNamara, "Convicting the Innocent," *Crime and Delinquency*, 15:57, 1969.
26. D. MacNamara, quoting then–Attorney General, Ramsey Clark, who was testifying before a subcommittee on criminal laws and procedures.
27. 428 U.S. 153 (1976).

28. Ibid at 364.

29. B. Bakst, "O'Connor Questions Death Penalty," Associated Press, July 2, 2001.

30. J. Fulwider, "O'Connor Lectures Lawyers," StatePaper.com., Nebraska, Oct. 18, 2001.

31. W.J. Brennan, "Neither Victim nor Executioners," *Notre Dame Journal of Law, Ethics & Public Policy*, 8:1–4, 1994.

32. Staff of the Subcomm. On Civ. And Const. Rights, of the House Comm. On the Judiciary, 103rd Cong. 1 Report on Innocence and the Death Penalty: Assessing the Danger of Mistaken Executions, Subcomm. Print 1993.

33. Note 24 at 22.

34. Ibid at 72.

35. M. Radelet, J. Lofquist, and H. Bedau, "Prisoners Released from Death Row since 1970 Because of Doubts about Their Guilt," *T.M. Cooley Law Review*, 13:907, 1996.

36. Ibid at 916.

37. R. Dieter, "Innocence and the Death Penalty: The Increasing Danger of Executing the Innocent," 1997.

38. S.R. Gross, "The Risks of Death: Why Erroneous Convictions are Common in Capital Cases," *Buffalo Law Review*, 44:472, 1996.

39. A. Rattner, "Convicted but Innocent: Wrongful Conviction and the Criminal Justice System," *Law and Human Behavior*, 12:203, 1988.

40. Antiterrorism and Effective Death Penalty Act of 1996, Public Law. No. 104–132.

41. Illinois Commission on Capital Punishment Report 1, 2002.

42. 196 F. Supp. 2d 416 (2002).

43. V. Novak, "The Death Penalty Under Fire," *Time Magazine*, Oct. 7, 2002.

44. L. Urs, "*Commonwealth* v. *Joseph O'Dell*: Truth and Justice or Confuse the Courts? The DNA Controversy," *New England Journal on Criminal & Civil Confinement*, 25:311, 1999.

45. J.C. Tucker, "May God Have Mercy: A True Story of Crime and Punishment" New York: W.W. Norton, p 51, 1997.

46. A.M. Moyes, "Assessing the Risk of Executing the Innocent: A Case for Allowing Access to Physical Evidence for Posthumous DNA Testing," *Vanderbilt Law Review*, 55:953, 2002.

47. M. Glod, "DNA Tests May Signal Shift in Death Penalty Debate," *Washington Post*, B5, Jan. 17, 2006.

48. W. Thompson, "Evaluating the Admissibility of New Genetic Identification Tests: Lessons from the DNA War," *Journal of Criminal Law and Criminology*, 84:22, 1993.

49. C.I. Lugosi, "Punishing the Factually Innocent: DNA, Habeas Corpus and Justice," *George Mason University Civil Rights Law Journal*, 12:233, 2002.

50. The Innocence Project at http://www.innocenceproject.org/.

51. E. Connors, T. Lundregan, N. Miller, and T. McEwan, *Convicted by Juries, Exonerated by Science: Case Studies in the Use of DNA Evidence to Establish Innocence after Trial*, Washington, DC: U.S. Department of Justice, p iii, 1996.

52. Ibid.

53. J. Hewitt and W. Podesta, "No Time to Wait: Rape Activist Debbie Smith Pushes to Clear Up the Huge Backlog in DNA Testing," *People Magazine*, June 3, p 147, 2002 .

54. Ibid.

55. N. Bendavid, "U.S. Targets DNA Backlog—Agency to Spend $30 Million to Aid State Crime Labs," *Chicago Tribune*, Aug. 2, 2002.

56. Note 51.

57. B. Scheck and P. Neufeld, "DNA and Innocence Scholarship," in S.D. Westervelt and J.A. Humphrey, eds., *Wrongly Convicted: Perspectives on Failed Justice*, New Brunswick, NJ: Rutgers Univ. Press, p 246, 2001.

58. D. Givelber, "Meaningless Acquittals, Meaningful Convictions: Do We Reliably Acquit the Innocent?" *Rutgers Law Review*, 49:1317–1320, 1997.

59. Note 8 at 59.

60. Bureau of Justice Statistics, US Dept. of Justice, "Sourcebook of Criminal Justice Statistics," 497, 1995.

61. Note 39 at 523.

62. Note 4 at 1343.

63. Note 57 at 242.

64. National Institute of Justice, US Dept. of Justice, "Post-conviction DNA Testing: Recommendations for Handling Request," Sept. 1999, at iii, quoting [then] Attorney General, Janet Reno.

65. *Herrera v. Collins*, 506 U.S. 390, 398 (1993).

66. K.A. Findley, "Learning from Our Mistakes: A Criminal Justice Commission to Study Wrongful Convictions, *California Western Law Review*, 38:333–351, 2002.

67. G. Castelle and E. Loftus, "Misinformation and Wrongful Convictions," in J.A. Humphrey and S.D. Westervelt, eds., *Wrongly Convicted: Perspectives of Failed Justice*, New Brunswick, NJ: Rutgers University Press, p 18, 2001.

68. D. Horan, "The Innocence Commission: An Independent Review Board for Wrongful Convictions," *Northern Illinois University Law Review*, 21:91, 2001.

69. Note 6 at 246.

70. Ibid.

71. Note 66 at 339.

72. J. King, *The Ordeal of Guy Paul Morin: Canada Copes with Systemic Injustice*,Washington, DC: The Champion, Aug. 1998.

73. Criminal Code of Canada, R.S.C. 1985 c.C-34 s.676.

74. F. Kaufman, "Executive Summary: Commission on Proceedings Involving Guy Paul Morin," Ministry of the Attorney General: Toronto, Ontario, 1, 1998.

75. Ibid.

76. The Inquiry Regarding Thomas Sophonow, http://www.gov.mb.ca/justice/sophonow/index.html.

77. http://indigenous bar.ca/cases/marshall.html.

78. "Where Justice Stumbles," *Globe and Mail*, Toronto, Mar. 4, 2002.

79. L. Griffin, "The Correction of Wrongful Convictions: A Comparative Perspective," *American University International Law Review*, 16:1241–1276, 2001.

80. Ibid at 1277.

81. Note 66 at 345.

82. S. Mills and K. Armstrong, "Death Row Justice Derailed," *Chicago Tribune*, Nov. 14, 1999.

83. "Illinois Commission on Capital Punishment Report," at i, 2002.

84. Office of the Attorney General State of Arizona, "Capital Case Commission Interim Report," 2001.

85. "Death Penalty Debate Slowly Shifts," *Chicago Tribune*, Jan. 31, 2001.

86. M.J. Saks, L. Constantine, M. Dolezal, and J. Garcia, "Model Prevention and Remedy of Erroneous Conviction Act," *Arizona State Law Journal*, 33:665–669, 2001.

87. Ibid at 270.

88. M.J. Saks, L. Constantine, M. Dolezal, and J. Garcia, "Toward a Model Act for the Prevention and Remedy of Erroneous Convictions," *New England Law Review*, 35:669–670, 2001.

89. "Mandatory Justice: Eighteen Reforms to the Death Penalty," *The Constitution Project*, Washington, DC: Georgetown University, p ix, 2001.

90. The Innocence Project at http://www.innocenceproject.org/causes/ policemisconduct.php.

91. S. Clark, "Procedural Reforms in Capital Cases Applied to Perjury," *John Marshall Law Review*, 34:453, 2001.

92. K. Armstrong and S. Mills, "Inept Defense Cloud Verdicts with Their Lives at Stake," *Chicago Tribune*, Nov. 15, 1999.

93. G. Castelle and E. Loftus, "Misinformation and Wrongful Convictions," in *Wrongly Convicted*, New Brunswick, NJ: Rutgers University Press, p 18, 2001.

94. Ibid.

95. G.L. Wells et al., "From the Lab to the Police Station: A Successful Application of Eyewitness Research," *American Psychologist*, 55:581–583, 2000.

96. G.L. Wells, "What Do We Know about Eyewitness Identification?" *American Psychologist*, 553, 1993.

97. D. Faigman, D. Kaye, M.J. Saks, and J. Sanders, *Modern Scientific Evidence: The Law and Science of Expert Testimony*, 1st ed., St. Paul, MN: West Group, 1997, & Supp. 2000.

98. Technical Working Group for Eyewitness Evidence, U.S. Dept of Justice, "Eyewitness Evidence: A Guide for Law Enforcement," 1999.

99. F.E. Inbau, J.E. Reid, J.P. Buckley, and B.C. Jayne, *Criminal Interrogation and Confessions*, 3rd ed., Sudbury, MA: Jones and Bartlett Publishers, 1986.

100. *Stephan v. State*, 711 P.2d 1156 (1985).

101. *State v. Scales*, 518 N.W.2d 587 (1994).

102. *Missouri v. Seibert*, No. 02–1371 (2004).

103. P.C. Giannelli, "The Abuse of Scientific Evidence in Criminal Cases: The Need for Independent Crime Laboratories, *Virginia Journal of Social Policy & Law*, 4:439, 1997.

104. J.L. Peterson, M.J. Saks, D.M. Risinger, and R. Rosenthal, *Forensic Evidence and the Police*, Washington, DC: National Institute of Justice, p 114, 1984.

105. A.A. Moenssens, "Novel Scientific Evidence in Criminal Cases: Some Words of Caution," *Journal of Criminal Law and Criminology*, 84:1–17, 1993.

106. National Institute of Justice, "Solicitation: Forensic Friction Ridge (Fingerprint) Examination Validation Studies," March 2000.

107. 509 U.S. 579 (1993).

108. M.J. Saks and J.J. Koehler, "What DNA 'Fingerprinting' Can Teach the Law about the Rest of Forensic Science," *Cardozo Law Review*, 13:361, 1991.

109. Federal Rules of Evidence, 702.

110. R. Liebman et al., "Capital Attrition: Error Rates in Capital Cases, 1973–95," *Texas Law Review*, 78:1839–1850, 2000.

111. *People* v. *Wilkins*, 268 N.E. 2d 756 (1971).

112. Colo. Rev. Stat. Section 21-2-101(1) (2000).

113. *The ABA Standards for Criminal Justice section 5–5.3 Commentary*, 3rd ed., 1992.

114. Federal Rules of Criminal Procedure, 16(a)(2).

115. A. Bernhard, "When Justice Fails: Indemnification for Unjust Conviction," *University of Chicago Law School Roundtable*, 6:73, 1999.

Selected Bibliography

Ambrosio, T.J. and V. Schiraldi. "From Classrooms to Cell Blocks: A National Perspective," Washington, DC: Justice Policy Institute, 1997.

Aptheker, H., ed. *A Documentary History of the Negro People in the United States.* Secaucus, NJ: Citadel, 1974.

Banner, S. *The Death Penalty: An American History.* Cambridge, MA: Harvard Univ. Press, 2002.

Beck, A.J. "State and Federal Prisoners Returning to the Community: Findings from the Bureau of Justice Statistics," report presented to the First Reentry Courts Initiative Cluster Meeting: Washington, DC, 2000.

Bloodsworth, K. and J. Junkin. *Bloodsworth: The True Story of the First Death Row Inmate Exonerated by DNA.* Chapel Hill, NC: Algonquin Books, 2004.

Borchard, E. "European Systems of State Indemnity for Errors of Criminal Justice," *Journal of Criminal Law and Criminology*, 3:684, 1913.

Bushway, S. "The Stigma of a Criminal History Record in the Labor Market," in J.P. May, ed., *Building Violence: How America's Rush to Incarcerate Creates More Violence.* Thousand Oaks: Sage, 2000.

Camus, A. "Reflections on the Guillotine," in *Resistance, Rebellion, and Death.* New York: Knopf, 1969.

Castelle, G. and E. Loftus. "Misinformation and Wrongful Convictions," in J.A. Humphrey and S.D. Westervelt, eds., *Wrongly Convicted: Perspectives of Failed Justice*, p 18, 2001.

Dieter, R. "With Justice for Few: The Growing Crisis in Death Penalty Representation," Death Penalty Information Center, October 1995.

Elkins, S. *Slavery: A Problem in American Institutional and Intellectual Life.* Chicago: Univ. of Chicago Press, 1976.

Gabel, K. and D. Johnston, eds. *Children of Incarcerated Parents*. New York: Lexington Books, 1995.

Ginzburg, R. *100 Years of Lynching*. Baltimore: Black Classic Press, 1988.

Hagan, J. and R. Dinovitzer. "Collateral Consequences of Imprisonment for Children, Communities, and Prisoners," Chicago: Univ. of Chicago Press, 1999.

Haines, H.H. *Against Capital Punishment: The Anti-Death Penalty Movement in America, 1972–1994*. New York: Oxford Univ. Press, 1996.

Huff, C.R., Rattner, A., and Sagarin, E. *Convicted but Innocent: Wrongful Conviction and Public Policy*. Thousand Oaks, CA: Sage Publications, 1996.

Jain, M. "Mitigating the Dangers of Capital Convictions Based on Eyewitness Testimony through Treason's Two-Witness Rule," *Journal of Criminal Law and Criminology*, 91(3), 2001.

Johnson, R. *Death Work: A Study of the Modern Execution Process*, Wadsworth Contemporary Issues in Crime and Justice Series. Belmont, CA: Wadsworth, 1998.

Levine, S., ed. *Death Row: An Affirmation of Life*. New York: Ballantine, 1972.

Liebman, J. "A Broken System: Error Rates in Capital Cases 1973–95," New York: Columbia University, 2000.

Loftus. E. *Eyewitness Testimony*. Cambridge, MA: Harvard Univ. Press, 1979.

Love, M. and S. Kuzma. *Civil Disabilities of Convicted Felons: A State-by-State Survey*. Washington, DC: Office of the Pardon Attorney, 1996.

Masur, L.P. *Rites of Execution: Capital Punishment and the Transformation of American Culture, 1776–1865*. New York: Oxford Univ. Press, 1989.

Mauer, M. *The Race to Incarcerate*. Washington, DC: The Prison Project, 2000.

Miller, G. *Invitation to a Lynching*. Garden City, NY: Doubleday & Co., 1975.

Miller, J.G. *Search and Destroy: African-American Males in the Criminal Justice System*. Cambridge: Cambridge Univ. Press, 1996.

Morgan, E.S. *American Slavery, American Freedom: The Ordeal of Colonial Virginia*. New York: W.W. Norton, 1975.

Mullin, G. *Flight and Rebellion: Slave Resistance in Eighteenth-Century Virginia*. New York: Oxford Univ. Press, 1974.

Oshinsky, D. *Worse Than Slavery: Parchman Farm and the Ordeal of Jim Crow Justice*. New York: Free Press, 1996.

Petersilia, J. *When Prisoners Come Home: Parole and Prisoner Reentry in the U.S.*, Chicago: Univ. of Chicago Press, 1999.

Prejean, H. *Dead Man Walking: An Eyewitness Account of the Death Penalty in the United States*. New York: Random House, 1993.

Radelet, M., H. Bedau, and C.M. Putnam. *In Spite of Innocence: Erroneous Convictions in Capital Cases*. Boston: Northeastern Univ. Press, 1992.

Redding, J.S. *They Came in Chains*. Philadelphia: Lippincott, 1973.

Reiman, J. *The Rich Get Richer and the Poor Get Prison; Ideology, Class, and Criminal Justice*, 4th ed. Boston: Allyn & Bacon, 1995.

Rossi, P.H. *Down and Out in America: Origins of Homelessness*. Chicago: Univ. of Chicago Press, 1989.

Scheck, B., P. Neufeld, and J. Dwyer. *Actual Innocence: Five Days to Execution and Other Dispatches from the Wrongly Convicted*, New York: Signet, 2000.

Sherman, L., D. Gottfredson, D. MacKenzie, L. Eck, P. Reuter, and S. Bushway. *Preventing Crime: What Works, What Doesn't, What's Promising.* College Park: Univ. of Maryland, 1997.

Stamp, K.M. *The Peculiar Institution.* New York: Knopf, 1956.

Tolnay, S. and E. Beck. *A Festival of Violence: An Analysis of Southern Lynchings, 1882–1930.* Urbana: Univ. of Illinois Press, 1995.

Wells, G.L. "What Do We Know About Eyewitness Identification?" *American Psychologist,* 48:553–571, 1993.

———. "Eyewitness Identifications: Scientific Status," in Faigman, D.L., Kaye, D.H., Saks, M.J., and Sanders, J. eds., *Modern Scientific Evidence: The Law and Science of Expert Testimony.* St. Paul: West Publishing, 1997.

Zinn, H. *A People's History of the United States.* New York: Perennial Classics, 2001.

Index

About the Author

RICHARD A. STACK, a lawyer and Associate Professor of Communication at American University, pioneered the field of litigation public relations after seven years of pro bono media advising for the National Coalition to Abolish the Death Penalty. He is the author of two previous books.